BAPTISM

AND THE
BATTLE FOR SOULS

Faith that Demands Obedience

By
Steven A. Carlson

GUARDIAN
PUBLISHING, LLC

Copyright © 2008, Steven A. Carlson
All Rights Reserved
ISBN: 978-0-9827915-0-9
Printed in the United States of America

This edition published in February 2008 in association with

Guardian Publishing, LLC
Holt, Michigan

The following copyright information is provided for the Bible passages quoted in this work...

All Scripture quotations, unless otherwise indicated, are taken from the New King James Version. Copyright © 1979, 1980, 1982 by Thomas Nelson, Inc. Used by permission.

Scripture portions cited and identified by the three-letter tag (KJV) are taken from the Holy Bible: King James Version.

Scripture portions cited and identified by the three-letter tag (ASV) are taken from the Holy Bible: American Standard Version.

Scripture portions cited and identified by the four-letter tag (NASB) are taken from the New American Standard Bible®, Copyright © 1960, 1962, 1963, 1968, 1971, 1972, 1973, 1975, 1977, 1995 by The Lockman Foundation. Used by permission.

Scripture portions cited and identified by the three-letter tag (NIV) are taken from the Holy Bible, New International Version®. NIV®. Copyright © 1973, 1978, 1984 by International Bible Society. Used by permission of Zondervan. All rights reserved.

Acknowledgements

This book is dedicated in part to my *faith only* friends who maintain that baptism is not a matter of salvation in our relationship with God. Without that motivation this treatise would never have been written. While it was a demanding and sometimes exhausting adventure, concern for their souls has lead me to perform a deeper study on the subject of baptism than I would ever have accomplished without them.

I would also like to dedicate this work to the memory of two men who have passed from this life in recent years. The first is Dr. Brandt Lee Doty who was, for many years, a professor at Great Lakes Christian College in Lansing, Michigan. The second, Mr. W. Robert Palmer, was a long-term minister in Lansing, Michigan. I have always considered these men giants in the faith. They have each played an important role in my life and my grasp of Scripture. I have a deeper understanding of the ways of God because of their mentoring. The spiritual impact on those who knew them was extraordinary.

Special gratitude goes out to my parents, Elton (a minister) and Edna Carlson and my brother Phil, as well as Mr. W. Robert Palmer, who unfortunately passed away prior to publishing, for their input. Thanks also go to Paul and Betty Stacy, a retired minister and his wife, who provided valuable insights into the subject matter of this book, and to my skillful proofreader, Annette Bobko. A friend and school teacher by the name of Debbie Schneider also aided immensely, offering helpful advice; while my two sons, Michael and Adam, were deeply involved in the editing process. I would also like to thank my remarkable wife, Denise, who was relatively patient as I spent hour upon hour in my office studying and writing.

Special acknowledgement must go to my friend and former minister, Greg Steere, who taught Greek and helped me immensely in assuring that the Greek presented in this book does not misrepresent the biblical authors' intended meaning. Most of all, however, I would like to recognize the invaluable contribution from my brother, Tim Carlson, who is also a minister and whose theological acumen far surpasses my own. His knowledge of biblical history has helped to make this book one that I am pleased to present. Thanks a lot, Tim.

Preface

The New Testament author of the book of Hebrews informs us that baptism should be considered an *'elementary principle of Christ'* in complement with other basic truths that include both repentance and faith (Hebrews 6: 1-2). Unfortunately, over the centuries the subject of baptism has developed into one of the most contentious issues in all of Scripture. The unity that the lesson of baptism is designed to generate within the church (Acts 2: 41; 1 Corinthians 12: 13; Ephesians 4: 5) has been impeded making it, ironically, the source of a great deal of bitter wrangling.

Engaging any topic that tends to cultivate controversy (e.g., water baptism, gifts of the spirit, baptism with the Holy Spirit, etc.) is always arduous. Passions often run high amid an assortment of beliefs as diverse as the colors of a spectrum. Given the emotionally-charged rhetoric that so often accompanies the debate on baptism we should begin this discussion by establishing certain basic principles that can provide us with some commonality. Therefore, the following paragraphs offer fundamental guidelines that will serve as a foundation for the discussion that follows.

* * * * *

Any worthwhile Bible-based discussion must begin with the understanding that the Bible is the one true and complete Word of God. No effective study can be performed absent this initial premise. When asked concerning belief in the Bible as God's divine message to mankind, some will agree that it is unquestionably God's Word. Others will absolutely deny the spiritual authority of Scripture. Still others, while boasting faith in God, will waver in their full acceptance of the infallibility of the Bible. This hesitation is most often based on an historical account or precept recorded or established in Scripture to which they are simply unwilling to subscribe. An answer such as this, however, ultimately denies the divine inspiration of Scripture. After all, if the Bible is truly God's Word, it must be received totally and unconditionally in that light. For those who are inclined to discard all or part of Scripture, the ideology discussed in this book will have little meaning. On the other hand, those who recognize the divine authority of Holy Writ will hopefully discover a genuine exegesis of the teaching of baptism as it is set forth in God's Word.

* * * * *

Any individual who believes that the Bible is the true Word of God must, accordingly, accept the predication that the words of the Bible, as they are written (especially in the original Hebrew and Greek text), are sufficient to deliver God's intended message. In essence, we must recognize that the design of Scripture is to communicate God's will in its entirety (2 Timothy 3: 15-17). Anything short of this renders a work whose inspiration could and should be challenged. If, however, the Bible is complete, it is reasonable that we should draw our beliefs from the teaching contained therein. Doctrine that can only be derived by circumventing the words of the Bible must be considered flawed.

* * * * *

As with any literary work, the context of a biblical passage is often quite relevant in determining the intended message of the text. The literary context encompasses: the theme of a particular chapter or book; the setting or circumstances behind the writing; and the nature of those being addressed. For example, the primary objective of the gospels (the books of Matthew, Mark, Luke, and John) is to acquaint us with Jesus' ministry as well as His death, burial, and resurrection. Additionally, Jesus often provided insight into the coming church age through His teaching that is recorded in these books. The Acts of the Apostles chronicles the events surrounding the establishment of the church and the introduction of the Holy Spirit into the lives of Christians. The epistles, which were written to various churches or individuals, were intended to provide teaching and edification to Christians both in the first century and throughout the ensuing church age. The context of each chapter and/or book, weighed against its surrounding biblical backdrop, is critical to the message it holds.

* * * * *

Quite often we are provided scriptural instruction through a method known as *direct command* or *assertion* by the author. For instance, who could doubt James' meaning concerning the bridling of the tongue or the care of orphans and widows (James 1: 26-27)? The words are straightforward and the meaning is clear. Yet there are times when reason and logic may be employed to help us determine the message from a passage, a method known as *necessary inference*. This method reasons that, while the text may not state a particular point explicitly, we can logically infer from the words that something is or is not true. For example, although the details of the teaching offered by Philip to the Ethiopian eunuch are not revealed, Philip must have directed him toward baptism since it was the eunuch who insisted on being baptized when they came upon water (Acts 8: 26-39).

However, when men claim that the apostle Paul was saved on the Road to Damascus, they ignore the fact that his sins were not forgiven until he met with Ananias three days later (Acts 9: 1-19; 22: 6-16). Since Scripture expressly conjoins redemption and forgiveness (Ephesians 1: 7; Colossians 1: 14), the proposal that he was saved on the road cannot withstand the facts provided in the account of Paul's conversion. This claim fails the test of *reasonable* inference, much less the test of *necessary* inference.

Simply stated, conclusions regarding the meaning of a biblical narrative must be objective and confined to the facts as they are presented in the words – a practice that is essential to all biblical analysis. One cannot attain understanding by abandoning or manipulating the words of the Bible in an effort to confirm his/her own belief, especially when the *prima facie* reading of the text conflicts with that belief. We must always draw our beliefs from the Bible (exegesis) and the original intent of the author, and avoid eclipsing Scripture by superimposing our own message onto the text (eisogesis).

* * * * *

Occasionally a doctrine may be developed from a passage without respecting what the balance of Scripture teaches. The most effective means of avoiding doctrinal misunderstanding is to take into account the full measure of God's Word. While certain passages speak broadly of God's will for mankind, no single verse reveals the message of God in its entirety. John 3: 16 is a compelling passage, but absent the history of the Old Testament and the supporting text in the gospels, we would have no insight into the meaning of this verse or what would be an appropriate response. Underlying this principle is the belief that, while Scripture does not contradict itself, it does complement itself; so insight into one passage may be enhanced or clarified by another. This foundation for biblical unity is based upon a notion of scriptural consistency resulting from divine inspiration of the whole (i.e., God would never disagree with Himself), and is well expressed in the axiom – *the best commentary on the Bible is the Bible itself.*

Some maintain that, if it was true that the Bible is its own best commentary, there would not be such a multitude of conflicting doctrines among men. In actuality, however, there is so much controversy only because many do not look at what the Bible says – they look at what *part* of the Bible says. Because of this many doctrines taught by men do not fully harmonize with Scripture. Not only does God's Word fail to impeach itself but, taken in its entirety, it provides us with an unclouded understanding of His will. A doctrine may be forged based upon a single passage of Scripture; yet, if the teaching that is derived from that passage challenges the theme of the Bible as a whole, we would do well to question the plausibility of that doctrine.

Paul admonished Timothy to be a discerning student of Scripture, *'rightly dividing the word of truth'* (2 Timothy 2: 15), in order to avoid being fooled by those who would misdirect him. Peter warned us that certain men would distort Scripture, resulting in doctrine that would mislead (2 Peter 3: 16). We find that this is often achieved by either portraying a single passage as comprehensive instruction concerning a specific doctrine, without regard for further scriptural guidance, or by simply disputing straightforward biblical edification. As an example, one sect has based their doctrine of baptism for the dead on the following words from Paul:

> Otherwise, what will they do who are baptized for the dead, if the dead do not rise at all? Why then are they baptized for the dead?
> (1 Corinthians 15: 29)

Paul's words fall considerably short of endorsing baptism on behalf of the dead. The fullness of God's Word, including additional statements by Paul himself, reveals that Scripture does not support this view (Luke 16: 20-31; 2 Corinthians 5: 10;

Hebrews 9: 27). Paul offers no warrant here, but merely recognizes that certain people are known to observe baptism for the dead. He clearly did not engage in the practice himself as is evident from his use of the word *they* in his query regarding those who are known to participate. Additionally, he does not suggest that their efforts provided any benefit for those who have passed. A reading of the entire fifteenth chapter of 1 Corinthians reveals that this remark by Paul is simply a passing comment in an entire discourse concerning whether or not people are *raised* from the dead. The statement does not establish Paul's advocacy of this custom. It is best to avoid deriving doctrine from a passage without weighing that teaching against the balance of Scripture.

* * * * *

At times in the New Testament, God intervened in the common lives of men in extraordinary ways as a matter of divine revelation and/or miraculous intervention. When God interacted with men in this way, the intended lesson or result was designed specifically for first century Christians in an effort to advance the work of the kingdom. We have no reason to believe that incidents of miraculous intervention were devised to establish biblical doctrine. They are not doctrinal in character. In each case God's purpose was to affect the outcome of a situation (Acts 12: 6-10), influence certain decisions (Acts 9: 3-8), or shape the structure of the early church (Acts 10: 44-46). For instance, God ignited the apostles with the power of the Holy Spirit so that they could perform miracles. He did this in order to demonstrate to the early church the special authority He had bestowed upon these men (Acts 2: 43; 2 Corinthians 12: 11-12).

The power granted the apostles is an example of miraculous intervention intended to profit the church in the first century. Its relevance to us lies in the fact that we can observe exactly how God used the apostles to establish the church. Through God's revelation that these men were chosen vessels, we can also discern that their words were God's words (John 17: 14). However, we cannot regard these miraculous powers as common in the church age, given the foundational role of the apostles in the kingdom (Ephesians 2: 20). On the contrary, it is evident that the power bestowed upon these men represents the greatest of exceptions as

God intervened in order to affect the establishment of the body of Christ.

Ananias and Sapphira perished instantly when they *'lied to the Holy Spirit'* (Acts 5: 1-10). Once again we find an incident of divine intervention. These deaths spread fear through the church body (Acts 5: 11) as God demonstrated to the early believers His hatred of sin and His total omniscience (complete knowledge) and omnipotence (complete power). Yet this was clearly an anomaly. While we can certainly learn from this occasion, we do not anticipate God employing this same method of discipline today.

God revealed Himself to the early church at this time in an extraordinary manner. Given the uniqueness of the event, we cannot develop biblical doctrine from this incident, nor do the apostles ever suggest that the episode carries with it doctrinal application. It does, however, provide further support for the authority of the apostles.

The Ethiopian eunuch received baptism after Philip presented the gospel message to him (Acts 8: 27-39). What is intriguing about this event is the fact that, after Philip had baptized the man, he disappeared from the eunuch's sight.

> And when they were come up out of the water, the Spirit of the Lord caught away Philip, that the eunuch saw him no more: and he went on his way rejoicing. (Acts 8: 39)

We do not know why Philip was taken away in this manner, but the implication from Scripture is that God had work for him in Azotus and Caesarea (v. 40).

If we could derive doctrine from this kind of miraculous intervention we might conclude that, for any man to be saved, the person administering the baptism must immediately vanish from sight. Of course, it would be foolish to believe such a tenet could be drawn from this incident. We have no reason to attempt to draw doctrine from such an exceptional case. Moments of miraculous intervention simply do not lend themselves to the establishment of biblical doctrine.

* * * * *

Finally, certain individuals may form a spiritual view completely independent from scriptural instruction. Often a person's life experiences may lead to a discounting of biblical teaching when it comes to developing his/her belief system. In such a case the written word is effectively discarded as a source of doctrine. However, a belief that is founded upon a personal experience rather than Scripture is a belief without substance. In fact, it is often simply a camouflaged attempt to elude God's direction. This is often expressed in terms of, *'I have a relationship with God but I don't need the church'* or, *'God and I have an understanding'*. Neither of these remarks can be considered sincere since the flippancy of the claim indicates little respect for the written instructions God has provided. According to Scripture, the way to Jesus is the church (1 Corinthians 12: 12-27; Ephesians 1: 22-23) and the way to the Father is through Jesus (John 14: 6). Any belief that proclaims a separate path to that relationship due to an earthly experience conflicts with God's own counsel.

* * * * *

Little dissension exists among believers regarding the salvation value of faith, confession, the deity of Christ, or a host of other creeds that hold a place of distinction in our walk with God. Baptism, however, seems to be the single subject that has the capacity to bring great division among those who believe in Jesus as the Son of God.

While this book is written to those who do not believe, or at least question, that water baptism is part of God's plan of salvation and for forgiveness of sins, it is also written to those who do believe baptism is essential. For those who have lacked the words or the Scripture to answer the arguments of men who dismiss baptism, this book will prepare you to make your belief clear through solid biblical teaching. The hope is that, upon reading this work, you will not only be able to defend your belief, but that you will boldly teach all that Scripture says about God's amazing covenant with man.

This book has been written with a single goal in mind. That goal is to discuss biblical instruction concerning baptism as honestly as possible. Honest presentation of God's teaching is essential if we are to honor Him. In that same vein the assignment for you, the reader, is to hold this work to biblical scrutiny to assure that what is written here does not misrepresent the inspired words of Scripture.

* * * * *

The biblical passages cited in this book are from the New King James Version of the Bible. At times the author has italicized certain words in cited passages as a matter of emphasis. When this occurs, the highlighting is noted by the words *emphasis added* at the end of the passage. However, there are times in the NKJ and other versions of the Bible where the translators have enhanced the English text by inserting words, (e.g., pronouns and prepositions) that are not included in the original Greek. For instance, in the following verse, the words *'it is'* have been incorporated into the English translation.

> For *it is* not possible that the blood of bulls and goats could take away sins. (Hebrews 10: 4)

These words are italicized in recognition of the fact that they are not part of the original manuscripts. The reasons for these insertions are simply to aid in the transition to English and generally do not affect the meaning of the verse. In an attempt to be faithful to Scripture, these insertions will remain italicized in this work.

Table of Contents

Title	Page
Chapter I - Beliefs Regarding Baptism - In Brief	**18**
Water Baptism Is Essential and by Immersion Only	18
Water Baptism Is Essential by Immersion, Pouring, or Sprinkling	19
Water Baptism Is a Sign	20
Water Baptism Is Immaterial	22
Baptism with the Holy Spirit	22
Chapter II - Baptism and the First Covenant	**28**
The Shadow Covenant	28
Elements of the First Covenant	29
Feasts of the First Covenant	29
Conversion in the First Covenant	30
Purification in the First Covenant	31
The Old Reflected in the New	32
Baptism and the Birthright of the First Covenant	35
The Baptism of John – A Transition	36
The Nature of Water	38
Chapter III - God's New Covenant	**41**
The Blood of the New Covenant	41
The New Ordinances	42
The Witness of the Spirit, the Water, and the Blood	44
Participation in the New Covenant	46
Chapter IV - When Is the Time of Salvation?	**53**
Salvation by Grace	53
Salvation by Belief	54
Salvation by Faith	55
Salvation by Repentance	56
Salvation by Confession	57
Salvation by Love	58
Salvation by Baptism	59
What About the Sinner's Prayer?	61
Salvation by Obedience	65

Title	*Page*
Chapter V - Must I Be Baptized?	**70**
Interpretation of the Word	70
The Principles of Baptism	72
Baptism in Matthew 28: 19	74
Baptism in Mark 16: 16	75
Baptism in Acts 2: 38	78
The Fallacy of Negative Inference	79
The Divine Inspiration of the Word	82
The Baptism of the Ethiopian Eunuch	83
The Baptism of Cornelius	84
Baptism – Duty or Privilege?	87
Chapter VI - Baptism and the Gospel	**90**
The Message of the Gospel	90
Approaching the Bible	91
The Philippian Jailer and the Message of the Gospel	93
A Profile of the Gospel in the Book of Acts	95
A Profile of the Gospel in the Epistles	97
The Relationship of Belief, Repentance, and Baptism	99
Paul's Alleged Disclaimer Concerning Baptism	103
Paul's View of the Relationship Between Baptism and Faith	108
Chapter VII - What Is the Purpose of Water Baptism?	**111**
Baptism as an Outward Sign of an Inward Change	111
The Efficacy of Baptism	112
The Purpose of John's Baptism	114
Christian Baptism for the Forgiveness of Sins	115
Christian Baptism for the Purpose of Regeneration	127
Christian Baptism for the Purpose of Salvation	129
The Gift of the Holy Spirit Bestowed in Christian Baptism	129
Christian Baptism and Membership in the Body	130
The Unifying Mettle of Christian Baptism	131
Effects of Baptism with Errant Motivation	132
The Purpose of Baptism for the Gentiles	135

Title	Page
Chapter VIII - What Is the Mode of Baptism?	**138**
The Baptism of John	138
The Meaning of Bapto, Baptizo, and Baptisma	138
Baptism – The Antitype	143
The History of Baptism in the Church	145
Paul's Portraiture of Baptism	147
Chapter IX - One, and Only One, Baptism	**152**
The Baptism the Apostles Taught	152
The Baptism of Rebirth – John 3: 5	153
Baptism with the Holy Spirit and with Fire	159
Baptism – A Once-In-A-Lifetime Experience	160
Chapter X - When Does Baptism Mean Water?	**162**
When Baptism Obviously Means Water	162
Death, Burial, and Resurrection - The Baptism of Jesus	163
When Water Is Not Intimated	164
The Day of Pentecost	165
Baptism in Samaria	166
The Baptism of Saul	166
The Symbolism of Baptism	167
Baptism in Corinth	168
The Baptism of 1 Corinthians 12: 13	171
The Baptism of Galatians 3: 27	174
The Baptism of Colossians 2: 12	175
The Baptism of 1 Peter 3: 21	175
Multiple Baptisms – Hebrews 6: 1-2	178
Chapter XI - Not of Works!	**181**
Works in the New Covenant	181
Obedient Faith Vs Works	182
Baptism Vs Works	187
Baptism – An Act of Man or God?	189
Faith – Man's Responsibility	191
Another Gospel	192

Title	Page
Chapter XI - Not of Works! (cont'd)	
Keeping God's Commandments Is Essential	194
God's Employment of Men in Administering Baptism	196
Chapter XII - Baptism Vs Special Circumstances	***200***
What If Baptism Is Not Possible?	200
The Day of Pentecost and the Gentile Conversion	202
From Saul to Paul	204
The Thief on the Cross	207
Chapter XIII - A Matter of Choice	***212***
The Nature of God	212
The Choice of Adam and Eve	212
The Fiery Serpent	213
David's Choice	214
Naaman, Moses, and the Blind Man	214
The Nature of God's Instructions	215
Chapter XIV - What Is Baptism with the Holy Spirit?	***218***
Power Received – The Day of Pentecost	219
The Day of Pentecost – A Proper Biblical Perspective	220
Baptism with the Holy Spirit – The Gentiles	224
Pentecost and Caesarea: One View – Two Perspectives	225
Gifts of the Spirit	224
The Moving of the Spirit – Acts 4: 29-31	227
Water and Holy Spirit Baptism Together	228
Baptism of the Three Thousand	230
Baptism *in* the Spirit, *with* the Spirit, or *by* the Spirit?	231
Instruction Vs Narrative Concerning Baptism	233
What is the Biblical Answer Concerning Spirit Baptism?	234
Chapter XV - In Whose Name Must I Be Baptized?	***237***
Chapter XVI - Paedobaptism: Scriptural?	***242***
Original Sin	24
New Testament Omission of Infant Baptism	24
The Candidate for Baptism	24

Title — Page

Chapter XVI - Paedobaptism: Scriptural? (cont'd)

What Is a Household? — 250
Baptism and Circumcision — 252
Circumcision and the Death of Christ — 256
Infant Baptism and the Day of Pentecost — 257
The Unnecessary Inference of Infant Baptism — 257
Paedobaptism and Immersion — 259
Forgiveness through Baptism Alone — 260

Chapter XVII - Baptism and Biblical Harmony — 264

Baptism in Harmony with Grace — 264
Baptism in Harmony with Faith — 269

Chapter XVIII - Baptism and Doctrinal Purity — 278

Doctrinal Significance — 278
The Doctrine of Baptism — 281
Doctrinal Purity Vs Sincerity of Heart — 283

Chapter XIX - The Apostles: Baptized in Jesus' Name? — 289

Baptized by John — 289
Baptized in the Name of Jesus — 290
Baptism of the Apostles – A Most Reasonable Conclusion — 295

Chapter XX - At the Feet of the Apostles — 297

The Apostolic Fathers — 297
The Ante-Nicene Fathers — 300

Conclusion — 305

Bibliography — 309

Chapter I
Beliefs Regarding Baptism - In Brief

Few topics in the Bible rival baptism in stirring controversy and discord among those who study God's Word and seek His ways. Numerous scholars have penned a multitude of books on the subject revealing a variety of perspectives concerning the mode and utility of baptism. Still, most views can be summed up in the few simple categories that follow.

Water Baptism Is Essential and by Immersion Only
A number of people believe that immersion in water is the only valid form of baptism, since this is the baptism portrayed within the pages of Scripture, and that it is essential for salvation. Those who propound this view believe that the decision to submit to baptism must be rendered by each man or woman once he/she reaches an age when the decision is his/hers to make. It is at the time of baptism, accompanied by repentance, that forgiveness of sins and the indwelling of the Holy Spirit are received. Regeneration (renewal) through Christ's blood is the central matter of the ceremony. While the water, in itself, owns no power to regenerate, the work of the Holy Spirit is to apply the blood of Christ to a person's sins in the waters of baptism, cleansing him/her of all guilt.

A vast number of disciples elected to dismiss the precept of immersion as a condition of salvation beginning in the early to mid sixteenth century. Its resurgence can be found in the work and writings of Alexander Campbell[1] (1788-1866) and Barton W. Stone[2] (1772-1844) in the nineteenth century. These may be considered the fathers of what is known as the Restoration Movement in America. It was their belief that the church should be *restored* to both the design and the ordinances that were established for the church of the first century as depicted in Scripture.

There exists a difference of opinion, although not an unfriendly one, even among those who profess that immersion is necessary for salvation. This discussion concerns baptism with the Holy Spirit. Among this group, some maintain that baptism with the Holy Spirit involved the miraculous outpouring of the Spirit that is portrayed in the book of Acts. It is believed that this occurred only twice in Scripture (Acts 2: 1-4; 10: 44-46) and that, once its mission was accomplished, God discontinued His use of that experience. Others hold a separate view of baptism with the Holy Spirit, having determined that this is what occurs at the time of immersion in water when we receive the *gift* of the Holy Spirit (Acts 2: 38).

Water Baptism Is Essential by Immersion, Pouring, or Sprinkling

Some men believe that, although water baptism is essential for salvation, immersion is not its only acceptable form. Accordingly, they consider sprinkling or pouring water over an individual as legitimate modes of baptism. Most who hold this view maintain that baptism can occur as early as infancy to cover what is deemed *original sin* (the notion that men are born with the guilt of sin). No decision on the part of the child is needed. A decision rendered by the parent on behalf of the child to receive baptism is adequate for redemption.

The hint that forms of a baptismal method other than immersion may have existed as early as the second century is found in a work known as the Didache[3], also called The Teaching of the Twelve Apostles, which can be traced back to that period. Notwithstanding the title, it is doubtful that the apostles were associated with its authorship since some of the teachings do not imitate apostolic practices. For instance, the Didache called for reciting the Lord's Prayer three times daily and prescribed specific prayers that were to be delivered both before and after partaking of the loaf and cup.

With respect to baptism, this work teaches that the person performing a baptism, the candidate for baptism, and other willing believers, should fast for two days prior to the event. No such teaching can be found in Scripture. The examples of the Day of Pentecost (Acts 2: 38-41), the Philippian jailer (Acts 16: 31-33), the Ephesian disciples (Acts 19: 1-5), and many others reveal that this was not a practice of the apostles. The custom of the apostles in Scripture was to baptize immediately those who wished to accept Jesus as Savior. While the apostle Paul did fast for three days prior, he was not instructed concerning baptism until the end of his fast (Acts 9: 1-18), at which time he received baptism immediately.

The <u>Didache</u> also suggests that sprinkling or pouring might be acceptable for baptism if water sufficient for immersion is unavailable. If, indeed, deviations of the method of baptism did emerge in the second century, it must have been on the rarest occasion since none are documented.

The first recorded incident of any form of baptism other than immersion is found in the third century when a man named Novatian[4], in AD 251, was ill and bedridden. While unable to arise and submit obediently to immersion, Novatian desired to be baptized. The church leaders determined that, due to Novatian's condition, they would merely pour water over him in lieu of immersion. Over the centuries more individuals and church leaders opted for either sprinkling or pouring water as a form of baptism. Finally, in AD 1311 at the Council of Ravenna,[5] the hierarchy of the Roman Catholic Church officially endorsed these as acceptable forms of baptism.

This is the perspective that most closely resembles Martin Luther's[6] (1483-1546) view of the role of baptism even as he opposed the formality of unauthorized rituals that were so prevalent in the church at the time. While Luther espoused a doctrine of salvation by *faith only*, he did not consider the efficacy of baptism antagonistic to that position. Luther's differences with the church developed out of his concern that the Roman Catholics held dear many sacraments *not* established in Scripture. Baptism was not a point of contention for him. This is the belief advanced today by the Lutherans, those who follow closely the teachings of Martin Luther.

Water Baptism Is a Sign

While it is true that many regard baptism, whether by immersion, pouring, or sprinkling, as essential for one's redemption, others see it as a deed that, although pleasing to God, is ineffectual with respect to salvation. Since this is a physical activity, it is held that baptism is a human *work* and, hence, can have no direct spiritual effect. Instead, baptism is considered a sign of the covenant of grace that has been commanded by God and is performed as witness that someone has made a commitment to Christ. Salvation and the indwelling of the Holy Spirit are experienced separate from water baptism. This view stems from a belief in the association of water baptism in the New Testament with infant circumcision as it is portrayed under the Old Testament law. This is the perspective taught today by evangelicals in America.

One well-known Bible scholar of Luther's time, William Tyndale[7] (1484-1536), who was an Englishman and early translator of the Bible, seemed to hold views more in line with evangelicals than Lutherans. While he held baptism in high regard, he apparently saw it as a sign of salvation rather than a requirement.

John Wycliffe[8] (1324-1384) was the first man to translate the Bible into English and the first to use Olde English variations of the words *baptize* and *baptism* in reference to this Christian rite. He was also one of the earliest to suggest, in opposition to the Roman Catholics, that baptism was not meant to wash away original sin. He determined *'that baptism doth not confer, but only signify grace, which was given before.'*[9] He did, however, consider baptism essential for church membership and partaking of the Lord's Supper.

Much of the discord that persists with respect to baptism can be attributed to the Reformation Movement of the sixteenth century, which resulted in a remarkable transformation of the religious community. A man by the name of Huldrych Zwingli[10] (1484-1531), a Swiss theologian and contemporary of Martin Luther, was the first of sufficient notoriety to successfully espouse the view of baptism as a mere outward sign of salvation circa 1525. Zwingli considered infant baptism to be legitimate – not for the benefit of salvation, but to join the child to the community of believers. Prior to the time of Zwingli, the understanding from the writings of the apostles was essentially universal that baptism was the manner in which men could attain eternal life.

John Calvin[11] (1509-1564) believed baptism to be an initiatory rite during which men were admitted into the fellowship of the body of Christ. To an extent, he saw some efficacy in baptism, although he viewed baptism as a new covenant sign in the same fashion that circumcision was a sign of the Abrahamic covenant. He did not believe baptism was a *means* to procure salvation, but saw it as a matter of man publicly *accepting* the promises of God.

John Wesley's[12] (1703-1791) perspective on baptism appears to be similar to Calvin's. Wesley, the founder of Methodism, considered no particular mode of baptism more or less scriptural than others. There is an impression in some of his sermons that he embraced baptism as man's acceptance of grace in some sense, as well as the manner of initiation into the church; yet he denied that baptism was the new birth of which Jesus and the apostles spoke. Wesley considered baptism to be an outward covenant sign that separated believers from nonbelievers. He contended in favor of infant baptism based on the belief that it represented a rite of admission into the church.

Water Baptism Is Immaterial

Baptism in water is considered to be of no consequence by many others who proclaim belief in Jesus as the Messiah. The fact that baptism is a command of Christ is apparently the single reason it is observed by these individuals if it is celebrated at all. As with those who view it as a sign, they reject regeneration at the time of baptism based on the belief that participation is a work of man and, therefore, is not a matter of salvation. The belief still originated from the work of Zwingli in the sixteenth century. Despite the fact that, prior to the time of Zwingli, baptism was universally understood as the moment salvation was attained, the past few hundred years have seen his teachings grow in popularity.

Baptism with the Holy Spirit

Finally, there are those who regard baptism with the Holy Spirit, not baptism in water, as the moment of salvation. Those teaching this doctrine submit that the outpouring of the Holy Spirit portrayed in the book of Acts is, by definition, baptism with the Holy Spirit. The belief is that the Holy Spirit *falls upon* men in this manner even today, unlike the earlier view that this experience was limited in nature. Accordingly, only through the outpouring of the Holy Spirit, as experienced on the Day of Pentecost, can one receive the seal of salvation. This (Holy Spirit) baptism is distinguished by the presence of spiritual gift(s) in one's life – most notably the spiritual gift of speaking in tongues – as a sign of salvation.

This view of baptism with the Holy Spirit has risen in popularity within what is known as the Pentecostal movement that had its beginnings within the United States in the early twentieth century. The most celebrated incident, often considered the foundation of the movement, took place on Azusa Street in Los Angeles in 1906. Many claimed to have received this baptism in the Spirit and the gift of tongues, much as it had occurred on the Day of Pentecost.

We do find some within the Pentecostal movement who, while teaching that the outpouring of the Spirit in this manner constitutes baptism with the Holy Spirit, do not deem this to be the time of salvation. To them this represents a second blessing that God bestows upon men as a matter of distributing miraculous gifts of the Spirit. They do not necessarily consider this experience a matter of redemption.

* * * * *

While these opinions may summarize the vast majority of views on the subject, certainly a wide variety of beliefs can be found intertwined among these few, covering an entire range of beliefs stretching from one end of the theological spectrum to the other. Since Scripture is forthright in its instruction regarding baptism and its value with respect to salvation, it is difficult to conceive how these disputes have risen to such prominence in religious circles. Since some of the claims openly clash, it is simply *impossible* for all of these beliefs to be valid. Therefore, given the seriousness of the debate and the eternal consequences involved, seeking biblical guidance is critical for those who wish to honor God.

NOTES FOR CHAPTER 1

1. The notion that immersion in water is essential for salvation must, in a sense, be qualified. Campbell held that a Christian is anyone who obeys God's instructions to the extent that he/she is aware of those instructions. According to Campbell an individual is responsible, *"in all things according to the measure of knowledge of his will."* One who is unaware of the charge for immersion could clearly not be held accountable for disobedience to that charge. This, however, is not intended to be license to ignore a call once one is cognizant of God's direction. Campbell, Extract from **"Any Christians Among Protestant Parties."** The Millennial Harbinger 8: (September 1837): 411; 33 (March 1862): 132. 2. Alexander Campbell

2. Perhaps the most significant difference between Alexander Campbell and Barton W. Stone lies in the ultimate goal each sought to achieve. Campbell focused on the Bible as the single ultimate guide for Christianity and salvation. Stone, on the other hand, while he held the Bible as the single authority by which men might seek God, considered *unity* of the brotherhood his highest priority. Thus the greatest difference lies in their view of the un-immersed. While Campbell refused to fellowship with those who rejected immersion for the remission of sins, Stone did not. He refused to draw a line of distinction, as Campbell did, between immersed believers and those who had not been immersed. His sentiment regarding these individuals is best expressed in his statement, *"I must believe that the household of Cornelius were made holy and received the Holy Spirit previous to their baptism yet before they were baptized they were not Christians nor united with the*

church of Christ." This statement, of course, does not speak to fellowship with those who simply reject immersion, but it does reflect a softer perspective toward those who did not receive immersion for the forgiveness of sins. Stone, Christian Messenger 4: 235.

3. While the Didache was not discovered until 1873 in a monastery in Constantinople, its existence was never in doubt. The writings of the Didache were referenced by several other authors in the early church. The author, and even the date of the writing, are unknown. Few ever consider a date later than AD 200 while others suggest a possible date of writing as early as AD 50.

The notion that sprinkling or pouring of water for the purpose of baptism when immersion was not possible is first mentioned in this particular work confirming that immersion was certainly the form of baptism practiced and taught by the apostles. The teachings of this work, however, do not seem to follow absolutely the apostolic example (e.g., fasting a day or two prior to baptism) as can be seen in this excerpt regarding baptism:

> **On Baptism**. *7:1 But concerning Baptism, this is how you shall baptize. 7:2 Having first recited all these things, baptize in living water in the name of the Father and of the Son and of the Holy Spirit. 7:3 But if you do not have running water, then baptize in other water; 7:4 And if you are not able in cold, then in warm. 7:5 But if you have neither, then pour water on the head three times in the name of the Father and of the Son and of the Holy Spirit. 7:6 But before the Baptism, let him that baptizes and him that is baptized fast, and any others also who are able; 7:7 And you shall order him that is baptized to fast a day or two before.* The Didache, Chapter 7. This revision into English is based on the translation of J.B. Lightfoot.

4. Novatian was a schismatic of the third century, and founder of the sect of the Novatians; he was a Roman priest, and made himself antipope. His name is given as Novatus (*Noouatos*, Eusebius; *Nauatos*, Socrates) by Greek writers, and also in the verses of Damasus and Prudentius, on account of the metre:

> **Biography** - We know little of his life. St. Cornelius in his letter to Fabius of Antioch relates that Novatian was possessed by Satan for a season, apparently while a catechumen; for the exorcists attended him, and he fell into a sickness from which instant death was expected; he was, therefore, given baptism by affusion as he lay on his bed. The rest of the rites were not supplied on his recovery, nor was he confirmed by the bishop. "How then can he have received the Holy Ghost? " asks Cornelius. Novatian was a man of learning and had been trained in literary composition. Cornelius speaks of him sarcastically as "that maker of dogmas, that champion of ecclesiastical learning". His eloquence is mentioned by Cyprian (Ep. lx, 3) and a pope (presumably Fabian) promoted him to the priesthood in spite of the protests (according to Cornelius) of all the clergy and many of the laity that it was uncanonical for one who had received only clinical baptism to be admitted among the clergy. The story told by Eulogius of Alexandria that Novatian was Archdeacon of Rome, and was made a priest by the pope in order to prevent his succeeding to the papacy, contradicts the evidence of Cornelius and supposes a later state of things when the Roman deacons were statesmen rather than ministers. The anonymous work "Ad Novatianum" (x2i) tells us that Novatian, "so long as he was in the one house, that is in Christ's Church, bewailed the sins of his neighbours as if they were his own, bore the burdens of the brethren, as the Apostle exhorts, and

strengthened with consolation the backsliding in heavenly faith." The Catholic Encyclopedia, Volume XI.

5. Interestingly, the decision to accept forms of baptism other than immersion caused a rift between the Roman Catholic Church and her ally, the Greek Orthodox. The Greek Orthodox could not abide any form of baptism but immersion, realizing the meaning of the original Greek words used to define baptism.

In a history of the Baptist Church David Benedict, a contemporary of Campbell and Stone, noted the following regarding the work of a man by the name of James Basanage (date unknown) who wrote regarding the decision of Pope Stephen 21 to allow sprinkling in the case of infants in danger of death.

> "The learned James Basanage makes several very proper remarks on this canon: as that 'although it is accounted the first law for sprinkling, yet it doth not forbid dipping; that it allows sprinkling only in case of imminent danger; that the authenticity of it is denied by some Catholics; that many laws were made after this time in Germany, France, and England, to compel dipping, and without any provision for cases of necessity; therefore that this law did not alter the mode of dipping in public baptisms; and that it was not till five hundred and fifty years after, that the Legislature, in a council at Ravenna, in the year thirteen hundred and eleven, declared dipping or sprinkling indifferent.'" David Benedict, A General History of the Baptist Denomination in America, and Other Parts of the World, 1813.

6. Those who believe Luther was responsible for trivializing baptism misunderstand his view completely. Luther merely wished to rid the church of manmade traditions and rituals. His view is well defined in this excerpt from his work:

> In these words you must note, in the first place, that here stand God's commandment and institution, lest we doubt that Baptism is divine, not devised nor invented by men. For as truly as I can say, No man has spun the Ten Commandments, the Creed, and the Lord's Prayer out of his head, but they are revealed and given by God Himself, so also I can boast that Baptism is no human trifle, but instituted by God Himself, moreover, that it is most solemnly and strictly commanded that we must be baptized or we cannot be saved, lest any one regard it as a trifling matter, like putting on a new red coat. For it is of the greatest importance that we esteem Baptism excellent, glorious, and exalted, for which we contend and fight chiefly, because the world is now so full of sects clamoring that Baptism is an external thing, and that external things are of no benefit. But let it be ever so much an external thing here stand God's Word and command which institute, establish, and confirm Baptism. But what God institutes and commands cannot be a vain, but must be a most precious thing, though in appearance it were of less value than a straw. If hitherto people could consider it a great thing when the Pope with his letters and bulls dispensed indulgences and confirmed altars and churches, solely because of the letters and seals, we ought to esteem Baptism much more highly and more precious, because God has commanded it, and, besides, it is performed in His name. For these are the words, Go ye baptize; however, not in your name, but in the name of God. Luther, Large Catechism X21, Part Fourth, Of Baptism. *Luther's Works*, 1551 edition, Vol. 2, p.76.

7. Regarding baptism, Tyndale wrote: *"If baptism preach me the washing in Christ's blood, so doth the Holy Ghost accompany it; and that deed of preaching through faith*

doth put away my sins. The ark of Noah saved them in the water through faith." Tyndale, Prologue to the Book of Leviticus.

This view of baptism to forgive sins seems to be contradicted in the following work by John Christian unless it is understood that Tyndale believed that water alone could not bring forgiveness.

> Upon the subject of baptism he is very full. He is confident that baptism does not wash away sin. 'It is impossible,' says he, 'that the waters of the river should wash our hearts' (Tyndale, *Works* 2. 30. London, 1831). Baptism was a plunging into the water (Ibid, 25). Baptism to avail must include repentance, faith and confession (21. 179). The church must, therefore, consist of believers (Ibid, 25). His book in a wonderful manner states accurately the position of the Baptists" Christian, A History of the Baptists, I, pp. 187-88).

8. Wycliffe held doctrinal views perhaps most closely associated with the Baptist denominational perspective. He wrote concerning the futility of infant baptism, though there does seem to be some confusion in his work concerning the fate of the unbaptized infant.

9. Walden, tom. ii. c. 98, 108

10. Zwingli viewed Christian baptism as not only equivalent to, but identical to, the baptism of John. His assertion was that no new covenant was instituted and that the church age was merely a continuation of the old covenant. To Zwingli, the forgiveness of sins in baptism suggested in Scripture was symbolic in nature. He viewed Holy Spirit baptism as the baptism that saves. Baptism in water, to Zwingli, was perhaps more important to the feeble Christian who needed to do something as assurance of salvation. He expressed his view of baptism accordingly:

> ...The inward baptism of the Spirit is the work of teaching which God does in our hearts and the calling with which he comforts and assures our hearts in Christ. And this baptism none can give save God alone. Without it, none can be saved – though it is quite possible to be saved without the baptism of external teaching and immersion. Zwingli, *Of Baptism, in Zwingli and Bullinger*, "Library of Christian Classics," Vol. 24. Ed. And tr. G.W. Bromiley (Philadelphia Westminster Press, 1953), p. 137

11. It seems somewhat ironic that men such as Zwingli and Calvin, who saw no salvation value in baptism, fought so vigorously in favor of paedobaptism. The following excerpt from the work of Calvin depicts his position very well as he associates baptism with circumcision:

> At length they object, that there is not greater reason for admitting infants to baptism than to the Lord's Supper, to which, however, they are never admitted: as if Scripture did not in every way draw a wide distinction between them. In the early Church, indeed, the Lord's Supper was frequently given to infants, as appears from Cyprian and Augustine, (August. ad Bonif. Lib. 1;) but the practice justly became obsolete. For if we attend to the peculiar nature of baptism, it is a kind of entrance, and as it were initiation into the Church, by which we are ranked among the people of God, a sign of our spiritual regeneration, by which we are again born to be children of God, whereas on the contrary the Supper is intended for those of riper years, who, having passed the

tender period of infancy, are fit to bear solid food. Calvin, Institutes of the Christian Religion, Book 4, Chapter 16, Section 30.

12. Wesley understood baptism to be the *outward sign of an inward change* as is expressed in his words from Sermon 45:

> 1. And, First, it follows, that baptism is not the new birth: They are not one and the same thing. Many indeed seem to imagine that they are just the same; at least, they speak as if they thought so; but I do not know that this opinion is publicly avowed by any denomination of Christians whatever. Certainly it is not by any within these kingdoms, whether of the established Church, or dissenting from it. The judgment of the latter is clearly declared in the large Catechism: [Q. 163, 165. -- Ed.] -- Q. "What are the parts of a sacrament? A. The parts of a sacrament are two: The one an outward and sensible sign; the other, and inward and spiritual grace, thereby signified. -- Q. What is baptism? A. Baptism is a sacrament, wherein Christ hath ordained the washing with water, to be a sign and seal of regeneration by his Spirit." Here it is manifest, baptism, the sign, is spoken of as distinct from regeneration, the thing signified. Wesley, Sermon 45, Part IV.

Chapter II
Baptism and the First Covenant

The Shadow Covenant

The Bible offers us the opportunity to understand God's character and His view of man. In it He has established a covenant that guides us in our relationship with Him and directs our steps on the path to eternal life. This covenant has its roots deep in the pages of history. The antecedents for water baptism that is introduced in the New Testament can be seen in the foundation that was poured by God in the old (first) covenant, initiated with Abraham and extended through Moses, so that the new covenant might be firmly established.

> 1. For the law, having a shadow of the good things to come, *and* not the very image of the things, can never with these same sacrifices, which they offer continually year by year, make those who approach perfect. 2. For then would they not have ceased to be offered? For the worshipers, once purified, would have had no more consciousness of sins. 3. But in those *sacrifices there is* a reminder of sins every year. 4. For *it is* not possible that the blood of bulls and goats could take away sins. (Hebrews 10: 1-4)

Through His servant Moses, God presented to the Israelites the law of the first covenant. This law was intended to secure the relationship between God and His chosen people, the children of Israel. Scripture reveals to us the continuity and consistency of God's plan through the ancestral-like relationship between the first covenant, founded upon the law, and the new covenant of grace that was instituted by Jesus' death, burial, and resurrection.

The apostle Paul addressed the idea of *shadows* found in the preceding passage (Hebrews 10: 1). In his letter to the Galatians, Paul identifies believers as those who have been freed from the bondage of sin by the blood of Christ and made heirs to the kingdom. Spiritually, he likens believers in the church age to the children of Abraham with whom God established His original covenant.

> 22. For it is written that Abraham had two sons: the one by a bondwoman, the other by a freewoman. 23. But he *who was* of the bondwoman was born according to the flesh, and he of the freewoman through promise, 24. which things are symbolic. For these are the two

covenants: the one from Mount Sinai, which gives birth to bondage, which is Hagar – 25. for this Hagar is Mount Sinai in Arabia, and corresponds to Jerusalem which now is, and is in bondage with her children – 26. but the Jerusalem above is free, which is the mother of us all. 27. For it is written:
> *Rejoice, O barren, you who do not bear!*
> *Break forth and shout, you who are not in labor!*
> *For the desolate has many more children than she who has a husband.*

28. Now we, brethren, as Isaac was, are children of promise. 29. But, as he who was born according to the flesh then persecuted him who was born according to the Spirit, even so *it is* now. 30. Nevertheless, what does the Scripture say? *"Cast out the bondwoman and her son, for the son of the bondwoman shall not be heir with the son of the freewoman."* 31. So then, brethren, we are not children of the bondwoman but of the free. (Galatians 4: 22-31)

Elements of the First Covenant

Various elements of the first covenant, intended to provide a mechanism for the Israelites to worship and honor God, were not the *same* as those in the new covenant, but rather *shadows* of what was to come. Throughout the New Testament inspired men of God, including the author of the book of Hebrews, cite distinct comparisons between the two covenants. Scripture reveals in detail the offerings the Israelites were commanded to sacrifice to God continually in order to atone for the sins they had committed against Him. Who can doubt that the sacrifice of Jesus was the reality of the *shadow* of animal sacrifices performed under the old covenant? The sacrifices of the first covenant that were offered by the priests on a daily basis were unable to afford men a clean conscience from the sins they had committed. Incapable of freeing men from the guilt of sin, these bore a shallow likeness to the one sacrifice that could offer what these priestly sacrifices could not.

Feasts of the First Covenant

The first covenant incorporated various celebrations that involved specific feasts and foods. Some of these feasts were intended only for the priests. For instance, it was the priests who were to partake of the sin offerings that were made in the temple (Leviticus 6: 24-30). Certain other feasts, such as the Feast of Weeks, the Feast of the Passover, and the Feast of the Tabernacles, were meant for the general Israelite population. The people observed each of these festivals for reasons detailed by Moses in

Deuteronomy 16: 1-16. The Passover Feast, also known as the Feast of Unleavened Bread, was celebrated in remembrance of their release from slavery as death came to the firstborn of each household in Egypt; but those households who obeyed His command were *passed over*, escaping this terrible plague. This was the final plague on the Egyptians, causing Pharaoh to decide to free the Israelites (Exodus 12: 17-23; Deuteronomy 16: 1-8).

The Feast of Weeks provided an opportunity for the children of Israel to remember their slavery in Egypt and show their gratitude, through free will offerings, for the freedom they now enjoyed (Deuteronomy 16: 9-12). Through the Feast of Tabernacles, the Israelites honored God for the fruitfulness of their work in the field that produced bountiful crops (Deuteronomy 16: 13-17).

The new covenant also provides a feast in which we commemorate our relationship with God through Christ. Jesus established this feast, known to us as the Lord's Supper, during the Passover on the night prior to His crucifixion (Matthew 26: 26-29). Like the feasts of the first covenant, they were to observe this feast as a memorial (Luke 22: 19-20). This time was intended to remind them of His death – a death that had not yet occurred, but was imminent. It is fair to say that the disciples did not fully grasp the significance of this breaking of bread until sometime after Jesus' resurrection.

Conversion in the First Covenant

Scripture indicates that God provided a means by which Gentiles could convert to Judaism (Acts 2: 11; 6: 5). The conversion process apparently included a ceremony involving water, historically referred to by some as *proselyte baptism*, that was comparable to the immersion performed by John the Baptist as well as Jesus' disciples. We have sufficient evidence in such writings as the Dead Sea Scrolls[1] and the Talmud[2] that various other ceremonies, also called baptisms, were employed prior to the time of Christ and John the Baptist for the purpose of purification.

While proselyte baptism is not addressed in Scripture, it is important to note that this ceremony is addressed in neither a positive or negative manner. If the Israelites were employing a rite of conversion unacceptable to God, it is reasonable to believe God would have highlighted that deed in Scripture. If, however, God provided a means for Gentiles to be accepted into the Jewish faith, as we know He did, He would not necessarily need to communicate that in Scripture. Those who participated in that conversion process would simply become subject to the Jewish law once converted.

Proselyte baptism should be considered more of an *indirect* precursor to Christian immersion for two distinct reasons. First of all, the fact that this practice is not communicated in Scripture as part of the old covenant is reason to dismiss it as a direct *shadow* of baptism. Secondly, Scripture reveals other purification ceremonies and events that truly *are* established in the Old Testament and are more befitting this role. Still, we should not lose sight of the fact that proselyte baptism was performed as a matter of conversion.

Purification in the First Covenant

While the Ten Commandments are delivered in the book of Exodus, it is in the book of Leviticus where we discover many of the finer points of the Mosaic Law. It is here, for the most part, that we find God establishing water as a means of purification for religious effect. The book of Leviticus reveals two different kinds of ceremonial washings performed by the Israelites. The first is represented by the Hebrew word כבס (*kabac*). While the word denotes cleansing for religious performance, we find that its use is generally limited to the ceremonial washing of clothing for purification purposes (Exodus 19: 10; Leviticus 11: 24-28). This word is employed metaphorically in passages like Psalm 51: 2 and Jeremiah 4: 14, but those references do not impact the literal meaning of the word, which is to *wash*.

Another washing in Leviticus also depicts a ritual cleansing by means of water – the Hebrew word רחץ (*rachats*), which is more often translated into English as *bathe*. While we find that there are certain times when רחץ refers to the washing of a man's hands and feet (Exodus 30: 19-21; 40: 31), it most often indicates a submergence (bathing) of one's entire body as a matter of cleansing (Leviticus 15: 16; 16: 4; 22: 6; Numbers 19: 19). Occasionally it denotes the washing of sacrifices prior to placing them on the altar (Leviticus 1: 2-23). This kind of washing, then, might fairly be viewed as a kind of progenitor to Christian baptism. Yet we can surmise from Scripture that God's foresight with respect to baptism far surpasses specific ritual washings like these.

It is not insignificant that God, beginning with the enactment of the Mosaic Law, has *always* demanded the combination of water and blood in the purification of His people. Those who offered sacrifices in keeping with the law, but failed to wash with water, were considered unclean notwithstanding the sacrifices that were made. While cleansing was offered through the shedding of blood, it was not affected without water. Washing with water and the sacrifice of blood labored jointly toward the purification of the Israelites. Failure to bathe according to the law was considered a breach of the covenant and grounds for separating that person from the assembly (Numbers 19: 20). This principle applied directly to Gentile converts as they experienced a conversion involving both water (proselyte baptism) and blood (circumcision).

A number of Old Testament passages point to cleansing with water in order for the Israelites to be presentable to God. Numerous washings are cited throughout the book of Leviticus as well as passages such as Numbers 19: 7-8. In fact, the entire nineteenth chapter of Numbers offers compelling evidence of the emphasis God has placed upon cleansing by means of water.

Scripture speaks of a myriad of events in which God's use of water for purification is demonstrated. In the Red Sea He buried in water those who opposed Him, thus liberating the Israelite nation (Exodus 14: 1-31). Paul explained to the Corinthians that this incident could be viewed as an *image* of baptism (1 Corinthians 10: 2) as the Israelites were freed from that which enslaved them. Naaman, a commander in the Syrian army, was required to wash seven times in the Jordan River in order to be cleansed of his leprosy (2 Kings 5: 1-14). Through the flood God removed from the earth all but Noah, who found favor in God's eyes, along with his family (Genesis 6: 5-8:22). The waters obliterated the evil of men. We are told that baptism does *correspond* to the waters of the flood (1 Peter 3: 21). Each of these instances illustrates the importance God placed upon the use of water in providing some kind of cleansing, both physical and spiritual, although mostly spiritual. These could arguably also be considered *shadows* of baptism that was to come. The apostle John, recognizing the divine role assigned to water, portrays it as an equal witness with the Holy Spirit and the blood to the eternal life we have available through Jesus (1 John 5: 6-11).

The Old Reflected in the New

It is the writer of the book of Hebrews who truly captures the essence of the relationship between the covenants. In providing a thorough examination of the old and new covenants he offers us the opportunity to realize the correlation, as well as the contrast, between the two. Embarking on an exploration of the old covenant in which the foundation for the new covenant was laid, the relationship between them becomes clear. A multitude of Old Testament references throughout the book that point to the coming Messiah and the establishment of the new covenant affirm this relationship beyond any doubt.

While the kinship of the old and new covenants may, at times, seem imprecise absent an affirming *this old covenant rite = that element of the new covenant*, the connection is still undeniable. The nature of a shadow is that its likeness to the original is often obscured. Various ceremonies and ordinances that formed the framework for the first covenant were designed to be temporary in nature. God's plan from the beginning was the covenant of grace in which we live. Having established that Jesus is now *the* High Priest through whom our approach to the Father is made possible, the author defines Jesus' role more precisely – He has risen to be with God and has established Himself as Mediator of the new covenant. The author of Hebrews indicates that it was unnecessary for Jesus to fill the role of priest here on earth. Through the lineage of Levi, priests under the Mosaic Law performed the rites that served as *a copy and/or shadow of heavenly things.* Jesus' role was to take the position of High Priest in the new covenant, considered a more excellent ministry (Hebrews 8: 4-7).

Within the new covenant, the significance of the temple and its design, as well as the articles located therein, were now obsolete (Hebrews 9: 1-5). Preparations of the priests prior to entering the temple and the inner sanctum, including various washings, as well as certain foods and drinks, were discarded (Hebrews 9: 6-10).

> 11. But Christ came *as* High Priest of the good things to come, with the greater and more perfect tabernacle not made with hands, that is, not of this creation. 12. Not with the blood of goats and calves, but with His own blood He entered the Most Holy Place once for all, having obtained eternal redemption. 13. For if the blood of bulls and goats and the ashes of a heifer, sprinkling the unclean, sanctifies for the purifying of the flesh, 14. how much more shall the blood of Christ, who through the eternal Spirit offered Himself without spot to God, cleanse your conscience from dead works to serve the living God? (Hebrews 9: 11-14)

Note the directional shift of verse eleven as the writer begins to feature the new covenant in contrast to the old. The weaknesses of the first covenant had been overcome through the blood of Christ. Still, while they had now been withdrawn, certain critical aspects of the Mosaic Law (ritual sacrifices, etc.) found themselves mirrored within the covenant of grace.

The temporal nature of these *shadows* (e.g., animal sacrifices, feasts, etc) was exchanged for the permanence of those images instituted under the covenant of grace. Rather than a temple constructed of mortar and stone, Jesus entered a spiritual Most Holy Place (Hebrews 9: 11). He now stood as the High Priest who would serve as *Intercessor* for mankind (Hebrews 9: 12). The animal sacrifices of the first covenant became obsolete once Jesus shed His own blood on our behalf (Hebrews 9: 13-14).

We find a similar, yet even more detailed, comparison of the covenants in the tenth chapter of Hebrews. The deficiencies of the previous covenant prevented it from offering redemption to mankind. The blood of bulls and goats, so central in covering man's sins under the law, could not offer the freedom from sin that was essential for mankind to be reconciled to God. Therefore, God replaced these with that which could accomplish the task – the sacrifice of Jesus (Hebrews 10: 1-11). We find that the one sacrifice in the new covenant replaced the many that are found in the first covenant. Just as we discovered a transition in verse eleven of the ninth chapter of Hebrews, we once again observe a change in the focus of the writer's treatise starting with the twelfth verse of chapter ten. While verses one through eleven address the weaknesses of the first covenant, beginning in verse twelve the author fully concentrates upon the characteristics of the new covenant in contrast with the old covenant.

Addressing the new covenant as the means of reconciliation to God (Hebrews 10: 12-14), the writer thoughtfully confers recognition upon specific elements found within the covenant (Hebrews 10: 12 – 11: 40). In a sweeping message he reveals the specifics of the covenant of grace. The *one sacrifice* for sin, in contrast to the many sacrifices required in the first covenant, can be found in Jesus' death on the cross (vs. 12-13). Through this one offering, *sanctification* was made possible (v. 14). The *Holy Spirit* stands as witness for those who would be saved (v. 15). True *remission of sins*, never before possible, is now realized (vs. 16-18). The role of *High Priest* has been assumed by the only one truly worthy (vs. 19-21). The combination of *faith, repentance,* and *one washing* (baptism), as opposed to the many washings of the first covenant, makes it possible for men to draw near to God (v. 22). *Confession* of Jesus as Lord is boldly spoken by the faithful (v. 23). *Love* and *good works,* as well as the *assembly* of Christ's followers, offer exhortation and support to all (vs. 24-25). Certainty of *judgment* awaits those who refuse to accept Jesus as Savior (vs. 26-31) while *eternal life* is the reward for those who do partake in God's covenant of grace (vs. 32-39). Faith (chapter 11), then, is the manner in which men respond to this offer of grace.

The numerous feasts of the old covenant that were intended to honor God were but chaff in the wind when contrasted with the loaf and the cup (the one meal replacing the many) that represent the holiness and purity of the sacrifice of Jesus' body and blood. God also discovered a more compatible dwelling place among men in the repentant hearts of those who choose to submit to Him. No longer would God separate Himself from those who love Him.

Performed alongside various blood sacrifices and continuing year after year, the purification practices of the first covenant were incapable of clothing the children of Israel with the perfection God desired (Hebrews 10: 1). No amount of washings or sacrifices in the first covenant could offer what the one sacrifice and one washing in the new covenant were able to convey. God instituted a new and more powerful covenant, the covenant of grace, built upon the only sacrifice that could be considered worthy. The first covenant, and those elements comprising it, paled in comparison to the power of the new covenant made available to us through the blood of Christ.

Baptism and the Birthright of the First Covenant

In the first covenant there was, of course, a unique event that occurred at which time a child was recognized as a descendant of Abraham and partaker in his covenant with God. It was the moment of childbirth. When an Israelite child was born, whether male or female, that child immediately inherited all the rights and privileges afforded anyone who was born into the lineage of Abraham, Isaac, and Jacob (Genesis 15: 17-21; 17: 1-8). This was an honor bestowed upon each Israelite, but not as a result of anything the child had done since, as an infant, he/she had obviously accomplished nothing. The inheritance was based solely upon the relationship Abraham had established with the Father.

While others were allowed to participate, the normal method of entry into the covenant was childbirth.

All serious students of the Bible would concede the New Testament teaching that there is a time, the determination of which is the source of endless controversy, in which an individual becomes a child of God. It is a time understood to be the moment of regeneration as God cleanses a man or woman of his/her sins and that person is reborn. In the tradition of the covenant of Abraham, and the fact that participation was recognized as a right of birth, the time of regeneration (renewal) is identified as rebirth (John 3: 3-8; Titus 3: 5). We discover that, just as the Israelites were born of Abraham, we must be born of God. Thus, inheritance of the kingdom of God is an inheritance that is a birthright for those who have been *born again* or *born of God* – by a spiritual birth (Galatians 4: 23-29; 1 Peter 1: 23; 2: 2; 1 John 2: 29; 3: 9) – into the family of God.

When the new birth, also called *new life* (Romans 6: 4), is presented in the New Testament, baptism is the time recognized as the moment of rebirth. As we consider the shadow that the new covenant of grace casts upon the first covenant, although the relationship between baptism and the ceremonial washings of old is easily established, its association with a child's birth into the Israelite nation must be considered genuine.

The Baptism of John – A Transition

In a search for some kind of transitional baptism between the old and new covenants, many look to the book of Acts and the water baptism that was conferred there. However, Christian immersion in water that is discussed throughout the New Testament would necessarily have ceased if God intended it to be temporary or transitional. The undeniable implication from the Great Commission is that baptism carries with it a sense of permanence. At no time in the New Testament do we discover any allusion to the cessation of water baptism.

It seems more reasonable to conclude that a baptism intended to provide connectivity between the two covenants would be found prior to the establishment of the new covenant in the book of Acts. Proselyte baptism should be ruled out since its role was to grant Gentiles access to the Mosaic Law. It is unlikely that a ritual such as proselyte baptism, which was not administered to the Israelites, would serve in a conjoining role between two washings (old covenant washings and new covenant baptism) that, at least initially, were applicable only to the Israelites.

As the beginning of Jesus' ministry drew nigh, God specially selected John to fill the role of forerunner for Christ (Mark 1: 1-3). One could easily argue that God specially *created* John the Baptist, given the extraordinary circumstances surrounding his birth. A complement to John's mission of preparing the way for the Messiah was his role as a great prophet.

> 7. As they departed, Jesus began to say to the multitudes concerning John: "What did you go out into the wilderness to see? A reed shaken by the wind? 8. But what did you go out to see? A man clothed in soft garments? Indeed, those who wear soft *clothing* are in kings' houses. 9. But what did you go out to see? A prophet? Yes, I say to you, and more than a prophet. 10. For this is *he* of whom it is written:
> "Behold, I send My messenger before Your face,
> Who will prepare Your way before You.'
> 11. "Assuredly, I say to you, among those born of women there has not risen one greater than John the Baptist; but he who is least in the kingdom of heaven is greater than he. (Matthew 11: 7-11)

John's ministry was marked by his emphasis on the rite of immersion in water. So central was baptism to John's ministry that the title by which he became known, the Baptizer, defined his ministry. John himself explained that he did not baptize of his own volition, but that he was instructed by God to baptize with water (John 1: 33).

John's baptism was distinct from proselyte baptism and the various washings of the old covenant. His was a baptism that offered forgiveness of sins (Mark 1: 4). Old covenant washings, admittedly inadequate to actualize God's desired effect of holiness, simply declared a man to be clean rather than unclean, or they prepared the priests to enter into the presence of God to perform sacrifices. No exact association can be found between proselyte baptism and forgiveness, although some do claim the relationship existed, but it did offer Gentiles conversion into the Jewish faith. Since John's baptism extended forgiveness prior to Jesus' death, it is most reasonable to view this as transitional, leading from the old covenant washings and/or childbirth to new covenant baptism in the name of Jesus.

A critical element that we must not overlook is the singular nature of John's ministry that is revealed through the prophets and the gospel writers. Isaiah indicated that a man was to make preparations for the coming of the Messiah, in essence, paving the road before Him (Isaiah 40: 3). Malachi also prophesied concerning an individual who would be Christ's forerunner (Malachi 3: 1) whose role it would be to prepare the Israelites for the coming Messiah. Both Matthew (Matthew 3: 3) and Mark (Mark 1: 2-3) quote Isaiah's prophecy and apply it directly to John the Baptist.

Through the words of these inspired writers the ministry of John the Baptist, of which baptism was an indispensable component, is seen and understood as preparatory for the appearance of the Messiah. If John and his ministry emerged in anticipation of Christ, the baptism he offered should be viewed in the same light. John's baptism provided for forgiveness of sins – yet it was not baptism in the name of Jesus, nor did it involve the Holy Spirit. Consequently, if the baptism of John was transitional between the covenants, water baptism in the name of Jesus that was instituted upon the establishment of the church in the book of Acts must be viewed with a sense of permanence.

The Nature of Water

When we consider the role of baptism, a factor that should not be discounted is the very nature of water. It is shortsighted to believe the relevance of God's use of water would be limited solely to its cleansing capabilities. Water has life-giving and life-sustaining qualities that nothing else in creation can claim. Tertullian, one of the early church fathers, pointed to these very characteristics of water as God's reason for using it as the means to enter His kingdom through immersion. Although Tertullian apparently endorsed the problematic view of baptismal regeneration (the notion that the water itself held the power to regenerate), that does not diminish the symbolism of water found in the following statement:

> What *of the fact* that waters were in some way the regulating powers by which the disposition of the world thenceforward was constituted by God? For the suspension of the celestial firmament in the midst He caused by "dividing the waters;" the suspension of "the dry land" He accomplished by "separating the waters." After the world had been hereupon set in order through *its* elements, when inhabitants were given it, "the waters" were the first to receive the precept "to bring forth living creatures." Water was the first to produce that which had life, that it might be no wonder in baptism if waters know how to give life.[3]

The symbolism evident in the life-giving and cleansing properties of water, the ceremonial washings of the old covenant that were but a shadow of the baptism of the new covenant, and the teachings of the apostles and Jesus concerning rebirth, intimate the magnitude of the celebration of Christian baptism.

NOTES FOR CHAPTER 2

1. The Dead Sea Scrolls were discovered in the late 1940's in some caves in the hills west of the Dead Sea. They were hidden in these caves, located in an area known as Khirbet Qumran, presumably by a Jewish community of believers, who traveled to these hills as a manner of setting themselves apart from other men in favor of their pursuit of a relationship with God. These Essenes, as they were known, established a monastery-like community where the goal was the attainment of the highest level of Spiritual commitment.

The exact relationship between the Essenes and the Dead Sea Scrolls is the source of much debate, although the two seem to hail from roughly the same time period (second century B. C.) and location (Qumran). Still, some claim that this is merely coincidence. The likelihood, however, is that the Essenes either wrote or collected the writings, or a combination of these two possibilities.

The Dead Sea Scrolls address, to an extent, certain ritual washings for the purpose of purification. Unfortunately the mutilated condition of certain scrolls prohibited them from being read and translated. One particular scroll that fits this description was entitled _Baptismal Liturgy_. Still, this is not the only portion of the scrolls to deal with ritual washings. For instance, the following excerpt holds reference to such cleansing. Note the relationship in this passage between spirit, water, and sanctification.

> **88. Purification of Initiates at Qumran 6** ...For it is by the Spirit of the Counsel of Truth concerning man's ways that all his iniquities shall be covered, so he may look on the light of life. And by a holy Spirit for union with his Truth shall he be cleansed from all his injustices. And by an upright and humble Spirit will his sins be covered; and by humbling his soul toward all that God prescribes his flesh shall be cleansed for sprinkling with purifying waters, and for sanctifying with cleansing waters. And he shall direct his steps to walk perfectly in all the ways of God, according to his command regarding the times appointed for his testimonies. And he shall deviate neither to the right nor to the left; and he shall not go beyond one of all his words. Then he shall be accepted by an atonement pleasing before God. And for him this will be for a covenant of Unity everlasting. – Dead Sea Scrolls, Community Rule (1QS) 3,6-12.

2. Throughout Old Testament times many oral rules were established by the scribes and priests of the Jewish faith. These rules became, for the most part, traditions of the Israelites that were often viewed as equal to the written law. The Talmud is a document dating back to the first century that stands as an attempt to form a written work of the oral laws that had been handed down over the centuries. Besides codifying these oral rules, the Talmud is also a source of commentary with respect to the Torah, offering the views of the scribes and priest regarding the writing of God's Word. These excerpts specifically address the ritual of proselyte baptism as a means of allowing entrance into the Jewish faith by Gentiles.

86. Essene Initiation - 137. There is no immediate initiation for those who are eager (to join the Essene) party. Rather, they give one a small axe, the loincloth mentioned above, and white garments, putting him under discipline for one year while he remains outside. 138. And during this examination period he gives evidence of his self-control, they lead him nearer to their discipline, letting him participate in cleaner waters for purification. But he is not yet received into their common life. For after proving his endurance, his character is tested for two more years. And then, if he appears worthy, he is admitted to the community. ---Josephus, Jewish War 2.137-138.

91. Rabbinic Proselyte Baptism 1 He who wants to be a proselyte is not received right away. They say to him:

--"Why do you want to be a proselyte? Have you not seen that this people is poorer and more oppressed and humiliated than all peoples? Troubles and trials come upon them, and they bury their sons and their sons' sons. They are killed on account of circumcision and immersion and all the rest of the commandments. And they do not behave in public like all the rest of the nations." **2** If he says, "I am not up to this!" they dismiss him and he goes his own way.

If he takes this on himself, they lead him down to the place of immersion (*beth tebilah*). **3** They cover him with water around the place of his nakedness, and they tell him some of the details of the commandments... **5** And they say good and comforting words to him:

--"Happy are you! Who have you joined? Him who spoke and the world was! The world was created only for the sake of Israel. Only Israel is called "sons of God" (cf. Deut 14:1), and there is none beloved before God except Israel. All the words that we spoke to you we told you only to increase your reward!" --- Babylonian Talmud (appendix), Gerim 1.1-5.

3. Tertullian, On Baptism, Chapter 21. Water Chosen as a Vehicle of Divine Operation and Wherefore. Its Prominence First of All in Creation.

Chapter III
God's New Covenant

The Blood of the New Covenant

Those of us who live in the church age, that is post-Pentecost, live in the covenant of grace that God established through the death of Christ. This *new* covenant is distinguished from the *first* covenant in that salvation (eternal life) could not be attained under the law due to some deep-seated weaknesses that were discussed in the previous chapter. The sacrifices of animals that were performed under the Mosaic Law failed to eliminate the guilt of sin that separated men from God (Hebrews 10: 4). Additionally, men were unable to keep the law perfectly. The transgression of one law was still transgression of the law (James 2: 10) and could not be undone.

> 47. Most assuredly, I say to you, he who believes in Me has everlasting life. 48. I am the bread of life. (John 6: 47-48)

Jesus, in teaching that He alone is the means by which men attain eternal life, revealed to His disciples His own existence as the sustenance of life. Those who would be partakers of Christ, eating His flesh, so to speak, have the opportunity for eternal life (John 6: 53). Failing to fully grasp His teaching, as was so often the case, many of the Jews were alarmed by the comment and began to argue about the prospect of eating a man's flesh. Jesus, however, was speaking of things spiritual – things they were not yet ready to understand.

Within the framework of a covenant, it is always the intent for blood to be a factor. At times blood is considered an agent of initiation during the inception of the covenant. We find that Noah sacrificed animals to God upon exiting the ark as the covenant was established between him and God (Genesis 8: 20). This is true even in a marriage where the mixing of the blood in marital relations is intended as a consummation of the covenant between a man and a woman. At other times it is blood that activates the covenant at a later date, such as a will, where an individual must die in order for the promises of the covenant to take effect. We are told that this is why the blood of animals was necessary in the first covenant.

Death, or blood, is required for a will or covenant to take effect, and this was true of the first covenant as well (Hebrews 9:18).

Jesus is the Mediator of the new covenant – a position He took once the covenant was established via His death and resurrection. Through His death, the promise of forgiveness (Matthew 26: 28) and eternal life is made available (Hebrews 9: 15). The New Testament contains the prescripts of the new covenant (the testament or will of Jesus) of which the writer speaks while the blood (death) of Christ is the dedication, or stamp, of that covenant – that which activates the covenant. Christ's death was necessary for the new covenant to become operative (Hebrews 9: 16-17). Absent His sacrifice of blood, the new covenant would not exist.

The New Ordinances

In James' discussion regarding good works that men might accomplish due to an earnest relationship with God (James 2: 14-26), he is not particularly concerned with statutes that we perform in obedience to God's commands as a matter of establishing and maintaining our relationship with Him. As we learn the character of God we realize that, like Him, we must be kind and loving and give of ourselves sacrificially to help others. These are inherent in our understanding of the type of character God wants His people to have.

Repentance, confession, baptism, and partaking of the Lord's Supper are commands of God. While repentance, to some extent, *may* occur naturally when we realize how our sins affect God, this is not true of other ordinances God has established. Who, simply because he/she wishes to have a relationship with God, would consider being immersed in water? It is not something that occurs instinctively – it is something that is taught. No one would even know to be baptized unless it was specifically commanded of us within the framework of the gospel message. Who would partake of the loaf and cup? This ceremony would not occur naturally simply because of the type of people we know God wants us to be, or because we understand the golden rule. The only means available for us to understand these things is the fact that they are specifically explained in the pages of the New Testament. These are not about character or good works, but about ordinance.

That God did away with *fleshly ordinances* when Jesus died and rose again (Hebrews 9: 10) undoubtedly feeds the notion of salvation without action on the part of man. It is true that God did away with the ordinances of the first covenant. However, these ordinances were temporary in nature in that they could not offer true freedom from sins (Hebrews 9: 9). If, however, God intended to eliminate all ordinances for His people, He would not have established communion – or baptism. The teaching that God removed fleshly ordinances, while at the same time establishing the Lord's Supper and baptism in the name of Jesus, indicates that He does not consider these to be fleshly, but spiritual ordinances.

Scripture is brimming with passages that reveal the need for men to honor God by keeping His commands (1 Corinthians 7: 19; 1 Thessalonians 4: 1-18; 2 Peter 3: 1-2; 1 John 2: 3-4; 5: 3; et al). Moreover, certain commands are required in man's pursuit of salvation (Acts 2: 38; 3: 19; Romans 10: 9-10).

> Now I praise you, brethren, that you remember me in all things and keep the traditions just as I delivered *them* to you. (1 Corinthians 11: 2)

The word translated as *traditions* in this passage is παραδοσις (*paradosis*) and is also translated *teachings* (NIV), or *ordinances*[1], (KJV) in this context. Paul beseeched the Corinthians to keep these traditions, or ordinances, precisely as he had taught them.

As the writer of Hebrews offers us counsel regarding the new covenant of God, he makes it clear that he considers the ordinances of the first covenant a thing of the past. However, we find that he does not consider ordinances, in general, obsolete. God has clearly provided a specific manner of purification in the new covenant.

> 19. Therefore, brethren, having boldness to enter the Holiest by the blood of Jesus, 20. by a new and living way which He consecrated for us, through the veil, that is, His flesh, 21. and having a High Priest over the house of God, 22. let us draw near with a true heart in full assurance of faith, having our hearts sprinkled from an evil conscience and our bodies washed with pure water. (Hebrews 10: 19-22)

The essence of baptism binds together man's faith and God's work as we are freed from an evil past. Yet the sequence of events is as significant as the results given in that baptism and a clean conscience with respect to our former life take place before we *'draw near to God.'*[2] The two phrases, *'having hearts sprinkled'* and *'having bodies washed,'* are written here in perfect participle form. This literally translates as *our hearts having been sprinkled* and *our bodies having been washed*. That is to say they occur prior to, or (at the very latest) in conjunction with, drawing near. Just as the priests of the first covenant did not enter God's presence prior to washing, so we prepare to enter His presence in baptism.

Man's responsibility in God's new covenant is a responsibility of faith. Man approaches God by faith, in baptism. This teaching from the book of Hebrews is confirmed in Peter's first epistle where the apostle identifies baptism as man's petition to God for a clean conscience (1 Peter 3: 21).

Paul considered the divisive nature of the abolished ordinances of the Mosaic Law in his letter to the Ephesians in the light of the first covenant that had so alienated the Gentiles (Ephesians 2: 15). Jesus' death eliminated these ordinances, offering reconciliation of both Jews and Gentiles *'to God into one body'* (Ephesians 2: 16), thus giving them each *'access to the Father by one Spirit'* (Ephesians 2: 18). Of particular interest in this passage is the fact that Paul ties together the Spirit and the body in much the same way that they have been linked throughout the New Testament. Peter instructed the Israelites on the Day of Pentecost to repent and be baptized. Those who were obedient received the Holy Spirit (Acts 2: 38) and were added to the church body (Acts 2: 41). Complementing Peter's remarks, Paul stated that we are all admitted to the body *'by one Spirit'* (1 Corinthians 12: 13).

The Witness of the Spirit, the Water, and the Blood

The apostle John, in his first epistle, spends a considerable amount of time proclaiming Jesus' identity as Savior. During that discourse he discusses the fact that God had given water the calculated role of *witness* in the covenant of grace (1 John 5: 1-8).

> 1. Whoever believes that Jesus is the Christ is born of God, and everyone who loves Him who begot also loves him who is begotten of Him. 2. By this we know that we love the children of God, when we love God and keep His commandments. 3. For this is the love of God, that we keep His commandments. And His commandments are not burdensome. 4. For whatever is born of God overcomes the world. And this is the victory that has overcome the world – our faith. 5. Who is he who overcomes the world, but he who believes that Jesus is the Son of God? 6. This is He who came by water and blood – Jesus Christ; not only by water, but by water and blood. And it is the Spirit who bears witness, because the Spirit is truth. 7. For there are three that bear witness in heaven: the Father, the Word, and the Holy Spirit; and these three are one. 8. And there are three that bear witness on earth: the

Spirit, the water, and the blood; and these three agree as one. (1 John 5: 1-8)

Gnosticism had begun to take root even in the first century. Gnostics believe Jesus' deity began with His baptism and departed from Him prior to the crucifixion. John disputes this teaching, explaining that Jesus is truly the Son of God as witnessed by the Holy Spirit (descending like a dove), the water (Jesus' baptism), and the blood (the crucifixion).

John declares that there are three who bear witness in the new covenant. These three are the Holy Spirit, the water, and the blood. Most scholars concede that the water refers to baptism and the blood to the blood of Jesus. This understanding is based on the fact that Jesus began His ministry when John baptized Him in the Jordan River. At that time he witnessed the Spirit descending and alighting on Jesus like, or in the form of, a dove (Matthew 3: 16). This ministry finally culminated in His death on the cross, a referral to the blood.

The witness of three has a direct correlation to the Mosaic Law and the weight of two or three witnesses (Deuteronomy 19: 15). Such testimony brings validity and substance to a case. The rationale behind the witness of three revolves around the notion that, if a man accuses another of wrongdoing, it is simply one man's word against the other. However, on the witness of two or three men, a believable case might be presented. Jesus, as well as the apostles, carried this same philosophy into New Testament teaching (Matthew 18: 16-20; 1 Timothy 5: 19).

If, as John suggests, we can believe the testimony of two or three witnesses, then the testimony of God's witnesses should stand unquestioned. God's witnesses are more reliable than men because God is true. He has no inclination to deceit; and God's witnesses are the Holy Spirit, the water, and the blood. To what, then, are these three considered witnesses?

> 11. And this is the testimony: that God has given us eternal life, and this life is in His Son. 12. He who has the Son has life; he who does not have the Son of God does not have life. (1 John 5: 11-12)

The testimony of the Holy Spirit, the water, and the blood continues even today. While Jesus' baptism and death had occurred more than fifty years prior to John's letter, their testimony is regarded as contemporaneous with this work. The word *testify* (v. 7) appears in present tense as does the statement, *'this is the testimony'* (v. 11). John has in view not only the Spirit descending upon Jesus, but also the Spirit descending on us. He has in sight not only Jesus' baptism, but ours. The indwelling of the Holy Spirit is promised to all those who are obedient to Christ. This obedience entails water baptism. Just as Jesus began His ministry here on earth with water baptism, to which the Holy Spirit bore witness, we begin our relationship with Christ in baptism.

After Jesus had been baptized, as He came up from the water, the Spirit descended on Him. It is not insignificant that the Spirit came upon Him as He rose from the water since it is at the time of baptism that we receive the promised presence of the Holy Spirit (Acts 2: 38). The Lord's Supper, then, continues to testify to the salvation we have through the blood of Christ. John closes this passage with a familiar thought, reminding us that, *'He who has the Son has life; he who does not have the Son of God does not have life'* (1 John 5: 12).

Admittedly, the correlation with Christian baptism and the Lord's Supper must be considered secondary in this instance. The primary focus is identification of Jesus as the Messiah. Witness to that truth is hereby given through the (Holy) Spirit, the water (of Christ's baptism), and the blood (of His death). Nonetheless, given the fact that these are the very elements by which eternal life is received, their eschatological significance cannot be ignored. John makes it very clear that these are witnesses to *our* eternal life and that life is attainable only through Jesus (v. 11).

As we discover the terms of the new covenant, the message is consistent that those who *have* Christ and have been promised the indwelling of the Holy Spirit are those who have been obedient in water baptism (Galatians 3: 26-27; Acts 2: 38; 5:32; 1 John 3: 24). The relationship depicted in the new covenant is one where God is Father and we are His children (Romans 8: 15-17; 1 John 3: 1) – a relationship that is established when we are born of God. It is a covenant relationship of blood. Now John, in the sunset years of his life, identifies water as a witness that we have received eternal life.

Participation in the New Covenant

A covenant defines the nature of a relationship and governs that relationship forward from the time it is instituted. God's new covenant with man is discussed at length in the eighth through the tenth chapters of the book of Hebrews.

In the same manner that childbirth offered the Israelite newborn participation in the first covenant, so a man must be reborn (born of God, born of Spirit, regenerated) in order to partake in the new covenant (John 3: 5; 1 Peter 1: 23). Participants in the new covenant are identified as the spiritual *seed* of Abraham (Galatians 3: 7-9). Yet no one may be called a descendant of Abraham without accepting the terms of the covenant that are spelled out in the New Testament.

Just as the first covenant incorporated various provisions, God has established conditions in the covenant of grace. The person who fails to accept the terms of the covenant relinquishes any claim to the inheritance that is offered there. These contingencies include belief in Jesus as the risen Messiah (Acts 16: 31), repentance of sins committed (Acts 3: 19), confession of Jesus as Lord (Romans 10: 8-10); and baptism in His name (1 Peter 3: 21). Finally, there is a call within the framework of the covenant for each one to live a life devoted to the holy ways of God in worship and actions (Romans 12: 1-2). Given the agreement of many concerning belief, repentance, and confession, we will focus on the Bible's characterization of baptism in the new covenant.

Perhaps no passage identifies the role of baptism within God's covenant of grace more clearly than Paul's words to the Colossians, a commentary offering insight into the work of God at the time of baptism. Paul spends much of his time in this book placing an emphasis on proper doctrine while, at the same time, filling the epistle with words of encouragement. In this vein, he accomplishes both goals as he reminds them of the first steps in an individual's relationship with God in this new covenant.

> 11. In Him you were also circumcised with the circumcision made without hands, by putting off the body of the sins of the flesh, by the circumcision of Christ, 12. buried with Him in baptism, in which you also were raised with *Him* through faith in the working of God, who raised Him from the dead. 13. And you, being dead in your trespasses and the uncircumcision of your flesh, He has made alive together with Him, having forgiven you all trespasses, 14. having wiped out the handwriting of requirements that was against us, which was contrary to us. And He has taken it out of the way, having nailed it to the cross. (Colossians 2: 11-14)

Before engaging the intricacies of this text, it is important to clarify that the apostle is not equating baptism in the new covenant with circumcision in the first covenant, despite the many voices espousing that view. Paul mentions physical circumcision in verse thirteen, but not in connection with baptism. According to the apostle, the Colossians had faced two major hurdles in their relationship with God. The first problem was that, like all men, they were sinners (dead in their trespasses). The second challenge they faced was the fact that they were Gentiles (*uncircumcision of their flesh*) and, therefore, not participants in the first covenant. Quite often in Scripture the Jews are identified as being *'of the circumcision'* (Acts 10: 45), *'the circumcised'* Galatians 2: 8), or *'the circumcision'* (Ephesians 2: 11) while Gentiles are deemed *'the uncircumcised'* (Romans 2: 26; Galatians 2: 7) or *'uncircumcision'* (1 Corinthians 7: 18; Ephesians 2: 11). Paul's remark concerning their uncircumcision is simply his way of acknowledging their Gentile heritage.

The apostle's point in verses thirteen and fourteen is that these challenges (their sin and their status as Gentiles) were no longer problematic for the Colossians. Paul explained that these obstacles had been removed through Jesus' sacrifice of Himself. They had not only been forgiven of their sins via the cross, but the requirements of the law, which separated Jew from Gentile, had been eliminated.

Paul's reference to circumcision in verse eleven is one that many people insist is the apostle's portrayal of baptism as a replacement for circumcision. Yet, Paul is not pointing to the ceremony of physical circumcision here, but to the manner in which God surgically removes sin from a person's heart, converting a carnal being into a holy one. It is replacement of the old man (flesh) with the new (spiritual) man. The thrust of Paul's statement is that, as the Colossians submitted to Christ in baptism they were, in essence, spiritually circumcised. Similarly, when Paul taught that we clothe ourselves with Christ at the time of baptism (Galatians 3: 27), he was not proposing that baptism was a substitute for physically dressing ourselves, but offered a picture of men spiritually covering themselves with Christ in baptism. Neither, in his words to the Colossians, is he supplanting physical circumcision with baptism. The characterization is purely analogous. In each passage, the apostle's aim is to demonstrate in recognizable terms exactly what occurs spiritually as we submit to Christ in water baptism.

In much the same way that the word *circumcision* is employed symbolically rather than physically in other passages, so it is applied here. *Circumcision of the heart* is intimated in the Old Testament to reflect the attitude of a man's heart toward God. Yet this kind of circumcision has no more relationship with physical circumcision than clothing ourselves with Christ is associated with a physical wardrobe. No one can mistake these writings of Moses and Jeremiah as a reference to literal physical circumcision. Neither should we make that mistake in Paul's letter to the Colossians.

> Therefore circumcise the foreskin of your heart and be stiff-necked no longer. (Deuteronomy 10: 16)
>
> Circumcise yourselves to the Lord, and take away the foreskins of your hearts, you men of Judah and inhabitants of Jerusalem…(Jeremiah 4: 4)

Scripture provides us with clarification concerning the meaning of Paul's phrase, *'made without hands'* in the Colossians passage (v. 11). A *'tabernacle not made with hands, that is, not of this creation'* (Hebrews 9: 11) depicts a temple existing on a purely spiritual plane. No one would deny that circumcision takes place in the physical realm, yet these words signify things that occur strictly in the heavenly arena. The circumcision of this Colossians passage is reiterated in Paul's letter to the Romans. We experience *'circumcision of the heart, by the Spirit'* (Romans 2: 29 – NIV). Paul speaks not of the *replacement* of physical circumcision in Colossians, but of the *presence* of spiritual circumcision at the moment of baptism.

In the first covenant purification involved both the sprinkling of blood and washing with water (Leviticus 1: 5; 3: 2; 5: 9; Numbers 19: 7-21). Under the provisions of God's new covenant, a man is circumcised with a *'circumcision of Christ'* (Colossians 2: 11), which is His death. His shed blood is applied to our sins as a purifying agent (Hebrews 10: 22; 11: 28; Revelation 1: 5). A direct link is established between baptism and the timing of the spiritual circumcision (cutting off) of our sins and our past in the Colossians passage (Colossians 2: 12). Once again we find the use of the perfect participle, revealing that this spiritual circumcision is performed in conjunction with baptism, *having been buried with*

Him. While this expression alone could suggest that the circumcision (of our sins) takes place subsequent to baptism, the balance of the passage provides sufficient evidence that the two occur simultaneously.

Man's approach to God in the covenant of grace takes place once our hearts have been *'cleansed from an evil conscience'* and our bodies have been *'washed in pure water'* through submission to baptism – not prior (Hebrews 10: 22). The person who has not yet received the circumcision of Christ is still dead in his/her trespasses (Colossians 2: 13). Therefore, if one has not received this *spiritual circumcision* (Colossians 2: 11), or has not yet clothed himself with Christ (Galatians 3: 27), then it stands to reason that the individual, prior to baptism, is still lost in sin.

In his letter to the Romans, Paul expounds on the relationship between baptism and Jesus' death, burial, and resurrection. He told the Romans that they had been buried with Christ in baptism as a matter of personal participation in Jesus' sacrifice of death. While for us it is symbolic, for Him it was true death. Additionally, as Jesus literally rose from the dead, we rise symbolically from the watery grave (Romans 6: 4). A man begins his walk in a new life in Christ when he is raised from the waters of baptism. The spiritual circumcision that takes place at this time (the cutting away of sin) frees the believer from his sins. Any claim that one might be saved prior to baptism, the time when his sins are washed away, does not follow this biblical pattern.

> 25. Husbands, love your wives, just as Christ also loved the church and gave Himself for her, 26. that He might sanctify and cleanse her with the washing of water by the word, 27. that He might present her to Himself a glorious church, not having spot or wrinkle or any such thing, but that she should be holy and without blemish. (Ephesians 5: 25-27)

Water is once again associated with God's new covenant in Paul's words to the Ephesians as he compares the relationship between Christ and the church with the covenant of marriage. What must be considered here is the role the water plays against the backdrop of the scene of marriage that is presented in the passage. We are told that Jesus loved the church and that He sacrificed Himself for her. If, however, Christ's sacrifice of Himself constitutes the whole of the equation, there would be no reason to incorporate a role for baptism into this illustration. Yet we do not find here that we are cleansed *directly* through Jesus' sacrifice, but through the medium of water. Christ's sacrifice does not automatically cleanse the bride. It does, however, make the offer of that cleansing available through the washing of water – the time at which the blood is applied to the sins of man.

The function of water in this passage is to *cleanse* – to *sanctify* – to *make holy*. Such is the role of baptism in the New Testament. Without the sanctifying benefit of baptism no one would be added to the church. No church body would then be available to be presented holy. Without the forgiveness offered in baptism the body of Christ cannot exist. Cleansing and sanctification are accomplished *'with the washing of water...'* (v. 26).

Is it possible that *water*, in this context, might be representative of something other than baptism? While some may be inclined to hope that is the case, no theologian of any standing would attempt it. Even John Calvin[3] and John Wesley[4], neither of whom was fully convinced of the spiritual efficacy of baptism, recognized that it is clearly depicted in this instance.

What can we make of the expression *'by the word?'* Consideration of this phrase in this instance may be regarded in two possible lights. The most reasonable view is that it means *according to (or in accord with) the word of God*. That is to say, the *message* concerning washing (baptism) is found *in* the Bible and the message of the gospel is the source of baptism's force. This same word, ρημα (*rhema*), represents the *word* (or message) of God in certain other passages (Romans 10: 17; Ephesians 1: 13; 6: 17). At other times it is also translated using such words as *spoken message* or *command*. This could also be a reference to the fact that it is in the name of Jesus that we are baptized. This, however, is unlikely since the word most often used to refer to the name of Jesus is the Greek word λογος (*logos*).

Salvation is offered through faith in the death, burial, and resurrection of Christ. The work of the Spirit during our washing with water (baptism) makes us presentable (holy) in God's eyes. This is precisely why, when addressing various churches and individuals in the epistles, the apostles presumed baptism by all (Romans 6: 3-4; 1 Corinthians 12: 13; Galatians 3: 26-27; Ephesians 4: 5; Colossians 2: 11-12; Titus 3: 5). The image of a Christian who had not been baptized is something never insinuated by the apostles simply because he/she would not yet be considered a follower of Christ. Therefore, while the apostles did not always *speak* of baptism within the pages of Scripture, they did recognize that everyone whom they addressed in the epistles was an immersed believer. We should be cautious about challenging this fundamental apostolic principle.

NOTES FOR CHAPTER 3

1. Tertullian wrote regarding the fact that baptism was an ordinance, addressing those who would negate the rite.

> Here, then, those miscreants[137] provoke questions. And so they say, "Baptism is not necessary for them to whom faith is sufficient; for withal, Abraham pleased God by a sacrament of no water, but of faith." But in all cases it is the *later* things which have a conclusive force, and the *subsequent* which prevail over the antecedent. Grant that, in days gone by, there was salvation by means of bare faith, before the passion and resurrection of the Lord. But now that faith has been enlarged, and is become a faith which believes in His nativity, passion, and resurrection, there has been an amplification added to the sacrament, viz., the sealing act of baptism; the clothing, in some sense, of the faith which before was bare, and which cannot exist now without its proper law. For the *law* of baptizing has been *imposed*, and the formula prescribed: "Go," *He* saith, "teach the nations, baptizing them into the name of the Father, and of the Son, and of the Holy Spirit." The comparison with this law of that definition, "Unless a man have been reborn of water and Spirit, he shall not enter into the kingdom of the heavens,"[140] has tied faith to the necessity of baptism. Accordingly, all thereafter *who became* believers used to be baptized. *Then* it was, too, that Paul, when he believed, was baptized; and this is the meaning of the precept which the Lord had given him when smitten with the plague of loss *of sight*, saying, "Arise, and enter Damascus; there shall be demonstrated to thee what thou oughtest to do," to wit-be baptized, which was the only thing lacking to him. That point excepted, he had sufficiently *learnt and believed* "the Nazarene" to be "the Lord, the Son of God." Tertullian, On Baptism, Chapter X21. - Another Objection: Abraham Pleased God Without Being Baptized. Answer Thereto. Old Things Must Give Place to New, and Baptism is Now a Law.

2. Gareth L. Reese notes the sequence of the two acts presented in Hebrews 10: 22.

> The Old Testament ceremony had the priests washing at the laver before entering the Holy of Holies. Just like the Levitical priest had to wash before drawing near to God, most commentators refer to the truth that baptism (immersion in water) is here identified as a second condition that must be met before men have free access to God's presence. Gareth L. Reese, The New Testament Epistles – Hebrews, Copyright 1992, page 178, Scripture Exposition Books.

3. http://www.ccel.org/ccel/calvin/calcom41.iv.i.html, John Calvin, Commentary on Galatians and Ephesians, Jun 2, 2007.

4. http://eword.gospelcom.net/comments/ephesians/wesley/ephesians5.htm, John Wesley, Notes on the Bible, June 2, 2007.

Chapter IV
When Is the Time of Salvation?

Man is saved by grace through faith (Ephesians 2: 8), a principle upon which all believers can agree. The question is not *if* man is saved by faith, but *at what time* in the journey of faith man initially realizes salvation. Some may consider the moment of salvation a trivial thing, suggesting that it is the *fact*, and not the *time*, of salvation that is significant. However, if the time of salvation is a mystery, how can the certainty of salvation be known? The apostle John indicated, when writing about the respective roles of *the Spirit, the water, and the blood,* that the very purpose of his writing was for people to know they had attained eternal life (1 John 5: 13). If then, we can *know* that we have attained salvation, Scripture must be clear in explaining the time it is received.

> For we are to God the fragrance of Christ among those who are being saved and among those who are perishing. (2 Corinthians 2: 15)

> Therefore we do not lose heart. Even though our outward man is perishing, yet the inward man is being renewed day by day, (2 Corinthians 4: 16)

A critical point concerning salvation, as these verses plainly indicate, is that it is a process that covers the span of an individual's life from the time he/she initially accepts Christ as Savior to the moment of death. That lifetime may last decades or days, depending on when one accepts Christ, but each of us continues to be saved daily by the blood of Christ. While there is a moment of initial salvation and regeneration, that instant when God bestows eternal life, each of us continues to be saved, or renewed, on a daily basis as we walk in the way of the Lord. The challenge we face, however, is determining the time at which salvation is initially conferred upon the believer.

Salvation by Grace

Often the idea that something other than grace[1] might have a place of significance within the covenant of grace seems offensive to those who refuse to embrace it, reasoning that anything added to grace must somehow be seen as an insult to God. Their disdain is often expressed in the equation *'grace* equals *grace* plus *nothing.'* If it is grace it must stand alone since *grace* plus *anything else* is no longer grace. Remarkably, no legitimate argument can resist this reasoning. It is true that grace, indeed, stands alone. Just as *one* plus *anything* is no longer *one*, so *grace* plus *anything* is no longer *grace*. Where this view errs, however, is in the presumption that grace is equivalent to salvation. If *grace* equals *salvation* we must consider all men saved. After all, it is not God's will that anyone would perish but that everyone would be saved (2 Peter 3: 9).

Grace is the *offering* of eternal life that God has presented to men through Christ's sacrifice of Himself. It is a *gift* in that men are not expected to pay the cost that is required to receive it. In truth, no man has the capacity to pay such a price. If, however, grace is the sum of the equation (if *grace* equals *salvation*) certainly all men must be saved. God, however, does not force His grace upon men, but merely offers it. Grace is not conferred upon an unwilling recipient. Hence, if it is not true that *grace* equals *salvation*, apparently something must be added to *grace* so that *salvation* may be received. No one, then, should take offense to the proposition that, at the very least, *belief* must be added to *grace* for *salvation* to be realized.

Salvation by Belief

A considerable number of believers maintain that salvation occurs at the moment a man or woman believes in the deity of Christ and His sacrifice for the sins of men. The essence of this position is that, while obedience is not insignificant, belief alone is sufficient for salvation and is the *sole requirement* addressed in the gospel message. This teaching finds its basis in passages of Scripture that indicate that believers will, indeed, be saved.

> Those by the wayside are the ones who hear; then the devil comes and takes away the word out of their hearts, lest they should believe and be saved. (Luke 8: 12)

> For since, in the wisdom of God, the world through wisdom did not know God, it pleased God through the foolishness of the message preached to save those who believe. (1 Corinthians 1: 21)

> In Him you also *trusted*, after you heard the word of truth, the gospel of your salvation; in whom also, having believed, you were sealed with the Holy Spirit of promise. (Ephesians 1: 13)

It is important, in the study of God's design for the redemption of men, that the *method* of salvation not be confused with the *time* of salvation. Belief is essential for eternal life as these passages indicate. Yet, while these verses substantiate the necessity of belief, no verse points to belief as the time when salvation is attained. Teaching *that* believers are saved does not automatically signify that they are saved *at the time of* initial belief. In fact, we will soon discover that, according to Scripture, the moment of belief is clearly *not* the time of salvation.

Salvation by Faith

Various elements of God's new covenant point men toward forgiveness, righteousness, and eternal life. It is a bit disingenuous to portray the passages cited above as relating belief alone to salvation as they seem to imply. The reading of a single verse normally cannot express the intentions of the author or speaker as fully as when the surrounding text is considered. Taken in context belief is always qualified, at a very minimum, by the faith[2] of the one who believes. Paul explained to the Corinthians that belief, absent adherence to the gospel message, was hollow.

> 1. Moreover, brethren, I declare to you the gospel which I preached to you, which also you received and in which you stand, 2. by which also you were saved, if you hold fast that word which I preached to you – unless you believed in vain. (1 Corinthians 15: 1-2)

The fact that belief, unless it is accompanied by faith, has no power to save is discussed thoroughly by James, noting that even demons believe (James 2: 19). The effect of their belief, however, is not salvation, but fear. John reveals that certain rulers also believed in Jesus, but refused to confess Him in fear of the Pharisees (John 12: 42). The proposition, then, that those who refused to confess Christ, much less the believing demons, should expect forgiveness or salvation at the mere moment of belief stands in stark contrast to teaching presented throughout Scripture.

For those who maintain that sins are forgiven and salvation is awarded at the moment of belief, it should now be evident that this is not the case. Such a view suggests that *belief* is the same as *faith*. Given the illustrations offered by James and John regarding the demons who believed, or those who refused to confess Christ even though they believed, this notion should be put to rest. Paul warned the Corinthians that it is possible to *believe in vain.* Scripture teaches that, while it is necessary to believe, not *everyone* who simply believes will be saved. Belief, unaccompanied by faith, cannot affect salvation.

> 1. Therefore, having been justified by faith, we have peace with God through our Lord Jesus Christ, 2. through whom also we have access by faith into this grace in which we stand... (Romans 5: 1-2)

> 8. For by grace you have been saved through faith, and that not of yourselves; *it is* a gift of God, 9. not of works, lest anyone should boast. (Ephesians 2: 8-9)

Belief and faith are closely associated, but they are not the same. While faith is impossible to achieve without belief, the reverse is not true. A man can believe without having faith. Therefore, the conditions for salvation have necessarily expanded to include *grace, belief,* and *faith.* Yet, certain elements of God's plan are still absent; therefore, the moment of faith cannot be deemed to be the time of salvation since more conditions of salvation must be fulfilled.

Salvation by Repentance

Few believers would ever deny the redemptive value of repentance.[3] A vital component of God's covenant with man is the call for men to repent, turn from their sinful ways, and return to Him.

> ...but unless you repent you will all likewise perish. (Luke 13: 3)

> For godly sorrow produces repentance *leading* to salvation, not to be regretted; but the sorrow of the world produces death. (2 Corinthians 7: 10)

Who, then, can doubt that repentance is essential for a man to be reconciled to God and thus, attain salvation? Scripture is crystal clear that no man may be saved short of repentance. However, repentance is not belief, nor is it faith. Repentance may result from faith, but is not faith's equivalent. Since repentance is necessary for a person to partake in the grace of God, it must surely be considered a condition of salvation. Thus, the components of God's plan of salvation have expanded to *grace, belief, faith,* and *repentance.* Yet, while all of these elements of God's plan explain the *method* of salvation, the *time* of salvation continues to elude. Scripture indicates that even though one believes, has faith, and repents of his sins, not all conditions for attaining salvation have been met.

Salvation by Confession

Unlike the teaching of many men who maintain that a simple private prayer asking God into one's life is sufficient, the following passages reveal the need for a verbal confession[4] of Jesus as Lord, spoken to others. What would be the reason for a spoken confession unless God meant for it to be heard as a witness to other Christians? If God intended our confession of Jesus as Lord and Savior to take place privately (between a man and God alone), no instruction for a vocal confession would be necessary. Paul confirms this very point in his letter to the Romans and his first letter to Timothy.

> 8. But what does it say? *"The word is near you, in your mouth and in your heart"* (that is, the word of faith which we preach): 9. that if you confess with your mouth the Lord Jesus and believe in your heart that God has raised Him from the dead, you will be saved. 10. For with the heart one believes unto righteousness, and with the mouth confession is made unto salvation. (Romans 10: 8-10)

> 12. Fight the good fight of faith, lay hold on eternal life, to which you were also called and have confessed the good confession in the presence of many witnesses. (1 Timothy 6: 12)

Some men may regard our confession of Jesus as Lord from the perspective that it reflects a *way of life* in both word and deed as opposed to a specific declaration before men. It is safe to say that confessing Jesus as Savior encompasses both ideas. Nonetheless, we have sufficient Scripture to support the view that God expects from each of us, as a matter of salvation, an open affirmation before witnesses of belief in Jesus as God's risen Son and Lord of our life. The apostle Paul highlights a verbal confession *'made unto salvation'* (Romans 10: 10).

To this point we have seen that a variety of conditions for salvation are revealed in the Bible. Belief is the first of these. Within God's design of the plan of salvation, without belief nothing can save – not even grace. Paul indicated to Timothy, *'I have fought the good fight, I have finished the race, I have kept the faith.'* (2 Timothy 4: 7). Belief is as important as the first step in a race. Indeed, it *is* the first step in that race of which Paul wrote. No one can finish a race in which the initial step is never taken. Faith, repentance, and confession cannot be present where belief is absent.

Faith, too, is essential to salvation. Nor can salvation be found in those who have not repented of, and turned from, their sins, or those who have failed to confess that Jesus is Lord. Since Scripture is clear in its instructions regarding these various elements of the course of salvation, it is only reasonable that the design of God's plan of salvation should include them all. Hence, we now must consider *grace, belief, faith, repentance,* and *confession* all essential for *salvation*. However, even with all of this understanding regarding *how* men are saved, the *time* of salvation has not been revealed in any of these passages.

Salvation by Love

It would be wise to avoid overlooking one particularly crucial element of God's plan. Jesus emphasized that which is undeniably the *most* critical component in our relationship with both God and other men when one Pharisee attempted to challenge Him.

> 35. Then one of them, a lawyer, asked *Him a question*, testing Him, and saying, 36. "Teacher, which is the greatest commandment in the law?" 37. Jesus said to him, *"'You shall love the Lord your God with all your heart, with all your soul, and with all your mind.'* 38. This is the first and greatest commandment. 39. And the second is like it: *'You shall love your neighbor as yourself.'* 40. On these two commandments hang all the Law and the Prophets." (Matthew 22: 35-40)

Love for both God and man is the quintessential theme in both the old and new covenants. Love is the basis upon which God has seen fit to offer salvation to those who have turned from Him; thus it is the reason Jesus gave His life on the cross. Love is not only God's motivation, but it is His character trait. As such, He expects love to be a character trait of all those who seek Him. Paul and the other apostles have offered some especially poignant remarks regarding the value of love with respect to the kingdom of God:

> 1. Though I speak with the tongues of men and of angels, but have not love, I have become sounding brass or a clanging cymbal. 2. And though I have *the gift of* prophecy, and understand all mysteries and all knowledge, and though I have all faith, so that I could remove

mountains, but have not love, I am nothing. 3. And though I bestow all my goods to feed *the* poor, and though I give my body to be burned, but have not love, it profits me nothing. 4. Love suffers long *and* is kind; love does not envy; love does not parade itself, is not puffed up; 5. does not behave rudely, does not seek its own, is not provoked, thinks no evil; 6. does not rejoice in iniquity, but rejoices in the truth; 7. bears all things, believes all things, hopes all things, endures all things. 8. Love never fails...13. And now abide faith, hope, love, these three; but the greatest of these *is* love. (1 Corinthians 13: 1-8; 13)

While this chapter in 1 Corinthians is a tiny fragment of the teaching regarding love that can be found in Scripture, it is one of the most eloquent treatises respecting the worth that God places upon love. Paul touches the reader with the nature of Christianity, which is love. Without love Paul considered himself as *a clanging cymbal.* Without love he saw himself as *nothing.* The love that is spoken here reveals itself vividly in Paul's words. It is love for brother and sister, friend and foe. It is a love of action and passion. It is the very message of God to mankind that is revealed in His Word. Since it is all of these things and more, it is also a love God deems essential in our relationship with Him.

Love binds us to God and to each other. God's promise is to those who love. While love is considered an element of Christian growth, a life void of love is a life that has not been converted. Moreover, it is presumably our love for Christ that leads us to obedience and salvation. Therefore, we can reason that some measure of love for Christ must be included among those elements that are critical even to our initial redemption. Thus, none of the following – *grace, belief, faith, repentance, confession,* and *love* – may be ignored when determining what man must *do* in response to the gospel message.

Salvation by Baptism

Beyond the grace that comes from God, a common thread runs through each of those prescripts that have, so far, been determined to be vital components in man's response to the gospel message. That common thread pertains to time. These various elements of redemption reflect not only the manner by which we are saved, but the manner in which we are to live. While there is a moment when a person *first* believes, it cannot end there. Belief involves not merely the initial moment of acceptance that Jesus is the Messiah, but a lifetime of commitment to that belief. So, too, faith and love must continue without end. Additionally, while there is a critical juncture when an individual first repents, all men should live a life that is directed by a repentant heart; and God forbid that any would ever cease to confess Jesus as Lord.

These conditions of salvation are simply that: *conditions of salvation*. They define *how* men are saved and, consequently, how we are to live in Christ. Yet there is no indication among these that any one of them defines the moment salvation is received. That is because one element still remains. Interestingly, it is a component of the plan of salvation that is distinguished in its relationship to time.

Both Mark 16: 16 and 1 Peter 3: 21 point specifically to baptism as conditional for salvation. Peter remarks that baptism is the means by which we are saved. In Acts 2: 38 he offers it in a prescription for forgiveness of sins and the gift of the Holy Spirit. Baptism, then, must be united with all other *conditions* that are essential to salvation. While baptism is a salvation issue, as these verses plainly testify, much is also revealed about the *time* of salvation in a thorough study of this rite.

With metaphoric eloquence Paul, in his letter to the Romans, draws a vivid picture of the death of Christ by which He overcame our sins. Death itself was defeated (Romans 6: 1-18). It is the means by which we are able, ourselves, to die to sin. Having completed, in the first few chapters of Romans, a thorough discourse of the grace of God through which righteousness is imputed to men, Paul now addresses his audience to stir them emotionally and spiritually by way of reminder of the moment they knew salvation. He makes some very specific points regarding baptism in this segment. Paul regards baptism as a burial with Christ. Who, then, should be buried but one who is dead. In baptism, upon death to the sinful life, men are buried with Christ. It is at the time of baptism that men die with Christ (Romans 6: 8) to sin (Romans 6: 2).

Death *to* sin and burial *with* Christ take place within the framework of baptism. Paul characterizes baptism not only as the time when we die to sin and are buried with Christ, but also as a symbolic act that represents His death in which we are united together (Romans 6: 5). Therefore, baptism is more than dying to sin and being buried with Christ. It is an act that provides unity, not between the new convert and Christ alone, but also among the members of the body of Christ as each person experiences this same death and burial.

Paul's portrayal of baptism does not end with death to sin and burial with Christ. We discover that, after we are buried, we rise to a new existence as Christ had done when He rose from the dead. (Romans 6: 4). Just as we are united together in a symbolic death, we shall also live a new life characteristic of His resurrection (Romans 6: 5). It is at the point of rising from the waters of baptism that, as after Christ, we begin a new life. It is the rebirth that Jesus explained to Nicodemus. It is a new life in that it is no longer the old life that was dominated by sin (Romans 6: 17-18).

In his epistle to the Colossians, Paul confirmed the notion that baptism is the time of salvation. He explained that we receive spiritual circumcision, the removal of our sins, in baptism through faith (Colossians 2: 11-14). It is a time when we are buried with Him and raised with Him. Once this has been accomplished we find that we have been made alive, our sins having been forgiven.

Baptism, like belief, faith, repentance, and confession, is a part of the *method* of salvation. What clearly differentiates baptism from these others, however, is that it is also the *time* of salvation. Certainly, unless baptism is accompanied by all precepts discussed here, it cannot affect eternal life. Baptism cannot stand by itself. Not one of these *conditions* can, alone, lead to salvation – not even belief or faith. Yet, of all the precepts God has set for us, baptism is designated as the moment when a person's sins are forgiven, he is freed from the law, and the new life that is promised is received. This is the reasoning behind Peter's statement that baptism saves (1 Peter 3: 21).

Baptism is set apart from all other precepts in God's plan of salvation by its uniqueness with respect to time. While God has designated all of these as fundamental in His design for men to attain salvation, baptism is the time He has appointed for the death of the old life and the resurrection of the new. Baptism, in the likeness of childbirth, occurs at one point in time, never to be repeated. No other time is prescribed to accomplish what is realized in baptism, which is salvation.

What About the Sinner's Prayer?

What are we to do with the Sinner's Prayer? Is this not the time of salvation? After all, many American evangelists teach that the way to salvation is actually through what has come to be known as the Sinner's Prayer. Of course, the greatest challenge we face with this path to Christ is that it has no scriptural warrant. Nonetheless, there are those who plead the case from sundry inferences that the notion of such a prayer could be derived from various passages. Let us, then, consider the history of this matter as well as its ostensibly scriptural foundation.

It is true that the Sinner's Prayer, as we know it, is not taught in Scripture. Whether on the Day of Pentecost, or with the Philippian jailer, or any other time when the apostles taught the manner whereby men might be saved, the Sinner's Prayer is not found. In the post-Pentecost era prayer is not intimated in Scripture as a matter of salvation for those outside of Christ. Men who seek to derive the Sinner's Prayer from the pages of Scripture claim that, while this teaching is not found in the Bible, it is somehow implied in certain passages.

> 13. "And the tax collector, standing afar off, would not so much as raise his eyes to heaven, but beat his breast, saying, 'God, be merciful to me a sinner!' 14. "I tell you, this man went down to his house justified..." (Luke 18: 13-14)

The prayer of the tax collector (above) may be considered the closest thing Scripture has to the Sinner's Prayer. Yet, there is no mention here of salvation through Jesus Christ or forgiveness through His blood. Nor does this man ask Jesus *into his heart*, the essence of the Sinner's Prayer. Instead, what Jesus has provided for His disciples, in this narrative, is an example of the humility God hopes to see in every man. Furthermore, this example, recorded in the gospel of Luke, occurred prior to the establishment of the new covenant on the Day of Pentecost and, hence, prior to the institution of immersion under the new covenant. Therefore, the episode offers no biblical support for the claim that humble acknowledgement of Jesus is somehow sufficient for salvation in the church age. The passage simply portrays the repentant heart that is essential for those who wish to seek forgiveness.

> As for me, I will call upon God; and the LORD shall save me. (Psalm 55: 16)

> The LORD is nigh unto all them that call upon him, to all that call upon him in truth. (Psalm 145:18)

These words from the book of Psalm seem to indicate salvation by *calling upon God*. However, it is important to recognize that these words were also written while the Israelites lived under the Mosaic Law, prior to Pentecost. Given that fact, the suggestion that verbally calling on the name of the Lord, in itself, leads to salvation ignores the law itself. Considering the minutiae of the Mosaic Law that are spelled out in Exodus and Leviticus, with the many continuing sacrifices and rituals, it was understood that the calling of which the Psalmist wrote must surpass a verbal declaration. In the Old Testament the notion of calling on the name of the Lord would have involved much more. Faithfulness to God's law was the manner in which men called upon Him.

Some men consider the expression *'calling on the name of the Lord'*, that is spoken on or after the Day of Pentecost (Acts 2: 21; 22: 16), a possible implication of something akin to the Sinner's Prayer. It seems, however, that we might more appropriately view these passages in a broader sense. On the Day of Pentecost, in the midst of his sermon to the crowd gathered in Jerusalem, Peter cited the prophet Joel (Joel 2: 32), declaring that those who call on the name of Jesus will be saved (Acts 2: 21). A few short sentences later the assembly, convicted by the message they heard, inquired of Peter and the other apostles what they should do (Acts 2: 37). Since Peter had just explained to them that those who call on Jesus' name would be saved, exactly what is the point of this question? Why did not those who sought salvation on that day simply cry out to Jesus for salvation, offering a Sinner's Prayer?

The truth is that they did not know *how* to call on His name. This is the reasoning behind their inquiry, *'what shall we do?'* They sought direction as to *how* they might call on the name of the Lord. In response, Peter instructed them to *repent and be baptized*. This was, according to the apostles, the manner in which men were to *call* on Him. Therefore, the *calling* of which Peter spoke may be more suitably understood to encompass the entire manner in which men respond to God rather than an allusion to the Sinner's Prayer, which was unknown at the time.

> 16. And now, why are you waiting? Arise and be baptized, and wash away your sins, calling on the name of the Lord." (Acts 22: 16)

As Ananias addressed Saul of Tarsus (Acts 22: 16), we find another undeniable example of baptism as the manner in which men *call on the name of the Lord*. It should be noted that Ananias spoke these words after Saul had fasted for three days, a reasonable indication that he was in a state of repentance. He was surely penitent, seeking direction from the Lord during that time. It is safe to assume that his repentance was much more intense and more grief-stricken than most men who cite the Sinner's Prayer today. Yet, this apparently did not satisfy the provision of calling upon Him since, as Ananias met with him, Saul's sins had not been forgiven. He was not saved despite his change of heart. His repentant prayer was not the manner by which Saul *called on the Lord*, otherwise Ananias would not after these three days, explain to him that he must *now* call on the Lord.

> 19. As many as I love, I rebuke and chasten. Therefore be zealous and repent. 20. Behold, I stand at the door and knock. If anyone hears My voice and opens the door, I will come in to him and dine with him, and he with Me. (Revelation 3:19-20)

This verse, written by the apostle John, is a verse highly favored by many who seek to dismiss Scripture's portrayal of baptism as a matter of forgiveness. It is considered an evangelical appeal to men everywhere, suggesting that by simply opening their hearts to Jesus, they can commune with Him. Of course, the greatest irony concerning this passage is the fact that it is not written to the lost multitudes, but to the church at Laodicea where they were *'neither hot nor cold'* (Revelation 3: 15). It is not an appeal to a lost and dying world, but a petition to those in the church who, at one time had been faithful but were now tepid in their service to the Lord. In order to derive legitimacy for the use of the Sinner's Prayer from this passage, scriptural context must be abandoned.

The truth is that the Sinner's Prayer was conceived out of necessity as a result of the Reformation Movement of the sixteenth century. As men cast aside the notion that salvation occurred at the time of baptism, which was a staple of Christian doctrine, a void developed within the plan of salvation that was taught among Protestant denominations. For a considerable length of time after the Reformation Movement, many men became confused concerning the time of salvation. As more men determined that baptism should not be seen as the moment salvation was received, the confusion broadened and it became necessary to replace baptism with something else – some occasion that could be recognized as the time of salvation.

Relying heavily on passages like Revelation 3: 20 many evangelists in the seventeenth and eighteenth centuries worked diligently to determine the moment at which an individual received redemption. In the 1700's preachers developed a time of confession that was considered the moment of salvation. Sometimes called the Mourners Seat, although other names were used, certain people were highlighted throughout the service with the challenge for them to accept Christ. Those who then admitted their sins and confessed Jesus as Lord were saved. They were not required to cite the Sinner's Prayer since it did not yet exist.

This practice continued for roughly two centuries as the *way* to salvation. It was the plea for *salvation without activity on man's part* that drove these doctrinal changes. Still, it is interesting that every event later developed to pinpoint the moment of salvation ultimately laid the responsibility at the feet of the sinner, requiring him to *do* something in response to the gospel message. So it is with the Sinner's Prayer.

The Sinner's Prayer, as we know it today, began to develop late in the nineteenth century. Men such as a minister by the name of Dwight Moody (1837-1899), Billy Sunday (1863-1935), who was a converted baseball player, and others were responsible for its widespread acceptance. Some even boldly suggested that it should be considered prayer *'for the forgiveness of sins'*, a tenet falling well outside the boundaries of scriptural teaching. Today, despite the absence of biblical support, the Sinner's Prayer is predominantly preached and accepted as the time of salvation. While this is an abbreviated history of the development of the Sinner's Prayer, we must consider it seriously. The fact that it did not exist for the first 1,800 years of the church age, along with its complete lack of biblical endorsement, gives us reason to fully dismiss the Sinner's Prayer as the time of salvation. It seems we may more aptly consider the Sinner's Prayer to be one of the *traditions of men* against which Paul offered the Colossians solemn warning (Colossians 2: 8).

Salvation by Obedience

Jesus closed the well-known Sermon on the Mount with a statement concerning those who were and were not saved (Matthew 7: 21-29). Hailed as one of the most intriguing passages in the New Testament, this is also arguably one of the most puzzling sections of all Scripture. It seems at the time of judgment many who had, in the eyes of men, accomplished great things in the Lord's name, will stand before Christ wishing to claim salvation for themselves. Yet Jesus' response will be that He never knew them. Who could be so enthusiastic for the cause of Christ and, in the end, not see heaven? While the answer is given, in that these have not *done the will of the Father,* it is not initially clear exactly how or where they had fallen short. What is even more fascinating is that, given Jesus' remark, *'I never knew you'* (Matthew 7: 23), we can conclude that they never had been saved.

If the astonishment that is evident in the words of these lost followers is any indication, the notion that they were undone for lack of belief can be immediately dismissed. Nor does Jesus point to unbelief as the reason for their state of condemnation. Jesus' declaration, *'everyone who hears these sayings of Mine, and does not do them'* (Matthew 7: 26) alleges that, while these believers may have been active and passionate in their efforts, there was something they had been commanded to do but, for some reason, simply had not.

Perhaps the point of greatest significance in this hypothetical exchange between Jesus and these lost men is the revelation that there is chasm that separates *activity* on behalf of the kingdom from *obedience* to the Father. It is a divide so critical that the good works of those who do not cross it are considered inconsequential. As He further explains the nature of the gulf that exists between activity and obedience, the meaning becomes clear. The word *'Therefore'* in the twenty-fourth verse indicates that an explanation of the judgment of these men/women is imminent.

Like the foolish builder, due to their disobedience the foundation for their relationship with Christ had never been properly laid. Jesus explains this fully as He concludes His comments with the parable of the wise and foolish builders (Matthew 7: 24-27). Thus, the statement, *'whoever calls on the name of the LORD shall be saved'* (Romans 10: 13) must be weighed against, *'Not everyone who says to Me, 'Lord, Lord,' shall enter the kingdom of heaven, but he who does the will of My Father in heaven.'* (Matthew 7: 21) *Calling on Him* evidently involves much more than simply speaking His name and encompasses obedience to the will of the Father.

There is no question that certain other inferences can be drawn from this passage. It is reasonable to conclude that Jesus' words suggest obedience to more than the precepts of belief, repentance, confession, and baptism. Nonetheless, the foundational aspect of the passage cannot be overlooked. The proper foundation can help keep one's faith from crumbling. Ignatius, a church leader who had studied under the watchful eye of the Apostle John, wrote, *'Let your baptism endure as your arms,'* [5] suggesting that submission to baptism can offer some protection from distractions or attacks upon our faith.

God has established a covenant of grace; however, grace alone does not equal salvation. The precepts of God are clear, and no one may enter the kingdom without doing the will of the Father. No one may be saved without initially laying the necessary foundation for a relationship with Christ. How that foundation is to be laid is determined and explained to us in God's Word. The words of Christ regarding God's will leave little doubt that man's salvation is contingent upon obedience to the precepts that God has established.

NOTES FOR CHAPTER 4

1. Justification and sanctification are available to man only by grace through the blood of Christ. Campbell addresses the essence of the bestowing of these as a matter of mercy in that man cannot achieve them on his own.

> What, then, is justification, the first fruit of this heavenly cluster of Divine graces? It is, indeed, a trite but a true saying, that the term justification is a forensic word; and, therefore, indicates that its subject has been accused of crime, or of the transgression of law. It also implies that the subject of it has not only been accused and tried, but also acquitted. Such, then, is legal or forensic justification. It is, indeed, a sentence of acquittal announced by a tribunal, importing that the accused is found *not guilty.* If convicted, he cannot be justified; if justified, he has not been convicted.
>
> But, such is not justification by grace. Evangelical justification is the justification of one that has been convicted as guilty before God, the Supreme and Ultimate Judge of the Universe. But the whole world has been tried and found guilty before God. So that, in fact, "there is none righteous; no, not one." Therefore, by deeds of law, no man can be justified before God. "For should a man keep the whole law, and yet offend in one point, he is guilty of all." He has despised the whole authority of the law and the Lawgiver. It is, then, utterly impossible that any sinner can be forensically or legally justified before God, by a law which he has in any one instance violated. Alexander Campbell, Christian Baptism, with Its Antecedents and Consequents, Chapter 2, Justification (1851).

In a specific, evangelical sense, sanctification is the act of separating a person or thing from a common to a special and spiritual use. In the following chapter on Sanctification, we have dilated, in a discursive way, on the whole subject of spiritual influence, in illumination and conversion, as terminating in sanctification. These, indeed, are concurrent means of self-consecration and of Divine sanctification or separation to God. But, in strict reference to our specific object, here, we have only to state, that the Christian is contemplated, not merely as adopted into the family of God, not merely as pardoned or justified, but, as also sanctified or consecrated to [285] God, both in state and character. Of this separation or sanctification to God, the Holy Spirit,--which, in the Christian, is the Holy Guest, commonly called the Holy Ghost, is the personal agent and author, his word the instrument, and the blood of Christ, apprehended and received by faith, the real, cleansing, purifying means. Alexander Campbell, Christian Baptism, with Its Antecedents and Consequents, Chapter 21, Sanctification (1851).

2. According to Campbell, there is a difference between mere belief (mental ascent or acceptance) in God and the leap to faith when the conviction of that belief leads to an alteration of one's lifestyle.

Every faculty of man has its proper object and its proper use. Has he the faculty of vision? There are objects to be seen, and advantages to be gained from seeing them. Has he the faculty of hearing? There are the harmonies and the melodies of nature and of the human voice to be heard and to be enjoyed. Has he the faculty of reasoning? There are objects to be compared, and conclusions of practical utility to be deduced from them. Has he the faculty of believing? There is the testimony of men, and there is the testimony of God, to be believed and appropriated. Now, as this is the noblest faculty which man possesses, conversant with things past, present, and future, proximate and remote, God has ordained that he shall walk by faith, physically, intellectually, and morally. Hence man is obliged to walk through his whole life more by faith than by his five senses, his own observations, or his own experience--probably more than by these all combined. This being a very fundamental fact, we shall be at some pains to develop it. Alexander Campbell, Christian Baptism, with Its Antecedents and Consequents, Chapter IV, Faith (1851).

3. While few would ever challenge the precept of repentance for salvation, nonetheless, the role of a repentant heart should be kept in perspective. Belief and faith have their respective roles, but it is sin that separates man from God. Clinging to a life of sin will continue to separate an individual from Him. It is necessary, then, to separate oneself from sin in order to draw close to God.

It is specially worthy of notice in this investigation that in the first and last communications of the Messiah we find an imperative *repent*. His harbinger, also, introduced his personal advent with the command, "Repent, for the reign of heaven approaches." In the commencement of his own personal ministry, his first discourse was, "Repent, for the reign of heaven approaches." His twelve Apostles, under their first commission, we are informed by Mark, went abroad proclaiming repentance to people. The same proclamation was made by the seventy evangelists sent to the lost sheep of the house of Israel. Indeed, the ministry of John is characterized as the proclamation of "the baptism of repentance for the remission of sins."[4] So that during the personal ministry of the Lord Jesus, and that of his harbinger, repentance was the burthen of every discourse to the people. Alexander Campbell, Christian Baptism, with Its Antecedents and Consequents, Chapter V, Repentance (1851).

4. B. W. Johnson views Romans 10: 10 as a call, not only for confession of Jesus as Lord, but as a confession to others in the brotherhood rather than a personal conversation between an individual and the Lord.

> The faith of the heart must be openly confessed. This is a test of the faith. Unless Christ had provided such tests as confession and obedience we could not know whether ours was really a belief of the heart. That our faith moves us to confession is to us an assurance of salvation. The whole Christian life is a confession. B. W. Johnson, People's New Testament (1891), Romans 10: 10

5. Ignatius, Anti-Nicene Fathers, Vol I, Chapter VI.—The duties of the Christian flock.

Chapter V
Must I Be Baptized?

The question, *'Must I be baptized?'* which has plagued men through the ages and brought bitter division among believers, lies at the heart of most disputes over baptism. The writings of Martin Luther, John Wesley, Alexander Campbell, John Calvin[1], and various other revered men of God reveal passionate deliberation on every side of this issue. How could men so knowledgeable in the things of God take such irreconcilable stands with respect to something that seems so basic? A thorough examination of every book, essay, or letter penned by these men would still fail to explain the inclination of some to derive from Scripture one belief regarding baptism while others come away with a completely different point of view.

The reflections of these men, however, are not the cornerstone upon which doctrine may be founded. The many intriguing schools of thought propounded by men on the subject of baptism cannot supersede God's own perspective. How can we discern God's view of baptism? Only through earnest consideration of all that the Bible teaches on the subject, and acceptance of that teaching, can this be accomplished.

Interpretation of the Word

Men often feel compelled to interpret the Bible in a manner that leads them to drift from the straightforward teaching contained within its pages. Yet it is the *study* of God's Word, not its *interpretation*[2], to which we are called (2 Timothy 2: 15). While it may seem there is a fine line between interpretation and study, it is reasonable that we should, at the very least, embrace those teachings found in Scripture that are presented in a plain and direct manner. For those who are prepared to devote the necessary time, God has delivered His Word in a manner that makes clear the things He desires for us to know. Those who are willing to apply themselves will find the words of the Bible sufficient to deliver God's message.

That is not to say that interpretation may be completely dismissed since, at times, the Bible demands it. Certainly the parables call for interpretation. However, when we must rely on interpretation, it is important that legitimate linguistic and interpretive principles be employed methodically and consistently. The same standards used to understand other literature should be applied to Scripture. It is critical that we consider the context, the original intent of the author or speaker, and the meaning the hearers would have reasoned at the time a statement was made. We must never allow our own ideology to lead the way in interpretation.

Furthermore, we have no reason to *force* interpretation upon the straightforward teaching found in the instructive writings of the apostles. While Jesus spoke mystically at times, that mystique was pertinent only for those who lived prior to the covenant of grace (Matthew 13: 10-12). We have been offered a much better understanding of Jesus' teaching than were those who listened to Him during His life here on earth.

Through the words of the apostles we have considerable insight into the constitution of the kingdom of heaven about which Jesus spoke. Unlike Jesus, the apostles' words are ordinarily presented in a conspicuous style. When an apostle employs symbolic speech in Scripture, we find that its figurative nature is ordinarily evident to the reader (Romans 11: 17-21; 1 Corinthians 3: 5-9; Galatians 4: 21-31). After all, God had placed upon their shoulders the task of revealing the kingdom to all nations. While Paul's epistles bear deep spiritual overtones, they are not written in cryptic code that few can understand, especially concerning matters of salvation.

Corinthians, Galatians, Ephesians, and certain other epistles, were written to the general membership of the church body rather than an elite group of theologians, and should be received with that in mind. When Paul wrote to the Ephesians concerning baptism (Ephesians 4: 5), they would have recognized it as the same baptism *in Jesus' name* that he taught and practiced when he was among them (Acts 19: 5). The Galatians would have pictured themselves being clothed with Christ as they were immersed in Christian baptism (Galatians 3: 27). As he wrote to the church at Corinth concerning baptism *'by one Spirit'* (1 Corinthians 12: 13), the members of the body there would have understood this to be the same baptism they had seen Paul administer while he was among them (1 Corinthians 1: 14-16). Therefore, unless the context offers commanding evidence to the contrary, we should embrace the apostles' words in the candid manner in which they are written.

The Principles of Baptism

Understanding that God is the ultimate author of the Bible should also lead us to recognize that He has not thrown it together haphazardly. Scripture is designed, in a methodical and meticulous manner, to instruct us. Through His Word He intends to direct us on a path that will restore us to Him. Within that structure there is an order to the teaching of baptism.

The seeds of the baptismal discussion within the pages of the New Testament are planted in the four gospels (Matthew, Mark, Luke, and John). Each of these authors begins this dialogue by addressing the baptism performed by John the Baptist. While it is not discussed in great depth, we learn that John's baptism was performed in water (Matthew 3: 11), that it had a purifying nature (John 3: 25), that it was combined with repentance for forgiveness of sins (Luke 3: 3), and that it was to be replaced by the baptism offered by the coming Messiah (Mark 1: 8). Each of these authors cites John's prophecy concerning a future baptism.

> I indeed baptize you with water unto repentance, but He who is coming after me is mightier than I, whose sandals I am unworthy to carry. He will baptize you with the Holy Spirit and with fire. (Matthew 3: 11)

> I indeed baptize you with water, but He will baptize you with the Holy Spirit. (Mark 1: 8)

> John answered, saying to all, "I indeed baptize you with water; but One mightier than I is coming, whose sandal strap I am not worthy to loose. He will baptize you with the Holy Spirit and fire." (Luke 3: 16)

> "I did not know Him, but He who sent me to baptize with water said to me, 'Upon whom you see the Spirit descending, and remaining on Him, this is He who baptizes with the Holy Spirit.'" (John 1: 33)

Looking toward the coming church age, John told of a baptism that would eclipse the water baptism his followers were witnessing. It would be a baptism that involved none other than the Holy Spirit Himself. John's prophecy concerning baptism with the Holy Spirit raises some intriguing questions as to the substance and makeup of this impending baptism. What does it mean to be baptized with the Holy Spirit? Who would perform this baptism? How would it differ from John's baptism?

Each book of gospel also provides us with insight into the time Jesus spent with His disciples after His resurrection. Complementing John's prophecy, two of the authors, Matthew and Mark, touch on Jesus' remarks about a coming baptism.

> 18. And Jesus came and spoke to them, saying, "All authority has been given to Me in heaven and on earth. 19. Go therefore and make disciples of all nations, baptizing them in the name of the Father and of the Son and of the Holy Spirit, 20. teaching them to observe all things I have commanded you, and lo, I am with you always, even to the end of the age." *Amen* (Matthew 28: 18-20)

> 15. And He said to them, "Go into all the world and preach the gospel to every creature. 16. He who believes and is baptized will be saved; but he who does not believe will be condemned." (Mark 16: 15-16)

While answering certain questions concerning John's prophecy, in that this new baptism would be performed by men under Jesus' authority, these passages raise some other questions. First of all, exactly what is the relationship between baptism and making disciples? These men were commanded to baptize men from all nations in the *process* of making disciples. Secondly, what does baptism have to do with eternal salvation? After all, this is the startling message from the passage in Mark. It is those who believe and are baptized who, according to Jesus, will be saved.

Having planted the seeds of baptismal instruction in the ministry of John the Baptist, and having watered that seed in Jesus' remarks to the disciples after His resurrection, God finally provides answers after Jesus' ascension as crowds were gathered together in Jerusalem.

> 38. Then Peter said to them, "Repent, and let every one of you be baptized in the name of Jesus Christ for the remission of sins; and you shall receive the gift of the Holy Spirit"...41. Then those who gladly received his word were baptized; and that day about three thousand souls were added *to them*. (Acts 2: 38, 41)

An explanation of the discussion in the gospels concerning baptism has been offered. Baptism is performed as a matter of receiving forgiveness of sins and the presence of the Holy Spirit in our lives. Additionally, we are, at the time of baptism, counted among those who belong to Christ. In baptism we are *'added to them.'* That is how baptism relates to becoming disciples. That is how baptism relates to salvation.

These three passages (Matthew 28: 18-20; Mark 16: 15-16; Acts 2: 38-41) set the stage for the lessons on baptism found in the balance of the New Testament. They help us to understand the basic principles underlying baptismal discussions in the book of Acts and the epistles. While Paul adds much to our understanding of baptism, including the symbolism upon which it is founded, these three passages identify the reasons for, and significance of, baptism. Therefore, a deeper exploration of these passages is necessary so that we might better understand the nature of baptism in the New Testament.

Baptism in Matthew 28: 19

Jesus commands certain things of His disciples in His final days on earth. Upon their shoulders He laid the burden of establishing His following among all nations.

> 18. And Jesus came and spoke to them, saying, "All authority has been given to Me in heaven and on earth. 19. Go therefore and make disciples of all nations, baptizing them in the name of the Father and of the Son and of the Holy Spirit, 20. teaching them to observe all things I have commanded you, and lo, I am with you always, even to the end of the age." *Amen* (Matthew 28: 18-20)

Baptism appears here as a *product* of initial instruction. Thus, they were to disciple and baptize men. Both discipleship and baptism are defined in terms of establishing men as Christ's followers. Additionally, baptism was to be performed by the authority of Jesus (v. 18) and in the name of the Father, Son, and Holy Spirit (v. 19). Once a person is established as Christ's follower, we understand that further instruction concerning *'all things...commanded'* is essential.

Two distinct kinds of teaching are proposed by Jesus. It seems a fundamental understanding of certain basic instruction (Greek: *matheteuo*) is necessary for one to become a disciple - instruction that, if accepted, would result in baptism. However, *becoming* a follower of Christ is one thing. Living a life that fulfills the expectations of a follower would require edification well beyond their belief in the Lordship of Christ and submission to baptism. Therefore, once the elements of basic instruction and baptism have been realized, further *teaching* (Greek: *didasko*) concerning the

Christian way of life would be necessary. From the moment of baptism each disciple should seek to understand exactly what is expected of those who would follow Jesus. They were to learn of His commands – His way of life.

Understanding that these instructions concerning discipleship, baptism, and teaching are aimed equally at us, it is upon us, as Christ's followers, to continue the tradition that Jesus established on that day. We are to disciple, baptize, and teach.

Baptism in Mark 16: 16

In determining the answer as to whether or not a person *must* be baptized as a matter of salvation, we have in Jesus' own words unequivocal confirmation regarding the significance of this rite with respect to redemption.

> 15. And He said to them, "Go into all the world and preach the gospel to every creature. 16. He who believes and is baptized will be saved; but he who does not believe will be condemned." (Mark 16: 15-16)

The fact that some men have raised questions concerning the canonization of Mark 16: 9-20, since Mark's authorship may be in doubt, must be acknowledged. Without going into much detail, the truth is Scripture provides sufficient evidence regarding the dependability of the material presented in these verses (Luke 8: 2; 24: 35-51; John 20: 1-23) even if it could be confirmed that Mark was not the author.[3] In addition, the text appears in *virtually* all early Greek and Latin manuscripts. Of the countless manuscripts available, only a few exclude this section. While respect for those particular manuscripts is significant, they still stand alone in omitting the passage. Furthermore, the fact that these verses were widely recognized as Scripture by some of the early church fathers of the second and third centuries speaks volumes concerning their legitimacy.

Interestingly, the discussion surrounding the ending of Mark is rarely focused on the accuracy of the verses. The debate primarily centers upon Mark's authorship rather than the substance of the writing. Most scholars agree that the contents of these verses should be considered reliable. Since those who ultimately made the decision regarding canonization saw fit to include them, and with adequate supporting Scripture for the validity of the material as well as God's undeniable influence upon scriptural content, they will be treated as divinely inspired in this book.

These things having been said, for those who wish to disregard this ending for the book of Mark, the role of baptism as a significant matter of redemption does not rely upon Mark 16: 16. Scripture offers conclusive testimony concerning the principles of baptism even in the absence of this passage. Nonetheless, this section does have something to offer as we consider baptism's standing in God's plan of salvation.

The objection to Mark 16: 16, with its obvious characterization of baptism as part of God's plan of salvation, hinges on the lack of the statement *he who is not baptized will not be saved.* The absence of these words leads many to deny that Jesus is presenting baptism as a redemptive matter. Yet the passage maintains that, to be saved, we are to believe *and* be baptized. Those are unambiguous instructions that are offered an abundance of support from many other passages of Scripture. Following this statement of simple instruction, Jesus maintains that those who do not believe will not be saved. Logically, what unbeliever would consider being baptized for salvation? The unbeliever is lost notwithstanding his baptismal status. In fact, an unbeliever *cannot* be baptized – he can only become wet. Once disbelief is ascertained, baptism is of no consequence and no further explanation on Jesus' part is necessary. Demanding of Jesus the clarification that unbelievers who are not baptized will not be saved begs redundancy from Him.

Furthermore, the belief of which Jesus spoke *presumed* a believer's submission to baptism just as it presumed repentance of sins (Acts 3: 19) and confession of Jesus as Lord and Savior (Romans 10: 9-10). Consequently, it would be pointless for Him to account for those who *believed and were not baptized.* Those who believed *were* baptized. The prospect that believers were not baptized is given no consideration since their baptism is understood. This truth finds support in Acts 2: 41 and Acts 8: 12 when those who believed *were* baptized. Those who did not believe were not baptized. Additionally, Peter offered no one exemption from baptism in his sermon on the Day of Pentecost as he commanded, *'let every one of you be baptized'* (Acts 2: 38). If Jesus considered baptism ineffectual relative to salvation, it would be completely out of place for Him to interject it at this time while neglecting the principles of repentance and confession. If baptism is unessential, no reasonable explanation can be offered for its appearance either here or in the commission given in Matthew's gospel (Matthew 28: 19).

Some may ask the question, *if belief presumes baptism, why has Jesus identified them individually in this verse?* The fact is Scripture provides us with only a small sample of the instruction Christ offered to the apostles. While Jesus had undoubtedly explained to them the significance of baptism in the coming kingdom prior to this occasion, these are some of His final words before His departure. Here, and in Matthew 28: 19, the purpose is to openly identify baptism as a critical component of the gospel message. No other reasoning seems to explain His mention of baptism at this time.

Of course, these words are meant for us at least as much as they were meant for the apostles. They were a prelude of what was to come. While the apostles surely understood the significance of baptism, until this point in Scripture *we* have only read about the baptism performed by John and Jesus' disciples (John 4: 1-2). There have only been allusions to a baptism that was to come (Matthew 3: 11; John 3: 5). Now baptism is laid down as a vital element of discipleship and salvation in the church age. Therefore, baptism is singled out in Jesus' final words in order to eliminate any question about the significance of the ceremony.

The combination of belief and baptism mentioned here also addresses another fundamental issue. Although disbelief, by itself, is enough for someone to be denied redemption, Jesus indicates that it takes more than mere belief to *attain* salvation. Those who charge that the phrase concerning unbelief somehow neutralizes the call to be baptized fail to appreciate the fact that Scripture does not recognize any claim of faith in God that disregards His commands (1 John 2: 4), including commands that lead to salvation. Other New Testament authors have clearly demonstrated the scale by which belief might be measured. These men inform us that the converse of belief in Jesus – the belief that saves – is disobedience to His commands. Consequently, the belief that saves is belief that embraces obedience.

> 18. And to whom did He swear that they would not enter His rest, but to those who did not obey? 19. So we see that they could not enter in because of unbelief. (Hebrews 3: 18-19)

> 7. Therefore, to you who believe, *He is* precious; but to those who are disobedient,

> 8.
> *"The stone which the builders rejected has become the chief cornerstone,"*
> and
> *"A stone of stumbling And a rock of offense."* (1 Peter 2: 7-8)

It is most fascinating the role that belief plays in Mark 16: 16 and how neatly it can be moored to examples of conversion throughout the book of Acts. This speaks to the complementary character of Scripture. Upon learning about Jesus, the eunuch asked to be baptized. Philip told him he could receive baptism *if he believed*. Belief was defined, not as the sole means to salvation, but as a prerequisite to baptism. The same is true concerning the Samaritans (Acts 8: 12-13). We are not told that they were saved when they believed, but that they were baptized when they believed. Additionally, we discover that the Philippian jailer, *when he believed*, was baptized (Acts 16: 33). So it is in this context as Jesus states that those who believe are candidates for baptism and salvation. Those who do not believe are unqualified for baptism.

Baptism in Acts 2: 38

A most compelling endorsement for the necessity of baptism within God's design for the salvation of men emerges during the initial proclamation of the gospel message to mankind.

> 38. Then Peter said to them, "Repent, and let every one of you be baptized in the name of Jesus Christ for the remission of sins; and you shall receive the gift of the Holy Spirit." (Acts 2: 38)

On the Day of Pentecost, the crowds in Jerusalem inquired of Peter and the other apostles what they should do. The answer is the first occasion within the church age where the path to salvation is identified. How can men be saved? Redemption comes by repentance and baptism. The teaching is unambiguous whether read in the Greek or English.

This verse, alongside certain other passages, offers us clarification concerning God's design for salvation. First, men must believe that Jesus is the Messiah (Mark 16: 16; John 3: 16) and that His death offered mankind the opportunity for reconciliation with God (2 Corinthians 5: 21). Secondly, realizing that separation from God came about because of our own sins, it is incumbent upon men to repent (Acts2: 38; 2 Peter 3: 9) of the sins that have so dishonored Him. Lastly, we are to proclaim Jesus as Savior (Romans 10: 9-10) and receive immersion in water, at which time we are promised God will forgive the penitent believer (Acts 2: 38; 1 Peter 3: 21).

Those claiming that Mark 16: 16 and Acts 2: 38 should not be accepted at face value contend that taking their meaning literally would intrude upon the message of the gospel portrayed in the balance of Scripture. Yet Mark 16: 16 does not infringe upon Peter's message of Acts 2: 38 or vice versa. These verses, in turn, do not violate the instructions offered in either 1 Peter 3: 21 or Matthew 28: 19-20. Nor do they disrupt the teaching found in Romans 6: 1-5, 1 Corinthians 12: 13, Galatians 3: 26-27, Colossians 2: 12, or Titus 3: 5, when we remember that those being addressed were immersed believers. Furthermore, these passages do not interfere with those that speak of salvation through belief (Galatians 3: 22) and/or faith (Romans 3: 28) when we accept that belief/faith in apostolic times presumed the believer's submission to baptism in water. In truth, the literal meaning of the words fully complement all New Testament instruction concerning salvation.

The Fallacy of Negative Inference

An appeal is often made to what is commonly known as the *fallacy of negative inference* theory in an effort to challenge passages that speak directly of the relationship between baptism and salvation. The basic premise of this philosophy maintains that, although a statement may be true, it does not automatically follow that the negative inference of that same statement is also true. Applied practically, if it is true that *a man who lives in Detroit lives in Michigan,* we cannot automatically infer that *a man who does not live in Detroit does not live in Michigan.*

Often men attempt to apply this same theory regarding *negative inference* specifically to the passages of Mark 16: 16 and Acts 2: 38. The claim is, while it may be true that, *'He who believes and is baptized will be saved,'* this does not necessarily translate into *He who believes and is not baptized will not be saved.* Likewise, Peter's command in Acts 2: 38, does not inevitably preclude those who are not baptized from receiving that same forgiveness.

However, rather than simply asserting that one statement does not *necessarily* reflect the negative, the essence of the teaching that results is that full equivalence can be found between two dissimilar statements. Thus, *'He who believes and is baptized will be saved'* equals *He who believes and is not baptized will be saved.* Similarly, *'Repent, and let every one of you be baptized in the name of Jesus Christ for the remission of sins'* equals *Repent for the remission of sins.*

The application of this theory to passages such as these, however, is fundamentally flawed in that the factual statements used to develop the argument are incompatible with those remarks that are the target of the test. The statement, *a man who lives in Detroit lives in Michigan,* is merely an observation of the man's status. This cannot be equally applied to verses that are clearly directional in nature, intended to guide us to a destination, any more than it can apply to other passages providing redemptive instruction. The following verses teach us what *will be* the outcome of obedience.

> Repent therefore and be converted, that your sins *may be* blotted out... (Acts 3: 19) - emphasis added

> ...if you confess with your mouth the Lord Jesus and believe in your heart that God has raised Him from the dead, you *will be* saved. (Romans 10: 9) - emphasis added

Can a man repent without being truly converted and still anticipate salvation? Does the man who refuses to either believe in or confess Jesus as Lord have any reason to be hopeful about his eternal existence? Of course, he does not. These verses are directional, intended to guide us to the goal of salvation.

When providing directions, men tend to offer the clearest, shortest route to a given destination. Deviation from any portion of the directions, as they are given, will prevent the one receiving those instructions from reaching the desired location. So, too, when God gives directions in order that men may realize a specific outcome, those directions are clear and sure. In Mark 16: 16 we discover what *will be* the status of those who believe and are baptized. Peter proclaimed in his statement of Acts 2: 38 that all who accept the invitation to repentance and baptism *will receive* forgiveness of sins and the gift of the Holy Spirit. These verses do not focus on where a man *is* (e.g., Detroit), but where he *will be* if he follows the directions he has been given.

Recognizing the character of these verses, as well as the shortcomings of this methodology in challenging the teaching found there concerning baptism, some have smartly addressed these passages taking into account their directional configuration. Therefore, the argument has shifted from *a man living in Detroit* to the suggestion that, if Jesus had said, *He who believes and reads his Bible every day will be saved*, it would not necessarily mean daily Bible reading was essential to salvation.

In this case, *negative inference* is offered as a challenge to the prescription of Bible reading, and consequently baptism, for salvation. In short, the argument states that, if daily Bible reading is not a matter of redemption, the same must be true of baptism. No reason is offered as to why we can equate baptism with daily Bible reading. Those making the claim simply assume that everyone fully understands their interchangeability based, no doubt, upon the innumerable passages of Scripture comparing the two (tongue-in-cheek).

Two noticeable flaws immediately surface with respect to this scheme. The first, and perhaps the most obvious, is the fact that those are not the words spoken by Jesus in this verse. Substituting unspoken words in an effort to discredit the spoken word is no argument at all and offers no legitimate insight into what Jesus actually did say. The fact that daily Bible reading is not assigned redemptive status in Scripture is undoubtedly a key reason Jesus did not declare it here.

Additionally, if we should consider this a proper means of biblical analysis why, in all of Scripture, is this methodology applied *only* to these two passages? Imagine the doctrinal possibilities if we were to employ this same logic through the balance of Scripture (once again – tongue-in-cheek). Yet honest biblical examination demands that we accept God's Word *as it is written*.

The second flaw, which is perhaps not so obvious, is that, had Jesus made the statement as proposed – inserting *Bible reading* rather than *baptism* – and the landscape of Scripture supported this teaching as it does baptism, we would be obligated to accept daily Bible reading as a redemptive matter. The instructive nature of the statement would require it.

Ultimately this attempt to discredit scriptural teaching concerning baptism challenges the very spirit of legitimate biblical interpretation. The entire proposition of negative inference, when applied to Mark 16: 16 or Acts 2: 38, contends that both Jesus and Peter capriciously integrated baptism into their instructions concerning what men must do to attain eternal life. Yet, Jesus has already explained to us those things He considers immaterial when it comes to following Him.

> 21. Then another of His disciples said to Him, "Lord, let me first go and bury my father." 22. But Jesus said to Him, "Follow Me, and let the dead bury their own dead." (Matthew 8: 21-22)

Not only does Jesus not mince words, but He also does not give commands frivolously. He considered taking the time to bury one's father, an apparent representation of anything that might delay or hinder our calling, as insignificant for someone who really cares to be a disciple. He does not consider baptism in that same manner. Given consistent New Testament instruction concerning the redemptive value of baptism (Matthew 28: 19-20; Romans 6: 1-4; Galatians 3: 27; Ephesians 4: 5; Hebrews 10: 22; Titus 3: 5), negative inference is, at the very least, an irreverent approach to understanding God's Word.

The Divine Inspiration of the Word

Returning to the premise that was established in the Preface of this book, that the Bible is the inspired Word of God, it is upon us to fully appreciate the fact that these passages were written the *way* they were written for a reason. The truth is, Jesus did say, *'He who believes and is baptized will be saved...'* (Mark 16: 16). Peter did proclaim, *'Repent, and let every one of you be baptized in the name of Jesus Christ for the remission of sins; and you shall receive the gift of the Holy Spirit'* (Acts 2: 38). The responsibility of any translator, beyond simply converting words from one language to another is, first and foremost, to ensure that the intended meaning of the words is not lost in the translation process. The message from these two statements regarding baptism is unmistakable. Yet, the failure of many to accept God's message has been, and continues to be, the source of considerable discord in the religious community.

Paul related to Timothy, whom he called his *'son in the faith'* (1 Timothy 1: 2), the high value that God has placed upon Scripture (2 Timothy 3: 16). Here we find that all Scripture comes from God and is to be treated as a source of doctrine, reproof, correction, and instruction. Note that *all* of Scripture, not just those points with which we agree ideologically, is given with this in mind. This is as true for Mark 16: 16 and Acts 2: 38 as for any other passage. Thus the teaching concerning baptism in these verses should be understood as significant rather than immaterial. The apostle John offers an ominous warning against the altering of the Scripture of the book of Revelation (Revelation 22: 18-19). Given God's view of the value of His inspired Word, it is safe to say that He would frown upon our attempts to modify any Scripture to fit our own resolve.

Of course, few, if any, would ever suggest that Mark 16: 16 should be revised to say, *'He who believes will be saved, but he who does not believe will be condemned,'* thus removing the phrase *'and is baptized'* from the text. Surely no one would dare rewrite the verse to say, *He who believes and is not baptized will be saved....* Yet, without eraser or pen in hand, these changes are made dogmatically every day by those who willfully deny the fact that Jesus and Peter, in these passages, proclaim the need for baptism.

The Baptism of the Ethiopian Eunuch

The Bible is replete with testimony concerning baptism and its integral role in God's plan of salvation. Numerous examples are provided depicting people who were baptized and the emphasis that was placed upon this ceremony. Perhaps one of the most compelling accounts depicting the importance of water baptism in the New Testament involves the episode of Philip and the Ethiopian eunuch (Acts 8: 26-39). Because the eunuch did not understand the Scripture he was reading, God arranged for Philip to teach him. Recognition must first be given to the fact that Philip was sent by an angel of God to minister to this man. If God would dispatch Philip, He surely would not send him with a false message. Nor should we suspect that Philip had any misconception concerning that message.

Philip taught the eunuch (Acts 8: 35), evidently revealing within his teaching the significance of immersion in water. When they came upon some water it was the eunuch who asked to be baptized (Acts 8: 36). His words indicate that he was not so much asking if he should be baptized, since he had evidently settled on that decision. Instead he asked Philip what would prevent him from being baptized *now*. Just as Peter had proclaimed on the Day of Pentecost, the eunuch must have perceived from Philip's teaching that forgiveness of sins and the gift of the Holy Spirit

(Acts 2: 38) were granted at the time of immersion in water. He understood baptism to be a matter of salvation. The eunuch sought baptism in water as a direct response to the teaching he had received from Philip.

Philip baptized the eunuch – in water. Once this was accomplished, *'the Spirit of the Lord caught Philip away, so that the eunuch saw him no more; and he went on his way rejoicing'* (Acts 8: 39). Based upon the principles of baptism about which we have read concerning its effects, the eunuch's rejoicing can rightfully be perceived as his recognition from Philip's instruction that he had received salvation. He seems to fully appreciate Philip's teaching. His delight was not in what many regard as baptism with the Holy Spirit, apart from water baptism, although he would have received the *gift* of the Holy Spirit described by Peter (Acts 2: 38) upon his obedience in water baptism. He was not ecstatic due to a miraculous spiritual gift granted to him; nor did his gladness show itself prior to baptism. The eunuch's excitement was, without a doubt, a direct result of his awareness of the redemptive power of baptism in water (Mark 16: 16) as taught by Philip. This episode emulates *instruction* concerning salvation in the New Testament and harmonizes fully with the initial instruction God has provided concerning baptism in the New Testament (Matthew 28: 18-20; Mark 16: 15-16; Acts 2: 38-41)

The Baptism of Cornelius

One of the more familiar accounts of conversion in the New Testament is that of Cornelius, a Gentile who was directed by an angel of God to send for Peter so that he might receive instructions concerning the things of God.

> 44. While Peter was still speaking these words, the Holy Spirit fell upon all those who heard the word. 45. And those of the circumcision who believed were astonished, as many as came with Peter, because the gift of the Holy Spirit had been poured out on the Gentiles also. 46. For they heard them speak with tongues and magnify God. Then Peter answered, 47. "Can anyone forbid water, that these should not be baptized who have received the Holy Spirit just as we *have?"* 48. And he commanded them to be baptized in the name of the Lord. Then they asked him to stay a few days. (Acts 10: 44-48)

Cornelius, along with his companions in Caesarea, was the first Gentile to be converted to Christianity. Luke informs us that he was a devout and God-fearing man (Acts 10: 1-2). Despite his faithfulness, he lacked knowledge that was *essential* to his salvation (Acts 11: 14) – the message of the gospel. Through His death, burial, and resurrection, Jesus had blazed the only trail that could lead to eternal life (Acts 4: 12). The narrative suggests an aspect of the gospel message that is too often overlooked – acceptance of the gospel is reliant upon a person's response to that message (Acts 10: 35). As the events of the day unfold, we discover that Cornelius did respond to the message Peter brought. Realizing that salvation was meant for Gentiles, as he witnessed the unmistakable work of the Holy Spirit, Peter commanded that they should be baptized in water.

Men are divided concerning the timing of salvation for these Gentiles. Those who allege the insignificance of water baptism commonly offer the account of Cornelius as an example to champion their cause. The manifestation of the Holy Spirit upon Cornelius preceding water baptism, it is charged, makes his salvation prior to immersion obvious. Quite often those who advance this view argue that baptism with the Holy Spirit, and not water baptism, is the path to salvation. This belief is grounded in the presumption that Holy Spirit baptism and water baptism *may* take place at two distinct times.

Others maintain that Cornelius and those with him received salvation at the time they were baptized in water (v. 48), based on the underlying principles upon which the discussion of baptism in the New Testament rests (Matthew 28: 18-20; Mark 16: 15-16; Acts 2: 38-41).

Both points of view can find encouragement within the pages of Scripture. The baptismal instruction found in the gospels and on the Day of Pentecost offers support for the proposal that salvation accompanied their baptism in water. Baptism is defined as the time of forgiveness (Acts 2: 38) and salvation (Mark 16: 16). However, Peter's words later in the book of Acts could be interpreted to suggest that they *may* have been redeemed as the Spirit came upon them. In a discussion concerning the relevance of the Mosaic Law to Gentiles in the new covenant, Peter states:

> 7. "...Men and brethren, you know that a good while ago God chose among us, that by my mouth the Gentiles should hear the word of the gospel and believe. 8. So God, who knows the heart, acknowledged them by giving them the Holy Spirit, just as *He did* us, 9. and made no

distinction between us and them, purifying their hearts by faith." (Acts 15: 7-9)

Did God purify (regenerate) their hearts prior to their immersion in water? No one may speak from either side of the aisle with complete confidence. It is possible; however, no absolute conclusion can be drawn from the text. Peter does not say exactly *when* God purified their hearts – only *that* He did so. On the other hand, Jesus explained to His disciples, while He was with them, that men of this world - that is to say, those who are of flesh rather than spirit - cannot know the Spirit (John 14: 17). Based on this verse it is not unreasonable to suggest that, as the Spirit came upon these Gentiles, God saw them as *men of Spirit* rather than *men of flesh*. Still, no exception is made at this time with respect to water baptism. These men were immersed in water.

Peter certainly recognized the uncommon nature of the events at the house of Cornelius. He had witnessed only one other time[4] when the Spirit manifested Himself in this way. Now God had once again poured out His Spirit in a mysterious and miraculous way – to the Gentiles. He had revealed His plan for the Gentiles in a manner that Peter acknowledged could only come from God. This was unquestionably a sign to Peter, and those with him, that salvation was not limited to the Israelites, but was intended for all men everywhere. This objective is revealed in the passage cited above as Peter explained the *reason* for the Spirit falling on the Gentiles in such a phenomenal manner. He stated that this was the means by which God acknowledged them.

In this case, the word for *acknowledged* (v. 8), which is μαρτυρεω (*martureo*), reveals that God was *bearing witness* to Peter and those with him concerning His acceptance of Gentiles into the kingdom. According to The New Strong's Exhaustive Concordance of the Bible the word means, 'to be a witness, i.e., *testify*...give testimony, (be, bear, give, obtain) witness.'[5] We find that various other Bible translations plainly bear this out.

> And God, which knoweth the hearts, *bare them witness*, giving them the Holy Ghost, even as he did unto us (Acts 15: 8, KJV) – emphasis added

> And God, who knoweth the heart, *bare them witness*, giving them the Holy Spirit, even as he did unto us (Acts 15: 8, ASV) – emphasis added

> God, who knows the heart, *showed that he accepted them* by giving the Holy Spirit to them… (Acts 15: 8, NIV) – emphasis added
>
> And God, who knows the heart, *testified to them* giving them the Holy Spirit, just as He also did to us (Act 15: 8, NASB) – emphasis added

The work of the Holy Spirit upon these Gentiles is an example of God's divine intervention, discussed in the Preface of this book, as He revealed to Peter and the Jews His intention to offer salvation to the Gentiles. This was the *purpose* of the occasion. It was not God's aim to establish a *new path* to salvation that ignores or alters the role of baptism, but to establish salvation for a *new people*. The focus is not on the *manner* by which men are saved, which has already been established (Mark 16: 16; Acts 2: 38), but on those to whom salvation was now made available. We find no instruction in this passage that would challenge the principles of baptism that were discussed earlier. According to Peter, the extraordinary nature of the event, as God bestowed these men with the Holy Spirit in an exceptional manner, was simply God's way of acknowledging His approval of Gentiles in the kingdom.

It is evident from his words that Peter understood the importance of baptism for the Gentiles. Absent a reason to prohibit it, baptism was the obvious course of action (Acts 10: 47). His call for baptism for the Gentiles was founded upon the principles of discipleship (Matthew 28: 19), forgiveness and the Holy Spirit (Acts 2: 38), and salvation (Mark 16: 16) to which Peter was a witness. He saw no reason to make any exception to the principles of baptism simply because of the unusual circumstances involved.

Baptism – Duty or Privilege?

In a real sense, there is a subtle tone of resistance hidden within the question, *'Must I be baptized?'* that is the title of this chapter and is, today, asked by so many. When men were approached with the teaching of baptism in the New Testament the response was not, *'Must I be baptized?'* as though it was a burden, but rather, *'When can I be baptized?'* as those who submitted to the rite did so with expectancy. Peter stated, concerning Cornelius and the other Gentiles, *'Can anyone keep these people from being baptized with water?'* (NIV - Acts 10: 47) The Ethiopian eunuch asked Philip, *'What hinders me from being baptized?'* (Acts 8: 36) The apostle Paul (Acts 9: 18), Lydia (Acts 16:14-15), and the Philippian jailer (Acts 16: 33), as well as many others anxiously participated in baptism, being baptized immediately, apparently recognizing that time was of the essence.

Disciples in the New Testament seemed to view baptism not as a burdensome obligation, but as an honor and opportunity eagerly anticipated. Perhaps this transformation from exuberance to encumbrance in our approach to baptism can be traced to the disparity that exists between the significance accorded this ceremony in the first century versus the manner in which it is trivialized in modern times. When, during the Reformation Movement, men began classifying baptism as a *work* rather than a spiritual experience, much of the appeal it had once known slowly began to dissipate. Yet, if we will allow the Bible to be our teacher, baptism can and should be a time of excitement and renewal today just as it was in the days of the apostles.

NOTES FOR CHAPTER 5

1. Martin Luther believed in Spirit regeneration at the time of baptism, *The Large Catechism by Martin Luther, X21 Part Fourth of Baptism*; yet he also held to the belief of infant baptism and sprinkling or pouring of water as acceptable, *The Large Catechism by Martin Luther, X21A Part Fourth of Baptism*. John Wesley, founder of Methodism, fell short of considering baptism a means of regeneration, but believed it was a sign equivalent to circumcision in the OT. Wesley also believed infant baptism was not only acceptable to God, but deemed it absolutely necessary for the salvation of a child, *Wesley's 25 Articles Of Religion, Article 15, Of The Ordinances*. John Calvin, along with Wesley, believed water baptism to be a sign of the new covenant as circumcision was of the old. For this reason he also believed infant baptism acceptable. Calvin believed in predestination and, therefore, only those whom God had chosen would be baptized. *John Calvin - The Institutes of Christian, Book IV, Chapter XV*. Alexander Campbell believed both in the regeneration effects of baptism and the necessity of immersion. He denied any scriptural basis for infant baptism. *Christian Baptism With Its Antecedents and Consequents, By Alexander Campbell*.

2. Campbell wrote of the misinterpretation of the Bible by scholarly men, noting that God's intent was for men to simply read the worth of the words rather than seek a hidden meaning. His reasoning was that if special rules apply to Biblical interpretation that apply nowhere else, how should man ever understand what God expected of men?

> *God has spoken by men, for men.* The language of the Bible is, then, *human* language. It is, therefore, to be examined by the same rules which are applicable to the language of any other book, and to be understood according to the true and proper meaning of the words, in their current acceptation, at the times and in the places in which they were originally written and translated.
>
> If we have a *revelation* from God in human language, the words of that volume must be intelligible by the common usage of language; they must be precise and determinate in signification, and that signification must be philologically ascertained--that is, as the words and sentences of other books are ascertained by the use of the dictionary and grammar. Were it otherwise, and did men

require a new dictionary and grammar to understand the Book of God,--then, without that divine dictionary and grammar, we could have no *revelation* from God; for a revelation that needs to be revealed is no revelation at all.

Again, if any *special rules* are to be sought for the interpretation of the sacred writings, unless these rules have been given in the volume, as a part of the revelation, and are of divine authority;--without such rules, the Book is sealed; and I know of no greater abuse of language than to call a *sealed book* a revelation. [54]

But the fact that God has clothed his communications in human language, and that he has spoken by men, to men, in their own language, is decisive evidence that he is to be understood as one man conversing with another. Righteousness, or what we sometimes call *honesty*, requires this; for unless he first made a special stipulation when he began to speak, his words were, in all candour, to be taken at the current value; for he that would contract with a man for any thing, stipulating his contract in the currency of the country, without any explanation, and should afterwards intimate that a *dollar* with him meant only *three francs*, would be regarded as a dishonest and unjust man. And shall we impute to the God of truth and justice what would blast the reputation of a fellow-citizen at the tribunal of political justice and public opinion! Campbell, Christian Baptism, with Its Antecedents and Consequents, Chapter 21, THE BIBLE-PRINCIPLES OF INTERPRETATION, (1851).

3. David Miller addressed the legitimacy of Mark 16: 9-20 writing for Apologetics Press.Org. After extensive exegetical discussion concerning evidence for both omission and inclusion, his findings are as follows:

For the unbiased observer, this matter is settled: the strongest piece of internal evidence mustered against the genuineness of Mark 16:9-20 is **no evidence at all**. The two strongest arguments offered to discredit the inspiration of these verses as the production of Mark are seen to be lacking in substance and legitimacy. The reader of the New Testament may be confidently assured that these verses are original—written by the Holy Spirit through the hand of Mark as part of his original gospel account. Apologetics Press: Reason and Revelation - Is Mark 16: 9-20 Inspired?

4. That this particular manifestation of the Spirit had occurred on one other occasion is clear from Peter's words in Acts 11: 15. Gareth Reese addressed the truth of this statement as follows:

The reference in the word "beginning" is to the day of Pentecost, Acts 2; and the "us" is limited to the apostles. It is strongly implied that there had been no common reception of the baptism in the Holy Spirit since Pentecost, for if it were something that all Christians were expected to and did receive, Peter could have simply pointed to the numerous other incidents and not have had to go back to Pentecost for an example. Gareth L. Reese, New Testament History – Acts, page 414, Scripture Exposition Books, 2002.

5. James Strong, LL.D., S.T.D., The New Strong's Exhaustive Concordance of the Bible, Greek Dictionary of the New Testament, p. 46, 1990, Thomas Nelson Publishers.

Chapter VI
Baptism and the Gospel

The Message of the Gospel

The gospel (good news) is the message of Christ through which salvation is made available to mankind. That message is revealed to us through Holy Writ. Although the Bible was written by men, we understand that these men were guided by the Spirit of God as they penned the words of Scripture. While the message of salvation is revealed in God's Word, the redemption of any individual is dependent upon his/her response to that message in the manner established in the teaching of the apostles – those men through whom Jesus would introduce His church on earth (Ephesians 2: 20).

Each facet of the gospel message, according to the apostles, is considered critical to our salvation. For instance, absent Jesus' death, burial, and resurrection, no man could anticipate salvation (eternal life in heaven). Additionally, without accepting (believing) the teaching that Jesus is the Son of God, that He died in our place for the sins we have committed, and that He rose again as a matter of conquering death and paving the way for our resurrection (Romans 10: 1-13) no one may be redeemed. Other elements of the gospel message include repenting of the sins we have committed against God and other men (Acts 3: 19), confessing Jesus as Lord and Savior before witnesses (Romans 10: 9-10), and submitting to immersion in water as a matter of remittance of sins (Acts 2: 38). Obedience to these fundamentals of the gospel is considered vital for anyone to attain salvation, but the message does not end there.

Once a person has attained salvation, it is incumbent upon him/her to honor God by living a life of faithfulness to Christ (Matthew 28: 20; John 5: 23). The manner in which we honor God, through Christ, is also taught in Scripture. Jesus, along with the apostles, offers us considerable insight into the attributes of a life that honors Him.

Those passages where the principles of baptism are initially discussed (Matthew 28: 18-20; Mark 16: 15-16; Acts 2: 38-41) offer compelling evidence that it is intended to be presented as an element of the gospel message. As we mentioned earlier, in Matthew's account of Jesus' proclamation of the Great Commission, he notes two kinds of teaching that Jesus commanded of His followers. First, they were to *disciple* men from every nation – *'baptizing them'* (Matthew 28: 19). This kind of instruction is distinct from *'teaching them to observe all things that I have commanded...'* (Matthew 28: 20). It is the initial instruction meant to bring men to a belief in Christ. It is teaching that culminates in baptism.

The fact that Jesus had in view the salvation value of baptism in Mark 16: 16, is evident from the immediate context of His words that is so often overlooked. Jesus links belief *and* baptism directly and incontestably to the gospel message. He instructed the disciples to *'Go into all the world and preach the gospel to every creature'* (Mark 16: 15). It is on the heels of this command to preach the gospel that Jesus explained who would be saved as a result. The saved were those who proved obedient to that proclaimed message – a teaching fully supported by both Peter (Acts 2: 38; 1 Peter 3: 21; 4: 17) and Paul (2 Thessalonians 1: 8). If, in response to hearing the gospel message, Jesus anticipated that men would believe and be baptized, we must recognize baptism as an element of that message.

The Day of Pentecost is the first time in the covenant of grace that the complete message of the gospel is revealed to mankind (Acts 2: 5-40). As Peter and the other apostles preached on that day, their words drew an exclamation from those who believed as they asked, *'what shall we do?'* (v. 37) Peter's response directs the listeners to repentance and baptism (v. 38). While the fact that the message of the gospel focuses on leading men to Christ through baptism may seem obvious, it is a point that many men are simply unwilling to accept, despite clear biblical instruction.

Approaching the Bible

Among those who profess Jesus as Lord, we discover a commonly accepted understanding that belief in Jesus as the risen Son of God is a basic principle of the gospel message. This broad consensus is primarily based on the many biblical passages that candidly call for belief in Christ.

> For God so loved the world that He gave His only begotten Son, that whosoever believes in Him should not perish but have everlasting life. (John 3: 16)
>
> So they said, "Believe on the Lord Jesus Christ, and you will be saved, you and your household." (Acts 16: 31)

A myriad of similar passages can be found strewn throughout the New Testament maintaining belief in Jesus as a condition of salvation. The reading of verses such as these has led some men to conclude that belief alone (or faith alone, where belief and faith are deemed to be equivalent) is sufficient for men to attain salvation. Individual verses, however, fail to provide a full view of the portrait of God's plan as it is painted in Scripture. In the pursuit of true scriptural doctrine, all that the Bible teaches concerning a particular matter, as well as the context of that teaching, must be considered. If only certain passages regarding salvation are examined, while others remain unheeded, the result may be misunderstanding of God's Word. In fact, selective use of Scripture such as this may be adopted to demonstrate biblical support for virtually any belief conceivable. For instance, applying God's Word in such a discriminating fashion could result in the conclusion that belief is, in fact, *not* necessary to secure salvation.

> 38. Then Peter said to them, "Repent and let every one of you be baptized in the name of Jesus Christ for the remission of sins; and you shall receive the gift of the Holy Spirit." (Acts 2: 38)

> There is also an antitype which now saves us–baptism... (1 Peter 3: 21)

Through the elimination of those passages that address the principle of belief in Jesus, we could conclude that salvation is attainable simply through repentance and baptism, as these verses signify. However, applying Scripture in such a restrictive manner denies God the opportunity to fully instruct the reader. In like manner this same technique could be employed to advocate a path to salvation that sets aside repentance.

> He who believes and is baptized will be saved; but he who does not believe will be condemned. (Mark 16: 16)

> Then Crispus, the ruler of the synagogue, believed on the Lord with all his household. And many of the Corinthians, hearing, believed and were baptized. (Acts 18: 8)

If we are to glean from Scripture the things God would have us know, we must be honest in our approach to His Word. The first thing we must do is allow Scripture to complement itself. We cannot gain understanding when we pit God's Word against itself. The fact that belief is presented in the Bible as essential to salvation does not mean that belief *alone*, exclusive of repentance or baptism, is sufficient. If we are intended to consider belief alone as sufficient to salvation, what are we to do with those passages that depict baptism as essential? The concepts are irreconcilable. This could explain why we do not find the phrase *belief alone* anywhere within the pages of God's Word.

Ironically, while the term *belief alone*, or *belief only*, does not appear in Scripture, the phrase *faith only* can be found there. However, *faith only* is not presented as the means to salvation.

> You see then that man is justified by works, and not by faith only. (James 2: 24)

While this remark from James is not specifically addressing one's initial salvation, this is the only time in the Bible when we find these words joined in this manner. Any other use of the terms *faith only* or *belief only* as a matter of redemption derives strictly from the teaching of men rather than from biblical edification.

The Philippian Jailer and the Message of the Gospel

The Philippian jailer was a man in search of answers. In response to his inquiry regarding what he must do to attain salvation, Paul explained to him that he must first believe in Jesus (Acts 16: 30-31). However, belief in Jesus was not the complete message that Paul delivered on that day; it was merely the introduction to his message. An earnest examination of the narrative reveals that, indeed, baptism was taught (Acts 16: 33) just as it had been taught to the eunuch (Acts 8: 36). As we read the account of the jailer, in order to accept that Paul's entire message consisted only of belief in Jesus as a matter of salvation, we must disregard the balance of the report.

> 30. And he brought them out and said, "Sirs, what must I do to be saved?" 31. So they said, "Believe on the Lord Jesus Christ, and you will be saved, you and your household." 32. Then they spoke the word of the Lord to him and to all who were in his house. (Acts 16: 30-32)

Having explained to his listeners that they must believe, Paul '*...spoke the word of the Lord to him...*' Those words resulted in baptism and, undoubtedly, repentance of their sins and open confession of Jesus as Lord (though these last two are not specifically cited). Paul's teaching would, no doubt, have been consistent with that of both the apostle Peter (Acts 2: 38) and Philip (Acts 8: 36-38). Beginning with the Day of Pentecost and venturing forward through the entire apostolic age, conversions reported in Scripture consistently involved water baptism. In fact, in *every* case where details of the conversion are offered, baptism is present.

Expressions such as *the word of the Lord* or *preach the word*, in the New Testament, pertained to the gospel message that was being preached (Acts 8: 4; 11: 19; 15: 35-36; 19: 10) by the apostles and evangelists in the first century. The New Testament writers used terms like *'preached the word of God'* (Acts 13: 5), *'preach the word'* (Acts 14: 25), *'preach the gospel'* (Acts 15: 7), *'preach the word of the Lord'* (Acts 15: 36), and similar phrases interchangeably (Acts 8: 25). We even discover, as Philip taught the Ethiopian eunuch, that the gospel message is represented simply by the name of Jesus as Philip, *'preached Jesus to him'* (Acts 8: 35).

The *word of the Lord* was, and is, the gospel message of salvation through Jesus that is to be preached to all. To many this is the message of *belief* in Jesus as Savior. Yet we find that, after Paul had explained to the Philippian jailer that he must *believe* in Jesus in order to be saved, *they continued to teach this man and others in his house concerning the word of the Lord.* Since Paul continued to speak the *'word of the Lord'* (the gospel), having already explained the need for belief, we can easily surmise that the substance of that message encompasses considerably more than belief. Of course, most will concede this point given the scriptural support for repentance of sins (Acts 3: 19) and confession of Jesus as Lord (Romans 10: 9-10), along with the fact that the *good news*, in itself, is the story of the death, burial, and resurrection of Jesus Christ (1 Corinthians 15: 3-5).

However, this narrative confirms that the *'word of the Lord'* included the teaching of baptism as part of the gospel message since the jailer, along with his family, was baptized that very night in response to Paul's teaching. Furthermore, while Paul would have undoubtedly introduced the entirety of the gospel message concerning salvation, we are not told that these Philippians repented or confessed, but that they were baptized. This suggests that their participation in baptism was the point Luke intended to convey to his readers as a matter of importance.

Some who seek to challenge the role of baptism in the plan of salvation have brought to our attention the fact that the episode with the jailer is the only time in Scripture when the question concerning salvation is actually framed, *'What must I do to be saved?'* Pointing to Pentecost, they note that, at that time the question asked of Peter and the other apostles was simply, *'What shall we do?'* Given the jailer's precise wording of the question, these men have determined that Paul's answer in this context is the only one we should consider relevant for those who seek salvation. Furthermore, this view insists that only the first sentence spoken by Paul at this time may be considered legitimate in discerning God's plan of salvation. Thus, only one sentence in all of Scripture (Acts 16: 31) is relevant to our salvation in the church age.

The sole objective of this observation, however, is to force personal doctrine upon the text. The question on the Day of Pentecost was clearly asked by men seeking salvation. In fact, Peter's single aspiration on that day was to present to the Israelites the opportunity to be saved. Additionally, numerous other statements made by Jesus (Matthew 7: 21; Mark 16: 16), Paul (Romans 6: 1-4; 10: 9-10), and Peter (Acts 3: 19; 1 Peter 3: 21) are focused on redemptive instruction. These passages are no less relevant when it comes to conversion than the incident with the jailer.

A Profile of the Gospel in the Book of Acts

The relentless challenges to baptism have led some to suggest that Scripture does not mention baptism frequently enough for it to be considered vital (apparently compared to belief). This same logic however, is not offered regarding confession. Yet, upon the founding of the church in the book of Acts, the narrative touches on confession in only a handful of passages (Acts 2: 21; 8: 36-37; 22: 16). The word *confess*, as a part of the plan of salvation, is absent from the book of Acts. Still, the examples of Peter's words on the Day of Pentecost (Acts 2: 21), the confession of the Ethiopian eunuch (Acts 8: 37), and Paul's *'calling on the name of the Lord'* (Acts 22: 16) provide evidence of its significance. Additionally, Jesus regarded the proclamation of the good confession made by Peter (Matthew 16: 16) as the basis (rock) upon which the church would be built (Matthew 16: 18).

In an effort to avoid any misrepresentation of Scripture, it should be noted that Acts 8: 37 is likely a late addition to the text and, therefore, is not included in certain versions (e.g., the NIV and NASB) of the Bible. If, however, this text is eliminated, only two verses remain in the book of Acts that could be cited as references to confession; and those passages (Acts 2: 21; 22: 16) are portrayed as *'calling on the name of the Lord.'* Whether or not this may be deemed a literal verbal declaration is perhaps a matter of opinion. For the sake of argument we will grant that this is the case, although, as we discussed earlier, it is apparent from Scripture that confession of Jesus as Lord would only be one element of the *calling* mentioned here.

The command to r*epent*, in one form or other, appears in the book of Acts eleven times. Twice reference is made to John's *'baptism of repentance'* (Acts 13: 24; 19:4). The remaining nine incidents speak either directly or implicitly of forgiveness and/or salvation.

Some derivative of the word *baptize* occurs twenty-seven times in the book of Acts. Some claim that Acts 1: 5 and Acts 11: 16 each carry specific reference to baptism with the Holy Spirit occurring separately from water baptism. Setting aside those passages, twenty-five instances specifically denote baptism in water. Of these twenty-five occasions, seven refer to the baptism performed by John the Baptist. Twice baptism is commanded as a matter of forgiveness of sins (Acts 2: 38; 22: 16). In sixteen other references to water baptism in the book of Acts, it is portrayed as an element of conversion as various men and women accepted Christ.

In some form the word *belief* appears in the book of Acts forty-four times. Four of these may be viewed as identifying belief specifically as a matter *leading to* salvation (Acts 10: 43; 13: 39; 13: 48; 16: 31). At certain other times belief is depicted simply as an antecedent to baptism (Acts 8: 12-13, 37; 18: 8). Four instances are concerned with those who failed to believe in Jesus (Acts 9: 26; 13: 41; 19: 9; 28: 24). On three occasions we find mention of belief in something or someone other than Christ (Acts 24: 14; 27: 11; 27: 25). Beyond these instances, ordinarily when *belief* appears in any form in the book of Acts, it is a general reference to *belief, believing,* or *believers* regarding those who were considered followers of Jesus.

The principle of *faith* is either written or spoken in the book of Acts on fifteen occasions. At times it denotes the faith exhibited by men as they were physically healed (Acts 3: 16; 14: 9). Often it simply expresses general reliance on the gospel message and/or Jesus (Acts 6: 5-8; 11: 24; 13: 8; 14: 22-27; 16: 5; 20: 21; 24: 24). Twice faith is depicted as having a purifying or sanctifying effect (Acts 15: 9; 26: 18).

A Profile of the Gospel in the Epistles

The third through the fifth chapters of Romans are often cited as Paul's declaration of the gospel of Christ and all that it involves. However, the message of the gospel within the epistles is not necessarily taught in a way that explains the manner in which men are saved. The gospel message that is discussed in the epistles is naturally retrospective since these letters were addressed to those who were already part of the body of Christ. The recipients of these letters were not seeking salvation since they had already *put on* Christ, a fact that Paul frequently recognizes (Romans 6: 4, 17; 1 Corinthians 12 13; Galatians 3: 27). They had heretofore accepted Jesus as their Savior and been baptized in obedience to His commands. Therefore, it would be unnecessary, even superfluous, to reiterate the conditions of salvation to those who had already been faithful to God in that respect.

Within the book of Acts we do not find the explicit *command* to openly confess Jesus as Lord as a matter of redemption. However, we do find Paul citing this as a matter of salvation in his letter to the Romans.

> 9. that if you confess with your mouth the Lord Jesus and believe in your heart that God raised Him from the dead, you will be saved. 10. For with the heart one believes unto righteousness, and with the mouth confession is made unto salvation. (Romans 10: 9-10)

While the passage drives much discussion, the most reasonable understanding of Paul's instruction is that God expects from us, as a matter of salvation, open confession before men that we accept Jesus as Savior. It is an act – a word spoken – derived from the words of Peter, that Jesus is the Son of God (Matthew 16: 16), also known as the *good confession*. Paul mentions this confession again, in his letter to Timothy, where he portrays it as a confession *'in the presence of many witnesses'* (1 Timothy 6: 12). Public confession of Jesus as Lord is also touched upon briefly in other passages (John 12: 42; 1 John 4: 15), but none as explicitly, or as boldly, as Paul's directive to the Romans.

While the word occurs thirteen times in the epistles, *repentance* as a device of initial redemption is found only four times (Romans 2: 4-5; 2 Corinthians 7: 10; and 2 Timothy 2: 25; 2 Peter 3: 9). Water baptism is mentioned seventeen times in the epistles. Four of these occasions attribute to baptism forgiveness of sins, newness of life, and salvation (Romans 6: 3-4; Galatians 3: 27; Colossians 2: 12; and 1 Peter 3: 21). Two verses depict baptism as a matter of unity (1 Corinthians 12: 13; Ephesians 4: 5). Four other passages denote the waters of baptism as a matter of cleansing or regeneration without explicit use of the words *baptize* or *baptism* (1 Corinthians 6: 11; Ephesians 5: 26; Titus 3: 5; Hebrews 10: 22). We discover, from the apostle Paul, baptism's relationship to the crossing of the Red Sea (1 Corinthians 10: 2) and the custom of baptism for the dead (1 Corinthians 15: 29). Other instances simply discuss baptism in relation to these various passages mentioned here.

The abundant teaching in the Pauline and general epistles concerning belief (it appears more than eighty times), as opposed to baptism, has lead many to rationalize that it carries with it greater significance. This is one of the reasons so many men have concluded that belief, to the exclusion of baptism, is sufficient for salvation. Like the book of Acts, however, the majority of these instances in the epistles simply use the word *believing* or *believer* as a means of identifying Christians. They do not speak of the manner by which men are saved.

Faith is the central theme of the epistles with well over one hundred fifty references. Oftentimes faith is defined as the path by which we are justified and, therefore, saved (Romans 5: 1; Galatians 2: 16). Not only are we saved by faith, but we are also told repeatedly that we must live by faith. In truth, one who does not actively live by faith is not saved by faith (Hebrews 10: 38; James 2: 24).

Those who claim that we are saved at the earliest twinkling of our faith fail to understand that faith does not sprout in a moment, but, like a seed, we absorb the nutrients of God's Word, allowing them to take root within us (Romans 10: 17). Our faith grows over time (2 Corinthians 10: 15; 2 Thessalonians 1: 3) as our knowledge of and trust in God increases. Faith identifies our *journey* with God (2 Corinthians 5: 7; Colossians 1: 23) rather than the moment of our salvation. That is how the writers of the epistles present faith to us. By faith we believe that Jesus was crucified for our sins

(Romans 10: 14-17). It is by faith in Christ that we repent of our sins (Acts 20: 21) and confess Him as Savior (Romans 10: 9-11). It is also by faith that the Spirit removes our sins from us in Christian baptism (Colossians 2: 11-12; Titus 3: 5).

The Relationship of Belief, Repentance, and Baptism

Baptism is intimately linked with belief and repentance within the pages of Scripture. In fact, the Bible portrays them as inseparable when it comes to salvation (Mark 16: 16; Acts 2: 38). Those who teach that belief/faith alone is sufficient for salvation insist that baptism can have no role in one's initial redemption. However, there are passages that impugn the claim of salvation by belief/faith only (2 Thessalonians 1: 8; John 12: 42) – including many passages involving baptism.

Quite often the *prima facie* reading of a passage or verse declares openly the redemptive value of baptism (Mark 16: 16; Acts 2: 38; Romans 6: 3-4; Colossians 2: 12; 1 Peter 3: 21). The contention that baptism is not required for salvation ultimately denies that these passages may be taken literally. After all, if baptism is deemed necessary for salvation, such a requirement would contradict what many consider overwhelming instruction throughout the New Testament that salvation comes through belief only or faith only. If then, Scripture does state on occasion that those who believe are saved (Acts 10: 43), or that we are saved by faith (Romans 3: 28) while, at the same time, presenting baptism as a matter of salvation, how can such a disparity be reconciled? The dilemma that this presents can be resolved, but only when we acknowledge the redemptive role of baptism.

The prospect of an impenitent Christian in the first century was as foreign to those who penned the words of the epistles in the New Testament as it is to us today. Similarly, someone who had not confessed Jesus as Lord and Savior would not have been considered saved (Romans 10: 9-10). So it is with baptism. The undeniable understanding of those who wrote the letters of the New Testament was that the *believers* to whom they were writing had been obedient to apostolic instruction concerning *all things* necessary to attain salvation (Romans 6: 3; 1 Corinthians 12: 13; Galatians 3: 27; Colossians 2: 12; 1 Peter 3: 21). When Paul wrote of believers being saved, it was with this in mind. Believers were, to Paul, those who had grieved to the Lord over their sins, confessed Jesus as Savior, and had been baptized in His name.

The apostles taught *'the things concerning the kingdom of God'* (Acts 19: 8). Variations of this theme, as noted earlier, can be found throughout Scripture regarding the gospel message that was preached by the apostles and evangelists. Although the specifics are not revealed in the narrative of each conversion portrayed in the book of Acts, the message must have been consistent given the uniformity of the results on a number of occasions (Acts 2: 38-41; 8: 12; 35-36; 9: 17-18; 10: 44-48).

As Luke chronicles the ministry of Philip, he offers a great deal of insight into the relationship between belief and baptism. One such incident concerns the Samaritans who, upon hearing the teaching from Philip about Jesus, believed and were baptized.

> 12. But when they believed Philip as he preached the things concerning the kingdom of God and the name of Jesus Christ, both men and women were baptized. 13. Then Simon himself also believed; and when he was baptized he continued with Philip... (Acts 8: 12-13)

As Philip preached the gospel message to the Samaritans, we find no mention of repentance. However, we understand from Scripture that this would have been a basic part of the message Philip delivered and that the Samaritans would have repented in response to that message.

Similarly, we can be confident that those who listened and responded to the gospel message on the Day of Pentecost believed in Jesus as the Messiah. While their belief is not specifically stated in the narrative, we understand from other passages that, absent their belief in Jesus, they would not be saved (Mark 16: 16; Romans 10: 9-10). The question that was asked of Peter and the other apostles, *'Men and brethren, what shall we do?'* presumes their belief.

Interestingly, among the conversions portrayed in the book of Acts, while belief and repentance are often inferred, we have no need to assume anyone's baptism. In each example of conversion, the believer's submission to baptism is openly discussed in the narrative. The only exceptions to this are the twelve apostles and Apollos (Acts 18: 24-28), both of whom had received the baptism of John the Baptist.

Baptism, like repentance, is depicted in Scripture as the expected and immediate response to the gospel message. Note that, when the Samaritans believed, they were baptized. Simon was also baptized when he believed. The text does not suggest that these believers opted to be baptized once they were saved, but that the decision regarding baptism was the obvious and anticipated outcome of belief. Luke's phrase, *'when they believed,'* presumes the resulting act of baptism. When men believed the gospel message, they were baptized. In each detailed account of conversion in the book of Acts baptism is portrayed, not as an afterthought for a person who had been converted, but the juncture to which the gospel message directs those who accept the substance of that message.

Lydia was a woman who heeded the gospel (Acts 16: 14-15). In accord with all other conversions, her immediate response to the message of the gospel, as spoken by one of God's teachers, was submission to baptism. The only credible explanation, the *necessary inference*, is that Paul directed her to submit to baptism in his presentation of the gospel. She apparently considered baptism an act of faithfulness to God, freely noting that they could judge her faithfulness by her response to their teaching. Narratives such as these provide us with practical examples of the principles of baptism that are discussed in certain other passages (Mark 16: 16; Acts 2: 38; 1 Peter 3: 21).

Just as we recognize that the Samaritans would have repented of their sins, despite scriptural silence on the matter, we presume that Lydia also repented of her sins and confessed Jesus as Lord as she accepted Him as her Savior. The apostles portray repentance and confession as vital elements of the gospel message (Acts 2: 38; 3: 19; Romans 10: 9-10). Philip and Paul would have taught nothing less than the full gospel of Christ on these occasions and those who believed would have followed their instructions. So it is with baptism. Although baptism might not be cited specifically in a passage that teaches belief as a means to salvation, like repentance, the presence of baptism is always couched within the message.

What is apparent in the several accounts of conversion in the New Testament is that the initial instruction offered by the apostles and other teachers in each case was determined by the state of the listener. Explaining to the Jews in Jerusalem on the Day of Pentecost that they must first believe, when it is evident from the narrative that they already believed (Acts 2: 37), would have been unnecessary. However, when the Philippian jailer inquired of Paul what he must do to be saved, Paul's first response was that he must believe in Jesus. Since the jailer did not yet believe, Paul met him at his level and explained what would be the first step on his journey of salvation. That first step was belief. It was not, however, the final instruction the jailer received from Paul. The apostle continued to teach the man until he understood sufficiently so that he could accept Jesus, repent of his sins, and receive baptism for the forgiveness of those sins.

> 1. And it happened, while Apollos was at Corinth, that Paul, having passed through the upper regions, came to Ephesus. And finding some disciples 2. he said to them, "Did you receive the Holy Spirit when you believed?" So they said to him, "We have not so much as heard whether there is a Holy Spirit." 3. And he said to them, "Into what then were you baptized?" So they said, "Into John's baptism." 4. Then Paul said, "John indeed baptized with a baptism of repentance, saying to the people that they should believe on Him who would come after him, that is, on Christ Jesus." 5. When they heard *this*, they were baptized in the name of the Lord Jesus. (Acts 19: 1-5)

In his encounter with the Ephesian disciples, Paul asked them if they had received the Spirit when they first believed. This question might appear to substantiate the claim that belief alone is sufficient for salvation, but for the subsequent conversation. In the ensuing text the passage is very telling as Paul clearly assumes that, if these men believed, they had been baptized. His question was not *if* they had been baptized, but *into what* they had been baptized. This query by Paul attests to his recognition that they would have received the promised Holy Spirit at the time of Christian baptism, a doctrine consistent with the principles of baptismal instruction (Acts 2: 38). Paul's words, indicating an intimate link between belief, baptism, and the Holy Spirit, convey his regard for the role of baptism in God's grand design.

As we noted earlier, it is often propounded by men that the third through the fifth chapters of the book of Romans constitute, in every sense, the fullness of the gospel message. Interestingly, at no time in that discourse does Paul teach baptism as critical to salvation – a point upon which the teaching of salvation by *belief only* relies heavily. We discover that this is also true of John's proclamation of life through Christ (John 20: 30-31) and Paul's reminder to the Corinthians concerning the gospel he had preached when he was among them (1 Corinthians 15: 1-11). Yet, the *fullness* of the gospel message that Paul declared, upon which so many hang their view of baptism, seems to also dismiss a contrite heart as a matter of salvation – at least, repentance is not mentioned openly within the text. Like baptism, however, it is implicitly present in relation to belief.

If we are to consider these writings of Paul as *complete* with respect to the gospel message, even though they fail to mention repentance, we must recognize that the belief of which he writes involves considerably more than acknowledgement of, or trust in, Jesus as Lord. Belief, as a response to the gospel, encompasses all that Scripture teaches as essential in our acceptance of Christ.

When addressing the various churches, groups, and individuals in the epistles, at no time did the apostles ever differentiate between believers and *baptized* believers, specifically because they saw no such distinction. All believers were baptized believers just as all believers were repentant believers. The words *believe*, *believer*, or *belief* embraced those who had been obedient to apostolic instruction concerning the gospel message. Those who were not fully submissive to these teachings were not considered believers. Therefore, these apostles simply identified the acceptance of, and obedience to, the gospel message as *belief*, and those who responded accordingly as *believers*.

Who among the Corinthians remained un-immersed? When Paul wrote to them concerning their inappropriate identification with the men who had baptized them (1 Corinthians 1: 1-17), there is no allusion to those who had not been immersed. He also recognized that the Galatians were *'all sons of God through faith,'* having been *'baptized into Christ'* (Galatians 3: 26-27). If we can grant that believers addressed by Paul had repented of sins and confessed Jesus as Savior, despite the fact that these are rarely cited in conjunction with belief, we can effortlessly presume their baptism. In that case, we can easily consider belief – obedient belief – as sufficient for salvation.

Paul's Alleged Disclaimer Concerning Baptism

In a hasty reaction to certain comments in his first letter to the Corinthians, it is oftentimes asserted that Paul's objective was to decry the Corinthians' overemphasis on water baptism. Wrongly identifying their own Christianity with the person who had baptized them, the Corinthians had begun to stray from the true gospel message that focused on Jesus as Savior. Paul responded by contending the insignificance, not of baptism, but of the one who performed the rite. His expression of relief that he personally had baptized few, thus averting claims of baptism in the name of Paul, testifies to his own humility toward his role as an apostle.

> 14. I thank God that I baptized none of you except Crispus and Gaius, 15. lest anyone should say that I had baptized in my own name. 16. Yes, I also baptized the household of Stephanas. Besides, I do not know whether I baptized any other. 17. For Christ did not send me to baptize, but to preach the gospel.... (1 Corinthians 1: 14-17)

Paul seems unsure how many he had baptized in Corinth, and uncertain if he had baptized any others (1 Corinthians 1: 14-17). In a life that had been marked by numerous baptisms in a variety of locations (Acts 16: 15; 33; 19: 5), his failure to recollect exactly whom he had baptized in Corinth is understandable. If Paul had only performed a few baptisms, it is likely he would be able to recall them more clearly.

A multitude of modern-day scholars take considerable liberty with Paul's statement respecting his role as a preacher. They reason that, in his remark, *'For Christ did not send me to baptize, but to preach the gospel,'* Paul was summarily dismissing baptism as a component of that gospel message. However, this is neither a fair nor honest assessment of the text since the content of the gospel message is not under examination at this time. What is being addressed is Paul's role of preaching in contrast to his physical participation in baptizing others. In keeping with that theme, this remark simply distinguishes between *baptizing* and *preaching.*

Those who wish to challenge the redemptive role of baptism insist that Paul, in this statement to the Corinthians, is contrasting baptism and the gospel. Thus they place the emphases of the statement on *baptize* and *gospel*. This rendering of the text ignores completely Paul's point of the narrative. He is distinguishing, not between an action (baptism) and a thing (the gospel message), but between two specific actions. In that case, we read, 'For Christ did not send me to *baptize*, but to *preach* the gospel.' Thus he contrasts the *action* of baptizing against the *action* of preaching. Given the context of the statement, this is the most reasonable understanding of the remark. Paul's focus on the inconsequence of the person performing the baptism testifies neither to the merit of baptism nor the substance of the gospel message he taught. Furthermore, since Scripture fully embraces baptism within the scope of the gospel

(Mark 16: 15-16; Acts 2: 38; Romans 6: 1-4; 1 Peter 3: 21), we have no basis for concluding that Paul is setting it aside here.

Paul's reflection upon his assigned role of preaching is a sterling example of an elliptical statement, a form of Greek syntax employed occasionally in Scripture to stress a significant point. More specifically, the speaker/writer uses the phrase '$ου...αλλα$' (*not...but*), as we find in this passage, to accentuate one matter over another. Paul's remark, *'For Christ did not (ου) send me to baptize, but (αλλα) to preach...'* simply punctuates his primary focus. This would not preclude Paul from baptizing, which he clearly did, but highlights his role as a teacher. Similar use of the ellipsis can be found in a number of passages in the New Testament.

> Do not labor for the food which perishes, but for the food which endures to everlasting life. (John 6: 27)
>
> You have not lied to men but to God. (Acts 5: 4).
>
> Little children, let us not love in word or in tongue, but in deed and in truth. (1 John 3:18)

By suggesting that men *should not labor for their food*, Jesus was not discounting the relevance of working for physical food, a basic teaching of Scripture, but was simply underscoring the importance of laboring for spiritual food. When Ananias and Sapphira lied to Peter, they had *'not lied to men but to God.'* While they had certainly lied to men, Peter was emphasizing the fact that, in doing so, they also had lied to God. Could John possibly be teaching that we should not love each other *'in word or in tongue?'* He was, of course, highlighting the need to love each other in deed and in truth since love expressed in words is exhibited in deeds. He had no intention of devaluing the verbal expression of love.

Elliptical statements can provide a powerful message as the writer seemingly overshadows a significant principle (labor for food, lying to men, or loving words) with the one where emphasis is placed. The point is not to diminish the former but to accentuate the latter. Additionally, the assumption that Paul's remark somehow rejects baptism as part of the gospel message can be dismissed with prejudice. The elliptical nature of the statement, accenting one element without excluding another, is confirmed by the very fact that Paul did baptize many believers. Evidently God did send him to baptize.

Contending that Paul's thankfulness for personally baptizing only a few at Corinth denotes a lesser role for baptism ignores the explanation Paul himself offers for this remark. His relief was in the fact that men could not look to him as their savior simply because he had baptized them. In fact, if Paul was concerned that members might look to him as savior based purely upon his incidental participation in baptism, it seems that both Paul and these Corinthian converts considered this rite to be a pivotal moment in the conversion experience. Therefore, rather than suggesting a fading role for baptism, the passage actually reveals the exceptional relevance placed upon its observance in the early church. A person who regards baptism as trivial is unlikely to be overly impressed with the person performing the rite. To place such a high level of distinction upon that person, baptism itself must have been held in high esteem.

It is evident from the narrative that the Corinthians perceived baptism as a matter of identification or association. Unfortunately, they had linked baptism to identification with other men rather than with Christ. They considered themselves to be *'of Paul...of Apollos...of Cephas'* as a result of baptism. Noting that Christ, not Paul, was crucified for them, he presses the Corinthians to remember that, having been baptized in the name of Christ, they were *of Christ*. They were not baptized in, and could not be saved by, Paul. Thus he assigns his concerns, not to baptism's irrelevance, but to its worth, hoping to avoid claiming for himself the glory that was meant for Christ alone.

The Bible offers no evidence of a change in Paul's teaching on baptism. Had such a transformation taken place it would necessarily have occurred in the period of time discussed in Acts 19: 8-10. In the nineteenth chapter of Acts, verses one through seven, Paul encountered the men from Ephesus who had received the baptism of John. He in turn baptized those men in the name of Jesus. Following this incident Paul remained in Ephesus for a time.

Over a period of between two and three years Paul spent his time in Ephesus teaching in the synagogue and in the school of Tyrannus. Scholars agree that he wrote his first letter to the Corinthians near the end of his time there. His statements in the first chapter of 1 Corinthians are the remarks most often quoted to suggest abdication of water baptism. Yet Luke offers nothing in his narrative that would give us reason to believe Paul's message was altered in any way. On the contrary, we find that *'...this continued for two years'* (Acts 19: 10) arguably indicating that his message remained consistent. A full reading of the entire nineteenth chapter of Acts will provide many of the details of Paul's stay in Ephesus. No change of doctrine and no declining role for water baptism are indicated. His teaching *continued* throughout his ministry.

It is imperative that Paul's role in the early church be given full consideration. His chief responsibilities, as revealed throughout the epistles, involved teaching the unsaved while edifying and exhorting those who were already converted to Christ. When he explained to the Corinthians that God did not send him to baptize (1 Corinthians 1: 17), it is most reasonable to conclude that, while Paul certainly baptized many of Christ's followers, physically baptizing new converts was not the primary task to which God had set his hand. Others could baptize, but few could teach in the bold and persuasive manner for which Paul was known. His was a role of instruction. In the twelfth chapter of this same letter to the Corinthians, Paul stresses the fact that diverse roles within the body of Christ are filled by a company of individuals. Scripture reveals, however, that Paul continued to teach water baptism unwaveringly through the end of his ministry.

Scholars estimate that Paul wrote the book of 1 Corinthians around AD 55, toward the end of his ministry in Ephesus, as previously noted. Regarding his view of baptism he also penned numerous other passages at various times throughout his ministry. The letter to the Romans, for instance, was written in or around AD 57. Colossians is dated approximately AD 60 and he wrote to Titus in AD 63.

> 3. Or do you not know that as many of us as were baptized into Christ Jesus were baptized into His death? 4. Therefore we were buried with Him through baptism into death, that just as Christ was raised from the dead by the glory of the Father, even so we also should walk in newness of life. (Romans 6: 3-4)

> 11. In Him you were also circumcised with the circumcision made without hands, by putting off the body of the sins of the flesh, by the circumcision of Christ, 12. buried with Him in baptism, in which you were also raised with *Him* through faith in the working of God, who raised him from the dead. (Colossians 2: 11-12)

> 4. But when the kindness and the love of God our Savior toward man appeared, 5. not by works of righteousness which we have done, but according to His mercy He saved us, through the washing of regeneration and renewing of the Holy Spirit. (Titus 3: 4-5)

The passages presented from Romans and Colossians, written years after his words to the Corinthians, portray a man who positively believed baptism to be a critical step in our walk with God. In his letter to Titus, Paul wrote concerning a cleansing that involves regeneration and renewal by or through the Holy Spirit. Translated *washing* in this instance, the Greek word, λουτρου (*loutrou*), literally means *bath*.[1] Given New Testament instruction concerning water baptism as the moment of rebirth (John 3: 5; Acts 2: 38; 1 Corinthians 6: 11) this, too, should be seen as water baptism as Paul again ties together washing (with water) and the Holy Spirit, much as Peter did on the Day of Pentecost. This also affirms Paul's comments to the Romans depicting our burial and resurrection in baptism as the moment we begin life anew. His view of baptism throughout his ministry is undeniably constant.

In Luke's account of Paul's journeys in the book of Acts, we find that he encountered the Jews in Jerusalem circa AD 58. Upon reflection of his own conversion, Paul described, from personal experience, the direct relationship between baptism and forgiveness of sins. He regards baptism, per the instructions he received from Ananias, as the time God forgave him of his sins (Acts 22: 16).

No passage in the Bible that reflects the life and teachings of Paul, whether written before or after 1 Corinthians, suggests that water baptism was no longer valid or necessary for the forgiveness of sins. Given the support found in Scripture for the importance of baptism, it is difficult to understand how the debate has reached such an elevated level.

Paul's View of the Relationship Between Baptism and Faith

The letter to the Galatians was presumably written about the time Paul wrote 1 Corinthians, but could arguably be dated earlier. Since many evangelicals claim that Paul, at some point in time, altered his position on the import of baptism, and since Galatians *may* have been written early in Paul's ministry, the book is not really a suitable tool to combat the misconceptions regarding

Paul's statements to the Corinthians. Nevertheless, his writing here does offer us a clear view of Paul's perspective regarding baptism:

> 21. *Is* the law then against the promises of God? Certainly not! For if there had been a law given which could have given life, truly righteousness would have been by the law. 22. But the Scripture has confined all under sin, that the promise by faith in Jesus Christ might be given to those who believe. 23. But before faith came, we were kept under guard by the law, kept for the faith which would afterward be revealed. 24. Therefore the law was our tutor *to bring us* to Christ, that we might be justified by faith. 25. But after faith has come, we are no longer under a tutor. 26. For you are all sons of God through faith in Christ Jesus. 27. For as many of you as were baptized into Christ have put on Christ. 28. There is neither Jew nor Greek, there is neither slave nor free, there is neither male nor female; for you are all one in Christ Jesus. 29. And if you *are* Christ's, then you are Abraham's seed, and heirs according to the promise. (Galatians 3: 21-29)

Paul places a great deal of emphasis on baptism in this passage even while faith is identified as the means of justification. He does not isolate baptism from faith, but thoughtfully binds them together. Baptism is relevant even in the presence of faith. Prior to faith men were kept under guard by the law. In faith baptism is a vital part of God's plan.

Commenting that we are baptized into (the body of) Christ, Paul perceived baptism as a passageway through which a man or woman could find his/her way into Christ. Rather than portraying baptism as merely *a* passageway, Paul depicts it as *the* passageway to Christ. His indicates that the *putting on* of Christ is limited to *'as many of you as were baptized'* (Galatians 3: 27). In a message where faith is a focal point recognizing that observation of the law was a thing of the past, Paul is dogmatic in his presentation of baptism as a step *into* Christ.

Having expounded fully upon the fact that we are justified by faith (vs. 23-26), Paul begins verse twenty-seven with a curious word. It is the word *for*, which is translated from the Greek word γαρ (*gar*). According to Strong's Exhaustive Concordance of the Bible this word *assigns a reason*[2] to the statement(s) made. Note the carefully designed progression of Paul's observation. *'But before faith came, we were kept under guard by the law...Therefore the law was our tutor to bring us to Christ...But after faith has come, we are no longer under a tutor. For (the reason is) you are all sons of God through faith in Christ Jesus.*

109

For (the reason is) as many of you as were baptized into Christ have put on Christ.'

It is extremely difficult to misconstrue Paul's meaning if we approach the text honestly, since the bond he establishes between baptism and our relationship with God is inescapable. The reason we have been justified *by* faith (v. 24) and are no longer under a tutor (v. 25) is that we are sons of God *through* faith (v. 26). The reason we are deemed to be sons of God *through* faith is that we, having been baptized *into* Christ, have *put on* Christ (v. 27).

While Scripture will always support itself, God needs to identify an element's redemptive value *only once* for it to be authentic. Therefore, if we are told in Scripture that we must repent to be saved (Acts 2: 38; 3: 19), then we must humble ourselves and repent. Confession in the pursuit of salvation being mentioned sparsely in Scripture (Romans 10: 9-10; 1 Timothy 6: 12) does not lessen its severity concerning eternal life. Therefore, since baptism is identified within the pages of Scripture as an integral component of the gospel message and a condition of salvation (Mark 16: 16; Acts 2: 38; 1 Peter 3: 21), we are compelled to acknowledge, and even embrace it, as part of the gospel.

NOTES FOR CHAPTER 6

1. *Loutron, on, to, (louw),* …a bathing, bath…used in the N.T. and in eccles. writ. of baptism. Thayer's Greek-English Lexicon of the New Testament, p. 382, 1977, Baker Books House.

2. James Strong, LL.D., S.T.D., The New Strong's Exhaustive Concordance of the Bible, Greek Dictionary of the New Testament, p. 20, 1990, Thomas Nelson Publishers.

Chapter VII
What Is the Purpose of Water Baptism?

Several views persist regarding the reasons for baptism. Some believe that the value of baptism is strictly cosmetic, contending that its true benefit lies in the witness to others that someone has made a commitment to Jesus. Others hold that baptism does have a greater worth than simply its outward appearance since it is a command of God. Baptism to them is an act of submission to God's will. Still others recognize a baptismal function that transcends the more evident accomplishments of witness and obedience. To these men baptism is seen as a spiritual act offering spiritual blessings. Those who respect the sanctifying effect of baptism understand that it is at the time of immersion that one's sins are forgiven. This tenet maintains that baptism has salvation value since, according to Scripture, no one may be saved without first being holy (1 Corinthians 3: 17; Hebrews 12: 14) and no one may be holy without first having his/her sins cleansed by Christ's blood (Colossians 2: 11-12; Hebrews 10: 22).

Baptism as an Outward Sign of an Inward Change
A favored maxim among those who deny the redemptive value of baptism is this – *baptism is an outward sign of an inward change* – a phrase made popular by John Wesley[1] and others. No reasonable person can dispute the fact that there is an obvious physical aspect to baptism. The Bible, however, does not present it as an outward sign whose worth is limited to its physical nature. When the Bible does address the objectives incorporated into baptism, its value is *never* confined to its tangible attributes. Admittedly, it is one facet of a person's faithfulness to which we can attest since men are able to witness baptism, but that is not its primary role as defined in God's Word.

> Then Peter said to them, "Repent, and let every one of you be baptized in the name of Jesus Christ for the remission of sins; and you shall receive the gift of the Holy Spirit. (Acts 2: 38)

> And now why are you waiting? Arise and be baptized, and wash away your sins, calling on the name of the Lord. (Acts 22: 16)

> Or do you not know that as many of us as were baptized into Christ Jesus were baptized into His death? (Romans 6: 3)
>
> For as many of you as were baptized into Christ have put on Christ. (Galatians 3: 27)
>
> There is also an antitype which now saves us - baptism... (1 Peter 3: 21)

The truth is no passage of Scripture suggests that the early church observed the rite of baptism as an outward sign of conversion, and the word *sign* is never applied to baptism by Jesus or the apostles.

The Efficacy of Baptism

From the time of the Reformation Movement in the sixteenth century, men have taught with conviction that the rite of Christian baptism embodies no real force. The changes that take place in a man's relationship with God, it is said, are realized prior to his immersion in water. It has even been proposed that one who has not previously been redeemed cannot legitimately submit to baptism. Our participation in the rite of baptism is simply considered obedience to a command of God and the role of baptism is to provide testimony to others of the change that has already occurred within us. This, however, is not the manner in which baptism is presented in Scripture.

While confession of Jesus as Lord and submission to baptism typically take place conjointly before many witnesses (Acts 2: 41; 1 Timothy 6: 12), that is not always true. In the case of Paul, or the Ethiopian eunuch, or even the Philippian jailer, baptism was administered somewhat privately. Apparently no other believers were present when Philip baptized the eunuch. He confessed his belief to Philip alone (Acts 8: 37). Just as Peter told the crowd on the Day of Pentecost, Ananias instructed Paul to be baptized as a matter of forgiveness. These people submitted to baptism for its spiritual value rather than as a physical sign to others. Even the baptism offered by John prior to Christ's death was considered much more than an exhibition of a person's commitment. It was joined with repentance *'for the forgiveness of sins'* (Luke 3: 3)

As we consider the biblical uses of the word *baptize*, something significant stands out. Baptism is efficacious. That is to say, the thing or person being baptized is altered *in the course of baptism*. This is true whether the subject is Christian baptism or any of a variety of other baptisms mentioned in God's Word. A distinguishing feature of baptism is that it affects change. According to Strong's Concordance, *'baptising...results in permanent change.'*[2]

Numerous incidents in Scripture are identified as baptism. Peter explained that baptism corresponds to the flood of Noah's day (1 Peter 3: 21). In his depiction of the relationship between the two, the apostle indicates that the waters of the flood are reflected in the waters of baptism. God destroyed the world via the flood. Water was God's *agent* of destruction and its power was realized as evil men of the world were destroyed *in the water*. It was a baptism of the earth that *resulted* in permanent change. This change did not take place prior to, but at the time of the flood.

Paul taught the Corinthians that baptism could also be pictured in the crossing of the Red Sea. He explained that the Israelites had been *'baptized into Moses'* (1 Corinthians 10: 2) at that time. This baptism, too, was effective as the evil of the Egyptians was extinguished *in the water*. The episode exhibits two distinct characteristics of Christian baptism: first, the Israelites crossed *through* the sea (on dry land), exiting the other side where they would begin a *new life*; and second, the threat from the world they had known was destroyed *in the sea* as they left their life of slavery behind them. While some may suggest that Pharaoh had already freed the Israelites prior to the incident at the Red Sea, there exists a considerable difference between Pharaoh's proclamation, which meant nothing, and the actions of God as the Israelites were baptized into Moses. Their freedom was realized in the sea.

Baptism with the Holy Spirit is a challenging subject. Many believe this experience has long since passed while others insist that every true Christian must realize baptism with the Spirit in some form. While the definition of baptism with the Spirit is one that divides many men, everyone recognizes the change that takes place at that time. Who would deny that this baptism, at the very least, identifies the *moment* that a man receives the Holy Spirit? It is a time of change. Men do not receive the Spirit prior to, but *at the time of*, baptism with the Spirit. One who has experienced baptism with the Spirit is not the same as he was prior to that moment of encounter.

As Jesus considered the path He would take, He questioned His disciples, whether they could withstand the *baptism* He Himself faced (Mark 10: 38). Jesus was, of course, contemplating the death, burial, and resurrection He would experience in order to redeem mankind. It was the sacrifice He must make. This, too, was a baptism wrought with power. Indeed, this should be considered the most powerful, most efficacious baptism of Scripture. It is the baptism (death, burial, and resurrection) of Christ that provides worth to Christian baptism (1 Peter 3: 21). It was a baptism that resulted not in mere permanent change, but in the establishment of an entirely new covenant – the covenant of grace.

Change takes place *during* baptism. That is the theme of baptism, whether it is the rite of Christian baptism in water or any other baptism mentioned in Scripture. Baptism *affects* change. Men of earth remained evil until the waters of the flood arrived. The Israelites were not free of their former life until their enemies were overcome in the waters of the sea. Men could not be saved by the blood of Christ prior to His experiencing the baptism of which He spoke. It was specifically *through* His baptism of sacrifice that the opportunity of *life* came to men.

Whether it was the purification of the baptism performed by John the Baptist (John 3: 25), or the ritual baptisms of the Pharisees as they attempted to purify themselves from the uncleanness of the company of Gentiles (Mark 7: 4), the intent has always been that change (cleansing) would occur in the course of baptism.

The Purpose of John's Baptism

The groundwork for Christian baptism, found in the ministry of John the Baptist, provides understanding regarding the effects of this ceremony. Luke's narrative reveals that forgiveness of sins is linked to the repentance and baptism over which John presided. We gain further insight into the efficacy of the baptism performed by John from a conversation he had with his disciples concerning purification.

> 25. Then there arose a dispute between *some* of John's disciples and the Jews about purification ($\kappa\alpha\theta\alpha\rho\iota\mu o\varsigma$). 26. And they came to John and said to him, "Rabbi, He who was with you beyond the Jordan, to whom you have testified—behold, He is baptizing ($\beta\alpha\pi\tau\iota\zeta\epsilon\iota$), and all are coming to Him!" (John 3: 25-26)

That the subject of purification would focus on baptism is certainly understandable for these men of Jewish descent. In Old

Testament Israel, purification was often closely linked to ritual cleansing by means of water to which they were often called (Numbers 8: 7, 21; 19: 9; 31: 23; Ezra 6: 20). The view that water baptism was a vehicle in which purification was achieved was clear to these men since God's use of water for religious cleansing was well known. Scripture teaches, in the various passages that depict John's baptism, that it was for the forgiveness of sin – a baptism providing purification (Mark 1: 4; Luke 3: 3).

Beyond the obvious feature of obedience (Luke 7: 29-30), purification seems to be the solitary consequence of the baptism of repentance offered by John. The sundry promises allied with Christian baptism, such as membership in the body of Christ, were simply not accessible during the time John was baptizing.

Christian Baptism for the Forgiveness of Sins

It was through the work of the apostles that Christian baptism was initiated. While there are undeniable similarities between the baptism of John and Christian baptism, some very discrete differences do stand out. The distinctions between the two were made manifest on the Day of Pentecost. As people gathered together in Jerusalem to celebrate Pentecost (Feast of Weeks), the account provides Peter's answer in response to the question, *'Men and brethren, what shall we do?'*

> Then Peter said to them, "Repent, and let every one of you be baptized in the name of Jesus Christ for the remission of sins; and you shall receive the gift of the Holy Spirit." (Acts 2: 38)

As with John's ministry, repentance and baptism are closely associated on the Day of Pentecost. These two acts are joined at the hip, directing the penitent believer toward forgiveness of sin and a new relationship with Jesus Christ. Christian baptism, like the baptism performed by John, continued to provide forgiveness of sins, but the nature and effect of baptism appear to have been expanded. The converts in the book of Acts were baptized *'in the name of Jesus'* and promised the *'gift of the Holy Spirit.'* Scripture does not mention John's baptism being performed in a specific name; nor was the Holy Spirit promised as a result of baptism prior to Pentecost as Peter proclaimed on that day.

During the ministry of John the Baptist, God's new covenant - which was established through the death, burial, and resurrection of Jesus - was not complete and the Holy Spirit had not yet presented Himself to men. On the Day of Pentecost, His indwelling presence was made available to those who were willing to repent and be baptized. The Day of Pentecost must be viewed in perspective. It stands as a pivotal moment in the history of mankind – a day when the new covenant of grace was instituted, offering men the promise of true and permanent cleansing from sins committed.

Despite the frankness of Peter's words, two primary trains of thought are offered to portray this passage (Acts 2: 38) as one that does *not* present baptism as a matter of forgiveness. The first contention is that the promises of forgiveness and the gift of the Holy Spirit (in the Greek text) refer only to the command to *repent*. This view is derived from the fact that *repent* and *you shall receive* are each written in second person plural while *be baptized* appears in third person singular form. This shift, however, is simply intended to personalize submission to baptism. It is a method occasionally utilized in the New Testament to emphasize personal responsibility (Acts 3: 26; 11: 29-30; 1 Corinthians 7: 24; Revelation 20: 13). Without delving too deeply, the fact that Greek scholarship finds forgiveness grammatically joined to both repentance and baptism in this verse should settle the issue.[3]

Concern over the link between baptism and forgiveness that this verse offers has led many men to contend that Peter's words have actually come to us broken and in need of mending. This has produced a remedy that highlights the singular-plural blend found within Peter's statement. In essence, their solution is to surgically fracture the verse, ever so gently, and reset it according to approved doctrine so that it might reflect the meaning they believe the apostle *intended* to convey, despite what he actually said. Having treated the statement to heal according to their specific baptismal creed, we find men teaching the more modern version illustrated below.

> Then Peter said to them, "Repent (and let every one of you be baptized in the name of Jesus Christ) for the remission of sins; and you shall receive the gift of the Holy Spirit."

The rejuvenated text depicted here, which casts the command to be baptized as a parenthetic comment, is essentially what evangelicals teach today concerning this verse. Of course, the transformed reading communicates a far different message than the original Spirit-breathed version. That being the case, perhaps we would do well to consider closely the consequences of reconstructing Scripture to suit our own ideological views.

The premise behind this approach to Acts 2: 38 is the assumption that Peter actually intended to sever baptism from the awarding of forgiveness. If that was Peter's goal he has disguised it well. In this critical passage that was inspired by the Holy Spirit and designed to lead men to eternal life, it is difficult to envision Peter inadvertently obscuring a key element of the message. The contention that he was presenting repentance alone as the means to forgiveness, while depicting baptism as an inconsequential rite performed after the fact, is not merely a strained interpretation, but a serious encroachment upon the text. It is a claim rooted in a sectarian view of baptism that exemplifies men speaking to Scripture rather than allowing Scripture to speak to men.

In truth, Peter's words openly reject the position stated above as he establishes an uncompromising bond between baptism and forgiveness. The fact that he purposed to include baptism as an element of forgiveness is corroborated in his first epistle where he states that *baptism saves* (1 Peter 3: 21). That is the sum and substance of his portrayal of baptism in this sermon on the Day of Pentecost. The canvas of Scripture upon which Acts 2: 38 is painted fully embraces Peter's command that these men and women should repent and be baptized in pursuit of forgiveness.

Criticism of Peter's portrayal of baptism on this day continues with a focus on the prepositional phrase, *for the remission of sins,* with specific emphasis on the word εἰς *(eis)*, which is pronounced *ice* and is translated in this passage as *for*. Charging that εἰς might also be interpreted *because of* or *with respect to*, many ardently insist that baptism is not for the *outcome* of forgiveness, but *a result of* forgiveness that has already occurred. If that is the case, however, Peter was telling the crowd that they must also *repent* because of the forgiveness of sins that had already taken place. This view places forgiveness before repentance when, in reality, repentance always precedes forgiveness – a formula that is taught deliberately within the pages of Scripture (Luke 3: 3; 17: 3; 24: 47; Mark 1: 4; Acts 3: 19; 5: 31; 2 Peter 3: 9). Of course, some men do tender the explanation that forgiveness occurs somewhere between repentance and baptism, but that is not the way it is depicted here.

The commands to *repent* and *be baptized*, in this passage, both fall squarely ahead of the realization of forgiveness.

A great deal of confusion is brought to bear by those who insist that one need not be *'baptized for the remission of sins.'* Much time and energy has been spent as men attempt to refute what is spoken plainly in Acts 2: 38. Since it lies at the heart of the debate over the need for baptism, a comprehensive look into the translation of the word εἰς is warranted at this time.

> 1519 εἰς ice – a primary preposition; to or into (indicating the point reached or entered), of place, time, or (figuratively) purpose (result, etc.); also in adverbial phrases:--(abundant-)ly, against, among, as, at, (back-) ward, before, by, concerning, + continual, + far more exceeding, for (intent, purpose), fore, + forth, in (among, at, unto, -so much that, -to), to the intent that, + of one mind, + never, of, (up-)on, + perish, + set at one again, (so) that, therefore(-unto), throughout, til, to (be, the end, -ward), (here-)until(-to), ...ward, (where-)fore, with. Often used in composition with the same general import, but only with verbs (etc.) expressing motion (literally or figuratively).[4]

> 1519 εἰς, Prep governing the Accusative, and denoting entrance into, or direction and limit: in, to, towards, *for, among.*[5]

The meaning of the word εἰς throughout the Bible, as with the word *for* in the English language, is largely dependent upon the context in which it is used. The word appears more than 1,750 times in the New Testament. In the vast majority of these cases it holds the meaning *to* or *into* while referencing a time or place. Of course, there are instances when it is translated into various other words, such as *for*. Quite often when this occurs the meaning can be most closely associated with the definition of *purpose*. Occasionally, however, the text does suggest another meaning.

> For what does the Scripture say? *"Abraham believed God, and it was counted to him for (εἰς) righteousness."* (Romans 4: 3)

Paul, explaining to the church in Rome the futility of seeking salvation through deeds of merit, portrayed Abraham as *being in a state of* righteousness as his belief was credited to him. This passage is probably not the best example, however, since we understand that Abraham's belief *led to* righteousness, thus supporting the position that baptism *leads to* forgiveness.

A preferred passage of those who teach the causal meaning for εἰς in Acts 2: 38, is found in the following words spoken by Jesus:

> The men of Nineveh will rise up in the judgment with this generation and condemn it, because they repented *at* (εἰς) the preaching of Jonah... (Matthew 12: 41).

Surmising that the people of Nineveh repented *at* (*in response to* or *because of*) Jonah's preaching that had already taken place seems to offer an opportunity for men to contend that we are baptized in response to forgiveness that has already taken place in Acts 2: 38. It should equally be noted, however, that the repentance of the Ninevites, while it was certainly in response to Jonah's preaching, was done *with a view to* his message and/or brought them *into* compliance with that message. This is the view many Greek scholars prefer.[6] Still, the translation *because of the preaching of Jonah* seems to fit the context well enough that we should consider its possible impact on the purpose of baptism proposed by Peter.

While this application (Matthew 12: 41) of the word εἰς can be found, it is extremely scarce not only in Scripture, but also in Greek literature generally, and is considerably less common than those times when the meaning of *purpose* is clearly intended. Nonetheless, the word appearing infrequently in this form still does not resolve the argument for or against a particular meaning in Acts 2: 38. Given this fact, we must determine Peter's intent on the Day of Pentecost based upon the context and phraseology of the spoken word.

Interestingly, a distinct characteristic can be found in Peter's sermon that clearly separates his use of εἰς from passages like this one from Matthew. In this instance, Peter uses the imperative commands, telling the people to *repent* and *be baptized*. While the word εἰς may be translated with various meanings depending upon the context, we know that this setting involves directives, in the form of imperatives, from Peter as he sought a decision from the crowd. That fact demands the translation of *purpose* and is the very thing that distinguishes this statement from others. In fact, if the causal translation, *because your sins have been forgiven*, was legitimate, given the imperative statements involved, it would evidently be the single instance in the whole of Greek literature where this was the case. The εἰς spoken in Matthew 12: 41 is simply incompatible with the εἰς found in Acts 2: 38. The vain attempts by numerous theologians to equate the two derive strictly from a predisposed view of baptism.

In the first chapter of Mark, Jesus encountered a leper as He traveled in Galilee. The man begged Jesus to heal him, which Jesus did willingly. This is a very telling episode since, once healed, Jesus provided the man with some instruction.

> And saith unto him, See thou say nothing to any man: but go thy way, shew thyself to the priest, and offer for (περι) thy cleansing those things which Moses commanded, for (εἰς) a testimony unto them. (Mark 1:44 - KJV)

As with the Day of Pentecost, in this passage εις follows an imperative as Jesus directed the man to *go* to the priests and make an offering according to the law. What makes this incident so enticing is the fact that the man was told to go to the priests and *offer* (imperative) *for* (in response to) a healing that had already taken place. The dilemma for those who claim that baptism is offered for forgiveness that has already been received is that the word here translated *for* is not the word εις, but rather the word περι *(peri)*. Even more challenging is the realization that the healed man was to make this offering *for* (εἰς), or *for the purpose of*, a testimony to the priests. This is the effect an imperative has on the meaning of the word εἰς.

Consideration must be given to the fact that, on the Day of Pentecost, Peter was responding to the Israelites' question regarding what they must *do* in order to alter their current condition. Had these Israelites, standing before Peter, already attained a state of righteousness, the reasonable answer from Peter should have been that nothing was required of them. Such was not the case, however. A specific response was necessary for them to be forgiven so that God might view them as holy.

> For this is My blood of the new covenant, which is shed for many for (εἰς) the remission of sins. (Matthew 26: 28)

Jesus proclaimed to the disciples that His blood was to be shed *'for the remission of sins.'* Many supporting passages throughout Scripture (Ephesians 1: 7; Colossians 1: 13-14) offer compelling evidence that the phrase *'for the remission of sins'* in this setting suggests *purpose*. Jesus' words indicate that He would *do* something (shed His blood), and that the *goal* of that action was to provide forgiveness of sins for the many. The meaning *because* is simply inapplicable or Jesus would have shed His blood *because men had been forgiven*.

Among believers there is no real dispute with respect to Matthew 26: 28. There is unity in the belief that the phrase *'for the remission of sins,'* as it is written here, speaks to the *intended result* of the shedding of Jesus' blood. In like manner, John the Baptist offered *'a baptism of repentance for remission of sins'* (Mark 1: 4; Luke 3: 3). The only reasonable conclusion is that this combination of repentance and baptism was also meant to bring about remission of sins. The same phrase employed by Jesus, $\varepsilon\iota\varsigma$ $\alpha\varphi\varepsilon\sigma\iota\nu$ $\alpha\mu\alpha\rho\tau\iota\omega\nu$, which defined the shedding of His blood for the forgiveness of sins, is found in conjunction with baptism and repentance associated with John the Baptist. In each instance, action was taking place where forgiveness of sins was the intended outcome.

In Acts 2: 38, the only reasonable rendering of the word $\varepsilon\iota\varsigma$ is *for the purpose of (*or *with a view to)*. As with the texts from Matthew 26: 28, Mark 1: 4, and Luke 3: 3, the context demands this meaning. The statement made by Peter on the Day of Pentecost, while injecting terms that individualize baptism and forgiveness, is the precise phraseology found in each of the other passages. If Jesus' death was intended to affect forgiveness (Matthew 26: 28) so, too, are the repentance and baptism discussed in Mark 1: 4 and Acts 2: 38.

Had Peter *intended* to teach that the men and women on the Day of Pentecost should be baptized *because they had received* forgiveness of sins, he had a much better option than the word $\varepsilon\iota\varsigma$. He had available to him the word in $\pi\varepsilon\rho\iota$ (Mark 1: 44). This would have portrayed one's participation in baptism as a *response to* forgiveness received rather than the means to receive that forgiveness. There can be no question that this rite of baptism was presented to those in the early church as the path necessary to receive forgiveness of sins.

What is so fascinating about the contention for the causal meaning of $\varepsilon\iota\varsigma$ in Acts 2: 38 is the fact that translator error is not alleged in any other passage of Scripture that employs this word. This suggests that out of nearly 1,800 instances where $\varepsilon\iota\varsigma$ appears in the New Testament, the translators got it right – save one. In fact, challengers to the translation in Peter's sermon often tout the accuracy of those instances where an alternative meaning is understood (e.g., Matthew 12: 41) in an effort to persuade us that, in this passage, it is wrongfully presented. Yet, if εις is misinterpreted in Acts 2: 38, what can be said about the trustworthiness of the nearly 1,800 other occasions when it is used (e.g. Matthew 12: 41)? Even more disquieting is the fact that the challenge to the translation of *for* (purpose) in this case is one built, not on a foundation of linguistics or Greek scholarship, but on theological exception to God's Word. Therefore, if we can trust that εις is translated correctly in all other passages, regardless of what that translation might be, it is reasonable that we should equally trust the translation, *for the remission of sins*.

Peter fully disavows forgiveness of sins (and salvation) prior to repentance and baptism on the Day of Pentecost. He concludes his sermon in verse forty with a call to salvation, appealing to the crowd to *'Be saved...'* or, as it is stated in the NIV, *'Save yourselves from this corrupt generation.'* Of course, Peter was not proposing that they had the capacity to actually save themselves. Yet as long as they stood guilty of Jesus' death, the very crime (sin) of which Peter had just accused them, they would remain lost. They could, however, make the decision to be obedient to those commands Peter had given, leading to their salvation. In that sense the decision concerning whether or not they would be saved rested upon the shoulders of each man and woman.

Many will charge that the word *saved*, in this instance (v. 40), may hold one of a variety of meanings – perhaps *healing* or *deliverance* - but the truth is that this is a call to salvation. Peter did not complete the day with a scant one-sentence plea for salvation. His entire discourse focused upon the decision his listeners faced. We are told that, *'With many other words he testified and exhorted them, saying, "Be saved..."'* encouraging them to choose in favor of salvation. After all, this is the Day of Pentecost. This is the day salvation has come to earth. To suggest that *saved* renders any meaning other than spiritual salvation, when this has been the sum and substance of his entire message, does great injustice to the text. Peter's plea, spoken on the heels of his command to repent and be baptized, is for his listeners to decide in favor of salvation.

Through the centuries it is very telling that interpreters have been ever consistent in their translation of the word εις in this passage. The relationship established here is one of cause and effect. Repentance and baptism *resulted in* forgiveness of sins. We have further support for this treatment of εις from scholars around the world. Over the pages of time the Bible has been translated into numerous languages. In every language and translation the interpreters have been remarkably consistent with respect to the meaning of this word. A review of the word εις as it has been translated into various languages in the context of Acts 2: 38, reveals uniform handling of this word by translators in various parts of the world.

Language	**Trans.**	**Definition**
French	pour	/pur/ prep **(a)** (in order) to; ~ **faire** to do; in order to do; **pour ne pas faire** so as not to do; **c'etait ~ rire** or **plaisanter** it was a joke; ~ **que** so that; ~ **ainsi dire** so to speak[7]
Latin	in	prep. (1) with acc., *into on to, towards, against*; of time, *until*; in omne tempus, *for ever*; in diem vivere, *to live for the moment*: **of tendency or purpose, for**; in adverbial phrases, indicating manner or extent: in universum, *in general*; in vicem, in vices, *in turn*.[8]
Polish	na	prep. –2. [czas, termin] for[9]
Portugese	para	[para] prep –2. [indica motivo, objectivo] (in order) to; **cheguei mais cedo ~ aranjar lugar** I arrived early (in order) to get a seat.[10]
Russian	для	*prep+gen* for; for the sake of; …in order to[11]
Spanish	para	prep. 1 : for 2 HACIA : towards 3 : (in order) to[12]

Scripture itself, however, effectively refutes the proposition that εις might be translated *because your sins have been forgiven*. In fact, we need not travel far from Acts 2: 38 to determine the truth concerning the meaning of εις in this context. One day, as Peter and John approached the temple, a man who had been lame his entire life asked them for money. Rather than giving him money, Peter reached out and lifted the man to his feet, healing him on the spot. As people gathered in response to this miracle, Peter began to preach. The following excerpt is taken from Peter's sermon on that day:

> Repent therefore and be converted, that (*εις*) your sins may be blotted out... (Acts 3: 19)

Once again, *εις* is employed concerning forgiveness of sins, although some Greek texts use *προς* (*hopos*) in its place. Yet, in this setting, the rationalization that repentance and conversion come *because of prior forgiveness* is not offered, not because the context has changed, but because this passage does not overtly infringe upon a specific creed concerning baptism. Repentance and conversion affect forgiveness of sins in this setting. The text as well as the context leave no other options and provide us with undeniable confirmation that forgiveness comes *as a result of* obedience to the commands given. Peter's words allow no alternative translation. If, in Acts 3: 19, forgiveness is defined as the outcome of obedience, it must be that this is also true in Peter's first sermon (Acts 2: 38). Peter was telling the crowd to repent and be baptized with their eyes fixed on the goal of forgiveness.

It may actually be a bit misleading to suggest that we repent *in order to receive forgiveness* – a point we should address before continuing. It is true, of course, that forgiveness does not come without repentance (Acts 3: 19) and, therefore, forgiveness always follows repentance; but our response of repentance is kindred to the pain of separation we experience with the death of a loved one. Repentance before God arises out of our sorrow when we realize that we have separated ourselves from God via our own sins. It is not a matter of presuming God's forgiveness *because* we have repented, but repenting *because* we realize we have wronged Him.

This is the repentance we saw in King David. He repented, not because he expected God to restore him, but because he realized that by his own actions he had grieved God. For this alone he was in agony. In this sense, if our motive behind repentance is to simply *seek* forgiveness, we have an unfortunate misunderstanding of the repentance of Scripture. True repentance comes only when we humble ourselves before God *because* we are distressed over the realization that our sins have grieved Him. The heartache we experience from our recognition that we have caused God pain must be the source of our repentance. If this is not the driving force then we dare not call it repentance. While God's Word does tell us that remission of sins results from repentance, if we do not *honestly* repent we should not anticipate forgiveness.

Our acceptance of responsibility when we have wronged someone, coupled with our remorse for what we have done, is not the same as asking forgiveness. It is true that the two walk hand in hand, but unless we truly repent, asking for forgiveness would be pointless. First then, we repent and turn from what we have done. Once we have repented we are in a position to ask for forgiveness – not before. What person, having refused to repent, would expect forgiveness?

As we consider the respective roles of repentance and baptism in Acts 2: 38, we should also note that we are not commanded in Scripture to repent *in Jesus' name* (or in the name of the Father, Son, and Holy Spirit as in Matthew 28: 19). A number of times, however, we are commanded to *be baptized* in the name of Jesus (Acts 8: 16; 10: 48; 19: 5; 1 Corinthians 1: 13; Galatians 3: 27). That fact helps us to understand that it is baptism *in Jesus' name* that is performed expressly to effectuate forgiveness. Repentance simply sets the stage for forgiveness. Like belief, repentance is an antecedent to baptism. First Peter told the crowd to *repent* of their sins. He then commanded that each one should *'be baptized in the name of Jesus Christ for (with a view to) the remission of sins.'* Baptism is specifically prescribed by God, upon a foundation of repentance (Acts 3: 19) and belief (Mark 16: 16; Acts 8: 37), as man's petition for forgiveness (1 Peter 3: 21). Upon repenting of their sins against God and receiving baptism as a matter of seeking cleansing from those sins, Peter explained the additional benefit of the gift of the Holy Spirit.

Until recently no Bible translation has ever seen fit to render Acts 2: 38 any differently than it has been translated for centuries, precisely because the text allows no other interpretation. Recently, however, the original translation of the International Standard Version (v1.1.0) stated that Peter told the crowd on the Day of Pentecost to *'repent and be baptized...since your sins are forgiven.'* It is illuminating that, in a subsequent translation of the ISV (v. 1.3.0), the passage was modified to read *'...for the forgiveness of sins.'* When asked concerning the rephrasing of this verse, Dr. William Welty responded:

> The change in the ISV text was made to correct an inadvertent divergence in that passage from our Principles of Translation... Our reading of Acts 2:38 in v1.1.0 is accurate in that baptism follows acknowledgment of forgiveness: hence our rendering originally read: "Be baptized, since your sins..." However, strictly speaking, the Gk.

text does read "for the forgiveness". We elected to go back to a more literal reading of the Gk. text.[13]

For those to whom scriptural integrity is of any consequence, the ripples from the impact of this particular pebble should send a veritable tidal wave across theological waters. Having initially dismissed the countless historical renderings of this verse, evidently the translators reconsidered their work, ultimately determining that their construction of the text failed the test of unblemished interpretation. It is only fair to elaborate that Dr. Welty does consider the meaning of the passage somewhat blurred since, when translated properly, it does not mix well with his theology. In fact, he is to be commended for his forthrightness in abiding by honorable principles despite this obvious internal tug-of-war. The fact that the translation is founded upon interpretive standards rather than personal philosophy objectifies the phrase *for the forgiveness,* which, in turn, only helps to reinforce the veracity of the resulting terminology. Therefore, for the thousands of scholars who for decades – even centuries – have hoped upon hope that εις might be interpreted *because*, it seems that door of opportunity should be considered permanently closed.

Those assembled in Jerusalem on that day clearly believed the gospel message the apostles preached; yet this belief was inadequate, on its own, to accomplish the goal of receiving God's grace. The question asked of the apostles, *'Men and brethren, what shall we do?'* demonstrates that the crowd was seeking direction in order to change their current state of sinfulness. Peter explained the means by which they could escape that condition. His response is clear and sure. As a complement to Peter's words, this promise of forgiveness of sins at the time of baptism is supported fully by the apostle Paul in his Colossians letter (Colossians 2: 11-14). That God made the penitent man alive, having forgiven his sins, is the undeniable theme. Exactly who has been forgiven? It is the man who has died to sin and been *buried in baptism.* It is the dead man, not the living (renewed), who is buried. It is the dead man, not the living, who is made alive. This is done *through our faith in the work of God.*

B. W. Johnson authored <u>The People's New Testament</u>, a commentary dating back to 1891. In it he provides one of the most thorough and reasonable explanations ever afforded this passage (Acts 2: 38), giving the author, Luke, and the Spirit of God due respect by expressing the meaning of the words of the passage as they were intended to be understood.

> 38. Repent, and be baptized. For the first time the terms of pardon under the New Covenant and the Great Commission are given; given once for all time, and always the same. The convicted, broken-hearted, sorrowing sinner, believing that Jesus is the Christ, is to repent and be baptized. Repent. Not sorrow. They already sorrowed; but a change of purpose; the internal change which resolves to serve the Lord. The Greek term rendered repent, means a change of mind. The act of obedience in baptism is an outward expression of both faith and repentance. In the name of Jesus Christ. "Upon the name" (Revised Version). Upon the ground of the name. In submission to the authority of Jesus Christ. For the remission of sins. Thus, by complying with the conditions just named, they shall receive remission of sins. No man can receive pardon without faith and repentance, nor can he without submission to the will of Christ. "Eis (for) denotes the object of baptism, which is the remission of the guilt contracted in the state before metanoia (repentance)."--Meyer. "In order to the forgiveness of sins we connect naturally with both the preceding verbs. This clause states the motive or object which should induce them to repent and be baptized."--Prof. Hackett. The gift of the Holy Spirit. Promised as a comforter to all who obey Christ, but whom "the world cannot receive."[14]

Christian Baptism for the Purpose of Regeneration

Baptism is a *time* of regeneration.[15] A sinful person enters the water and a new creature rises from the water. This new creature is now heir to the kingdom of God.

> Therefore we were buried with Him through baptism into death, that just as Christ was raised from the dead by the glory of the Father, even so we also should walk in newness of life. (Romans 6: 4)

> 4. But when the kindness and the love of God our Savior toward man appeared, 5. not by works of righteousness which we have done, but according to His mercy He save us, through the washing of regeneration and renewing of the Holy Spirit, 6. whom He poured out on us abundantly through Christ Jesus our Savior, 7. that having been justified by His grace we should become heirs according to the hope of eternal life. (Titus 3: 4-7)

Of course, the notion that baptism is a time of regeneration calls for an understanding of the concept of regeneration and all that it involves. We should make an effort to realize the nature of the believer who rises from the waters of immersion. Scripture points to three distinct principles of regeneration, none of which is necessarily more significant than the others.

The first principle of regeneration that must be grasped is justification (1 Corinthians 6: 11). Justification is viewed by men as forgiveness of sins but, to an extent, it is more than that. It is the means by which we are separated from our old self and made a new creature (Romans 6: 3-6). Justification, which embodies the application of Christ's blood to our sins, eclipses the mere pronouncement that a man is *no longer* guilty of sins committed and suggests that, by faith and the grace that is offered through the blood of Christ, God confers a sinless condition upon the obedient believer. He replaces our old carnal being with a new life (Galatians 6: 15). God is able, in His omnipotence, to offer the new Christian a life absolutely free of sin. While we certainly recall our previous sins, God does not. To Him it is as if those sins never occurred.

Justification is the essence of salvation to which Paul referred when he suggested what it is that man is unable to accomplish through works (of the law). Man cannot, through any deed, blot out sins committed. No feat performed by man reaches the level of righteousness necessary to achieve justification. Only God has that capability. This is not to say that our active participation in responding to the gospel message plays no part in justification. According to Scripture it is at the time of baptism that God has chosen to grant justification (Romans 5: 1 - 6: 7).

Sanctification (1 Corinthians 6: 11), the setting apart of an individual, is another vital aspect of regeneration that occurs at the time of baptism. Sanctification alone is not necessarily salvation-related. We discover that there are times in Scripture when reference is made to sanctification without the automatic bestowal of salvation (1 Corinthians 7: 14). Yet, in relation to baptism, sanctification is directly linked to redemption. Within the design of salvation we are sanctified, just as we are justified, as we are washed in baptism (1 Corinthians 6: 11; Ephesians 5: 26).

Finally, regeneration is the time when a person is adopted as a child of God (Romans 8: 15; Galatians 4: 5). In truth, no one may be saved without experiencing the adoption process. It is through adoption that we are able to become heirs of God – heirs to the kingdom of God. Like justification and sanctification, adoption is available to us by our faith, through the blood of Christ, at the time of baptism (1 Peter 1: 17-25).

Regeneration, and all that it involves, is essential to salvation. No one may be saved without experiencing the new birth of which Jesus spoke in His conversation with Nicodemus (John 3: 1-6). No one may be saved without first becoming a true child of God (Romans 8: 14-17). While there is considerable disagreement regarding the moment at which regeneration occurs, Scripture is teeming with testimony that God has set aside baptism for that very purpose.

Christian Baptism for the Purpose of Salvation

Salvation (eternal life) is a corollary of baptism so closely associated with forgiveness and regeneration that any attempt at severance presents an unimaginable challenge. Without forgiveness and regeneration one cannot be saved and, for the forgiven/regenerated man or woman, the promise of salvation is instantaneously fulfilled. The new and eternal life of the Christian convert, which is conferred at the time of baptism (Romans 6: 4-5), is the ultimate destination of faith (1 Peter 1: 9) and, by reason thereof, a legitimate motive for baptism. Jesus proclaimed all who satisfied the twofold command of belief and baptism who would be saved (Mark 16: 16), Peter echoed this sentiment, stating unequivocally that salvation is found in baptism (1 Peter 3: 21). If salvation is the consummate *goal* of our faith, salvation may justifiably be viewed as the *primary* effect of baptism.

The gospel leads to salvation. Baptism is *for* the forgiveness of sins and regeneration. These, in turn, are *for* the purpose of salvation. Belief (John 3: 16), repentance (2 Corinthians 7: 10), and confession (Romans 10: 9) are all identified by Scripture as leading to the objective of salvation/eternal life. Even Jesus' life, death, burial, and resurrection were designed so that man might realize salvation by God's grace through faith (Ephesians 2: 8). Essentially everything God has wrought on earth from the time of man's fall has been focused on nothing else. The scriptural teaching that baptism is for the purpose of salvation is a principle that must never be frustrated.

The Gift of the Holy Spirit Bestowed in Christian Baptism

A very fine line can be drawn between the stated purpose of baptism and the benefits conferred upon the believer who submits to this rite in Jesus' name. Forgiveness (Acts 2: 38), regeneration (Titus 3: 5), and salvation (1 Peter 3: 21) are stated objectives of baptism. Intimacy with God through the Holy Spirit, however, is portrayed in Scripture as more of a distinguished honor, perhaps better perceived as a divine blessing, for one who is obedient in submitting to water baptism. Peter did not charge the people on the Day of Pentecost with the command to be baptized *for the gift of the Spirit*. The promise of the Spirit was added as a point of additional privilege for those who believed (Acts 2: 38).

Often called the *indwelling* of the Holy Spirit, the gift of the Holy Spirit seems to be portrayed in Scripture as a one-on-one relationship with God the Father through the work of the Holy Spirit. The fact that the gift of the Spirit (Acts 2: 38) is the *presence* of the Spirit rather than a gift *from* the Spirit is easily derived from a variety of New Testament passages that speak of His role in our lives (2 Corinthians 1: 22; 1 Thessalonians 4: 8). While the word *indwelling* does not appear in God's Word, based on 2 Timothy 1: 14 it is widely accepted as depicting the presence of the Holy Spirit who rests upon us (1 Peter 4: 14) and lives in us (Romans 8: 9). He resides in our inner being (Ephesians 3: 16). It is by His presence that we are able to exhibit the fruit of the Spirit (Galatians 5: 22). The Holy Spirit abides with us to help us in our daily walk. He provides *unity* (Ephesians 4: 4), *hope* (Romans 15: 13), *sanctification* (Romans 15: 16), *discernment* (1 Corinthians 2: 14), *joy* (1 Thessalonians 1: 6), *spiritual sustenance* (2 Corinthians 3: 6) and a host of other spiritual advantages. Occasionally, within the context of His indwelling presence, the Spirit is even able to intercede for us when necessary (Romans 8: 26-27). In essence, the Spirit walks with us as we serve the Lord daily in order to enhance our relationship with God and with each other.

Christian Baptism and Membership in the Body

Beyond the role of baptism to provide forgiveness, regeneration, salvation, and the gift of the Spirit, an additional benefit is revealed on the Day of Pentecost following Peter's words to the assembly. Having explained what the Jews in Jerusalem must do to receive redemption, many responded with obedience.

> Then those who gladly received his word were baptized; and that day about three thousand souls were added *to them*. (Acts 2: 41)

The connection between baptism and souls being '*added to them*' is unmistakable; but to what, or to whom, were they added?

When we consider this verse in conjunction with other Scripture (Acts 2: 47; 1 Corinthians 12: 13; Colossians 1: 18), we can easily determine that those who believed his word and were baptized on that day were added to the church, also called the body of Christ.

Baptism is portrayed as a mechanism through which people were added to the body of Christ for fellowship and support, identifying this as an additional benefit of baptism. It is one of the steps involved in the process through which one is added to the church, thus *putting on* Christ (Galatians 3: 27), offering endorsement for what Luke penned in Acts 2: 41 regarding those who were added to Christ's body.

The Unifying Mettle of Christian Baptism

Paul, in addressing the church at Ephesus, offered a lesson concerning unity within the body of Christ (Ephesians 4: 4-6). He compelled them to keep hold of the unity that had been taught by the apostles. Within this lesson, baptism is identified as a source of unity along with various other unique elements of the faith. This is a lesson taught forthrightly within Scripture. Not only was baptism considered a matter of unification within the body, but also a matter of oneness with Christ. Paul offered edification to the Romans concerning their oneness with Christ at the time of baptism.

> 4. Therefore we were buried with Him through baptism into death, that just as Christ was raised from the dead by the glory of the Father, even so we also should walk in newness of life. 5. For if we have been united together in the likeness of His death, certainly we also shall be *in the likeness* of *His* resurrection. (Romans 6: 4-5)

The unifying nature of baptism reaches beyond harmony within the body. These words to the Romans reveal that unity with Christ is central in the matter of baptism. It is the time men are united with Christ, not just in this earthly life, but for eternity. From Paul's words we can rightly deduce that it is those who have *experienced unity with Him in His death through baptism* who will for eternity experience *unity with Him in His resurrection*, a ratification of Jesus' own claim discussed earlier (Mark 16: 16).

Whether in the gospels, the book of Acts, or the many epistles where it is addressed, the significance of baptism in the New Testament is undeniable (though many deny it). In baptism men acknowledge and, in a symbolic manner, participate in the sacrifice of Jesus as a matter of experiencing death from sin, burial in water, and resurrection to a new life (Romans 6: 3-5). We must not trivialize the value Scripture places upon this rite as a pivotal moment in a man's conversion. Baptism, an act commanded by Jesus, is intended to draw men closer to God and to each other. It is in baptism that we may be cleansed from sin and become a part of the body of Christ. In baptism, we are regenerated by the Spirit and able to begin a new life. It is also at this time that the Holy Spirit takes an active role in the life of a convert. No doubt, submission to baptism is vital for those who wish to be united with Christ.

Effects of Baptism with Errant Motivation

Of course, consideration of the purpose of baptism inevitably gives rise to one especially engaging question. If someone is baptized without having in mind the obvious biblical teaching of forgiveness-regeneration-salvation, is baptism for that person profitable? In other words, will that person receive the benefits promised to the baptized believer even though he/she does not accept that these things occur at that time? After all, Jesus did say that baptized believers would be saved (Mark 16: 16) without seemingly slipping the yoke of a particular doctrine around the neck of this remark. So then, does baptism received in the name of Jesus qualify one for the spiritual benefits ascribed to the rite regardless of the intricacies of one's belief concerning its value or purpose?

It is important to realize that the act of immersion in water in itself has no power or spiritual value. Changes in our relationship with God that do occur at the time of baptism take place based fully upon two factors. First, it is up to the individual to have faith in the promises of God at the time of baptism. Second, substantively speaking, God works directly in response to the faith of the one who submits to baptism. Paul states that we are resurrected with Him through faith (Colossians 2: 12). Therefore, the assurance of salvation is *dependent* upon the person's faith concerning God's fulfillment of His promise.

In Paul's letters to Timothy there exists a theme specifically concerning doctrine that is undeniable. Sound scriptural doctrine is *vital* in shaping one's faith (1 Timothy 1: 3; 6: 1-5), a fact that cannot be overstated. Salvation itself, according to Paul, is dependent upon the teaching of, and adherence to, biblical doctrine (1 Timothy 4: 16). Errant sincerity is given no standing in

Scripture with respect to salvation. Paul warned the Corinthians that their belief in Jesus could be *in vain* unless they *hold fast* to the gospel message he had preached (1 Corinthians 15: 2). We learn from Scripture that false doctrine misleads (2 Peter 3: 16) and that any gospel other than that taught by the apostles is no gospel at all since it derives from men rather than God (Galatians 1: 6-9).

Apostolic instruction concerning baptism concerns not only the necessity of the act itself, but also the reasoning and motivation so intimately linked to baptism. In fact, the apostles taught the essentiality of baptism by virtue of its consequences (Acts 2: 38; Romans 6: 1-4; Titus 3: 5). Given this fact, we can conclude that baptism cannot be severed from God's intended purpose (Acts 2: 38; Romans 6: 1-4; Galatians 3: 26-27; 1 Peter 3: 21-22).

From Paul's words to the Romans we learn that our walk as a new creature not only follows, but is contingent upon, our unity with Christ in the baptismal waters (Romans 6: 5-8). This is a truth of which Paul acknowledges these disciples were fully aware (Romans 6: 6). Emphasis is placed upon the piety of the individual and his/her consideration of the spiritual activity that is embedded within the act of baptism.

> 5. For if we have been united together in the likeness of His death, certainly we also shall be *in the likeness* of *His* resurrection, 6. knowing this, that our old man was crucified with Him, that the body of sin might be done away with... (Romans 6: 6)

> 8. Now if we died with Christ, we believe that we shall also live with Him, 9. knowing that Christ, having been raised from the dead, dies no more... (Romans 6: 8-9)

The subject matter here is, of course, baptism in water (Romans 6: 1-4). Each of these remarks by Paul, tied so closely together in this letter, contains an '*if*' statement. Additionally, the outcome in each case appears to be contingent upon the proposition found within the '*if*' statement. Those who *will share in the likeness of His resurrection* are those who *have participated with Him in the likeness of His death* (v. 5), which is baptism (v. 4). Yet, Paul does not end it there. He highlights the fact that there is an awareness of these things among the Romans, stating that there is a *knowing* ($\gamma\iota\nu\omega\sigma\kappa o\nu\tau\varepsilon\varsigma$), or recognition, of these truths.

In the same vein, those who will live with Him are those who have died with Him (v. 8) in baptism (v. 4). Paul explains that,

'...if we died with Christ, we believe...knowing that Christ...dies no more' (vs. 8-9). Here the word *knowing* (ειδοτες) is a perfect active participle, plural in number, and is linked directly to the verb *'believe.'* This suggests that our *belief* that death with Christ (v. 4) will ultimately allow us to live (eternally) with Him hangs, at least partially, upon our perceiving or understanding His victory over death in relation to baptism.

Some latitude must be granted when it comes to our comprehension at the time of baptism. For instance, in verse eight above it is likely that Paul is simply offering these converts greater insight into the meaning of baptism rather than reflecting on things they understood fully when they accepted Christ. Suggesting that a person must have full understanding of all the intricacies of baptism at the time he/she submits to this rite most likely overstates the case. Many scholars who have studied the Bible for years often find themselves discovering some truth in Scripture that previously had escaped them. It is possible that the Philippian jailer did not fully comprehend *all* the benefits the night he was baptized even though Paul surely taught him well (Acts 16: 32-33). In fact, Paul spent much time and effort in his epistles educating the various churches concerning the deeper meaning of baptism (Romans 6: 1-4; Colossians 2: 11-12). Yet Scripture does seem to place an emphasis on a basic understanding that baptism is the time God has chosen to redeem the repentant sinner and grant the gift of the Spirit (Acts 2: 38; 19: 2). Other benefits, such as membership in the body, often appear to be explained after submission to baptism (Acts 2: 41).

God has, through the words of the apostles, fully demonstrated the purpose for which baptism was designed (forgiveness, regeneration, etc.). If we are, in the spirit of discipleship, to observe all that Jesus has commanded (Matthew 28: 20), and it was He who commanded baptism, as a matter of honoring God we must regard it appropriately. What, then, is to become of the person who approaches God believing that forgiveness and other benefits assigned to baptism will not occur as God has promised, assuming that salvation has somehow already been attained despite biblical instruction? If the actuality of God's work is reliant upon our faith in God's promise that this will occur, and we have not that faith, in His omniscience God will know it. Consequently, if we disrespect God's purpose for baptism we have no assurance, and are in no position to presume, that He will sanction self-derived doctrine by granting baptismal benefits to those who are fixed on denying them.

The Purpose of Baptism for the Gentiles

Our review of the purpose of baptism provides an excellent opportunity to address an enduring challenge to the meaning of baptism – a challenge that specifically zeroes in on the baptism of Gentiles. Some men have proposed that, while water baptism may have been essential for the Jews in the first century, this is not necessarily true for those who are not descendants of Abraham. After all, those passages that *directly* link forgiveness to baptism seem to be aimed specifically at the Jews (Acts 2: 38; 22: 16). At least they appear to be uttered in defined Jewish settings. Gentiles, it is asserted, never received the command to be baptized *for the remission of sins*.

This view, of course, completely disregards Paul's teaching on the subject including his re-baptism of the men at Ephesus (Acts 19: 1-7). He emphasized to the Romans *newness of life* and *freedom from sin* in baptism (Romans 6: 1-7) and explained to the Galatians that this was the moment when they *'put on Christ'* (Galatians 3: 27). Additionally, Peter, when writing to the Christians scattered throughout Asia, proclaimed that *baptism saves* (1 Peter 3: 21).

In His final instructions to the apostles, Jesus suggested no limit to the significance or efficacy of baptism among Gentiles. He commanded them to *'...make disciples of all nations, baptizing them...'* (Matthew 28: 19). His statement concerning the salvation of men through the combination of belief and baptism is offered without qualification in conjunction with the command to, *'Go into all the world'* (Mark 16: 15-16). Later, through the book of Acts and the epistles (many of which were written to Gentiles) we gain much of our insight into the meaning of baptism. Scripture simply does not distinguish between the baptism of Jews and the baptism of Gentiles. Jesus' inclusion of baptism in His all-encompassing final command speaks volumes concerning its effect for *all* men.

NOTES FOR CHAPTER 7

1. John Wesley, credited as the founding father of Methodism, was previously a priest in the Anglican Church. Adapting the Thirty-nine Articles of Religion from the Anglican Church, Wesley developed his own Twenty-five Articles of Religion. Viewing the

sacraments as signs of faith he penned the following regarding first, the sacraments in general, and then baptism specifically.

Article 16—Of the Sacraments
Sacraments ordained of Christ are not only badges or tokens of Christian men's profession, but rather they are certain signs of grace, and God's good will toward us, by which he doth work invisibly in us, and doth not only quicken, but also strengthen and confirm, our faith in him.

There are two Sacraments ordained of Christ our Lord in the Gospel; that is to say, Baptism and the Supper of the Lord.

Those five commonly called sacraments, that is to say, confirmation, penance, orders, matrimony, and extreme unction, are not to be counted for Sacraments of the Gospel; being such as have partly grown out of the corrupt following of the apostles, and partly are states of life allowed in the Scriptures, but yet have not the like nature of Baptism and the Lord's Supper, because they have not any visible sign or ceremony ordained of God.

The Sacraments were not ordained of Christ to be gazed upon, or to be carried about; but that we should duly use them. And in such only as worthily receive the same, they have a wholesome effect or operation; but they that receive them unworthily, purchase to themselves condemnation, as St. Paul saith. Wesley, Twenty-five Articles of Religion, Article 16 – Of the Sacraments.

Article 17—Of Baptism
Baptism is not only a sign of profession and mark of difference whereby Christians are distinguished from others that are not baptized; but it is also a sign of regeneration or the new birth. The Baptism of young children is to be retained in the Church. Wesley, Twenty-five Articles of Religion, Article 17 – Of Baptism.

2. Strong's Concordance
http://cf.blueletterbible.org/lang/lexicon/lexicon.cfm?Strongs=G911&Version=KJV, Accessed January 15, 2005.

3. Just a few of the scholars who speak with confidence concerning the link between forgiveness and both repentance and baptism in Acts 2: 38 include the following:

Bruce Metzger was the editor of the *Textual Commentary on The Greek New Testament*, published by the United Bible Societies.

Arthur L. Farstad was the chairman of the New King James Executive Review Committee and general editor of the *NKJV New Testament*.

John R. Werner is the International Consultant in Translation to the Wycliffe Bible Translators. He was also a consultant to Friberg and Friberg with the *Analytical Greek New Testament*.

Barclay Newman and **Eugene Nida** edited *The Translator's Handbook On The Acts Of The Apostles*.

Dr. H. B. Hackett and Dr. Alvah Hovey, both of these are Baptist theologians.

Dr. C. B. Williams, a long-time professor of Greek in Union University, Jackson, Tennessee.

4. James Strong, LL.D., S.T.D., The New Strong's Exhaustive Concordance of the Bible, Greek Dictionary of the New Testament, p. 26, Thomas Nelson Publishers, 1990.

5. Joseph Henry Thayer, D.D., Thayer's Greek-English Lexicon of the New Testament, p. 183, Baker Book House, 1977.

6. http://www.isv.org/musings/musings 15.htm [Online] May 5, 2007.

7. Marianne Chalmers and Martine Pierquin, Pocket Oxford Hachette French Dictionary Second Edition, p. 337, Oxford University Press, 2000.

8. D. P. Simpson, Cassell's Latin English Dictionary, p. 111, Hungry Minds, Inc., Macmillan Publishing, 1987.

9. Stownik Kieszonkowy, Larouse Polish English Pocket Dictionary, p. 116, Larousse/SEJER, 2004.

10. Luzia Araujo and Valerie Grundy, Larouse Portuguese English Pocket Dictionary, p. 233, Larousse/VUEF, 2003.

11. Della Thompson, The Oxford Russian Dictionary, p. 43, The Berkley Publishing Group, Oxford University Press, 1997.

12. Webster's Everyday Spanish - English Dictionary, p. 129, Federal Street Press, 2002

13. http://www.sermoncentral.com, "The Preposition "eis" in Acts 2:38" [Online] May 7, 2007.

14. B. W. Johnson, , The People's New Testament, Volume 1, The Acts of the Apostles, Christian Publishing Company, 1891.

15. That regeneration occurs at the time of baptism is addressed thoroughly by Alexander Campbell.

> I. The change which is consummated by immersion, is sometimes called in sacred style, "*being quickened,*" or "*made alive,*" "*passing from death to life,*" "*being born again,*" "*having risen with Christ,*" "*turning to the Lord,*" "*being enlightened,*" "*conversion,*" "*reconciliation,*" "*repentance unto life.*" These, like the words propitiation, atonement, reconciliation, expiation, redemption, expressive of the various aspects which the death of Christ sustains, are expressive of the different relations in which this great change, sometimes called a "new creation," may be contemplated. The entire change affected in man by the Christian system, consists in four things:--a change of views; a change of affections; a change of state; and a change of life. Alexander Campbell, The Christian System, page 62.
>
> We have the phrase "*washing of regeneration*" once, in contradistinction from the "renewal of the Holy Spirit," (Titus 2i. 5) but never, by itself, as indicative of this four-fold change. Alexander Campbell, The Christian System, page 63.

Chapter VIII
What is the Mode of Baptism?

The mode of baptism, where *mode* defines the physical manner in which the rite is administered, is certainly the source of a great deal of discord. A variety of forms of this ceremony have been passed down from one generation to the next. While immersion is preferred by many, some also recognize either sprinkling or pouring water on an individual as acceptable methods of baptism. However, the Bible has much to say with respect to the mode of baptism that was established by Jesus for those who would enter His kingdom.

The Baptism of John

New Testament water baptism was first introduced through the life of John the Baptist as it is portrayed in the four gospels. We find that a number of passages in Scripture demonstrate categorically that John baptized with water (Matthew 3: 6-13; Mark 1: 5-8; Luke 3: 16; John 1: 26; Acts 1: 5).

Designated as the forerunner of Christ, John's role was to prepare the people (more specifically, the Israelites), through teaching and baptism, for the appearance of Jesus onto the scene as He began His ministry on earth. The fact that John's baptism involved water is easily determined and is essentially an undisputed point among scholars and laymen alike. The more formidable task is seeking the biblical *method* of baptism. This involves a careful examination of the original Greek since the meaning of the word *baptism* in the English language has become somewhat diluted.

The Meaning of Bapto, Baptizo, and Baptisma

It is with the Greek word $\beta\alpha\pi\tau\omega$ (*bapto*), from which are derived the extensions $\beta\alpha\pi\tau\iota\zeta\omega$ (*baptizo*)[1], $\beta\alpha\pi\tau\iota\sigma\mu\alpha$ (*baptisma*), and others, that this investigation must begin. $\beta\alpha\pi\tau\omega$ indicates that some sort of dipping or submersion is taking place, but not *just* dipping. It is a dipping that results in permanent change.

> $\beta\alpha\pi\tau\omega$ 1) to dip, dip in, immerse. 2) to dip into dye, to dye, colour. The clearest example that shows the meaning of baptizo is a text from the Greek poet and physician Nicander, who lived about 200 B.C. It is

a recipe for making pickles and is helpful because it uses both words. Nicander says that in order to make a pickle, the vegetable should first be 'dipped' (bapto) into boiling water and then 'baptised' (baptidzo) in the vinegar solution. Both verbs concern the immersing of vegetables in a solution. But the first is temporary. The second, the act of baptising the vegetable, produces a permanent change.[2]

In one form or other this word appears four times in the New Testament, each occasion depicting the act of an individual dipping something in liquid and then removing from the liquid what was dipped.

Upon his death a rich man found himself in Hades where he was in torment in the fire. Lazarus, a beggar who was mistreated by the rich man while they were both alive, also died and was taken to Abraham's bosom, which is presumably Paradise. In his agony, the rich man called out to Abraham to have Lazarus *dip* (βαψη) his finger in water (Luke 16: 24). His desire was for Lazarus, with that drop of water on the tip of his finger, to cool the rich man's tongue.

In the account of the Last Supper (John 13: 26), a form of the word βαπτω appears twice, both referring to Jesus *dipping (βαψας)* the bread in the dish, which presumably contained some kind of dressing or wine. Removing the bread from the dish He passed it to Judas, His betrayer.

The apostle John witnessed a robe that was *dipped*, literally *having been dipped (βεβαμμενον)*, in blood and then removed so that it may be worn (Revelation 19: 13). The word *dip* in our English language implies the action of immersion in, and removal from, some kind of liquid or container. Something dipped presumes removal. While the use of the word *bapto* depicts the act of *dipping* or *immersion*, its transformation into *baptizo*, according to the definition provided, suggests that some kind of permanent change may be the result.

The words *baptize, baptism*, etc., were actually fabricated by those responsible for the translation of the Bible from Greek into the English language. Interpreters formed these words from their Greek counterparts for use in the English Bible. These words appear a number of times in the New Testament, generally with respect to the water ritual performed by John and his disciples, Jesus' followers (John 4: 1-2), and men in the church age beginning on the Day of Pentecost. Occasionally, however, those men upon whose shoulders this mission was laid did translate this word into English rather than falling back on their manufactured word, which was *'baptize.'* In those instances the verbiage resulting from the translation is most often found to be some form of the word *wash* (e.g., wash, washed, washing, etc.).

> 9. It *was* symbolic for the present time in which both gifts and sacrifices are offered which cannot make him who performed the service perfect in regard to the conscience – 10. *concerned* only with foods and drinks, various washings *(βαπτισμοις)*, and fleshly ordinances imposed until the time of reformation. (Hebrews 9: 9-10)

Assorted rituals of the first covenant were performed on a regular basis by the Israelites (Hebrews 9: 9-10). The function of these ordinances varied depending on the circumstances involved. Feasts were generally intended as a manner of celebration – a means of honoring God. The bathing commanded under the first covenant provided a means of religious purification either for the priests prior to entering the temple or for any person (Israelite) who, for some reason stipulated within the confines of the law, found himself/herself in an unclean state.

> 1. Then the Pharisees and some of the scribes came together to Him, having come from Jerusalem. 2. Now when they saw some of His disciples eat bread with defiled *(κοιναις)*, that is, with unwashed *(νιψωνται)* hands, they found fault. 3. For the Pharisees and all the Jews do not eat unless they wash *(νιψωνται) their* hands in a special way, holding the tradition of the elders. 4. *When they come* from the marketplace, they do not eat unless they wash *(βαπτισμος)*. And there are many other things which they have received and hold, like the washing *(βαπτισμος)* of cups, pitchers, copper vessels, and couches. 5. The Pharisees asked Him, "Why do Your disciples not walk according to the tradition of the elders, but eat bread with unwashed *(κοιναις)* hands?" (Mark 7: 1-5)

> 37. And as He spoke, a certain Pharisee asked Him to dine with him. So He went in and sat down to eat. 38. When the Pharisee saw *it*, he marveled that He had not first washed *(βαπτιζο)* before dinner. 39. Then the Lord said to him, "Now you Pharisees make the outside of the cup and dish clean, but your inward part is full of greed and wickedness. 40. Foolish ones! Did not He who made the outside make the inside also?" (Luke 11: 37-40)

These passages from Mark and Luke are quite popular among those who hope to challenge the significance of immersion since the text seems to address the washing of an individual's hands or inanimate objects such as pots and pans. In all honesty, however, these statements shine a distinctly favorable light on the doctrine of baptism by immersion.

The *'tradition of the elders,'* of which the Pharisees spoke, did not entreat Old Testament law as we might suspect. Often Jesus rebuked the religious leaders of His day for demanding rituals not ordained by God (Matthew 12: 1-13; 15: 1-20). Men had established this washing of the *fists* depicted here not in search of physical cleanliness at the table, but as a pseudo religious ceremony developed and taught by men. Appropriately $νιψωνται$, a form of $νιπτω$ (*nipto*), is spoken specifically acknowledging the washing of a portion of the body such as the hands or the face.

A distinction must be drawn between the custom of hand washing ($νιψωνται$) discussed in verses two and five, where the topic is the Pharisaic practice of ceremonially washing their hands prior to eating, and the washing[3] ($βαπτιζο$) depicted in verse four. Mark detours slightly, touching briefly on other ritual washings practiced by the Pharisees but not condoned by God. The ceremonial washing of hands was one of many counterfeit rituals, but it brought to mind a practice that was truly contemptible, one that concerned their interaction with Gentiles.

Contact with Gentiles by a Jew must, in the minds of the Pharisees, certainly defile the entire body. Returning from a public setting like the marketplace, where they would have encountered Gentiles, the Pharisees ritually *bathed* ($βαπτιςο$) prior to eating that they might once again be considered clean. The reference to washing in verse four is not to the hands or face or another *portion* of the body, nor is that inferred. Hand washing (or unclean hands) is not cited in reference to $βαπτιςο$ but is linked to $νιψωνται$ and $κοιναις$ (vs. 3 and 5). The transition from $νιψωνται$ to $βαπτιζο$ is intentional and significant since verse four suggests an immersion of the body quite similar to the way dishes are submerged ($βαπτισμος$) in water for washing. The passage implies that even the washing of dishes had taken on a ritual-like personality for the Jews.

The same rule must apply to Luke 11: 37-40. Having arrived directly from a place where *'the crowds were thickly gathered together'* (Luke 11: 29), the Pharisee did not question Jesus about neglecting to ceremonially wash His hands, nor is hand washing mentioned here. Instead the man inquired about His failure to *bathe* (βαπτιςο) His body since He had been among Gentiles. Given Jesus' response in verses thirty-nine and forty we cannot mistakenly identify this washing as a reference to the hands alone. Thus the Pharisees developed two types of washing that were required. The first involved washing (νιψωνται) the hands or fists (though some perhaps legitimately claim that it was a cleansing *of* or *up to* the wrists). The second (βαπτιςο) was required for those who, prior to sitting down for a meal, had been in the company of Gentiles (v. 4).

Lest the word *couch* in the passage in Mark cause confusion, an explanation must be given. Does this suggest that these individuals *dipped* a piece of furniture into water as a means of washing? This word indeed identifies the so-called dining couches that were prevalent in homes of that day. It is reported that the Pharisees had carried their ceremonies to such an extreme that they did actually dip some of their furniture as a matter of ritual cleansing.

While acknowledging that *bapto (βαπτω)* certainly means to *dip* or *immerse*, many deny that this meaning must apply to derivatives such as *baptizo* (βαπτιςo). Yet we uncover in Strong's own definition an acknowledgement that the individual or object being *baptized* is presumed to be *fully wet*.

> 907. βαπτιςo baptizo, bap-tid'-zo; from a der. of *911*; to make whelmed (i.e., *fully wet*); used only (in the N.T.) of ceremonial *ablution*, espec (techn.) of the ordinance of Chr. *baptism*:-baptist, baptize, wash.[4]

Occasionally in Scripture when the word *wash* appears in English it is translated from Greek wording that is not a form of βαπτω. One such account recalls the time when Jesus washed the feet of the disciples (John 13: 5-9).

The English word *wash,* appearing twice here, is translated from two Greek words, each a derivative of the root word νιπτω, which was encountered previously with respect to Mark 7: 3, meaning *to cleanse*. More precisely, they are used in connection with washing *especially the hands or the feet or the face.*[5] Given the context in this passage, their use seems most appropriate.

Support for this translation of the word is recorded in the book of John where this same word is once again translated as *wash*. Early in His ministry Jesus came upon a man who had been blind from birth (John 9: 1-7). Forming clay from a mixture of dirt and saliva and placing the clay upon the man's eyes, Jesus told him to go and wash his eyes in the Pool of Siloam. Having obeyed, he then returned to Jesus with his eyesight restored. The word $\nu\iota\pi\tau\omega$, employed here as Jesus told the man to *'Go, wash...,'* in its various forms, fairly depicts the kind of washing that was taking place. God's Word is thoroughly consistent in its application of language as His will is disclosed through the writing of men inspired by Him. No doubt God was meticulous as, through the hands and minds of men, He knitted together the books through which His plan would be revealed.

> 37. And behold, a woman in the city who was a sinner, when she knew that *Jesus* sat at the table in the Pharisee's house, brought an alabaster flask of fragrant oil, 38. and stood at His feet behind *Him* weeping; and she began to wash ($\beta\rho\varepsilon\chi\varepsilon\iota\nu$) His feet with her tears, and wiped *them* with the hair of her head; and she kissed His feet and anointed *them* with the fragrant oil. (Luke 7: 37-38)

> 1. So it was, as the multitude pressed about Him to hear the word of God, that He stood by the Lake of Gennesaret, 2. and saw two boats standing by the lake; but the fishermen had gone from them and were washing ($\varepsilon\pi\lambda\upsilon\nu o\nu$) their nets. (Luke 5: 1-2)

The word $\beta\rho\varepsilon\chi\varepsilon\iota\nu$ (*brechein*) is derived from $\beta\rho\varepsilon\chi\omega$ (*brecho*), which means: *to moisten (espec. by shower): - (send) rain*[6], while $\varepsilon\pi\lambda\upsilon\nu o\nu$ (*eplunon*), a form of $\alpha\pi o\pi\lambda\upsilon\nu\omega$ (*apopluno*), renders a meaning: *to rinse off*[7]. Given such honest characterizations of the actions involved, once again God's Word checkmates the challenge of literary dependability. So it is when $\beta\alpha\pi\tau\omega$, $\beta\alpha\pi\tau\iota\varsigma o$, or $\beta\alpha\pi\tau\iota\sigma\mu\alpha$, appear in Scripture, having undoubtedly been selected for their capacity to accurately portray the events of the scene to the reader.

Baptism – The Antitype

Innumerable attempts to disprove the biblical teaching that immersion in water is the baptism of the church age simply fall short. Scripture is not only pregnant with instruction concerning immersion (Romans 6: 1-4; Colossians 2: 12), but it is noticeably barren when seeking evidence that the first century church practiced baptism in any other form. This fact is corroborated most effectively in Peter's first epistle with rather conclusive evidence regarding the form of water baptism as it was practiced in New Testament times.

> 18. For Christ also suffered once for sins, the just for the unjust, that He might bring us to God, being put to death in the flesh but made alive by the Spirit, 19. by whom also He went and preached to the spirits in prison, 20. who formerly were disobedient, when once the Divine longsuffering waited in the days of Noah, while *the* ark was being prepared, in which a few, that is, eight souls, were saved through water. 21. There is also an antitype which now saves us--baptism (not the removal of the filth of the flesh, but the answer of a good conscience toward God), through the resurrection of Jesus Christ...
> (1 Peter 3: 18-21)

God chose water as the vehicle by which He would cleanse the world of the evil that had consumed mankind. Peter transcends simply implying that baptism was a counterpart to the waters of the flood. Translated as *antitype,* the word $\alpha\nu\tau\iota\tau\upsilon\pi o\nu$ (*antitupon*) reveals a great deal more concerning the relationship between baptism and the flood. The implication for us can be best determined by considering the two Greek words from which this word is formed. The prefix $\alpha\nu\tau\iota$ (*anti*), in colloquial English, is most often understood to mean *against* or *opposed to*. However, Funk & Wagnals renders a meaning of *opposite to or reverse*[8]. Strong's defines it as opposite...*Often used in composition to denote contrast...* [9]. The second half of the word *antitupon* finds its origin in the Greek word $\tau\upsilon\pi o\varsigma$ (*tupos*) which, while it has many synonyms, essentially refers to *form* or *manner*.[10] Thus is incorporated the English word *type* into the word *antitype.*

A better grasp of the word *antitype* is attained once an individual understands both the means of Noah's salvation and the relationship between the testaments. New Testament baptism is a counterpart to the waters of the flood in much the same fashion that a mirror reflects the image before it in an opposite manner. Drue Freeman describes this reciprocal effect in the following excerpt from his work:

> There is a distinct vocabulary found in the New Testament that references the Old Testament. The Greek word HUPODEIGMA means that which is shown privately as an example or pattern. TUPOS is an impression that is left from the blow of a hammer... An ANTITUPON is a counterpart like an echo.[11]

The hammer will leave an impression that is opposite in nature. The result of the hammer's strike is a depression while the hammerhead protrudes. Noah was saved through water in that this was the device used by God to separate him from the evil by which he was surrounded. So it is in baptism as God has again chosen water as the instrument in which He separates a man from the evil of sin. Yet, Noah was saved as God lifted him above the water – the antitype of immersion. Today we are saved, not through escaping the water, as was Noah, but by the *opposite* ($αντι$) *form* or *manner* ($τυπος$). We are immersed. Concerning this verse, one popular commentary testifies:

> Opposite of imagery which pictures those who floated safely above the waters within the ark is that of a complete immersion which "saves us."[12]

In actuality, given God's choice of water to cleanse the earth of evil, nothing short of total immersion would suffice. A slight sprinkle or even torrential rains would ultimately fail to provide the cleansing that God deemed necessary. It was critical that God flood the earth completely in order to accomplish the task at hand. Since Peter considered baptism a correspondent to the flood, where we find immersion was essential, perhaps we should consider closely the import we place upon the mode of baptism we employ.

The History of Baptism in the Church

The Roman Catholic Church deserves recognition for their passion for history, having spent extraordinary amounts of time and money to assure that accurate records of the history of the church are available to us. For this reason the Catholic Encyclopedia is an invaluable source of information for those in search of the history of religion. The following excerpt from the Catholic Encyclopedia regarding baptism provides insight into the history of the form of baptism from the earliest times.

> Scripture is so positive in its statements as to the use of true and natural water for baptism that it is difficult to see why it should ever be called in question...The remote matter of baptism, then is water, and this taken in its usual meaning...The proximate matter of baptism is the ablution (cleansing) performed with water. The very word "baptize", as we have seen, means a washing. Three forms of ablution have prevailed among Christians, and the Church holds them all to be valid because they

fulfill the requisite signification of the baptismal laving. These forms are immersion, infusion, and aspersion. The most ancient form usually employed was unquestionably immersion. This is not only evident from the writings of the Fathers and the early rituals of both the Latin and Oriental Churches, but it can also be gathered from the Epistles of St. Paul, who speaks of baptism as a bath (Ephes, v, 26; Rom., vi, 4; Tit., 2i, 5). In the Latin Church, immersion seems to have prevailed until the twelfth century. After that time it is found in some places even as late as the sixteenth century. Infusion and aspersion, however, were growing common in the thirteenth century and gradually prevailed in the Western Church.[13]

Immersion was recognized from the beginning of the church as the form of baptism by water. Through much of history we discover that *'immersion seems to have prevailed.'* It was long after the time of the apostles that church leaders made the decision to begin accepting other forms of baptism.[14]

Essentially all scholars concede that the water baptism of the New Testament was by immersion. The general consensus among theologians is that $\beta\alpha\pi\tau\iota\varsigma\omega$, $\beta\alpha\pi\tau\iota\sigma\mu\alpha$, and $\beta\alpha\pi\tau\iota\sigma\mu o\varsigma$ depict the act of immersion. Evidence is abundant that sprinkling and pouring of water were never used in Scripture with respect to the ceremony of baptism. Had these methods been employed, we would expect that words more accurately portraying sprinkling or pouring would have been utilized. $P\alpha\nu\tau\iota\varsigma\omega$ (*rhantizo*) and $\varepsilon\kappa\chi\varepsilon\omega$ (*ekcheo*) are Greek for sprinkling and pouring, respectively. Yet, in the pages of Scripture these words are never used in conjunction with this ceremony of baptism. Had they been accurately descriptive, no doubt they would have been utilized where appropriate, but they are not. For this reason immersion is universally viewed as the water baptism taught in the Bible. It seems a bit presumptuous then that we should take it upon ourselves to alter this ceremony that God has established.

The International Standard Bible Encyclopedia offers these thoughts about the Greek use of the words that form our English words of baptize and baptism – root word $\beta\alpha\pi\tau o$. This is a passage that adds considerable insight into the method of baptism.

> The Greek language has had a continuous history, and Greek [baptizo] is used today in Greece for baptism. As is well known, not only in Greece, but all over Russia, wherever the Greek church prevails, immersion is the unbroken and universal practice. The Greeks may surely be credited with knowledge of the meaning of their own language.[15]

As we read or hear the words *baptize* or *baptism* in English, each one develops a picture in his/her own mind as to what these words mean. To some it would mean immersion while others may envision sprinkling or pouring. Yet, when the people of the first century heard these words spoken, they would have heard and pictured the following.

> Go therefore and make disciples of all the nations, *immersing* them in the name of the Father and of the Son and of the Holy Spirit. (Matthew 28: 19)

> He who believes and is *immersed* will be saved. (Mark 16: 16)

> Repent, and let every one of you be *immersed* in the name of Jesus Christ for the remission of sins... (Acts 2: 38)

> Or do you not know that as many of us as were *immersed* into Christ were *immersed* into His death? (Romans 6: 3)

> For as many of you as were *immersed* into Christ have put on Christ (Galatians 3: 27)

> There is also an antitype which now saves us – *immersion*. (1 Peter 3: 21)

Paul's Portraiture of Baptism

While the Greek terminology used to define baptism attests to its form, even more compelling evidence is found in Paul's vivid portrayal of this ceremony (Romans 6: 3-4; Colossians 2: 11-12). Baptism is intended to be representative of the death, burial, and resurrection of Christ. One method alone offers this symbolism as Paul described it.

We discover that when God designed the form of baptism it was with this specific symbolism in mind. Sprinkling or pouring water on an individual fails to exhibit the characteristics that Paul has presented here. The symbolism in baptism (immersion) should be obvious in that one who is baptized is buried into death and raised to a new life. In Colossians 2: 12 the word συνθαπτω (*sunthapto*), translated as *buried with Him*, conveys a joint burial with Christ. Once again, the words from which this one is formed offer additional insight into Paul's teaching. The first of these is συν (*sun*), which means *with* or *together.*[16] The second portion, θαπτω (*thapto*), means *to bury* or *to celebrate funeral rites.*[17]

Paul's emphasis here indicates that the representation of Christ's death and resurrection in baptism may not be as trivial as many claim.

From Paul's words in the book of Colossians emerges a passionate plea for these Christians to remain faithful to God. Through his insight into human character he recognized that, if an individual could psychologically and emotionally return to that moment of decision and conversion, that person's commitment could be strengthened. His strong point regarding these attributes of burial and resurrection is undoubtedly an effort to awaken a precious memory in the minds of his readers. The discourse concerning these specific characteristics of baptism continues well into the third chapter. Had these individuals not actually participated in a symbolic burial and resurrection, Paul's words would certainly not provide the emotional spark that he sought in order to refresh their faith.

Interestingly, Paul's focus in these passages is not on the mode of baptism, but on the significance of baptism to the Christian life. Depicting the mode of baptism is not Paul's intent. The envisioning of immersion (burial) that Paul offers is present simply by default as he embraces the symbolism found in the act of baptism. Immersion was understood by his readers and simply reflected that symbolism. There was no need for Paul to dwell on the mode of immersion for two reasons. First of all, the wording in the Greek language depicts immersion. Secondly, those to whom he penned these words had experienced the very baptism (immersion) of which he wrote.

God's Word plainly binds the form of baptism to its very purpose. If regeneration occurred prior to baptism, a persuasive argument could be put forth that the form of baptism is of little consequence. Forgiveness and salvation prior to baptism would truly relegate it to the role of the mere illustration of salvation. However, given Paul's articulation of the symbolism and the labors of God that are involved, the mode and purpose of baptism may not be dissociated without destroying completely the role of baptism as it is presented in Scripture.

Challenges to immersion as the baptism of Scripture rely mostly upon the claim that baptism need not mean immersion, and/or that the examples or teaching about baptism found there are inconclusive in determining the method used. Could not Philip and the eunuch both have entered the water where Philip then poured water over him as a matter of baptism (Acts 8: 38)? Did John baptize where there was *much water* because he required it for immersion or because the many who came out to see him would simply need water for personal use (John 3: 23)? Is Paul's reference to burial in connection with baptism purely symbolic with no real reference to the mode of baptism (Romans 6: 4; Colossians 2: 12)? If we ignore the meaning of βαπτιςω in the Greek and the historical records depicting baptism as immersion in the first century, these questions might be considered reasonable. However, ignoring Greek terminology and historic records is a questionable approach to understanding Scripture.

The Bible offers an abundance of evidence not only that the form of baptism was by immersion, but that this form was meaningful for its characterization of the death, burial, and resurrection of Christ. If Paul considered significant the manner in which people were baptized, perhaps we would do well to consider its significance today. The meaning of the words employed in the original Greek, as well as the symbolism expressed in the baptism of which Paul wrote, point specifically to immersion as the form that was used in New Testament times. The burden of proof for the acceptance of another mode, then, must lie with those who profess it. Absent testimony in Scripture to repudiate immersion as the single mode of baptism, the offering of such evidence lies beyond the reach of men.

NOTES FOR CHAPTER 8

1. Alexander Campbell addressed well the meaning of the word baptizo as *immersion* or *dipping*. He makes the important point that the origin of a word, in this case bapto, must not be ignored when determining a word's intended meaning. Citing a multitude of independent historically authoritative works, he notes that *all* consider the word baptizo, unless a figurative use is explicit in the text or implicit in the context, should always be understood as immerse, dip, or plunge. Following are examples of those references as found in Alexander Campbell, Christian Baptism, with Its Antecedents and Consequents, (1851).

> We shall first hear the venerable Scapula, a foreign lexicographer, of 1579. On *bapto*, the root, what does this most learned lexicographer depose? Hear him: "*Bapto*--mergo; immergo, item tingo (quod sit immergendo)." To translate his Latin--To dip, to immerse; also, to dye, *because that may be done by immersing*. Of the passive *baptomai* he says, "Mergor, item lavor--to be immersed, to be washed." Of *Baptizo*--"Mergo seu immergo, item submergo, item abluo, lavo--To dip, to immerse; also, to submerge or overwhelm, to wash, to cleanse."

> Next comes the more ancient Henricus Stephanus, of 1572. *Bapto* and *baptizo*--"Mergo seu immergo ut quae tingendi aut abluendi gratia aqua immergimus--To dip or immerge, as we dip things for the purpose of dyeing them, or immerge them in water." He gives the proper and figurative meanings as Scapula gives them.
>
> Schleusner, a name revered by orthodox theologians, and of enviable fame, says, (Glasgow ed. 1822,)--"1st. Proprie, immergo ac intingo, in aquam immergo. Properly it signifies, I immerse, I dip, I immerse in water. 2d. It signifies, I wash or cleanse by water--(quia haud raro aliquid immergi ac intingi in aquam solet ut lavetur)--because, for the most part, a thing must be dipped or plunged into water that it may be washed." Thus he gives the reason why *baptizo* figuratively means to wash, because that it is frequently the effect of immersion. Alexander Campbell, Christian Baptism, with Its Antecedents and Consequents, (1851).

2. Strong's Concordance
http://cf.blueletterbible.org/lang/lexicon/lexicon.cfm?Strongs=G911&Version=KJV, Accessed January 15, 2005.

3. T. J. Conant offers insight into the separation of these two washing ceremonies that were performed by the Pharisees:

> The unvarying sense of the word (baptizo) is expressly distinguished from the application of water to some portion of the body denoted by other words. In Mark 7: 3, it is said that the Pharisees "eat not" (i.e., never eat) "except they wash their hands," these being always liable to ceremonial defilement; and that when they come from a public place, as the market (the whole body having been exposed), "except they IMMERSE (BAPTIZE) THEMSELVES, they eat not." In the former case, the writer uses the appropriate word (NIPTEIN) for washing any portion of the body; as the *face* (Matt. 6: 17), the *hands* (Matt. 15: 2), the *feet* (John 13: 5). In the latter case he uses, in distinction from it, the word BAPTIZEIN, which by constant usage expressed an entire submersion of the object spoken of. As there is here no limitation ("they IMMERSE THEMSELVES"), the whole body of course is meant. Conant, The Meaning and Use of Baptizein, Published by The Wakeman Trust 2002, page 119.

Alexander Campbell also addresses quite effectively this particular episode between Jesus and the Pharisees:

> These washings before dinner, reported by Mark and Luke, contain the only two instances in which any part of *baptizo* is ever translated by *wash*, in the New Testament. And, fortunately, the antithesis between the washings here mentioned, indicated by the words employed in the original, and the facts stated, not only does not sustain the common version in translating both words by the same word, *wash;* but clearly intimates that the latter term, *baptizo*, ought here to have been rendered immerse. In verse 3d, it is *nipto* with *pugmee*, a word already shown to mean washing the hands, face, or feet, always when applied to the human person. This is true in every case in the Bible. Moreover, it has *pugmee*, the fist, in construction with it; that is, as Lightfoot and others interpret it, to the wrist, or so far as the fist extends. When the hand is shut, says Pollux, as quoted by Carson, the outside is called *pugmee*.[1] Now, as this limits the first washing, the second, being expressed by *baptizo*, and having no part of the body mentioned as its peculiar regimen, according to the usage of

the Greeks, (and the Romans, in the case of *lavo,*) the whole body is meant. Hence, they dip or bathe themselves after being to market; whereas, ordinarily, they wash their hands only up to the wrist. [166] Alexander Campbell, Christian Baptism, with Its Antecedents and Consequents, Book Second, Chapter 10 (1851).

4. James Strong, LL.D., S.T.D., The New Strong's Exhaustive Concordance of the Bible, Greek Dictionary of the New Testament, p. 18, 1990, Thomas Nelson Publishers.

5. James Strong, LL.D., S.T.D., The New Strong's Exhaustive Concordance of the Bible, Greek Dictionary of the New Testament, p. 50, 1990, Thomas Nelson Publishers.

6. James Strong, LL.D., S.T.D., The New Strong's Exhaustive Concordance of the Bible, Greek Dictionary of the New Testament, p. 19, 1990, Thomas Nelson Publishers.

7. James Strong, LL.D., S.T.D., The New Strong's Exhaustive Concordance of the Bible, Greek Dictionary of the New Testament, p. 15, 1990, Thomas Nelson Publishers.

8. Funk & Wagnals Desk Dictionary Volume 1 A-M, p. 27, 1980, Lippincott & Crowell,, Publishers.

9. James Strong, LL.D., S.T.D., The New Strong's Exhaustive Concordance of the Bible, Greek Dictionary of the New Testament, p. 12, 1990, Thomas Nelson Publishers.

10. James Strong, LL.D., S.T.D., The New Strong's Exhaustive Concordance of the Bible, Greek Dictionary of the New Testament, p. 73, 1990, Thomas Nelson Publishers.

11. http://www.realtime.net/~wdoud/topics/hermeneutics.html, Lesson 11, Types, Symbols, and Parables.

12. The General Epistles: A Practical Faith, Practial Christianity Foundation,L. L. Speer, Founder, Green Key Books, p. 174.

13. The New Advent Catholic Encyclopedia, Volume 2; Matter and Form of the Sacrament (1) b.

14. *A GENERAL HISTORY OF THE BAPTIST DENOMINATION IN AMERICA, AND OTHER PARTS OF THE WORLD* was written by David Benedict in 1813. In this work is found the following excerpt with respect to the history of the various modes of baptism. "The Council of Ravenna, 1311, legalized the baptism of sprinkling, but the practice of 'clinical,' or bedside baptism had long been in use and spread from the sickroom into the churches." David Benedict, A General history of the Baptist Denomination in America and Other Parts of the World, 1813.

15. *International Standard Bible Encyclopedia.*

16. James Strong, LL.D., S.T.D., The New Strong's Exhaustive Concordance of the Bible, Greek Dictionary of the New Testament, p. 68, 1990, Thomas Nelson Publishers.

17. James Strong, LL.D., S.T.D., The New Strong's Exhaustive Concordance of the Bible, Greek Dictionary of the New Testament, p. 35, 1990, Thomas Nelson Publishers.

Chapter IX
One, and Only One, Baptism

The Baptism the Apostles Taught

Scholars have not completely agreed on the date that the book of Ephesians was written. In truth, not everyone acknowledges that Ephesians was actually authored by Paul. It is difficult to attribute this work to another, however, based upon the initial salutation in chapter one and Paul's reference to himself in chapter three. It is, of course, possible that the letter was dictated, but authorship ultimately falls upon Paul. Some believe Ephesians could have been written from Ephesus, although this is unlikely based upon close examination of certain statements contained within the text.

That Ephesians was written at some point in time after Paul's ministry there can be reasonably concluded from the personal concern about Paul's welfare that he discusses in his closing remarks. He was undoubtedly addressing people who knew him and cared a great deal about his well being. Paul twice alludes to the notion that he was a prisoner at the time he wrote the epistle. While some believe he may have been a prisoner in Ephesus, it would have been for a very short period of time. He was also imprisoned in Caesarea for a time around AD 58-60. Yet the sense is, from the narrative of the book, that it had been a while since Paul had seen these friends.

While pinpointing the exact date of this epistle is most difficult, it is likely that the book was written between AD 61 – 62 when Paul was a prisoner in Rome, approximately four or five years after he had completed his ministry in Ephesus. Paul finds no fault with the faith or works of the Christians at Ephesus. His words are offered as a preventative measure in an effort to guard this group of believers against those elements of darkness that may lead men to fall from grace and cause division within the body.

Logic dictates that the *one baptism* of which Paul wrote (Ephesians 4: 5) in his letter to the Ephesians must be the same water baptism he taught while he was with them. This is the very baptism he administered in Ephesus in the nineteenth chapter of Acts. He does not suggest to the Ephesians that the *one baptism* mentioned here is anything other than what they had already been taught – by him.

Peter's message that baptism in water is the *'antitype which now saves us'* (1 Peter 3: 21) is corroborated by the many baptisms in which Paul participated and about which he wrote. Baptism, as it is presented in Paul's words to the Romans, is an occasion when we are buried and raised (Romans 6: 3-8). This can only be the same water baptism experienced by such individuals as the Ethiopian eunuch (Acts 8: 38), Cornelius (Acts 10: 48), Lydia (Acts 16: 15), the Philippian jailer (Acts 16: 33), and Paul himself (Acts 22: 16). It is the very moment, as Paul suggested to the Galatians, that we *put on Christ* (Galatians 3: 27). Two apostles, composing by the inspiration of the Holy Spirit, would not – could not – contradict each other by writing concerning two separate baptisms, each of which held the capacity to save.

The Baptism of Rebirth – John 3: 5

Each of the apostles whose works were canonized wrote concerning water baptism. Paul's epistles are flowing with instruction regarding the meaning and redemptive value of baptism (1 Corinthians 6: 11; Galatians 3: 27; Ephesians 4: 5). His writings teach that baptism is a time of renewal or rebirth (Romans 6: 1-4; Titus 3: 5). Peter consistently identifies baptism as a matter of forgiveness and salvation (Acts 2: 38; 1 Peter 3: 21). Each one recognized the work and gift of the Holy Spirit that are associated with water baptism (Acts 2: 38; 19: 1-3).

Matthew wrote about the ministry of John the Baptist in his gospel letter and recorded John's prophecy concerning baptism with the Holy Spirit (Matthew 3: 11). Much of the apostle John's writing concerning baptism also deals with that performed by John the Baptist. Mark and Luke, who were not apostles, identified the baptism of John the Baptist as a *'baptism of repentance for the remission of sins'* (Mark 1: 4; Luke 3: 3) and the apostle John revealed its purifying nature (John 3: 25-26).

In his opening remarks in the first chapter of the gospel that bears his name, the apostle John addressed the idea of spiritual rebirth (John 1: 12-13). He regards those who have received Christ as having been *'born of God.'* The topic resurfaces in his account of Nicodemus' visit with Jesus as He informed Nicodemus that a man must be *'born again'* or he could not *'see the kingdom of God'* (John 3: 3). When Nicodemus inquired exactly how a man might be born again, Jesus answered him plainly.

> Jesus answered, "Most assuredly I say to you, unless one is born of water and the Spirit, he cannot enter the kingdom of God." (John 3: 5)

Many men have vigorously argued that Jesus' reference to water in this setting is indicative of childbirth, since amniotic fluid envelopes the fetus in the womb, and that being *born of Spirit* reflects being born again. Others view this as either a figurative use of the term *water*, as it is occasionally portrayed in the New Testament, or denoting the Spirit Himself. Still others conclude that Jesus is pointing to a direct correlation between immersion in water and salvation as God has defined it in His plan. The quagmire this presents can only have one true answer. For the sake of the salvation of many, we cannot afford an errant determination as to what that answer is.

It seems rather awkward to suggest that Jesus would, as many have determined, teach Nicodemus that he must experience physical childbirth in order to enter the kingdom of God. Yet, this is what lies at the very core of the belief of many with respect to His words to Nicodemus. Instruction regarding childbirth would be extraneous, especially as it relates to salvation, since all men were brought into the world through childbirth. Additionally, this approach to Jesus' remark effectively dissects a statement, *'born of water and the Spirit,'* that is too tightly woven to allow it. His answer is in direct response to Nicodemus' question regarding what constitutes being born again. Jesus' explanation is that a person must be *'born of water and the Spirit.'* This statement offers Nicodemus clarification of the phrase *born again.*

When the subject arises in Scripture, childbirth is consistently given the designation *'born of woman'* (Job 14: 1; 15: 14; 25: 4; Matthew 11: 11) or *'born of flesh'* (John 3: 6; Galatians 4: 23). It is never deemed *'born of water,'* nor is that the case in Jesus' conversation with Nicodemus. Conversely, *water* often refers to baptism and/or being born again or regenerated (Acts 8: 36; 10: 47; Hebrews 10: 22; Titus 3: 5; 1 Peter 3: 21). Explaining to Nicodemus exactly how a man might be *'born again,'* Jesus denotes a critical union between being *'born of water'* and *'born of Spirit,'* indicating that the two are inseparable and that neither may be discarded by those who would *'see the kingdom of God'* (v. 5). In fact, His words signify that this is not two births, one *'of water'* and one *'of the Spirit,'* but a single birth involving *both* water and Spirit.

In His thoughts immediately following the expression *'born of water and the Spirit,'* Jesus actually differentiates between being *'born of flesh'* (childbirth) and *'born of Spirit'* (v. 6). He would not bind these two births so tightly in verse five only to distinguish between them in His next breath. This can only lead us to conclude that *'born of water'* must indicate something other than childbirth – something that is an element of rebirth (v. 3).

There is a tendency to overlook the relevance of the Jewish culture to this conversation. The truth is that Nicodemus, raised as an Israelite, had always understood that the relationship between God and the children of Israel was established as a (physical) birthright. In His response to Nicodemus that a man must be born again, Jesus knew the perspective from which Nicodemus viewed his relationship with God. Rather than suggesting that childbirth was somehow a condition of salvation, this passage clarifies, in verse six, that it was *no longer* human birth that determined man's relationship with God. For that reason Jesus could not be presenting childbirth as a condition of salvation. On the contrary, childbirth was being removed as a matter of participation in the covenant and being replaced with a new birth – a *birth of water and Spirit.* Therefore, despite insistence by many that the terminology reflects childbirth, this is not a practicable option in identifying the meaning of the phrase *born of water.*

Others assert that the water of which Jesus spoke figuratively embodies either the Word of God or the Spirit or some kind of eternal symbolic water one might drink in order to attain eternal life. Certainly, there are other times when water is employed figuratively in the New Testament. On a number of occasions in His ministry Jesus spoke of quenching a spiritual thirst with *'living water'* (John 4: 7-10). Later the apostle John also wrote about the *'waters of life'* (Revelation 21: 6; 22: 1, 17).

What is evident, however, in instances where water is applied in such a figurative manner, is that the symbolic nature of the water is plainly expressed by the author or speaker. Jesus gives no such indication in His conversation with Nicodemus. Here the word *water* stands on its own without reference to *'living water'* or *'waters of life.'* Each time in Scripture that Jesus spoke of water without direct figurative application, His meaning was of the physical substance of water (Matthew 10: 42; Mark 9: 41; 14: 13; Luke 5: 4; 7: 44; 13: 15; 16: 24; 22: 10; John 2: 7; Acts 1: 5). No exception to this consistency should be made regarding the dialogue recorded between Jesus and Nicodemus.

Despite overwhelming evidence, insistence that Christian baptism could not be Jesus' point to Nicodemus continues since, while both proselyte baptism and John's baptism were available at the time, Christian baptism was still to come. Recognition of this fact has led men to postulate that Jesus would not have instructed Nicodemus concerning baptism in the church age since it was not yet instituted. This raises the question, *'exactly what does it mean to be born of Spirit?'* Was this an element of the baptism of John? Did the forgiveness offered through John's baptism constitute spiritual birth, or does this phrase have something more in view?

Jesus surely realized that a Pharisee such as Nicodemus would recognize *'born of water'* as the baptism of John. This would have been a reference point for Nicodemus. Furthermore, forgiveness was available through John's baptism. Thus, Jesus was undoubtedly pointing Nicodemus toward baptism as a matter of forgiveness. That is certainly Jesus' most immediate meaning for the Pharisee, notwithstanding the fact that he lived under the Mosaic Law. While baptism was not yet mandated as a matter of salvation, it was recognized as ordained by God. Those who refused John's baptism were deemed to have *'rejected the will of God'* (Luke 7: 30). Therefore, Jesus was undoubtedly telling Nicodemus that he should be baptized with the baptism of John.

We must also realize that Jesus' conversation with Nicodemus, like most of His teaching, is equally meant for those of us who live in the covenant of grace. Jesus quite often spoke about things involving the coming kingdom. The beatitudes (Matthew 5: 1-11), as well as the parables, were certainly reflective of the new covenant. He also alluded to the Lord's Supper prior to introducing it to the disciples (John 6: 49-58). A feature of Jesus' role on earth was to speak of things yet to come. In these instances, His listeners did not always grasp the reaching significance of His words (Matthew 13: 13; Mark 4: 11-12), nor was that Jesus' intent.

Given John the Baptist's prophesy concerning *baptism in the Holy Spirit* (Matthew 3: 11), it seems most reasonable to conclude that birth of Spirit involves the gift of the Spirit that was reserved for the church age (Acts 2: 38). John the Baptist did not see a direct link between the water baptism he performed and the kind of relationship men would have with God through the Spirit in the new covenant. Furthermore, from Jesus' own lips we learn that the

Holy Spirit would not be given until after He had ascended to heaven (John 7: 39). What's more, the notion that *'born of water and the Spirit'* reflects *Christian* baptism fits masterfully with Paul's words to Titus concerning *'the washing of regeneration and the renewing of the Holy Spirit'* (Titus 3: 5). The two phrases, one by Jesus and one by Paul, appear to express the very same thought.

If being born of Spirit is limited to the church age, Nicodemus could not, at this time, be born of Spirit in the Christian sense (with the gift of the Spirit). Such a rebirth would not occur until the new covenant was established. Thus, Jesus' words implicate a time when it would be possible to be *'born of water and the Spirit.'* The fact that those Ephesians who received John's baptism were later baptized in the name of Jesus (Acts 19: 5) indicates that John's baptism was insufficient once the new covenant was inaugurated, and that being *born of Spirit* is intended to direct us to Christian baptism.

Consequently, if the water in this passage reflects the waters of baptism, Jesus is solidly placing upon mankind the specific condition of baptism in water as an indispensable component of rebirth, purporting that short of baptism a man *'cannot enter the kingdom of God'* (John 3: 5). Later in this book some of the writings of the early church fathers will be examined. In their communications we find that they considered Jesus' conversation with Nicodemus a clear directive for water baptism.

In truth, the idea that the water of which Jesus spoke in His words to Nicodemus constitutes baptism simply harmonizes with Scripture. This is hardly the only instance where baptism is portrayed as the time of the new birth. Paul calls it, *'newness of life,'* (Romans 6: 4). He also told the Corinthians that they had been, *'washed...in the name of the Lord Jesus and by the Spirit of our God'* (1 Corinthians 6: 11). Peter notes that being born again comes as a result of purification, which in turn comes through obedience to the truth (1 Peter 1: 22-23) - a comment that is offered just prior to his claim that baptism saves (1 Peter 3: 21). He also defines baptism as the time of forgiveness (Acts 2: 38). These words of Jesus are in complete accord with numerous other instructive passages concerning baptism, including His own words (Matthew 28:19; Mark 16: 16).

The view that Jesus had baptism in mind in His exchange with Nicodemus is further supported as John, who recorded this dialogue, later echoes Jesus' use of the term *water* in place of the word *baptism*. In challenging the Gnostics of his day in his first epistle, John deemed water, in a pointed reference to Jesus' baptism by John the Baptist, as a witness of Christ's deity and, hence, our salvation (1 John 5: 6-11). John must have understood, given his parallel use of the word, that when Jesus spoke of being *born of water and the Spirit*, His focus was baptism.

Men are often relentless in their insistence that the water of John 3: 5 *might* be considered *childbirth, the Holy Spirit, symbolic water*, or even limited to the *baptism* performed by John the Baptist. Most consider the meaning of water in this passage inconsequential as long as it is *not* deemed to be Christian baptism; therefore, any of these viewpoints is considered acceptable. Admittedly these same men cannot certify its absolute meaning; they can only tell us what they are profoundly convinced it does not mean. However, if men can only speculate on its meaning, how can those very same men say with any confidence the meaning that it does *not* carry? In a statement made by Jesus that conspicuously denotes eternal consequences, it seems somewhat slack to be content with uncertainty. Yet the single reason men remain uncommitted about the meaning of the phrase *'born of water'* is simply an enduring reluctance to grant the only meaning that suits the message, which is baptism.

Paul spoke of one baptism that was unique within the kingdom (Ephesians 4: 5). This one baptism, so distinct that Paul should go out of his way to identify its significance, can be none other than the baptism identified by both Peter and Paul in their writings. In speaking to Nicodemus, Jesus pointed to a birth of water so meaningful that failure to experience it would preclude one from entering God's kingdom (John 3: 5). Peter stated boldly that baptism saves (1 Peter 3: 21). The connection between baptism and salvation to which the apostles bear witness leaves no room for maneuvering. The birth of water in John 3: 5 can be nothing other than the one baptism of Ephesians 4: 5 – Christian immersion in water for the remission of sins.

God has sewn a sinewy thread throughout Scripture that is undeniable. Through the use of this thread the Bible always explains itself fully, at least on those issues that are of utmost importance. Often clarification comes by such elementary means that a supplementary verse escapes us. Such is the case with the account of the discussion between Jesus and Nicodemus. Their dialogue, which begins in the second verse of the third chapter of

John, continues through the twenty-first verse. It is the twenty-second verse that provides a wake-up call regarding this account.

> After these things Jesus and His disciples came into the land of Judea, and there He remained with them and baptized. (John 3: 22)

Jesus not only explained in His discussion with Nicodemus that being born again involved being baptized; but He followed that teaching by example.

Baptism with the Holy Spirit and with Fire

Notwithstanding Paul's statement that there is *one baptism* (Ephesians 4: 5), two additional baptisms are prophesied by John the Baptist. In his role as forerunner to Christ, John the Baptist took every advantage of the opportunities afforded him to prepare the people for Jesus' coming. In seeming contrast to the water baptism he offered, John points to baptism with the Holy Spirit and baptism with fire (Matthew 3: 11) as two baptisms that would be administered by the coming Messiah. His words suggest that, in New Testament times, certain kinds of baptism may, in fact, transcend his own water baptism. (Since an entire chapter is dedicated to *baptism with the Holy Spirit*, details concerning it will not be discussed here.)

While this incident in Matthew, and its corresponding passage in the gospel of Luke (Luke 3: 16), is the only reference in the New Testament specifically to a *baptism* with fire, it is not a particularly encouraging picture. The image of fire as a means of *purification* and/or *punishment* was not a new concept for the Israelites to whom John was speaking. Sacrifices in the Old Testament were burned on an altar as a means of cleansing the people from their sins. It is possible that Abel, the son of Adam and Eve, offered burnt offerings to God, but fire is first introduced in the Old Testament when Noah and his family exited the ark (Genesis 8: 20).

Abraham, it is discovered, offered burnt offerings to God (Genesis 22: 8) and, in like manner, the Israelites were commanded to provide burnt offerings for their sins (Leviticus 9: 8-10). Such sacrifices were central among the rituals commanded by God. Records of these offerings are scattered through the Old Testament and stand as a witness to God's use of fire for the purpose of purification.

Occasionally, however, God employed fire as a more direct means of purging evil. When God destroyed the cities of Sodom and Gomorrah, He did it with fire (Genesis 19: 24). As Joshua was leading the Israelites, God had him destroy the enemy cities with fire (Joshua 6: 24; 8: 8-19; 11: 11). Elijah called down fire from heaven to destroy the enemies of God (2 Kings 1: 9-14). In many other instances we discover that God used fire to rid the earth of evil. These accounts suggest that baptism with fire is something from which we should flee. An expanded look at the excerpt from Matthew will reveal additional relevant information concerning baptism with fire (Matthew 3: 10-12).

Baptism with fire, as the phrase implies, seems to point to a judgment that is to come. The fire of baptism will consume sinners at the time of judgment in much the same way that men are overwhelmed by water in baptism. This baptism, then, is one that should be feared, but only by those who are unfaithful to God. Whether the fire is literal or figurative in nature, it offers a frightening portrait of the wrath of God (Hebrews 12: 29).

The baptism with fire prophesied by John cannot be mistaken for the one baptism iterated by Paul and taught by the apostles. At no time in the New Testament epistles do the apostles ever contemplate baptism with fire. It is certainly not identified as a matter of salvation. On the contrary, it seems to be more a matter of condemnation.

Baptism – A Once-in-a-Lifetime Experience

The essence of Paul's reference to *one baptism* in the book of Ephesians is often hotly contested. Some view it as confirmation of immersion in water as the one baptism that is endorsed by Paul. Others have maintained, and perhaps justifiably so, that it may not be completely fair to assume that this statement regarding baptism points specifically to the *method* of baptism due to the conspicuous absence of any reference to the *one Lord's Supper* among this grouping. The presumption is that *one baptism* is not meant to suggest a single mode of baptism, but the fact that this event is intended to occur only once in the life of each Christian.[1] Such a claim cannot be made with respect to the Lord's Supper. The rite of Communion was never intended to be a one-time observance, but a continuing celebration of the sacrifice of Jesus' body and blood. Baptism is a single ceremony through which our sins are forgiven. One who has been baptized need never again submit to this rite. The Christian's sins are forgiven, once and for all, through the one baptism. The author of the book of Hebrews employs this very rationale in the ninth and tenth chapters as the writer explores the distinct contrasts between the old and new covenants. Of course, forgiveness of future sins of the immersed believer is still reliant upon a continued life of repentance.

This view of *one baptism* does not diminish the fact that, throughout his ministry, Paul certainly advocated immersion in water as the baptism of entrance into the kingdom. The claim is merely that the method of immersion in water may not be the intent behind Paul's words in this case. Still, it is in the one-time immersion in the waters of baptism that each man is cleansed permanently from a guilty conscience of sin and presented, pure and holy, to Christ.

NOTES FOR CHAPTER 9

1. Tertullian, was a strong advocate of the teaching that immersion in water was essential for an individual's salvation. Nonetheless, his view regarding the one baptism mentioned in Ephesians takes the perspective that this passage more accurately denotes the once in a lifetime occasion of the rite rather than the singular method in which it is administered.

Chapter X
When Does Baptism Mean Water?

A source of confusion with respect to the subject of baptism is the fact that some scriptural accounts utilize the words *baptize* or *baptism* in a context that cannot possibly signify immersion in water. Several other passages reference baptism without clearly explaining precisely what is involved. Still other New Testament texts are quite detailed regarding the type of baptism being addressed. This apparent incongruity has cultivated varying schools of thought regarding biblical teachings with respect to baptism. A thorough examination of the many references to the ceremony throughout the Bible does, however, provide answers to the concerns raised by this seeming disparity.

When Baptism Obviously Means Water

The certainty that water is involved in baptism is easily determined in a number of passages in the gospels where baptism is discussed. Often the message is crystal clear in that the use of water is plainly stated (Matthew 3: 5-16; Mark 1: 4-9; Luke 3: 16; John 1: 25-33).

...for John truly baptized with water... (Acts 1: 5)

The baptism performed by John the Baptist was unquestionably a baptism in water. Nowhere in Scripture can inference be found that John employed any instrument other than water for baptism. It can be reasoned, then, that when the baptism being addressed is that performed by John, it is *always* baptism in water. Consequently, in certain other passages, the vehicle must be water despite its omission from the text (Matthew 21: 25; Mark 11: 30; Luke 3: 2-12; 21; 7: 29-30; 20: 4; Acts 1: 21-22; 10: 37; 13: 23-24; 18: 25; 19: 3-4).

Given the fact that John's baptism was performed in water, and through the application of some simple reasoning, a conclusion can easily be reached that certain other times when baptism is mentioned, water is certainly the instrument of reference. For example, the baptism performed by Jesus' disciples was undoubtedly a baptism in water inasmuch as the Bible offers no distinction between the baptism performed by John the Baptist and that of Jesus' followers (John 3: 22-26). A thorough examination of the gospels (the books of Matthew, Mark, Luke, and John) reveals no record of baptism being *performed* in any medium other than water.

Advancing beyond the ministries of Jesus and John, the baptism in which people participated subsequent to Jesus' resurrection and ascension must be given consideration. It is this baptism that is relevant to the church age. Several instances from the book of Acts depict water as the device in which men and women were baptized. Such are the accounts of Philip teaching the gospel to the Ethiopian eunuch (Acts 8: 36) and Peter's visit to the house of Cornelius (Acts 10: 46-48). The conclusion that both the Ethiopian eunuch and those present at the house of Cornelius were baptized in water is undeniable. At times, however, the Bible is not quite so explicit in identifying the agency of baptism. An assessment of those passages, then, is certainly in order. However, it would be wise for us to first consider certain other baptisms cited in the Bible in an effort to provide better insight into some passages that may be in question.

Death, Burial, and Resurrection - The Baptism of Jesus

In addition to baptism with fire and baptism with the Holy Spirit (Matthew 3: 11), which are contrasted with water, the gospels indicate another occasion that may be justly viewed as a baptism. The mother of James and John, as a matter of pride, approached Jesus asking that her sons be granted positions of prominence in the kingdom that is to come. Jesus responded with the following remarks directed toward her sons:

> But Jesus answered and said, "You do not know what you ask. Are you able to drink the cup that I am about to drink, and be baptized with the baptism that I am baptized with?" (Matthew 20: 22)

Luke addresses this same baptism in a somewhat different setting, but there can be no mistaking the unique event of which Jesus is speaking.

> But I have a baptism to be baptized with, and how distressed I am till it is accomplished. (Luke 12: 50)

Some may contend that Jesus was speaking figuratively. This was certainly not an allusion to water, fire, or Holy Spirit baptism.

While the use of the word *baptism* may be considered somewhat symbolic in this instance, the event of which Jesus was speaking was all too real as He was looking forward with great angst to His own death, burial, and resurrection. These are the very elements after which water baptism was designed (Romans 6: 3-4).

When Water Is Not Intimated

While baptism with water and fire, as well as Jesus' death and resurrection, to which He refers as a baptism, may be easily understood, we must now contend with numerous passages where some form of the word *baptize* is intimated without specifying a medium for that baptism. These passages often find themselves at the heart of the discord that persists among many believers. An exegetic study of each one of these instances should provide sufficient insight to make a determination regarding the kind of baptism conveyed in each passage.

Jesus spoke the Great Commission (Matthew 28: 19-20), as it is so often called, to His followers after His resurrection. His apostles were to go into the world and lead people to follow Him, *baptizing them.* The baptism characterized in this passage must be seen as a baptism that was to be performed by men since it is a command Jesus clearly charged to them. A study of the prophecies of Jesus (Acts 1: 5) and John the Baptist (Matthew 3: 11) regarding baptism with the Holy Spirit and baptism with fire suggests that these were not to be performed by men, but by God. Perusing through the book of Acts, the narrative reveals that the baptism performed by those whom Jesus had commanded to baptize was indeed baptism in water. The incontrovertible conclusion, then, based on the available evidence in Scripture, is that the baptism commanded in the Great Commission was baptism in water.

> 15. And He said to them, "Go into all the world and preach the gospel to every creature. 16. He who believes and is baptized will be saved; but he who does not believe will be condemned." (Mark 16: 15-16)

The final chapter of Mark, like the last chapter of Matthew, is a brief synopsis of Jesus' resurrection and ascension. Included here are some of Jesus' final instructions to His followers prior to His ascension, a fact that lends considerable gravity to the teaching. This is a charge by Jesus to His disciples for men to believe and be baptized while declaring the consequences for those who refused to obey God's commands. Since baptism is employed in conjunction with belief, and belief lies upon the shoulders of man as his responsibility, we may rightfully hold that this baptism is also an obligation of man. It is something commanded of men. The only baptism that is taught in Scripture as man's responsibility is baptism in water (Matthew 28: 19; Acts 2: 38).

The Day of Pentecost

When the Day of Pentecost arrived, Peter called upon those who wished to follow Christ to *'repent and be baptized'* (Acts 2: 38). With no mention of water in this account, the fullness of Scripture must be considered in order to make a determination concerning the baptism of which Peter is speaking.

The question asked of Peter by those who believed his teaching about Christ carries with it a sense of timelessness. It is a question asked in one form or other by all those who come to the realization that they are lost in their sins. They asked, *'...what shall we do?'* (Acts 2: 37) In his answer that they should *'repent and...be baptized,'* the responsibility to accomplish these tasks is placed squarely on the shoulders of those who sought direction. Peter saw them as having the capacity to decide to follow, as well as the ability to carry out and submit to, his instructions. No decision to be baptized with the Holy Spirit or with fire could be made since these were to be administered by God. Given this, along with the fact that only days had elapsed since Jesus had commissioned His followers to go and baptize *with water*, no other explanation can be reasoned. A review of Cornelius' conversion (Acts 10: 47) reveals that the baptism commanded by Peter at that time was water baptism. Although Peter had witnessed the Holy Spirit being poured out on these Gentiles, he still commanded water baptism just as Jesus had ordained it. He would have done no less on the Day of Pentecost.

A significant characteristic of the baptism on the Day of Pentecost is that it was united together with repentance. The only prior baptism that was tied to repentance was the baptism of John the Baptist and, by association, the baptism of Jesus' disciples. No other determination can be made, then, but that the baptism commanded by Peter on the Day of Pentecost must be baptism in water.

Baptism in Samaria

While Philip was in Samaria preaching to the crowds we are told that *'both men and women were baptized'* (Acts 8: 12). Once again Luke offers a report involving baptism in which no instrument for that baptism is identified. Yet, we are provided with clear evidence that establishes the baptism in Samaria as baptism in water.

As Philip taught in Samaria an angel of God directed him to head south toward Gaza. At this time Philip left Samaria and joined with the Ethiopian eunuch. As the incident unfolds we find Philip teaching the eunuch the gospel, to which the eunuch responded, *'See, here is water. What hinders me from being baptized?'* (Acts 8: 36) Once again Philip's teaching resulted in baptism – a baptism in water. Given this corresponding text we can, with confidence, conclude that the baptism performed in Samaria was also baptism in water.

The Baptism of Saul

Saul of Tarsus was a man who waged war against Christianity. Extraordinary events turned him from an enemy of the church into Paul, an apostle who spent the remainder of his life teaching others about Christ. Luke chronicles the events surrounding Saul's conversion, first in a narrative (Acts 9: 1-19) and later in Paul's own words as he took the opportunity to reflect personally on his conversion experience (Acts 22: 6-16).

As in other situations, identification regarding the mode or substance of baptism is lacking. Still, the text reveals a recurring scenario. As was true concerning baptism on the Day of Pentecost, in Samaria, and with the eunuch, Saul appears to have power over the decision to be baptized. He was not told that if he believed God would baptize him with the Holy Spirit. Baptism is a matter of response by Saul. Ananias' instruction is that *he should not hesitate*, but that he should, *'Arise and be baptized.'* Once again God's Word offers abundant support for the determination that this was baptism in water.

For those who insist that *'calling on the name of the Lord'* (Acts 22: 16), aside from baptism, was the means by which Saul's sins were washed away, Scripture simply offers no evidence for that verdict. Peter, on the Day of Pentecost, instructed the people that they must be baptized for forgiveness of their sins. Interestingly, the incident between Ananias and Saul is actually quite similar to the events surrounding Peter's meeting with Cornelius. Each man was advised what he must *do*. Peter instructed Cornelius just as Ananias directed Saul regarding how he should respond to the gospel. In these two cases, one of the first instructions provided was that each of these men should be baptized – in water. This is the precise instruction Peter spoke to the Jews on the Day of Pentecost, Philip offered to the Samaritans and the eunuch, and Paul taught to Lydia and the Philippian jailer. This same instruction is no less important for us today.

Through some simple deductive reasoning we can easily determine that several other incidents also involve baptism in water (Acts 16: 15, 33; 18: 8; 19: 5). In each case, it is evident that men and women made a personal decision to receive baptism and that humans administered the rite. No legitimate debate can be raised that these were not accounts involving water.

The Symbolism of Baptism

A number of scholars claim that, in his writings, Paul does not specifically stipulate water as a vehicle for baptism. When he does broach the subject he refers to it simply as baptism. Of course, this view completely ignores those passages where Paul does regard the cleansing of God's people through the washing of water (Ephesians 5: 26; Titus 3: 5) and the fact that Paul, at times, administered baptism. We can, however, ascertain what Paul intends by baptism. The answer, as always, lies in the study of God's Word.

When Paul wrote to the church in Rome he had not yet journeyed there. Apparently none of the apostles had yet been to Rome. Others had carried the gospel message to the people there and a church body was formed.

> 3. Or do you not know that as many of us as were baptized into Christ Jesus were baptized into his death? 4. Therefore we were buried with Him through baptism into death, that just as Christ was raised from the dead by the glory of the Father, even so we also should walk in newness of life. 5. For if we have been united together in the likeness of His death, certainly we also shall be *in the likeness* of *His* resurrection, 6. knowing this, that our old man was crucified with *Him*, that the body of sin might be done away with, that we should no longer be slaves of sin. (Romans 6: 3-6)

The imagery of baptism here is absorbing, providing what G. R. Beasley-Murray refers to as '...*the most extensive exposition of baptism Paul has given....*'[1] His instruction concerning baptism begins with a question to his readers, *'Or do you not know that as many of us as were baptized into Christ Jesus were baptized into His death?'* (Romans 6: 3). This query is rhetorical in the same vein as Jesus' question to Nicodemus in the third chapter of John when He asked, *'Are you a leader of Israel, and do not know these things?'* (John 3: 10). It was not a question to which Paul was seeking an answer, but a reminder of those things of which they were already aware.

Paul was a man who always selected his words deliberately and efficiently. His intent is to portray baptism in terms of the burial and resurrection of Christ. The *only* baptism of Scripture that embodies this imagery is immersion in water. The New Testament never suggests that another baptism (Holy Spirit, fire, etc.) might be representative of such symbolism. This likeness is specific to immersion in water.

The ceremony of baptism, as defined by Paul in the sixth chapter of Romans, is a baptism through which we are united together in a portrait of His death (Romans 6: 5), being *buried with Him*. He also identifies their submission to baptism as obedience in the ensuing verses (vs. 16-18). This is the same baptism in which Paul participated throughout the book of Acts, whether in submission as he was baptized by Ananias, or as one who administered baptism to others. We have no reason, then, to speculate that Paul was speaking of any baptism other than the one he experienced in Damascus and had administered to Lydia and the Philippian jailer, which was water baptism.

Baptism in Corinth

The book of 1 Corinthians is one that is often bitterly contested with respect to baptism. As Paul initially addresses the issue that the Corinthians faced, the narrative also provides additional insight into the baptism of which Paul wrote. He rebuked the Corinthians for sadly associating themselves too closely with the men who had performed their baptism, thus taking the focus off of Christ. Once again we discover a baptism administered by men. Paul even acknowledges that he had baptized some of those at Corinth. Reference is specifically made to the conversion of Crispus, whom Paul claims to have baptized. His baptism, mentioned in

Acts 18: 8, is one we have already determined could be nothing other than baptism in water.

Concerning the Corinthians' error, as they wrongly identified themselves with those who had performed the rite of baptism, Paul's instruction does not end with the first chapter. In the third chapter we find him still teaching on the same topic and still addressing their claims that they are *'of Paul'* or *'of Apollos'*. He supplements his teaching with an illustration of two men, one who plants (preaches) and one who waters (baptizes), at the same time recognizing that despite these efforts, no crop can grow without God (1 Corinthians 3: 4-7). In this context, the identification of *planting and watering* as the *preaching and baptism* of the first chapter is inescapable.

Even if nothing more was written, we already have sufficient evidence that baptism in the first chapter of 1 Corinthians is baptism in water, but Paul has not yet finished. As we reach the sixth chapter we discover yet another declaration concerning the baptism of the people at Corinth. Explaining that they could no longer be identified with their former sinful life, Paul defines the very reason they were now separate from the world.

> ...But you were washed, but you were sanctified, but you were justified in the name of the Lord Jesus by the Spirit of our God. (1 Corinthians 6: 11)

At what time does Scripture teach that we are sanctified (Ephesians 5: 26) and justified (Romans 5: 1 - 6: 7) in Jesus' name – by the Spirit? It is at the time of immersion in water. While there are those who wish to distinguish the *washing* of the sixth chapter from the *baptism* of the first chapter, the construction of the writing will not allow it. Paul binds the teaching together too meticulously in these chapters for us to even imagine that they are distinct. Thus, not only does baptism in the first chapter speak directly of water baptism, so, too, the *watering* and *washing* of the third and sixth chapters respectively point to the same.

Later in this epistle, in the tenth chapter, we find an allusion to the baptism in the sea as the Israelites escaped the Egyptians by crossing the Red Sea on dry land (1 Corinthians 10: 2). Through his detailing of the essence of this baptism we can discern that Paul is not discussing Christian baptism in water. He notes in the subsequent verses how these Israelites of old succumbed to temptations even after they had been freed (baptized) in the sea. The warning to the Corinthians was, in their freedom, to avoid the same mistakes. Here the word is employed in a somewhat figurative sense since the Israelites obviously were not, themselves, immersed in the Red Sea. It was, however, the evil of men (Egyptians) that was immersed, much like the flood of Noah's day. Furthermore, we would do well to remember that the Israelites were freed through water. This baptism might also be considered an *antitype* of Christian baptism.

As we continue our journey through the book of 1 Corinthians, the subject of baptism surfaces two additional times. In one instance it is in response to skepticism on the part of certain disciples in the church at Corinth regarding the resurrection of the dead. Paul, in response, purported that some people are even *baptized for the dead* (1 Corinthians 15: 29) in search of the resurrection.

Various perspectives have been proposed regarding this passage. Some view this statement as an indication that someone might be discharging a promise made to a loved one who has already passed from this life, thus being *baptized for them*. This mindset suggests that prior to death, a Christian may have offered a plea to a close friend or family member, that they might be converted and, thus, see them beyond the grave. Others have speculated that some may have been baptized out of a profound respect for a deceased believer. Still others see this simply as a statement about the Corinthians' own baptism in anticipation of the resurrection from the dead. This is unlikely, however, given the third person reference to those who participated in the baptism for the dead. It is most likely that Paul is alluding to a man making a decision to be baptized *on behalf of* one who had died in an effort to save that person's soul.

Regardless of the motivation behind the deed, this message clearly reveals a baptism that consists of water since it is, once again, decided upon and administered by men. It is something men *chose* to do. Additionally, other than its aspiration of salvation for those already deceased, Paul draws no distinction between their performance of this baptism and that discussed in the first chapter. The only baptism to which Paul could be referring is water baptism, even if it was for a purpose he could not sanction.

These remarks to the Corinthians regarding baptism for the dead demonstrate an undeniable link between water baptism and salvation. While he may not have condoned the practice of baptism for the dead (2 Corinthians 5: 10), Paul recognized that the ceremony was being performed in an effort to attain salvation, even if it was for those who had already passed on. This lesson of salvation in baptism is taught throughout Scripture, although clearly the intent of the New Testament is to apply that lesson to those who are living.

The Baptism of 1 Corinthians 12: 13

Manmade divisions within Scripture, such as chapters and verses, while often beneficial, can occasionally obscure the intended message. While they certainly make it much easier to locate various passages, what must be understood is that this is the very reason they were developed. Those who designed the segmentation of Scripture must have done their utmost to prevent interference in the flow of any passage. Yet, at times these divisions can be somewhat distracting. Viewing 1 Corinthians simply as a letter that Paul composed to a church yields a much clearer picture of the baptism discussed in this epistle.

> For by one Spirit we were all baptized into one body—whether Jews or Greeks, whether slaves or free—and have all been made to drink into one Spirit. (1 Corinthians 12: 13)

The lesson that the work of Holy Spirit, at the time of water baptism, involves the regeneration of that person who has decided to submit his/her life to God has been covered at length. Despite the clarity of this biblical principle (Acts 2: 38; Colossians 2: 12; Titus 3: 5), many view Paul's words in 1 Corinthians 12: 13 as specific to baptism with the Holy Spirit, contending that this occurs separately from water baptism. Six times in this letter Paul mentions baptism (1 Corinthians 1: 11-17; 3: 1-9; 6: 11; 10: 1-5; 12: 13; 15: 29). Beyond a doubt the baptism discussed in the first through the sixth chapters involves water. This is also true of baptism for the dead in the fifteenth chapter. The tenth chapter holds an allusion to a figurative Old Testament baptism at the crossing of the Red Sea. Now we encounter the baptism of the twelfth chapter. Many men have determined from Paul's words at this time that he is depicting baptism with the Holy Spirit in lieu of immersion in water. After all, it does say baptism comes *'by one Spirit'* with no apparent reference to water.

The point was made in the Preface of this book that the context of a word or text might be very material when attempting to discern its true meaning. Just as Paul was not sanctioning baptism for the dead when he wrote concerning it, neither is he distinguishing between immersion in water and baptism with the Holy Spirit in this case.

In the <u>New International Version of the Bible</u>, the twelfth chapter of 1 Corinthians is prefaced by a subtitle just above the first verse. It is titled *Spiritual Gifts*. This is one of those manmade labels that can sometimes distract us from the objective of the text since it suggests that Paul's intent is to instruct his audience about spiritual gifts. Even his introduction to this portion of the letter, as he states, 'Now concerning spiritual gifts...' (1 Corinthians 12: 1), may lead the reader to believe this is his objective.

While the topic of spiritual gifts is addressed, the focus of Paul's lesson is not on the gifts themselves, but on the lack of unity present among the brotherhood with respect to these gifts. In fact, the Corinthians' lack of unity is the theme of the entire epistle beginning with Paul's distress in the first chapter over their divisions with respect to baptism. This lesson of disharmony is now applied to the difficulties that have surfaced among the people, perhaps out of jealousy or confusion, from the distribution of spiritual gifts. Paul is not so concerned with the intricacies of the gifts themselves, but that they should be an opportunity for accord rather than division within the church.

Atop the twelfth verse of this chapter, the NIV inserts another heading which is, *One Body, Many Parts,* a title that is much more descriptive of the substance of the writing. Having addressed in the first several verses the discord regarding spiritual gifts, Paul adjusts his focus and takes a look at the bigger picture of unity in what he refers to as the body of Christ. The lesson taught is that, while men have many unique characteristics and abilities, believers are bonded together through unity in Christ. As Paul scans this larger horizon with respect to unity he highlights the diverse roles of the members of the body that help men complement each other's work in Christ. Enveloped by this notion of oneness in Jesus is verse thirteen; and it must be read and understood in the light of this theme of unity.

Paul's instruction that members of the body must be unified in Christ is the framework upon which 1 Corinthians 12: 13 rests. The focus of the words in the first eleven verses is on singleness of purpose rather than on the significance of spiritual gifts. It is this theme that leads us to Paul's comment concerning baptism. If, as Paul suggests, Christians are *'baptized into one body,'* it stands to reason that the baptism of which he speaks is baptism that results in membership in that body. Since the issue here is unity, we can also gather that this is the baptism that unites the members of that body not only with each other, but with Christ (Romans 6: 5). It is the same baptism Paul addressed earlier when he stated to the Corinthians, *'But you were washed, you were sanctified, you were justified, in the name of the Lord Jesus Christ and by the Spirit of our God.'* (1 Corinthians 6: 11). Luke wrote, in the book of Acts, that water baptism is the mechanism through which men receive cleansing from sin, fulfillment of the promise of the Holy Spirit, and membership in His body (Acts 2: 38-47). The church, then, is unquestionably the body of Christ to which Paul refers in his letter to the Corinthians (Colossians 1: 24).

The claim that Paul's words represent a doctrine of baptism with the Holy Spirit that somehow supplants immersion in water is unsupported by the context of this passage within the epistle. In this letter, save the reference to the Red Sea (1 Corinthians 10: 2), Paul has in mind immersion in water (1 Corinthians 1: 13-15; 3: 6; 6: 11; 15: 29). If the baptism expressed in 1 Corinthians 12: 13 was anything other than the baptism in water that is addressed in the balance of this letter, we could reasonably expect Paul to make that distinction. Yet he does not. There is no need to differentiate between them since they are one and the same.

Two serious gaffes are made by those who view the baptism of 1 Corinthians 12: 13 as a lesson regarding baptism with the Holy Spirit, independent from the act of water baptism. The first, quite obviously, is the assertion that this is a baptism without water. In his words Paul simply recognizes the association with, and work of, the Holy Spirit during water baptism that is noted at various times in the New Testament (Colossians 2: 11-12; Titus 3: 5). Furthermore, in order to determine that this is not water baptism we must somehow be able to sever any connection with Paul's comments in the sixth chapter. There he similarly denotes a washing that takes place *'in the name of Jesus and by the Spirit of our God'* (I Corinthians 6: 11). Yet any attempt to disjoin the two statements is hopeless. Paul unites purification *'by the Spirit'* with a washing that takes place *'in the name of Jesus'*. The only cleansing that is offered *'in the name of Jesus'* is baptism in water

(Matthew 28: 19; Acts 2: 38). If the washing of the sixth chapter *'by the Spirit'* represents water baptism, which it surely does, the claim that 12: 13 does not is untenable.

Furthermore, many fail to notice the connection between Paul's depiction of baptism in 1 Corinthians 12: 13 and the baptism of the first chapter. He begins the letter by chastising the Corinthians for making baptism an issue that divides (1 Corinthians 1: 10-17). He now explains the gravity of their mistake. They have become divided over something that was intended to unite men in Christ

The other error in judgment offered up by those who insist that Paul is not citing water baptism is the speculation that a separate *baptism with the Spirit* or *by the Spirit* grants membership into the body. This is a dictum foreign to Scripture. Since it is the members of the body who will inherit the kingdom (Ephesians 3: 6), we must apply to this passage the scriptural principle that membership in the body (Acts 2: 41) and unity with Christ are realized when one is baptized in water (Romans 6: 5). This occurs in unison with forgiveness of sins and the gift of the Holy Spirit (Acts 2: 38). This is why Paul boldly identifies baptism as a crucial unifying element of Christianity (Ephesians 4: 5). The leap to a separate baptism with the Spirit is a leap made by modern men rather than Paul.

The Baptism of Galatians 3: 27

> For as many of you as were baptized into Christ have put on Christ. (Galatians 3: 27)

In this context we find that baptism is accompanied by faith and justification (v. 25), linking it directly to the forgiveness granted at the time of baptism (Acts 2: 38; 1 Corinthians 6: 11). It is also a time when we become sons (children) of God (v. 26) offering a direct connection to the notion of rebirth (John 3: 3-5; Galatians 6: 15).

Baptism is portrayed as the time when the Galatians' effectively *put on* Christ Jesus. Had this text related an unforeseen act from God, as with Cornelius (Acts 10: 44), Paul might have said that Christ *had been put on them* but, instead, they *had put on Christ,* indicating that the decision belonged to each one. Baptism is depicted here as a response of faith. If it is a response of faith, it is once again baptism initiated and administered by men as opposed to baptism that is involuntary and is not administered by men, but by God (e.g., baptism with fire). Paul's claim that there is but one baptism only confirms that this is water baptism.

The Baptism of Colossians 2: 12

More than once Paul compares baptism to the death, burial, and resurrection of Christ. In his epistle to the Colossians the lesson is expanded, however, as he instructs them regarding the work God performs on the believer at the time of baptism. As in his depiction of baptism to the Romans, this is once again a baptism where we are *buried* and *raised:*

> 11. In Him you were also circumcised with the circumcision made without hands, by putting off the body of the sins of the flesh, by the circumcision of Christ, 12. buried with Him in baptism, in which you were also raised with *Him* through faith in the working of God, who raised Him from the dead. (Colossians 2: 11-12)

Immersion in water is the only form of baptism that is representative of Jesus' death, burial, and resurrection. Therefore, it must apply to Paul's writing to the Colossians. Baptism is a physical act of faith. However, it is through this physical act that God does some of His most magnificent work. Through the sacrifice of Jesus, whose death, burial, and resurrection are symbolized in baptism, God accomplishes some specific things. He forgives us of our sins. We are provided the indwelling of the Holy Spirit. Each one is added to the body of believers. Finally, we are presented with eternal life.

The Baptism of 1 Peter 3: 21

> 18. For Christ also suffered once for sins, the just for the unjust, that He might bring us to God, being put to death in the flesh but made alive by the Spirit…20. …when once the Divine longsuffering waited in the days of Noah, while the ark was being prepared, in which a few, that is, eight souls, were saved through water. 21. There is also an antitype which now saves us—baptism (not the removal of filth from the flesh, but the answer of a good conscience toward God), through the resurrection of Jesus Christ… (1 Peter 3: 18, 20-21)

Many argue that Peter was not proposing in this passage that the *baptism that saves* is baptism in water, contending that Noah was not saved through water, but that he was saved in the ark – separated from the water. In truth, Noah was saved by faith, a point on which all can agree, but the baptismal connection in 1 Peter is a direct reference to the flood waters.

Peter's words are not vague. The baptism intimated in the twenty-first verse is openly compared, not to the ark, but to the water. Those on the ark *'were saved through water.'* This is not a timid suggestion that baptism might be likened to the waters of the flood, but a bold proclamation of that fact. Through water Noah and his family were saved, and it is the antitype of that water – baptism – through which men are saved today.

The aside that is offered to complement the main thought of the text, which is that baptism saves, is intended to provide further clarification of the statement. Peter remarks parenthetically, *'not the removal of the filth of the flesh, but the answer of a good conscience toward God.'* A return to the original Greek text is central in identifying the true meaning of the statement. The erroneous claim that this comment denotes a baptism that does not have the *ability* to cleanse the flesh ignores completely the essence of the words as they are written.

Various words in the Greek language can be translated as *but* in English. Most often the word δε (*de*) is used, carrying the meaning of *now, therefore, then, verily,* or *in truth*[2], etc. Occasionally it is the word και (*kai*), which tends to mean *and, also* or *even*[3]. However, as with other elliptical remarks, Peter employs the word αλλα (*alla*) in this passage. The application of this word implies an exception or limitation to a general rule or a particular thought. Some of the primary definitions of the word are *objection, exception,* or *restriction*[4]. Strong defines it as *contrariwise.*[5] Spiritual purification that is offered to men at the time of baptism is exclusive to baptism. Peter's statement, *'not the removal of filth...'* differentiates the water of baptism from the physical cleansing with which water is normally associated. This statement of qualification regarding baptism is out of place unless the baptism of which Peter is writing is baptism in water.

> Not everyone who says to Me, 'Lord, Lord,' shall enter the kingdom of heaven, but (αλλ) he who does the will of My Father in heaven. (Matthew 7: 21)

> But He said to them, "All cannot accept this saying, but (αλλ) only *those* to whom it has been given." (Matthew 19: 11)

Peter said to Him, "Even if all are made to stumble, yet (αλλ) I *will* not *be*." (Mark 14: 29)

59. So it was, on the eighth day, that they came to circumcise the child; and they would have called him by the name of his father, Zacharias. 60. His mother answered and said, "No (but) (αλλα); he shall be called John." 61. But they said to her, "There is no one among your relatives who is called by this name." (Luke 1: 59-61)

These verses reflect the meaning of *exception* for the Greek word αλλα. For instance, many people are willing to verbally *call out* to the Lord, believing that is the way to salvation. However, it is those who are obedient, those who are the exception, who will enter the kingdom. Also, Peter claimed he would be the exception to the many who would deny Christ. Similarly, at the time Elizabeth gave birth to John the Baptist it was customary to name a son after his father or one of his ancestors. John's parents, Zacharias and Elizabeth, broke with tradition in naming their son John, following the instructions given by the angel of the Lord. This was truly an *exception* to the perceived, though unwritten, rule. The custom was that a son would be named after a relative, but *(αλλα)* John was not. Peter's clarification that it is not the physical cleansing value of baptism but *(αλλα)* its spiritual worth that is important, confirms baptism in water.

This passage (1 Peter 3: 21) must also be considered within the greater context of the entire epistle. The work is addressed, at least in part, to those who were new in Christ. This observation may even be considered an understatement since Peter suggests that they had *most recently* accepted Christ as Savior (1 Peter 2: 1-2). Some men have speculated that this entire epistle is actually a sermon offered at a baptismal service that was later sent in written form to provide greater instruction concerning baptism. Thus, Peter's words cannot be severed from the context of the audience and the setting of their conversion. Peter recognized that they had been *obedient* (1 Peter 1: 14). They had actually *purified their souls through obedience* and, as a result, were *born again*, which is identified as the beginning of their eternal life (1 Peter 1: 22-23).

Through the second and third chapters Peter continues his instructions to these *babes* in Christ and exactly what changes they might anticipate as well as what it was that God expected of them. This culminates in Peter's words concerning baptism in the third chapter and is followed in the fourth chapter with instruction about

Christian attitudes and accountability. The fifth and final chapter is an exhortation to those of the fellowship, especially the elders, to care for those who are new in Christ and for each other.

In determining the kind of baptism to which Peter is referring in 1 Peter 3: 21, it may help to consider not only the context of this epistle, but also to examine the greater context of the works of Peter. What must be taken into account in this text is Peter's reason for the letter. The apostle's goal in writing both 1 Peter and 2 Peter is one and the same and is spelled out clearly in his second epistle.

> Beloved, I now write to you this second epistle (in *both of* which I stir up your pure minds by way of reminder), 2. that you may be mindful of the words which were spoken before by the holy prophets, and of the commandment of us, the apostles of the Lord and Savior... (2 Peter 3: 1-2)

Peter wrote his epistles to help his readers recall the words of the prophets and the commandments given to them by the apostles. If this was not the initial intent of the first epistle, which is possible given its context as well as Peter's parenthetic remark here, he certainly recognizes the first work as having that effect. Thus, it is unimaginable that Peter was addressing anything other than the baptism that was commanded by the apostles. It is the very baptism he had proclaimed on the Day of Pentecost and at the house of Cornelius. It is the baptism Paul administered to the Corinthians and the Ephesians. It is water baptism.

Multiple Baptisms – Hebrews 6: 1-2

Faced with the fact that some disciples were not growing spiritually simply because they still could not progress beyond some of the simple doctrinal principles from the teaching of the apostles, the author of the book of Hebrews wrote:

> 1. Therefore, leaving the discussion of the elementary *principles* of Christ, let us go on to perfection, not laying again the foundation of repentance from dead works and of faith toward God, 2. of the doctrine of baptisms, of laying on of hands, of resurrection of the dead, and of eternal judgment. (Hebrews 6: 1-2)

Often, when the word doctrine is considered, it brings to mind the notion of *thou shalt do this* or *thou shalt not do that*! In truth, the word for doctrine is διδαχη (*didache*) and simply means *teaching* or *instruction*. While it is possible that the word *baptisms* suggests the great number of believers who had been baptized, it most likely references instruction that was certainly given regarding various types of purification in much the same way that they have been portrayed in this chapter. Paul wrote about the baptism of the Israelites in the Red Sea. The gospels address baptism with the Holy Spirit and baptism with fire as well as the full account of Jesus' death, burial, and resurrection, also called a baptism, not to mention the ceremonies of the first covenant. Were the Hebrews taught about diverse baptisms? Certainly they were. This passage is evidence of that. The *baptisms* mentioned in this passage, then, undoubtedly refer to the host of baptisms, both figurative and literal, of which we have already spoken.

* * * * *

Many look to the baptism discussed in the epistles of Paul, Peter, and others, with the view that it is most certainly a Spirit baptism *rather than* water baptism, believing the two are distinct. Most will concede that certain passages depict the act of water baptism that is administered by men (e.g., 1 Corinthians 1: 10-17). However, other passages (Romans 6: 3-4; 1 Corinthians 12: 13; Galatians 3: 27; Ephesians 4: 5; Colossians 2: 12; 1 Peter 3: 21) are seen as *baptism with the Holy Spirit* that does not involve the use of water.

It is important to note, at this point, that the proposition of a separate spiritual baptism with respect to the epistles actually originated in the nineteenth century with an Anglican clergyman by the name of E. W. Bullinger (1837-1913). Until that time the word *baptism*, whether found in the gospels, the book of Acts, or the epistles was generally recognized as a direct reference to the rite of water baptism. Therefore, in order to be true to apostolic doctrine, we are obliged to regard Paul's use of the word baptism in that same vein. Of course, the word is employed figuratively on occasion, as we have discussed. Nonetheless, it is difficult to credit Paul with a baptismal doctrine that was established nearly two thousand years after his death.

The New Testament consists of many incidents or narratives where a form of the word *baptism* is mentioned. In each case, the use of water can be easily determined from either the context or other corroborating passages. Still, there are those who deny that

Paul taught water baptism, even rejecting that his references to baptism in his letters to churches and/or individuals reflected water baptism. Yet the conclusion that certain passages of Scripture, such as 1 Corinthians 12: 13, do not involve water can only be reached if the full extent of biblical teaching regarding baptism is dismissed.

NOTES FOR CHAPTER 10

1. G. R. Beasley-Murray, Baptism in the New Testament, William B. Eerdmans Publishing Company, 1994, p. 126.

2. Thayer's Greek-English Lexicon of the New Testament, p. 131, 1977, Baker Books House.

3. James Strong, LL.D., S.T.D., The New Strong's Exhaustive Concordance of the Bible, Greek Dictionary of the New Testament, p. 39, 1990, Thomas Nelson Publishers.

4. Thayer's Greek-English Lexicon of the New Testament, p. 27, 1977, Baker Books House.

5. James Strong, LL.D., S.T.D., The New Strong's Exhaustive Concordance of the Bible, Greek Dictionary of the New Testament, p. 10, 1990, Thomas Nelson Publishers.

Chapter XI
Not of Works!

Perhaps the most prominent philosophy advanced in opposition to the teaching of water baptism as an essential component of God's plan of salvation is that it is a *work*[1] and, in Paul's own words, men cannot earn salvation through works (Ephesians 2: 8). This is a topic that deserves considerable discussion since it is critical to the debate, but it would be much better to first review exactly what Scripture teaches regarding the actions of a righteous man.

Works in the New Covenant
Contrary to the teaching offered by many, from the inspired words of Scripture we learn that no one can be saved without works. Peter taught Cornelius that God would not accept the man who does not perform righteous works (Acts 10: 35). He also stated that our works are the means by which other men will recognize us as God's children and, consequently, give glory to God (1 Peter 2: 11-16). Paul explained to King Agrippa that repentance must be joined with works according to the *heavenly vision* (Acts 26: 19-20). James emphasized that one who is not full of good works is dead spiritually (James 2: 20). Hence, the person who has no works has no faith (James 2: 14). The conclusion that works are a part of the character of a faithful person is inescapable. Since one cannot be saved without faith, we can presume that no one can be saved without works. These remarks concerning the relationship between faith and works are not presented to substantiate the need for baptism, but rather to dispel the myth that works are not necessary for salvation. Man is not justified by faith only, but by faith and works (James 2: 24).

Known as the faith chapter of the Bible, the eleventh chapter of Hebrews defines faith in terms of works. God respected Noah, Abraham, Jacob, Joseph, Moses, and others for their *works* of faith. Their actions directly resulted from the intimate relationship each one had with God. That kind of relationship with Him naturally produces actions. If there are no deeds it is because there is no relationship and there is no faith. It is those who *do* the work of the Father who will be saved (Matthew 7: 21).

Certainly works, or acts of righteousness, cannot be dismissed in one's devotion to Christ. In fact, immediately following Paul's instruction that men are not saved by works (Ephesians 2: 8-9), he wrote that we as men were created to perform good works (Ephesians 2: 10). During a study of the book of James a dear friend named Debbie suggested to the group that it seems God expects His children to have a *deedful heart,* a phrase that has stuck with this author since that day. It illustrates the kind of character a child of God will have with respect to deeds.

Obedient Faith Vs Works

Nonetheless, the proposition that baptism is an act during which men are saved, when the Bible clearly indicates that no one can be saved *through* works, still has not been addressed. The question that must be answered is this: *Is baptism a deed of merit whereby men attempt to earn salvation, or is it an act of faith in obedience to God's instruction without which one cannot be saved?* For those who see baptism as a creditable work the following verse is often promulgated in an effort to overcome the many passages of Scripture that portray the redemptive value of baptism:

> 8. For by grace you have been saved through faith, and that not of yourselves; *it is* the gift of God, 9. not of works, lest anyone should boast. (Ephesians 2: 8-9)

While those to whom Paul was writing in this instance were already Christians, it would be insincere to suggest that he is not speaking here of initial salvation. As we consider the context of this statement, we cannot deny that Paul is, in retrospect, addressing the time of conversion as a man is transformed from spiritual death to spiritual life (Ephesians 2: 5). Paul is speaking not only of their continuing daily salvation as cited in other epistles (2 Corinthians 4: 16), but also of the manner in which the Ephesians first received the grace of God, which was through faith.

In James' letter to the Israelites, while the combination of faith and works is the focus, his remarks are offered in the setting of an enduring relationship with God where faith inspires works and works reflect faith. The inseparable link between true faith and the works evident in the Christian life is at the very heart of our walk with God. This is confirmed in Paul's letter to Titus when he explained that we must maintain our life in Christ through good works (Titus 3: 8).

These things having been said, the passage in Ephesians concerning salvation *not of works* still does not repudiate scriptural teaching concerning the redemptive role of baptism, despite the fact that initial salvation is the clearly defined subject matter. As we take in the whole of Scripture, just as we must be forthright in accepting that Ephesians 2: 8 has the sinner's conversion in view, we must honestly approach Scripture in every sense. It is the only way we can truly honor God with respect to His Word. The truth is that the scriptural backdrop against which Paul wrote these words teaches that while salvation is not earned, when it comes to atonement faith is invariably combined with obedience on the part of men.

For those who attempt to equate works and obedience, a basic dilemma that arises from Scripture is the seeming contradiction between the words of Paul and the words of Jesus. While Paul states that no one will earn salvation (Ephesians 2: 8-9), Jesus emphasizes the teaching that men and women who fail to obey the commands of God will not be saved (Matthew 7: 21; John 14: 21). Additionally, both Peter and John recognize obedience as a matter of *attaining* one's initial salvation (1 Peter 4: 17; 1 John 2: 3-4). Complicating the matter even more is the fact that Paul appears to counter his own statements in Ephesians regarding works when he remarks on the necessity of keeping God's commands and obeying the gospel message (1 Corinthians 7: 19; Thessalonians 1: 8-9).

How can such seemingly incompatible statements within Scripture be reconciled? The only reasonable conclusion is that these various points are not contradictory. The obedience addressed in these verses is not the righteous works of which James wrote, but the obedient faith by which we receive grace. In his letter to the Thessalonians, Paul ties together the notion that those who do not know God are those who have failed to obey the gospel. Jesus mirrored this view regarding the importance of keeping His commands.

10. If you keep My commandments, you will abide in My love, just as I have kept My Father's commandments and abide in His love. (John 15: 10)

In the covenant of grace, the separation between Jew and Gentile that had persisted under the Mosaic Law was now abolished. Adherence to rules and regulations, such as existed under the Old Testament law, no longer defined man's relationship to God. Under the new covenant men could only approach God via the blood of Christ. We discover that Paul's letters to the Romans and Galatians mirror the sentiments concerning works of which he warned the Ephesians.

> And if by grace, then *it is* no longer of works; otherwise grace is no longer grace... (Romans 11: 6a)

> This only I want to learn from you: Did you receive the Spirit by the works of the law, or by the hearing of faith? (Galatians 3: 2)

The primary distinction between the dispensation of the law and the dispensation of grace is manifest. The manner in which man reached out to God under the Mosaic Law, with the many continuing rituals and sacrifices, was phenomenally different from how men would reach out to Him in the covenant of grace. In his epistles, Paul does not suggest that believers have no responsibility to keep the precepts of Christ in order to be saved, but that no one was saved by means of the law. Many passages in the Bible evince a call for each man and woman to act upon his faith by responding appropriately to the gospel message. Paul would teach nothing less.

> Circumcision is nothing and uncircumcision is nothing, but keeping God's commands *is what matters.* (1 Corinthians 7: 19)

> Neither circumcision nor uncircumcision means anything; what counts is a new creation. (Galatians 6: 15) - NIV

According to the apostle Paul, it is *'keeping God's commands'* that is vital to our Christian walk. That is what counts. Similarly, we discover the interchangeable personality of *keeping God's commandments* and *being reborn* in a parallel passage written to the Galatians. Whether or not one has been circumcised is once again deemed inconsequential, while that which really matters is whether one is a *new creation* (Galatians 6: 15). Can we say that Paul placed more emphasis on *obedience* or on a *new creation*? It seems the two elicit equal force here as obedience in Corinthians is rephrased in terms of rebirth/renewal in the Galatians text. The two thoughts are one. Who can deny, then, that short of obedience to the commands of God there is no regeneration?

Apostolic doctrine charges that salvation is unattainable short of obedience to the gospel (2 Thessalonians 1: 8; 1 Peter 4: 17). Thus, if the gospel message is something to be obeyed, there must be something within that message that *can* be obeyed. The gospel, as taught by the apostles, calls for action on the part of the believer in response to that message. Those actions (as opposed to works of merit) include repentance, confession, and baptism – in water. What separates these actions from deeds that do not have salvation value? It is faith in the death, burial, and resurrection of Jesus. The meritorious works suggested by Paul (Ephesians 2: 8-9) are distinct from those that fall under the umbrella of faith. Salvation by merit has no relationship to salvation through faithful obedience to God's precepts. Eternal life is not earned through baptism any more than it is earned through belief, repentance, or confession. Unlike obedience to the gospel that we perform within the arena of faith, works that are accomplished outside that realm are simply irrelevant to God's plan of salvation.

The Christians in Rome existed in a state of grace as opposed to living under the law[2] (Romans 6: 14). A man cannot reside in both camps. He may either live under the law or under grace. Those who lived under the law were considered *slaves of sin* while those living in grace Paul viewed as *slaves of righteousness* (Romans 6: 16). At one time, however, even those who now lived under grace had been under the law as slaves of sin. The fact that they no longer dwelt there can only lead to the conclusion that at some point in time a transformation had occurred.

Despite his clear teaching that earning salvation through works was impossible (Ephesians 2: 8-9), Paul explained to the Romans that salvation *did* come by obedience (Romans 6: 1-18). He told them that it was expressly through their obedience (in this instance he is specifically citing obedience in baptism) that they had escaped the law and found themselves within the fold of grace. Furthermore, they were under the law and slaves of sin *until* they obeyed the doctrine they were taught (v. 17), at which time they became slaves of righteousness (v. 18). Therefore, if this state of grace can be attained by obedience, but not by works, these two pursuits cannot be considered equals. Thus, a conscientious approach to Scripture demands that we acknowledge the difference that exists between the two. For this reason, the apostles consistently portray obedience to the gospel message as essential to salvation (Romans 6: 16-18; 10: 16; 2 Thessalonians 1: 8; 3: 14; Hebrews 5: 9; 1 Peter 1: 2; 3: 1; 4: 17) despite their insistence that salvation can never be earned.

In his first epistle, Peter provides penetrating insight into the value of baptism (1 Peter 3: 18-21), a passage already discussed at length. While Peter's discourse on the redemptive benefit of baptism is compelling, perhaps his most illuminating statement concerns his observation of the means by which baptism provides salvation. Rather than portraying the rite of baptism as a deed of merit through which we can earn our salvation, Peter explains that the effect of salvation in baptism is granted to us *'through the resurrection of Christ'* (1 Peter 3: 21). Yet the objective of a meritorious deed as a matter of salvation, as characterized by Paul (Ephesians 2: 8-9), is to circumvent the grace that is offered through Christ's death. That is what Paul condemned. Salvation in baptism achieves what meritorious works cannot since the entire focus in baptism is the death, burial, and resurrection by which grace is made available. Beasley-Murray, addressing Peter's proclamation that baptism saves (1 Peter 3: 21), demonstrates the fact that the source of the saving power of baptism is the resurrection of Christ:

> The chief lesson of this passage is its emphatic denial that the external elements of baptism constitute either its essence or its power. The cleansing in baptism is gained not through the application of water to the flesh but through the pledge of faith and obedience therein given to God, upon which the resurrection of Jesus Christ becomes a saving power to the individual concerned.[3]

One of the most effective metaphors in Scripture concerns the woman who touched the hem of Jesus' garment in order to be healed (Luke 8: 43-48). While we have no reason to doubt the authenticity of Luke's account, there is no denying the portraiture that can be derived from the story. The woman represents a lost world full of sickness – hemorrhaging with sin. Jesus is the only means by which healing (forgiveness/salvation) is possible. Just as the woman fought through the crowd to reach Jesus we, too, must overcome obstacles that would prevent us from turning to Him. When the woman reached out and touched Him (His garment) she was restored to a life without the sickness that had tormented her.

In like manner, when we reach out to Jesus we are provided newness of life absent the sins that had enslaved us. Yet, Jesus did not tell the woman that touching His garment had healed her, but that her faith had made her whole. The effort she put forth, fighting through the crowd in her weakened state and reaching out to touch Him despite the impediments she faced, does not detract from the fact that she was saved/healed by faith. On the contrary, her actions were the very means by which she was healed through faith. It was not the touching of the garment, but the work of God at that moment that healed her. So it is with baptism. Rather than diminishing salvation by grace through faith, our response in baptism demands the utmost of faith and it is the work of God at that moment by which we are saved.

Baptism Vs Works

Scripture itself distinguishes between baptism and the good deeds of a faithful man or woman. In His final words to the disciples, prior to His ascension, Jesus told them to, *'Go therefore and make disciples of all the nations, baptizing them in the name of the Father and of the Son and of the Holy Spirit'* (Matthew 28:19). Once they had accomplished these tasks of going, teaching, and baptizing, they were to instruct those who had been taught and baptized to *'observe all things that I have commanded you'* (Matthew 28:20). Jesus separates baptism from all other *things commanded* (works). Even repentance and confession, as important as these may be, are lacking in Jesus' final words. Baptism is presented, not in relationship with *all things commanded*, but as a distinct critical matter in the *making of disciples*. The apostles faithfully followed Jesus' lead in distinguishing between baptism and works. In that vein, Paul enlightened the Ephesians respecting the singularity of baptism that sets it apart from what may be considered righteous works.

> 4. *There* is one body and one Spirit, just as you were called in one hope of your calling; 5. one Lord, one faith, one baptism; 6. one God and Father of all, who *is* above all, and through all, and in you all. (Ephesians 4: 4-6)

Certain components of God's covenant are deemed vital in providing a sense of unity within the brotherhood. These include *one baptism* as well as *one body* (church), *one* (Holy) *Spirit*, *one hope*, *one Lord* (Jesus), *one faith*, and *one Father*. Such close association with these foundations of the faith offers some pretty impressive credentials for the force of baptism in God's plan. The notion that works are incapable of helping one attain salvation, a point made clear earlier in the epistle (Ephesians 2: 8-9), does not deter Paul from pointing to the significance of baptism in the same letter.

Baptism is portrayed as distinct from the works of the faithful Christian. The apostle effectively elevates this rite to a place of prominence that eclipses the good deeds of the Christian life to which we are called. At some point Scripture identifies each of these unique figures as vital to our salvation. For instance, Jesus is Savior specifically for those who are members of His body (Ephesians 5: 23). We are told that the Holy Spirit is the seal of our salvation (2 Corinthians 1: 22). It is through faith in Jesus that we accept God's offer of grace (Ephesians 2: 8). Additionally, Paul explained to the Romans that we are saved by hope of things yet unseen (Romans 8: 24). God the Father sent His Son as sacrifice for our sins (John 3: 16). Finally, baptism is the time designated by God that we should receive forgiveness of sins (Acts 2: 38). Paul distinguishes baptism here in a manner not proffered either repentance or confession.

An unqualified contrast specifically between meritorious deeds and faithful obedience in baptism is established in Paul's letter to Titus as he discusses how men are saved. He told Titus, in a deliberate reference to baptism, '*...not by works of righteousness which we have done, but according to His mercy He saved us, through the washing of regeneration and renewing of the Holy Spirit.*' (Titus 3: 4-5). Bible scholars who teach that baptism is a *work of righteousness* struggle heavily with this verse. Most will (reluctantly) acknowledge the reference to baptism, but still emphatically deny that '*He saved us, through the washing of regeneration (baptism).*' Yet cleansing through baptism is a principle wholly in line with New Testament teaching. The abundance of other Scripture identifying the redemptive role of baptism (Matthew 29: 19; Mark 16: 16; Acts 2: 38; 22: 16; Romans 6: 1-5; Galatians 3: 27; Colossians 2: 12; Hebrews 10: 22; 1 Peter 3: 21; et al) simply impugn the view that it is a meritorious work.

Baptism is a command of God linked to two specific promises – forgiveness of sins and the gift of the Holy Spirit – which, in turn, are tied to salvation throughout the New Testament. Peter confirmed Jesus' words from the Great Commission concerning baptism (Matthew 28: 19-20) on the Day of Pentecost when the Jews in Jerusalem heard and responded to the message being spoken. The people inquired as to what they should do in response to Peter's words (Acts 2: 37). It is somewhat curious that these people so long ago, on the occasion of the gospel first being declared, realized that they must *do* something in response to the message. Two thousand years later, with their account readily available as witness, many maintain resolutely that no such response is necessary. Even more interesting is Peter's answer in that he does, indeed, tell them what they must do: first they must repent, and then they are to be baptized (Acts 2: 37-38).

Peter's instructions on the Day of Pentecost are not only valuable regarding what he explained were necessary steps to salvation, but with respect to what he so noticeably omitted. He did not say, *'You do not need to do anything, since Jesus already took care of everything on the cross.'* Nor are statements such as, *'If you believe you are already saved,'* or, *'Ask Jesus into your life and say a prayer, and you will be saved,'* part of the gospel message delivered on that day. Yet these are the instructions offered by many teachers in our modern age concerning what one must do to attain salvation. Peter, however, responded to these men based upon Jesus' command. He told them to repent and be baptized.

Baptism – An Act of Man or God?

In contrast to work performed by us, Paul perceives the work that is performed in baptism as work that God accomplishes specifically through our faith. Writing to the Colossians, he affirms that baptism is not an act of man, but a spiritual act in physical form through which God does *His* work (Colossians 2: 11-12). We are buried and raised with Christ in baptism. It is something that occurs *'through faith in the working of God.'* Our sins are washed away in baptism. That washing away of sins is an act of God, not man. Baptism, then, is an act of God to which men submit (passively) and cannot justifiably be considered a meritorious work of man.

A special point should be made regarding Paul's letter to the Colossians. While he spends some time reviewing baptism and the role it plays in God's plan, his statements just prior to these remarks are equally important.

> 4. Now this I say lest anyone should deceive you with persuasive words. 5. For though I am absent in the flesh, yet I am with you in spirit, rejoicing to see your *good* order and the steadfastness of your faith in Christ. 6. As you therefore have received Christ Jesus the Lord, so walk in Him, 7. rooted and built up in Him and established in the faith, as you have been taught, abounding in it with thanksgiving. 8. Beware lest anyone cheat you through philosophy and empty deceit, according to the tradition of men, according to the basic principles of the world, and not according to Christ. 9. For in Him dwells all the fullness of the Godhead bodily; 10. and you are complete in Him, who is the head of all principality and power. (Colossians 2: 4-10)

This lesson on baptism provides a clear sense that, if there are *'persuasive words that are deceiving,'* or a *'philosophy through which they may be cheated,'* or *'traditions of men,'* or *'basic principles of the world,'* baptism is not among them. These *'traditions of men,'* whether of drinks or festivals or Sabbaths, are discussed through the balance of the chapter. They do not entail baptism. Moreover, our symbolic death in baptism is defined as the moment of separation from rules of the law (Colossians 2: 20-22). The cry that baptism is a work of man is clearly refuted as Paul draws a clear distinction in his words to the Colossians between the *'traditions of men'* and the celebration of the death, burial, and resurrection of Christ in baptism.

The false doctrine of salvation by works, which contradicts the biblical teaching of salvation by grace, suggests that a man could actually offer to God something of such value that he might be worthy of eternal life. Yet nothing within the design of baptism suggests that God is indebted to us in any way. We bring nothing to baptism but a repentant heart and a desire to have our sins forgiven. This does not mean that we are entitled to forgiveness. Still, Scripture teaches us that God has promised to forgive the repentant believer at the time of baptism (Acts 2: 38) – and we know that God keeps His promises.

The debate concerning whether baptism is a human work or a spiritual act of obedience bears an uncanny likeness to a discussion between Jesus and the chief priests and elders regarding the baptism performed by John the Baptist. Jesus asked them bluntly, *"The baptism of John – where was it from? Was it from heaven or from men?"* (Matthew 21: 25). We would do well to ask ourselves this same question in conjunction with water baptism today. If we could honestly answer that Christian baptism is of human design, a much more reasonable defense could be offered that it is man's flagrant attempt to somehow *earn grace* (an obvious oxymoron). If, however, baptism is of heavenly design, it is not our prerogative to deem irrelevant a ceremony that Scripture ties directly to our salvation (1 Peter 3: 21).

Faith – Man's Responsibility

Man is saved by grace. Grace alone, however, is not the fullness of God's plan. Each one is called upon to take defined steps to accept this grace. That involves faith. Grace is God's part of the plan of salvation while faith is that portion that man must fulfill. Therefore, the question is not whether man has any role in the salvation process, since a man clearly must have faith; the real question that must be answered is, *'What is involved in this faith that is man's charge in God's plan?'* This is where men have varied ideas and opinions. Those who would have us accept that faith means a person must only believe Jesus is the Son of God will cite the following Scriptures in support of this position:

> And this is the will of Him who sent Me, that everyone who sees the Son and believes in Him may have everlasting life. (John 6: 40)

> So they said, "Believe on the Lord Jesus Christ, and you will be saved, you and your household." (Acts 16: 31)

Apostolic doctrine, however, cannot be determined by selecting certain passages and deeming them to be the complete message. This is why the Psalmist stated, *'The entirety of Your word is truth'* (Psalm 119: 160). The NASB puts it a little more precisely by stating, *'The sum of Thy word is truth.'* We must consider the *sum* of God's Word if we are to understand His ways. The call to obedience as a matter of salvation that is presented throughout Scripture is no less relevant than biblical instructions regarding the necessity of faith, and cannot be neglected. We find that the gift of the indwelling of the Holy Spirit, promised to us through faith, is conferred specifically upon the obedient.

> And we are His witnesses to these things, and *so* also *is* the Holy Spirit whom God has given to those who obey Him. (Acts 5: 32)

> Now he who keeps His commandments abides in Him, and He in him. And by this we know that He abides in us, by the Spirit whom He has given us. (1 John 3: 24)

God bestows the gift of the Holy Spirit upon those who obey Him. The Holy Spirit abides in those who keep His commandments. Thus, obedience to God must influence our receiving the indwelling of the Holy Spirit. To what obedience does God call us in order to be afforded such an honor? We can ascertain that it is obedience to the very precepts He has commanded us to keep in order for us to receive the promised Holy Spirit – repentance and baptism (Acts 2: 38).

Another Gospel

The presumption that baptism is a deed of merit is a relatively recent development historically speaking. While the church has existed for nearly two thousand years, this view has become popular only within the last five hundred years. Yet, it is a view that has led many to take a pugnacious attitude toward both baptism and those who teach that it does, indeed, have redemptive value. In fact, many openly proclaim that any teaching concerning the efficacy of baptism actually constitutes *preaching another gospel*, thus eternally condemning those who would participate.

> 6. I marvel that you are turning away so soon from Him who called you in the grace of Christ, to a different gospel, 7 which is not another; but there are some who trouble you and want to pervert the gospel of Christ. 8. But even if we, or an angel from heaven, preach any other gospel to you than what we have preached to you, let him be accursed. 9. As we have said before, so now I say again, if anyone preached any other gospel to you than what you have received, let him be accursed. (Galatians 1: 6-9)

Later in this very epistle Paul identifies baptism as the time when we *'put on Christ'* (Galatians 3: 27). It seems that if this was what he so effectively taught the Galatians at the time of this writing, and then later changed his doctrine concerning baptism as many suggest, he would be condemning himself by his very own words in verse eight above.

Still others maintain that if baptism is necessary for salvation, it means that millions of believers are not saved; therefore it must not be a requirement. This, however, is not a position based upon scriptural teaching, but is an emotional lament suggesting that such a tenet must be unfair if, by its mandate, many are lost. However, biblical doctrine is to be founded upon the words of Scripture rather than our own personal wishes. Still, we would do well to consider these views in proper perspective.

Throughout the first fifteen hundred years of the existence of the church, the general understanding of apostolic teaching held that baptism was the moment a man received forgiveness of sins and the gift of the Holy Spirit. This was a doctrine handed down by the apostles and postulated by believers everywhere. The first view stated above, which claims that teaching baptism as a path to forgiveness of sins and salvation is equivalent to *preaching another gospel*, invariably assumes that until the early sixteenth century the true gospel of Christ was not taught by anyone. This view, by default, also implies that no one prior to Huldrych Zwingli, in the 1520's, comprehended the teaching of the apostles concerning baptism, including those who received teaching directly from the lips of the apostles. As a matter of fact, Zwingli made this very claim, stating unequivocally that all previous theologians were wrong in their assessment of the role of baptism and that he alone had come to a true understanding of the apostles' doctrine.

> "In this matter of baptism -- if I may be pardoned for saying it -- I can only conclude that all the doctors have been in error from the time of the apostles. . . . All the doctors have ascribed to the water a power which it does not have and the holy apostles did not teach."[4]

Those, then, who refute the view that baptism is for the forgiveness of sins find the foundation of their beliefs not in Scripture, but in the works and writings of Huldrych Zwingli nearly fifteen hundred years after the establishment of the church.

If it is true, as the Bible teaches, that baptism is essential for salvation, no doubt millions of believers, those who have not been baptized, are sadly lost. Conversely, however, if we accept the premise that teaching baptism as a matter of salvation is *another gospel*, and if those who willingly teach another gospel are condemned, we are faced with another serious dilemma. The only reasonable conclusion is that from the beginning of the church until the time of the Reformation Movement, a period spanning roughly fifteen hundred years, none were saved.

We know that Peter recognized a parallel between the waters of the flood and the waters of baptism (1 Peter 3: 21), stating that baptism is the *antitype* of the flood. The NIV states that the waters of the flood *symbolized* baptism. In truth, Peter's words may be considered as prophetic as they are profound. Given the predominant view of baptism in modern times, its identification with the waters of the flood may be considered disturbing and perhaps even a little eerie. Within the world of religion today the vast majority vigorously deny the redemptive character of immersion even though it is plainly revealed in Scripture. According to Peter, in the days of Noah it was not the modest number who would be saved (eight) or the multitudes that would be lost that determined God's actions (2 Peter 2: 4-5). Noah and his family were saved due to their faithful obedience to the clear commands of God. Men today will undoubtedly be saved in the same manner.

Keeping God's Commandments Is Essential

For those who are so fervently opposed to the idea that some kind of response, or action, may be required from an individual for his/her salvation, please consider the following verses. These articulate the fact that one *cannot be saved* without keeping God's commandments.

> Not everyone who says to Me, 'Lord, Lord,' shall enter the kingdom of heaven, but he who does the will of My Father in heaven. (Matthew 7: 21)

> He who has my commandments and keeps them, it is he who loves Me. (John 14: 21)

> 5. But in accordance with your hardness and your impenitent heart you are treasuring up for yourself wrath in the day of wrath and revelation of the righteous judgment of God, 6. who *"will render to each one according to his deeds."* (Romans 2: 5-6)

> 16. Do you not know that to whom you present yourselves slaves to obey, you are that one's slaves whom you obey, whether of sin *leading* to death, or of obedience *leading* to righteousness? 17. But God be thanked that *though* you were slaves of sin, yet you obeyed from the heart that form of doctrine to which you were delivered. 18. And having been set free from sin, you became slaves of righteousness. (Romans 6: 16-18)

> But they have not all obeyed the gospel... (Romans 10: 16)

> And having been perfected, He became the author of eternal salvation to all who obey Him. (Hebrews 5: 9)

> But be doers of the word, and not hearers only, deceiving yourselves. (James 1: 22)
>
> Since you have purified your souls in obeying the truth through the Spirit... (1 Peter 1: 22)
>
> For the time *has come* for judgment to begin at the house of God; and if *it begins* with us first, what will *be* the end of those who do not obey the gospel of God? (1 Peter 4: 17)
>
> 3. Now by this we know that we know Him, if we keep His commandments. 4. He who says, "I know Him," and does not keep His commandments, is a liar and the truth is not in him. (1 John 2: 3-4)
>
> Now he who keeps His commandments abides in Him, and He in him. (1 John 3: 24)

Many men struggle heavily with the idea that God has established conditions for receiving His grace. Such conditions, they say, tend to diminish the characterization of grace as a gift. If receiving grace is contingent upon any action performed by man – or in the case of baptism, an act to which man submits – then it can no longer be considered a gift. The receiving of grace based upon a man meeting certain provisions that God has set forth suggests that God owes salvation to all who complete the task. Yet the grace that God bestows as a result of men keeping His precepts is simply His fulfillment of a promise. It is not a matter of debt.

A striking example of how God links faith with works to accomplish His will is provided in the story of Jericho. God told Joshua, *'I have given Jericho into your hands'* (Joshua 6: 2). Nothing the Israelites could do would earn them the city of Jericho. It was a gift God was giving them. Yet, while it was a gift in that it was *given*, their receiving of Jericho was conditional. The Israelites were required to march around the city six days in a row. On the seventh day the priests were to blow their trumpets and the people would shout, at which time the walls of the city would crumble (Joshua 6: 3-5). Of course, the marching and the trumpets and the shouting did not collapse the walls, nor did these actions in any way earn the Israelites a right to enter the city. Still, their possession of the city was contingent upon fulfillment of God's command. So it is with salvation. While it is a gift, in that it cannot be earned, it is still conditioned upon our faithfulness to the precepts He has established.

If God expects nothing from man for redemption, as many maintain, what is it that separates those who are saved from those who are lost? If we say it is the fact that those who are saved are forgiven of their sins, this begs the question, exactly *why* are they forgiven? If it is through belief, repentance, confession, and the Sinner's Prayer, the saved have done something – performed some action or fulfilled some proviso – in response to the gospel message *in order to be saved*.

Contrary to the predominant view that salvation comes through belief/faith only, if we are completely honest in our approach to Scripture, we will recognize that the New Testament writers unswervingly portray salvation as a matter of faithful obedience to the gospel message. This, rather than faith only, is unquestionably the prevailing theme of the Bible. Redemption is not a matter of meritorious works, but it is undeniably a matter of obedience, including submission to the precept of baptism. If we deny this we find ourselves challenging the inspired instructions offered by Peter, Paul, James, and John as well as Jesus Himself. Those, then, who deny baptism as a redemptive matter in response to the gospel transcend the biblical teaching of salvation without works and present a doctrine that teaches salvation without obedience.

God's Employment of Men in Administering Baptism
The fact that God employs the hands of men in the administration of baptism is often seen an indication of the purely physical nature of this rite, making it a human work. However, historically God has consistently turned to men in the administration of His commands. We discover that this is especially true of baptism.

The various baptisms depicted in Scripture reveal a harmonious relationship between the efficacy of the baptism being performed and man's active role in its implementation. Noah did not bring the waters of the flood; yet we cannot help but notice that the salvation of Noah and his family came through the work of his hands as he built the ark, a complement to God's work in sending the rain. While the purpose of the water was to destroy, the work performed by Noah was the means by which he and his family were lifted to safety. God certainly could have saved Noah without the ark, but He wanted Noah to participate in the saving of his family. In a similar fashion, He has decided to have baptism administered by the hands of men. He has chosen to have men participate in the saving of men

As the Israelites were *'baptized into Moses'* at the crossing of the sea (1 Corinthians 10: 2), God worked through Moses to rescue them from their life of slavery. It was a baptism where God sought Moses' assistance in freeing the Israelites. Additionally, Jesus received water baptism at the hands of John the Baptist. According to Matthew's account of the event, God the Father chose the occasion to extend His blessing upon the ministry of God the Son (Matthew 3: 16-17). John provided the physical component of immersion in water while God the Father supplied the spiritual effect as the Spirit descended and He voiced His approval.

Perhaps most significant, however, is the relationship between the crucifixion of Christ, considered a baptism of the highest order, and the meaning of that baptism. This was a baptism administered by humans in that it was men who crucified Him. Men participated in the physical aspect of this baptism (the crucifixion) while God administered the spiritual side, as Jesus rose from the grave. Yet the involvement of men seems to have given this baptism, through which eternal life was made possible, even greater meaning. God intended for this baptism to be personal. We nailed our own sins to the cross (2 Corinthians 5: 21). When we as men are forgiven of our trespasses, not only are we no longer guilty of past sins, but we are also united with Him personally at that time (Romans 6: 5). No other baptism offered this kind of intimacy. Paul focuses on the very personal nature of the efficacy of Christian baptism in the sixth chapter of Romans. While the flood and the Red Sea represent corporate baptism, as a number of people were rescued, the significance of Christian baptism is that it is a personal matter between a man or woman and God as each one shares in the crucifixion of Christ.

* * * * *

In New Testament times, baptism was not considered an act of achievement, but a spiritual experience that was common for all believers (Acts 2: 41; Romans 6: 1-4; 1 Corinthians 12: 13; Galatians 3: 27; Colossians 2: 11-12; Titus 3: 5; Hebrews 10: 22). Despite the many voices proclaiming it today, the apostles never suggested that baptism could or should be considered a human work. When it is presented in the New Testament, water baptism is steadfastly portrayed as a matter of man's response to the gospel message. If men wish to teach baptism as a human accomplishment, the burden is on these individuals to ascribe Scripture to this claim. Without scriptural support for such a doctrine, however, we are obliged to accept the words of Jesus and the apostles concerning the efficacy of the rite of baptism.

NOTES FOR CHAPTER 11

1. Many look to Martin Luther as a great advocate of salvation through faith only. While this is certainly a concept taught by Luther, his view of salvation through faith only, absent works of men, stands in stark contrast to the modern-day perspective regarding faith without works. Luther understood that the precepts of God, such as baptism in water, were not works of men, but works of God without which man could not attain salvation. Following are some of his remarks regarding baptism:

> [I] affirm that Baptism is no human trifle, but that it was established by God Himself. Moreover, He earnestly and solemnly commanded that we must be baptized or we shall not be saved. No one is to think that it is an optional matter like putting on a red coat. It is of greatest importance that we hold Baptism in high esteem as something splendid and glorious. The reason why we are striving and battling so strenuously for this view of Baptism is that the world nowadays is full of sects that loudly proclaim that Baptism is merely an external form and that external forms are useless.... Although Baptism is indeed performed by human hands, yet it is truly God's own action. Luther, Martin (1978), _Luther's Large Catechism_, (Saint Louis, MO: Concordia) pp. 98-99.

> But our know-it-alls, the new spirit people, claim that faith alone saves and that human works and outward forms contribute nothing to this. We answer: It is of course true that nothing in us does it except faith, as we shall hear later. But these blind leaders of the blind refuse to see that faith must have something in which it believes, that is, something it clings to, something on which to plant its feet and into which to sink its roots. Thus faith clings to the water and believes Baptism to be something in which there is pure salvation and life, not through the water, as I have emphasized often enough, but because God's name is joined to it.... It follows from this that whoever rejects Baptism rejects God's word, faith, and the Christ who directs us to Baptism and binds us to it. Luther, Martin (1978), _Luther's Large Catechism_, (Saint Louis, MO: Concordia) pp. 101-102.

Prior to the time of Luther, perhaps the one man who stood out as an advocate of salvation through faith alone was Augustine of Hippo (354-430 AD). His remarks here reflect that very view:

> All the blessings which God hath bestowed upon man are of his mere grace, bounty, or favour; his free, undeserved favour; favour altogether undeserved; man having no claim to the least of his mercies. It was free grace that "formed man of the dust of the ground, and breathed into him a living soul," and stamped on that soul the image of God, and "put all things under his feet." The same free grace continues to us, at this day, life, and breath, and all things. For there is nothing we are, or have, or do, which can deserve the least thing at

> God's hand. "All our works, Thou, O God, hast wrought in us." These, therefore, are so many more instances of free mercy: and whatever righteousness may be found in man, this is also the gift of God. Preached at St. Mary's, Oxford, before the University, on June 18, 1738.

Yet, as with Luther, Augustine's understanding of salvation through faith only did not suggest that the precepts of God were unnecessary, but that they were essential with respect to salvation.

> "There are two REGENERATIONS...the one ACCORDING TO FAITH, which takes place in the present life BY MEANS OF BAPTISM; the other according to the flesh, which shall be accomplished...by means of the great and final judgment." Augustine, Book 20, Chapter 6 [commenting on the Revelation:].

2. The law to which Paul refers in his letter to the Ephesians may not be limited strictly to the law of Moses, but to law in general, as men are held accountable for those laws to which they are subject. Adherence to any law is ineffectual when it comes to righteousness and/or salvation; otherwise salvation could be *earned* without the blood of Christ. No matter how much an individual obeys the law, he will fall short. If, then, salvation relied upon man's obedience to law – any law – no one would be saved. Thus, salvation is available only through the blood of Christ.

3. G. R. Beasley-Murray, Baptism in the New Testament, William B. Eerdmans Publishing Company, 1994, p. 262.

4. Huldreigh Zwingli, "Of Baptism," in Zwingli and Bullinger, "Library of Christian Classics," Vol. 24, ed. And tr. G. W. Bromiley (Philadelphia Westminster Press, 1953), p. 153.

Chapter XII
Baptism Vs Special Circumstances

What If Baptism Is Not Possible?

Occasionally someone will challenge the necessity of baptism by suggesting circumstances when this kind of precept would *seem* unfair. For instance, imagine that a soldier on the battlefield wishes to accept Jesus as his Savior but, due to obvious circumstances, has no opportunity for baptism. They reason that, if the soldier died on that battlefield, God would not be so unjust as to deny him/her eternal life for failure to submit to baptism when there was no opportunity for it at the time. The same question might also arise regarding those who, on a deathbed, want to follow Jesus but are simply physically unable to participate in baptism.

Of course, invoking a situation that involves an individual who *cannot* be baptized does not address the salvation or condemnation of the person who simply denies God's call to baptism, which is the focus of this book. Nor is such a case suitable to challenge baptism as a condition of salvation. The notion that God might have compassion for someone who *cannot* be baptized demonstrates nothing. It is simply an attempt to persuade us that if a convincing exclusion to the command for baptism can be unearthed, then we are somehow obliged to accept that there is no such command.

Human laws are written with the intent that they should be applied evenly and universally. Still, who among us does not understand that, while speed limit laws are to be obeyed, exemption might apply under exceptional conditions, such as rushing someone to the hospital in a life or death situation? The punishment for taking the life of another human being is severe, yet we understand that in the case of self-defense, a life or death situation, the circumstances overshadow the law. While we recognize these exceptions, the laws still apply to everyone who does not find himself/herself in such an extreme position. If we as men, created in the image of God, can discern these things, surely we can expect even greater wisdom from God. This is not meant as an endorsement of the view that God makes these exceptions, but as an explanation that an exemption should not be construed as license to ignore God's command.

Ironically, there is a fully unintended upshot from the scenarios presented here. Given the extreme setting where water is inaccessible in a catastrophic situation, the subtle implication is that the person involved *would be baptized* if at all possible. This does not disavow, but sustains the significance of baptism. While the point is to refute the necessity of baptism, the suggestion that God would make an exception for someone *desiring to obey* is a clandestine acknowledgment of baptism's importance. Therefore, if God would make such an exception, the command for baptism would invariably apply to those to whom water is accessible. Nonetheless, we should take note that Paul, in his letter to the Romans, addresses the fact that some may never have the opportunity to partake in the covenant that is established by the blood of Christ.

> 11. For there is no partiality with God. 12. For as many as have sinned without law will also perish without law, and as many as have sinned in the law will be judged by the law 13. (for not the hearers of the law *are* just in the sight of God, but the doers of the law will be justified; 14. for when Gentiles, who do not have the law, by nature do the things in the law, these, although not having the law, are a law unto themselves, 15. who show the work of the law written in their hearts, their conscience also bearing witness, and between themselves *their* thoughts accusing or else excusing *them*) 16. in the day when God will judge the secrets of men by Jesus Christ, according to my gospel. (Romans 2: 11-16)

It is honestly difficult to discern if the scenario of the soldier on the battlefield, or any similar situation, is addressed within the scope of this text. Whether one who has perhaps previously rejected God at a time when he/she did have the capacity to meet Him in baptism might, in the end, bypass that precept with a sincere heart when baptism is not possible, is a determination that men cannot make. What we can say unequivocally, however, is that Scripture offers no such exemption. Still, Paul delivers a clear message that God views differently those who hear and reject His precepts and those who never hear.

At best we can only acknowledge that situations such as these are not addressed in Scripture. Perhaps the reason for this omission is simply that God does not want us to agonize over the person whose circumstances might prevent him/her from obedience. After all, in such a setting we can have no effect. Therefore, they are His concern alone. Our role is simply to teach the gospel message to those on whom we can have some saving influence.

The Day of Pentecost and the Gentile Conversion

Certain narratives in the Bible are often the focus of those who seek to refute the water/Spirit relationship of baptism. The Day of Pentecost is one such case. On that day the Holy Spirit was poured out (Acts 2: 1-4). The assertion is that surely this *must* be the baptism prophesied by John. This *must* be the baptism that saves. Yet, it is in Acts 2: 38 rather than Acts 2: 1-4 that the word *baptism*, as a command of God, is first associated with the reception of the Holy Spirit. Nor was this outpouring of the Spirit the baptism that was commanded by Jesus to His disciples (Matthew 28: 19), since His direction was for them to baptize others – men baptizing men.

The story of Cornelius and the other Gentiles who were with him in Ceasarea is also central in the debate surrounding water baptism (Acts 10: 1 – 11: 18). This incident, shoulder to shoulder with the experience of Pentecost, is considered key by those who reject the salvation value of water baptism. What is very telling, however, is the reason that these passages are at the heart of the discussion; it is because these are the only recorded instances in the church age when anyone received the Holy Spirit prior to water baptism.

These incidents are fundamental to the debate, but not in the manner most often noted. What makes these occasions significant is the unrivaled magnitude of the events. A mighty wind accompanied by tongues of fire cannot be considered a normal circumstance in either pre- or post-Pentecost Jerusalem. Pentecost was pivotal in that God's new covenant came into being. It was a moment greater than the day God established His covenant with Abraham or provided the Ten Commandments to the Israelites, for this covenant was established by the blood of Christ.

In order to portray these episodes as representative of the manner in which men in the first century received the Holy Spirit, a marked skewing of Scripture must take place. Either incidentally or intentionally, the biblical fact that no others received the Spirit in this manner must be overlooked. For instance, on the Day of Pentecost, in the second chapter of Acts, we find no indication that anyone, save those in the house where the Spirit was poured out, experienced the same phenomenon or received spiritual gifts (e.g., speaking in tongues). In the accounts of the Ethiopian eunuch (Acts 8: 26-39), Lydia (Acts 16: 13-15), and the Philippian jailer (Acts 16: 25-34), no such manifestation of the Spirit is noted. Not even in the report of Saul's conversion (Acts 9: 1-19) is any such phenomenon recorded.

An examination of the conversion experiences of the Samaritans (Acts 8: 1-17) and the Ephesians (Acts 19: 1-7) reveals that the Holy Spirit did not *fall upon* them, and no spiritual gifts were witnessed, until an apostle had laid hands on them. Upon their submission to baptism it is not unreasonable to expect, given the principles of baptism, that these men and women would have been saved and received the gift (*indwelling*) of the Spirit prior to the touch of the apostles' hands. Peter proclaimed on the Day of Pentecost that the promises of forgiveness and the gift of the Spirit were for everyone who repented and submitted to baptism, including *'all who are afar off'* (Acts 2: 39). This would seem to include the Samaritans as well as anyone upon whom the apostles did not lay their hands. This was surely true of Lydia and others where no supernatural gifts are evident. Based upon the information available to us, we can only conclude that the manifestation of the Spirit on these two occasions (Pentecost and Ceasarea) was not the normal manner by which men would receive the Spirit, but the greatest of exceptions. Additionally, we cannot ignore the fact that these occasions involved apostles. Their agency for the distribution of miraculous works of the Spirit in the first century is significant to these events and must not be overlooked.

Pointing to markedly extraordinary events such as these and concluding that they are the manner by which all men are saved, when they clearly are not, is a questionable approach to developing scriptural doctrine. Furthermore, while many have adopted the stance that water baptism is a *sign* of salvation, these two occasions indicate that it was not water baptism, but the outpouring of the Spirit, along with the accompanying tongues, that served as a sign to others that God was present. This is confirmed as Paul wrote to the Christians at Corinth concerning gifts of the Spirit.

> Therefore tongues are for a sign, not for those who believe but to unbelievers… (1 Corinthians 14: 22)

On the Day of Pentecost this served as a sign to those who had traveled to Jerusalem for the festivities. The members of the crowd were unbelievers until they heard the apostles speak in tongues. In Caesarea, the outpouring of the Spirit was clearly intended for Peter and those who were with him so that they would recognize the handiwork of God and understand His plans for the Gentiles. Peter was unsure that Christianity was for Gentiles until God offered witness on their behalf by bestowing them with the Spirit and they, too, spoke in tongues.

It appears that the events of Pentecost and the conversion of the Gentiles were moments of God's miraculous intervention, as discussed in the Preface of this book, meant to convey a message to those who witnessed these events – lessons we are able to see in retrospect. For this reason, it is generally ill-advised to attempt to establish doctrine from passages with narrative rather that instructional character. The uniqueness of these events prohibits ideological conclusions. Just as they were characteristically unique, we understand from Scripture that they were also purposefully unique. Pentecost unveiled the Holy Spirit and the authority of the apostles while Caesarea affirmed God's plan for the Gentiles. These episodes must be recognized for their distinction rather than reasoning that they somehow reflect common experience.

From Saul to Paul

As Saul of Tarsus journeyed to Damascus in search of Christ's followers, the Lord intercepted him (Acts 9: 1-19). A bright light blinded Saul as the Lord introduced Himself and questioned him regarding his persecution of the church. Following the instructions given to him, Saul had those men who were with him lead him to Damascus where he would *'...be told what you must do.'* Three days of prayer and fasting ensued as Saul sought answers to some deep and soul-searching questions.

> 17. And Ananias went his way and entered the house, and laying his hands on him he said, "Brother Saul, the Lord Jesus, who appeared to you on the road as you came, has sent me that you may receive your sight and be filled with the Holy Spirit." 18. Immediately there fell from his eyes *something* like scales, and he received his sight at once; and he arose and was baptized. (Acts 9: 17-18)

> 12. Then a certain Ananias, a devout man according to the law, having a good testimony with all the Jews who dwelt *there*, 13. came to me; and he said to me, "Brother Saul, receive your sight." And at that same hour I looked up at him. 14. Then he said, "The God of your fathers has

chosen you that you should know His will, and see the Just one, and hear the voice of his mouth. 15. For you will be his witness to all men of what you have seen and heard. 16. And now, why are you waiting? Arise and be baptized, and wash away your sins, calling on the name of the Lord." (Acts 22: 12-16)

God sent a reluctant Ananias to provide answers for Saul. Other than the fact that Ananias was a disciple, little is known of this man. It is also unknown whether he had received the spiritual gift of healing through the hands of the apostles or if the healing of Saul was a singular event in his life. Indicating to Saul that God had sent him so the he could regain his sight and receive the Holy Spirit, he then laid his hands on Saul and his sight was restored. Saul, when his sight had returned, was immediately baptized as instructed by Ananias.

Many theorists point to these accounts of the conversion of Saul and draw conclusions that are not reflected in the text, hypothesizing, for instance, that Saul was actually saved on the Road to Damascus when the Lord met him. Yet a thorough examination of the text reveals that this claim completely oversteps the narrative. Saul addressing Jesus as *Lord* during the encounter cannot be construed as salvation. When he initially addressed Him as *Lord*, it was in the form of an inquiry regarding the identity of this powerful being as he said, *'Who are You, Lord?'* (Acts 9: 5) This cannot be considered submission to Christ since he did not know to whom he was speaking. Upon learning the identity of his accuser, Saul simply asked, *'Lord, what do You want me to do?'* (Acts 9: 6) Within this question, while there is a sense of submission, the impression is that Saul knew he was facing God. The passage offers no indication that he was saved – only that he wished to know what was expected of him. His demeanor seems to be one of concern and foreboding as he fasted for three days. Contrasted against others, such as Cornelius and the eunuch, who rejoiced in their salvation, there is little doubt that salvation for Saul was yet to come.

As Paul (Saul) reflects on his conversion (Acts 22: 6-17), the essence of the narrative is that it was after he had received his sight that Ananias proceeded to explain to him the message of the gospel and what God expected from him. Concluding that he was granted salvation during his encounter on the road when the narrative plainly reveals that he had neither heard the gospel message or received forgiveness of sins until he met with Ananias in

Damascus three days later extends the boundaries of biblical analysis beyond reasonable limits.

An additional claim, that Saul received the Holy Spirit at the time that he regained his sight as Ananias laid hands on him, is also absent from the text. We are not told that Saul received the Spirit when Ananias laid hands on him. We are told only that he regained his sight at that time. Concluding that he received the Spirit at the same time eclipses the narrative.

In order to reach the conclusion that Saul received the Holy Spirit at the moment he received his sight, the text of the passage must be cast aside. The twofold mission of Ananias' presence was that Saul might recover his sight *and* that he might be filled with the Holy Spirit. The first portion of this mission was fulfilled as Ananias laid hands on Saul and his sight was restored. Having regained his sight, Ananias instructed him that he should be baptized. We understand from Acts 2: 38 that the Spirit was to be received by those who were baptized. We find nothing in the narrative that suggests that this principle would not apply equally to Saul. Consequently, we can reason that he would have received the Spirit at the time of his baptism in accord with scriptural instruction. This would have constituted fulfillment of Ananias' dual mission.

Finally, that Saul's sins were washed away by *calling on the name of the Lord*, independent from the faithful act of baptism is, at best, a precarious rendering of the text. Since Scripture teaches that sins are washed away at the time of baptism (Acts 2: 38), the view that it was some kind of *calling*, absent submission to *baptism*, that washed away his sins would contradict the association that has already been provided in Scripture between baptism and forgiveness. Ananias' point concerning *washing* allies much more cleanly with the waters of baptism than with what many insist is Paul's verbal plea to God for forgiveness. While confessing Jesus as Lord is deemed critical to salvation (Romans 10: 10), in itself it is not considered the moment of forgiveness in any passage. However, invoking the Lord's name in baptism as a matter of calling on Him, to which the context here clearly points, simply connects the *calling* to the *baptism* in which Saul's sins would be forgiven. Submission to baptism is portrayed as the very manner by which Saul called on the name of the Lord.

Once again, the incident with Saul on the Road to Damascus was a matter of divine revelation that was designed specifically to convert him into an apostle to the Gentiles. Scripture offers this as the sole reason for God's intervention (Acts 22: 14-15). We cannot derive a doctrine of salvation without baptism from this episode since Scripture offers no claim that Saul was saved prior to baptism. In fact, we have a wealth of evidence that this was not the case. What we can glean from the Damascus experience is a better understanding of the growth and dynamics of the early church as Paul was sent to minister to the Gentiles. Instances of miraculous intervention such as this are simply not intended to provide us with doctrinal instruction.

The Thief on the Cross

> 39. Then one of the criminals who were hanged blasphemed Him, saying, "If You are the Christ, save Yourself and us." 40. But the other, answering, rebuked him, saying, "Do you not even fear God, seeing you are under the same condemnation? 41. And we indeed justly, for we receive the due reward of our deeds; but this Man has done nothing wrong." 42. Then he said to Jesus, "Lord, remember me when You come into Your kingdom." 43. And Jesus said to him, "Assuredly, I say to you, today you will be with Me in Paradise." (Luke 23: 39-43)

Most discussions concerning baptism as a condition of salvation seem to eventually drift to the topic of the thief on the cross. Often, the cry is, *I want to be saved like the thief on the cross!* What those making this petition fail to realize is that the only means to accomplish this begins with a reversal of time by roughly two thousand years. It then involves their painstaking death in a manner that was deemed fit only for the lowest form of character in society (Galatians 3: 13). Perhaps, however, the claim of a desire to experience salvation in such a manner is merely being employed metaphorically. It could be that he/she simply wishes to live a life of sin and deceit and, at the moment prior to death, have the good fortune of being in the right place at the right time to be forgiven and attain salvation.

Ultimately, the cry to be saved *like the thief* is merely the reflection of one's desire to be saved specifically without water baptism. Pointing to the fact that baptism cannot be found in the narrative regarding the thief, who clearly had no opportunity for it at the time, the assumption is that anyone may be saved in like manner, without submitting to water baptism. The demonstration that the thief lived, not under the new covenant of grace, but under the law of the old covenant, is often deemed to be meaningless by those who either do not understand or, worse yet, do not care.

It is admittedly a bit embarrassing when, in defense of baptism's redemptive value, someone suggests that *perhaps* this thief was baptized by either John the Baptist or Jesus' disciples. While it is certainly within the realm of possibilities, since he did recognize who Jesus was, it is highly unlikely. Although little is known regarding this man, what is known is the fact that he was a thief. His guilt is never in question. The man's point to the other thief who was opposite him that their punishment was justified is a confession as clear as any that was ever made. The likelihood of a baptized thief diminishes when it is realized that his petition to Jesus was not made on the basis of a baptism that he might have received. Yet, it was not merely the good fortune of being nailed next to Christ that brought salvation to this man. Two thieves were present but only one was saved. It was his willingness to recognize Jesus as the Son of God and his request to be remembered in Jesus' coming kingdom that saved him. While Scripture does not characterize it specifically as such, this may be seen as reasonably inferring the man's repentant heart, which Jesus apparently recognized.

Why, then, should men today expect to attain salvation any differently than the thief on the cross? He believed and was saved; therefore, salvation today must be achieved in the same manner. This is the case presented by those who turn to the thief as an illustration of salvation without baptism. What must be addressed, then, for those who either do not understand, or do not care that this man lived under the old covenant, is how the details of the new covenant affect us in a manner very different from the thief.

In a passionate message to the Romans, Paul expressed his deepest desire for those Israelites who still attempted to live under the law, to come to an understanding of grace (Romans 10: 1-13). He regards confession of Jesus as Lord, along with belief in the resurrection, as essential to salvation both for the Israelites and for the Romans. If anyone refuses to confess Christ he should not anticipate eternal life with Him. In like manner, given the fact that the resurrection of Jesus is the very thing by which death was conquered and, thus, eternal life was offered, belief in, and acceptance of, that resurrection is deemed by all to be indispensable to our salvation.

Those who charge that the thief's salvation – without baptism – is a model for salvation in the church age should realize that the thief did not, and in fact could not, believe in the resurrection. Christ had not yet died when He told him, *'Assuredly, I say to you, today you will be with Me in Paradise.'* Consequently, if we accept the argument that *'what was true for the thief must be true for us,'* we have no need to believe in the resurrection.

This inconsistency is irrelevant to those who insist that baptism has no salvation value. Yet, it is no small thing. Belief in the resurrection of Jesus is at the very core of man's opportunity for eternal life in the church age. This was not true for the thief. Using the example of the thief to confound the role of baptism, when the circumstances surrounding that incident clearly are not relevant to salvation in the church age, is a perilous calculation. If it is applicable at all it must be universally applied, thus relegating trust in the resurrection to a place of insignificance in the covenant of grace. Since belief in the resurrection cannot be dismissed in the church age, it must be the case that the manner in which the thief was saved is not pertinent to the salvation of men today.

Who would accept that anyone could be saved without the Holy Spirit? Belief that the manner in which men are saved in the church age is consistent with the case of the thief must, naturally, minimize the relevance of the work of the Holy Spirit. Regardless what one believes with respect to baptism with the Holy Spirit few would ever consider trivializing the role of the Spirit within the kingdom of God. In Jesus' own words we find that, absent spiritual birth, no one may enter the kingdom (John 3: 5). Later, John portrays the Spirit as a witness, *'that God has given us eternal life, and this life is in His Son.'* (1 John 5: 11). Despite the contention that the thief did, somehow, receive the Holy Spirit prior to his death, Scripture does not support this claim, nor is it remotely implied in the text. The indication from Scripture is that the Holy Spirit would not be given until after Jesus had ascended to heaven (John 7: 39).

This discrepancy regarding the Holy Spirit is, once again, inconsequential to those who are adamant in their rejection of baptism for forgiveness of sins. Yet, as with the case of belief in the resurrection, it is no small thing if failure on our part to be *born of Spirit* is a matter to forbid entrance into the kingdom. In order to experience salvation in the same manner as the thief, one must be willing to shun a spiritual birth. If spiritual birth is essential, as it clearly is, the case of the thief must not apply to men in the church age.

Paul spends a great deal of time teaching disciples regarding the body of Christ, which is the church. As with baptism and the Holy Spirit, Paul refers to the body of Christ as one of the unique unifying elements of Christianity (Ephesians 4: 4). According to Scripture, all who are saved are incorporated into the body of Christ (1 Corinthians 12: 13). For a saved person membership in that body is not optional, but essential and automatic. According to Paul, it is the members of that body who are heirs to the kingdom (Ephesians 3: 6). Who, then, would wish to escape membership? Yet, the thief on the cross was not a part of the body of Christ. He could not have held membership in the body since it was not established until Pentecost, weeks after his death.

While many who wish to be saved in the manner of the thief may consider this disparity insignificant, it is a fair assessment of Scripture that God does not. Once again, if the thief is a useful example of salvation for the church age, to be saved in the same manner one must forego membership in the body. If, however, inheritance of the kingdom of God in the church age is limited to those who are part of the body of Christ, membership in that body must carry considerable import with respect to salvation. In that case, the manner in which the thief was saved can have no bearing on the manner in which men are saved today.

These truths concerning the effects of the new covenant vs. the first covenant would have applied to all those with whom Jesus came in contact during His ministry on earth. Jesus forgave a number of people while He was on earth, including a paralytic (Matthew 9:2) and the woman who washed His feet (Luke 7: 47-48). He declared, and even demonstrated, His own authority to forgive sins while He was on earth when He was questioned by the Pharisees (Mark 2: 5-11). These, however, are not examples of salvation in the church age. The incessant effort to portray them as the manner by which we must be saved challenges the very heart of the gospel message that is presented in Scripture.

While Jesus' disciples, as well as John the Baptist, performed water baptism prior to the death of Christ, that baptism must be placed in proper perspective. Certainly it was considered a baptism for the forgiveness of sins (Mark 1: 4; Luke 3: 3), but it was limited in scope since its symbolic nature was yet to be realized. John's baptism was performed in anticipation of Christian baptism in the same manner that his ministry was intended to prepare the way for Christ. The baptism of John was never identified as essential for salvation.

The *requirement* of baptism for salvation was introduced after Jesus' resurrection (Mark 16: 16, Acts 2: 38, 1 Peter 3: 21) and well after the death of the thief. Pointing to the thief on the cross to support a doctrine of salvation without baptism is equivalent to offering Moses, Elijah, or Abraham as suitable examples. It is true that, in the end, it is the blood of Christ that saves even these great men of God. What is not true, however, is that the manner in which men of the old covenant were saved has direct bearing on the manner of salvation in the covenant of grace.

Chapter XIII
A Matter of Choice

The Nature of God

God is gracious – of that there can be no doubt or disagreement. Mankind is His created being whom He loves. Instilled within man, who was created in the image of God (Genesis 1: 26), is free will – the ability to make choices regarding his own actions (Judges 5: 8; Proverbs 1: 29; 1 Peter 5: 2). It was essential that God create man with this ability since it was God's plan to have a true relationship with this creature of earth. He wanted man's love; not a love dictated by God, but a love that was chosen by men. Without free will it would not be possible for men to make such a choice.

God is holy (1 Peter 1: 16). Indeed, it is His nature is to be holy (2 Peter 1: 4). This holy nature of God that is revealed in Scripture provides us with the understanding that God is pure, undefiled, virtuous, and divine. He is a God who not only has never done wrong but, because of His nature, cannot do wrong (Titus 1: 2; James 1: 13). God is also completely righteous (Exodus 9: 27). Righteousness, however, encompasses much more than a mere understanding of right and wrong. The essence of righteousness is a sense of fairness or justice. Inherent within the character of righteousness is the recognition that good must be rewarded and evil must be punished. The righteous nature of God reveals that He is always fair and that His judgments are immanently just.

Much as a parent, knowing right from wrong as well as what is in the best interest of the child, sets down rules for the sake of that child, so God has established parameters meant to guide us in our walk with Him. It is God's desire for men to be holy in order to commune with Him. This is the very reason He has provided us with guidelines – so that we may be a holy people presentable to Him.

The Choice of Adam and Eve

Man's resistance to God's guidance is evidenced near the very outset of the relationship. Adam and Eve were the first to encounter the boundaries God had set in place for mankind. Assuming familiarity with the account of Adam and Eve, it is sufficient to note that God had provided these two with one simple instruction – they must not eat of the *tree of knowledge of good and evil*. While His command was not a burdensome one, it was one they simply could not abide. The lesson learned not only regards the weakness of man, but the deceptive nature of Satan. His persuasiveness convinced them, ironically, that God was the liar when, according to Eve, He forewarned them:

> You shall not eat it, nor shall you touch it, lest you die. (Genesis 3: 3)

Yet Satan, speaking oh so cunningly, persuaded the woman that God's way was not the only way and not necessarily the best way. He told Eve:

> You will not surely die. (Genesis 3: 4)

Thereafter, man became easily duped by Satan to turn from the instructions of God, leading us on a path where many, while alleging a life of obedience, will freely defy God's directions for any one of a variety of reasons.

The Fiery Serpent

Scripture provides countless illustrations of individuals and groups who were faced with choices. While men were free to choose what path they would walk, each decision involved either a reward or a consequence. So it is with the gospel message. While each man or woman is free to choose whether he/she will embrace the precepts of God, rewards and consequences are fully dependent upon the choices made. In a rebellious manner, the children of Israel spoke out against God who then sent serpents among them as punishment. As they repented God made available to them a means to survive the poison of the serpents.

> Then the Lord said to Moses, "Make a fiery serpent, and set it on a pole; and it shall be that everyone who is bitten, when he looks at it, shall live." (Numbers 21: 8)

While each one could choose not to gaze upon the serpent, the foolishness of that decision should be obvious. Why would someone refuse something so simple when the reward of obedience is life and the consequence of refusal is death? The notion that one might disregard an opportunity for life seems absurd.

David's Choice

God had forbidden all but the Priests to lay hands on the Ark of the Covenant. Included in His instruction with respect to the Ark was a design of how it should be carried – the ark should be carried on poles (Exodus 25: 13-15). However, King David and his captains and other leaders decided to build a new cart to carry the Ark from a place called Kirjath Jearim back to Judah where David believed it should be. David was undoubtedly very sincere in his desire to please God with the new cart. Two men, Uzza and Ahio, drove the cart that carried the Ark.

> 9. And when they came to Chidon's threshing floor, Uzza put out his hand to hold the ark, for the oxen stumbled. 10. Then the anger of the Lord was aroused against Uzza, and He struck him because he put his hand to the ark; and he died there before God. (1 Chronicles 13: 9-10)

No doubt Uzza's actions were carried out in an earnest attempt to prevent the ark from falling to the ground. Had David followed God's instructions, Uzza would not have died because an ox happened to stumble. As a consequence of David's choice to discard the guidelines offered by God, Uzza, an innocent, died even in his sincere effort to protect the ark. His action, no matter how sincere, was contrary to the command of God. God became angry with Uzza, and he died in his sincerity.

Naaman, Moses, and the Blind Man

Naaman, a commander in the army of Syria who happened to develop leprosy, was another who faced a decision whether he would heed God's instructions. Through the advice of his wife's maidservant he sought audience with Elisha, the prophet, seeking a cure. Elisha instructed Naaman to wash (dip or bathe) in the Jordan River seven times. Naaman was not particularly thrilled about the prospect of bathing in such a filthy body of water and would have preferred either the Abanah or the Pharpar. However, he eventually capitulated and was immediately healed (2 Kings 5: 10-14).

Few, having considered this narrative, would truly believe that Naaman would have been healed of his leprosy had he approached the Abanah or the Pharpar and dipped himself seven times. Who would believe he would have been healed had he gone to the Jordan and dipped himself three...four...five...even six times? None would expect that. In truth, the *only* course of action for Naaman to be healed was for him to, '*Go and wash in the Jordan seven times...*'

* * * * *

Moses knew God's command. He was to speak to the rock in the Wilderness of Zin and water for the Israelites would come forth (Numbers 20: 7-12). While the command could be easily followed, Moses saw fit to defy God. As a consequence he was not allowed to enter into the Promised Land.

* * * * *

At a certain time during His ministry Jesus came upon a man blind from birth. Jesus formed some mud with a mixture of saliva and dirt and placed it on the man's eyes. He then told the man to go and wash his eyes in the Pool of Siloam (John 9: 1-7). Who would believe, if this man had said to himself, *Jesus already touched me; therefore I need not to go to the pool of Siloam,* his blindness would have been healed? Of course, no one would believe that. Nor did he seem to question Jesus' directions. His response was simple obedience.

The Nature of God's Instructions
Of note concerning the response of so many throughout Scripture regarding the obedience or disobedience of God's direction is that the nature of the instruction given was never in question. Gideon knew what God expected of him. He realized that he was to lead the Israelites in defeat of the Midianites. He laid out a fleece, not as a manner of determining what God wanted, but to assure himself that it was actually God who was calling him (Judges 6: 36-40). Noah did not question God's instructions for building an ark, but followed them precisely without wavering (Genesis 6: 22). So it was with those to whom Jesus gave direction in the Great Commission concerning making disciples through teaching and baptism (Matthew 28: 18-20).

God has made a practice of making clear His instructions for mankind. It is not, nor has it ever been, the nature of the instruction that is in doubt. In simple words God has made His intentions known. Those who heard these words of the Great Commission unquestionably understood what was expected. Throughout the book of Acts, as the word spread and the church, the body of Christ, was established, it was understood that in baptism sins were forgiven, the Holy Spirit was received, and souls were added to the body of Christ.

It may be beneficial at this time to consider the nature of the remarks in the Great Commission. The recorded words spoken by Jesus after His resurrection are extremely limited in number. While He undoubtedly offered the disciples much teaching prior to His ascension, for they surely had much to learn, a mere handful of comments are offered up in Scripture. This is a reliable indicator that these words should be considered significant. A review of the Great Commission reveals the timelessness of the message.

'All authority has been given to Me in heaven and on earth.' No one would suggest that this authority was fleeting. For all time Jesus held within Himself all the authority of heaven and earth. *'Go...and make disciples of all nations.'* Surely no one would doubt that this call to *make disciples* is as applicable today as it was on the day the words were originally spoken. He then stated, *'...teaching them to observe all things that I have commanded you.'* The timeless value of this statement is beyond challenge. *'And lo, I am with you always, even to the end of the age.'* This one speaks for itself.

Amid all of these words that speak so boldly of the perpetual nature of the Great Commission, it is, *'baptizing them in the name of the Father and of the Son and of the Holy Spirit'* that so many refuse to regard in that same light. Yet timelessness is undoubtedly Jesus' intent – an intent that was grasped plainly by those who stood before Him.

It is important to understand that there is a distinction between the *will* of God and the *instructions* of God. God's *will* is about His purpose or desire. Certainly it is God's *will* that man should be faithful to Him as a holy being. Instructions received by man from God establish the manner in which He guides us to accomplish His will. While His instructions are not forced upon us, neither are they burdensome. Each one has the freedom to choose whether he/she will follow the path God has chosen for us to become a holy people. The biblical roadmap leads the way. As, throughout Scripture, men were charged to decide whether or not to accept God's instructions, so we are challenged. So, too, will men reap the rewards or suffer the consequences of decisions made.

Having received instruction regarding baptism throughout the New Testament by men of God, many simply refuse to accept it. Perhaps it is because, unlike Naaman or the blind man, the consequences are not so immediate. Unwilling to believe that these two would have been healed without obeying the instructions given, many claim exemption for themselves regarding God's precept of baptism.

* * * * *

Perhaps one difficulty regarding baptism is that it is generally viewed from an improper perspective. Often the question is posed, *Does baptism save one?* The more appropriate question that should be asked is, *Can one be saved without baptism?* Certainly belief alone does not save anyone. James made this abundantly clear when he explained that belief without action is a useless belief (James 2: 20). Therefore, none can attain a saved status through belief alone. Yet, can anyone be saved without believing? Of course, the answer is an unwavering "No!"

Like teaching can be applied to confession and repentance. Neither repentance nor confession can, in itself, yield salvation. Nonetheless, no one can be saved without them. The question regarding baptism is just as pertinent. Can one be saved without baptism? God has made it clear in Scripture that baptism is an integral component of His plan of salvation – a component that must not be ignored by man. Each one has a choice to make with respect to baptism. It is not, however, a choice as to whether or not baptism is God's instruction to man, but a choice regarding our submission to directions clearly given.

Chapter XIV
What Is Baptism with the Holy Spirit?

The controversy surrounding baptism can be traced partially to the diverse opinions that exist regarding the roles of various baptisms as they appear in Scripture. Of particular concern are the characteristics and respective functions of *water baptism* and what both Jesus and John the Baptist referred to as *baptism with the Holy Spirit*.

References to baptism with the Holy Spirit, *per se*, are extremely limited in Scripture. The truth is God's Word does not reveal, in so many words, the precise meaning of this expression. That being the case, it is probably best to approach the topic without pre-conceived notions as to exactly what is meant by this phrase. Regeneration is tied to the work of the Holy Spirit in certain passages, such as Romans 15: 16, 1 Corinthians 6: 11, and Titus 3: 5. Whether or not this represents *baptism* with the Spirit is something upon which many cannot agree.

Most men are so fixed on a specific belief concerning the substance of baptism with the Holy Spirit that nothing will change their minds. Yet it is possible that we as men have approached the subject of baptism with the Holy Spirit from a rather finite perspective. As we consider those times in Scripture where the term is actually used, there seem to be some incongruities that make harmony with the commonly held views very difficult. Four of the passages where we find this phrase spoken (Matthew 3: 11; Mark 1: 8; Luke 3: 16; John 1: 33) must be considered as one since they simply address the same incident four different times as each of the gospel writers wrote concerning John the Baptist's prophecy about baptism with the Spirit. The next incident where it is used finds Jesus, after the resurrection and prior to His ascension, reiterating John's prophesy that is found in the four passages mentioned above.

> 5. for John truly baptized with water, but you shall be baptized with the Holy Spirit not many days from now. (Acts 1: 5)

Later, in Caesarea, Peter uttered the same verbiage as he witnessed the Holy Spirit *falling upon* the Gentiles (Acts 11: 16), associating this event with Jesus' prophecy prior to Pentecost, which is akin to the prophecy by John the Baptist. Furthermore, Paul, as he considered the divisions among the Corinthians, told them that they had been *'washed...sanctified...justified...by the Spirit...'* (1 Corinthians 6: 11). He also wrote that we, as the body of Christ, can find unity in the fact that *'by one Spirit we were all baptized into one body'* (1 Corinthians 12: 13). The challenges that these passages present are numerous given the circumscribed views of men concerning the meaning of *baptism with the Holy Spirit*. We will address these difficulties after we have taken a look inside the disparate ideological stands men have taken concerning this terminology.

Power Received – The Day of Pentecost

One belief with respect to baptism with the Holy Spirit is that it speaks of a mysterious manifestation of the Spirit by which God imparts phenomenal gifts, such as the ability to speak in unknown tongues or to prophesy. Some also teach that this is the time of salvation or regeneration. Others hold a somewhat similar view, believing that this manifestation of the Spirit represents a second blessing – a supernatural whelming of the Spirit, including speaking in tongues, that often occurs *after* one has been saved. This view maintains that the event portrayed in the following passage is the very definition of baptism with the Holy Spirit about which both John the Baptist (Matthew 3: 11) and Jesus (Acts 1: 5) prophesied:

> 1. When the Day of Pentecost had fully come, they were all with one accord in one place. 2. And suddenly there came a sound from heaven, as of a rushing mighty wind, and it filled the whole house where they were sitting. 3. Then there appeared to them divided tongues, as of fire, and *one* sat upon each of them. 4. And they were all filled with the Holy Spirit and began to speak with other tongues, as the Spirit gave them utterance. (Acts 2: 1-4)

The notion that baptism with the Holy Spirit is a spiritual event initiated directly by God is reasoned from the remarks made by John the Baptist (Matthew 3: 11; Luke 3: 16) that seem to contrast water and Spirit baptism. The word *baptism* suggests an immersion – in this case it would be an immersion in or with the Spirit. The portrayal of the Spirit being *poured out* on these men on the Day of Pentecost could easily harmonize with the idea of immersion. Note that the *house was filled*. Just as the earth was completely submerged in the flood, so the Spirit was poured out on that day.

A miraculous event occurred on the Day of Pentecost as the apostles were overwhelmed by, and filled with, the Holy Spirit and began to speak in other languages. They then proceeded to preach to the crowds gathered in Jerusalem – probably many of the same Jews who were present at the time of Jesus' crucifixion. Perhaps some had even seen the risen Christ. This was almost certainly true of the disciples mentioned in the first chapter of Acts. Those who were not present for the crucifixion were most likely familiar with the incident as friends and family shared the details of Jesus' death. They understood those things of which the apostles spoke. When the people heard what the apostles had to say they asked what they should do in response to this message. Given the circumstances, it is understandable why the message resonated with them and three thousand were saved.

We understand in retrospect that the event described by Luke in Acts 2: 1-4 was the *initial* outpouring of the Spirit upon mankind for the church age, and this through the apostles. The fact that the apostles received power on that day is quite interesting when you consider that Jesus had already granted them the ability to drive out demons and heal the sick (Matthew 10: 1). If they could already do these things, what power were they to receive at Pentecost?

Evidently, on the Day of Pentecost the apostles realized an expansion of the powers already given. The *authority* awarded them earlier in Jesus' ministry was somewhat limited in nature. Once Pentecost arrived and the power of the Holy Spirit was unleashed, we discover that the apostles performed works in ways not possible prior to that day. They spoke in foreign tongues they had never studied (Acts 2: 1-13), performed miracles beyond casting out demons and healing the sick (Acts 2: 43), and they were now able to distribute spiritual gifts to other believers by laying hands on them (Acts 8: 17-18; Romans 1: 11).

The Day of Pentecost – A Proper Biblical Perspective

Given the confusion that exists among men concerning the Day of Pentecost, this seems like a good time to offer a brief commentary about the activities leading up to and including the outpouring of the Holy Spirit that was experienced on that day (Acts 2: 1-4). Insight into the first two chapters of the book of Acts is vital since they are the source of considerable theological disparity. For instance, prior to His ascension, Jesus promised His listeners that they would receive power as the Spirit came upon them (Acts 1: 8). Some men maintain that this promise of *power* was meant for all men and women who accept Him as Savior. There is also widespread belief that, as the Holy Spirit first fell upon men on the Day of Pentecost and they were filled with the Spirit (Acts 2: 1-4), the experience involved more than the twelve apostles. Yet an honest reading of the text frustrates those arguments.

It is evident from Scripture that when Jesus prophesied about the coming of the Holy Spirit and the power these men would receive, He was specifically addressing the apostles. We know this from the details of the text. First of all, Luke specifically references the apostles in the narrative (Acts 1: 1-11). Secondly, when two angels appeared to the men after Jesus had ascended, they addressed them as, *'Men of Galilee'* (Acts 1: 11), a pointed reference to the apostles who were chosen while Jesus was in Galilee (Matthew 4: 18-21; 9: 9 – 10: 4). As these men returned to Jerusalem from the Mt. of Olives, Luke provides us with their exact identity.

> 12. Then they returned to Jerusalem from the mount called Olivet, which is near Jerusalem, a Sabbath day's journey. 13. And when they had entered, they went up into the upper room where they were staying: Peter, James, John, and Andrew; Philip and Thomas; Bartholomew and Matthew; James *the son* of Alphaeus and Simon the Zealot; and Judas *the son* of James. (Acts 1: 12-13)

Later, in the same chapter, we are told of a gathering where Peter addressed the entire body of believers in Jerusalem, a group numbering roughly one hundred twenty disciples (Acts 1: 15). During that assembly Matthias was selected to replace Judas as an apostle. We learn that, *'he was numbered with the eleven apostles'* (Acts 1: 26). Finally, on the Day of Pentecost, we discover that *'they were all with one accord in one place...'* (Acts 2: 1).

Given the sequence of events, many maintain that the word *all* in this verse represents the many disciples whom Peter addressed in the previous chapter. These same men insist that the entire one hundred twenty disciples received the outpouring of the Spirit on that day (Acts 2: 1-4). Yet the nearest antecedent for the word *they*, regarding those who were gathered together, is found in the previous verse (Acts 1: 26), which is a reference to the twelve as Matthias was added to the number of apostles. This is easily realized when one disregards the chapter break that has been inserted between these verses. Of course, while identification of the nearest antecedent is a strong grammatical argument, in itself it is not conclusive. Still, we have rather impressive evidence in the balance of the text supporting the view that only the apostles were gathered together on the Day of Pentecost as the Spirit came upon them (Acts 2: 1-4).

First of all, the crowd in Jerusalem recognized that all of those who were speaking in tongues were from Galilee (Acts 2: 7). This was true of the apostles (we can assume that Matthias was from Galilee) as well as other disciples, including Jesus' family and Mary Magdalene. However, in order to conclude that all of the disciples received this same gift we must not only assume that every one of them hailed from Galilee, but that the crowd would actually be able, with relative ease, to recognize all one hundred twenty as Galileans. This is not only highly unlikely, but is essentially unrealistic considering the diversity of Jesus' early followers. Many of His disciples were from Galilee, but many were not. Mary, Martha, and Lazarus came from Bethany, a short distance from Jerusalem, and were very likely part of this family of believers. Barnabas was from the Island of Cyprus while Zaccheus and Bartimaeus both came from Jericho on the eastern border of Judea. Also, let us not forget Joseph, the disciple from Arimathaea who asked Pilate for Christ's body so that he might give Him a proper burial (Matthew 27: 57).

Most convincing, however, is the fact that John Mark, who was the author of the gospel of Mark and a cousin to Barnabas (Colossians 4: 10), along with his mother Mary, were from Jerusalem and were certainly not Galileans. Yet they were among Jesus' earliest disciples and undoubtedly numbered among these followers. Certain incidents in the life of Christ that are mentioned in Mark's gospel indicate that he was an eyewitness to the events. Furthermore, a great many scholars assume that the upper room where the disciples prayed together (Acts 1: 13) was located at Mary's home, believing this to be the same room where Jesus shared the Last Supper with the apostles the night before His death (Mark 14: 15). The early church met there at least occasionally (Acts 12: 12) and probably regularly.

If, by chance, the house where Jesus shared the Lord's Supper was not Mary's house, it was undoubtedly the home of another Judean disciple – perhaps Joseph of Arimathaea or someone else – since we understand that it was someone unknown to the apostles prior to Passover (Matthew 26: 17-18; Mark 14: 12-16). Therefore, we can easily determine that not all of the one hundred twenty disciples were transplanted from Galilee, which means that not all of the one hundred twenty disciples were *'with one accord in one place...'* (Acts 2: 1). Hence, the one hundred twenty did not all receive the outpouring of the Spirit.

Secondly, Peter specifically identifies those men who were speaking in tongues as the apostles, defending them against the accusation of drunkenness (Acts 2: 13-15). Additionally, when the people responded to the gospel message being spoken, they did not respond to the one hundred twenty disciples, but to those who were doing the preaching, who were the apostles (Acts 2: 37). Since all those who were gathered together received the gift of tongues (Acts 2: 4), based upon the compelling evidence available to us in Scripture, it is clear that only the apostles *'...were all with one accord in one place...'* (Acts 2: 1). No other fair-minded conclusion may be derived from the text.

Of course, some will argue tenaciously that the narrative could still be construed, however awkwardly, to allow all of the disciples the outpouring of the Spirit and the gift of tongues. However, this conclusion is possible only if we are willing to ignore the details of the text. It is by no means an objective view; nor does this position harmonize with Jesus' promise of power (*dunamis - suggesting something beyond normal human capabilities*) when the Holy Spirit came upon them (Acts 1: 8). These men were given powers well beyond the miraculous spiritual gifts (*charisma*) experienced by others later in the book of Acts. The gift of tongues was merely one example of the power received by these men on that day. In order to reach the conclusion from Luke's account that all of the disciples were involved, we would need to accept that the Holy Spirit bestowed this one gift (tongues) on all the disciples while granting greater powers only to the apostles (Acts 2: 43). No such scenario can be inferred from the text.

Despite irrefutable biblical evidence to the contrary, many still insist that the phenomenon on the Day of Pentecost was experienced by all of the one hundred twenty disciples. Many men continue to argue that, on that day, each of these disciples received the ability to speak in tongues in the same manner, and at the same time as the apostles. Then again, others may wonder what difference it makes who received the Spirit miraculously on the Day of Pentecost. Does it really matter if it was the entirety of the disciples or only the apostles?

The significance of the matter is actually twofold. First of all, the contention that all of the disciples received the outpouring of the Spirit has resulted in a somewhat skewed perception of the significance of the occasion and the role of the apostles in the early church. The position of the apostles was unique within the kingdom. They were the conduit through whom the Holy Spirit was introduced to mankind. The Spirit came *to* other men *through* the apostles, both in a general sense and even more specifically in relation to the special powers that were experienced in the first century church. Insisting that each of the one hundred twenty disciples received the Spirit in the same manner as the apostles, despite overwhelming biblical evidence, undermines the nature of the apostles' role in the church.

Secondly, the example of Pentecost, as men insist on overlooking what Scripture says in favor of personal views, demonstrates the boldness with which men tend to discount biblical teaching, no matter how forthright, when it does not harmonize with what they believe. If men are willing to disregard uncomplicated information such as this with such ease, how much more might they be willing to abandon biblical edification on issues of even greater significance if they simply disagree?

In order to gain proper perspective concerning the Day of Pentecost, and as a matter of respect for the Word of God, we must put aside this view and acknowledge the exceptional status bestowed upon the apostles on that day. Hopefully, highlighting this example of doctrinal inconsistency will challenge men to reconsider many of the lessons they have learned generally about what Scripture actually says.

Baptism with the Holy Spirit – The Gentiles

The prophecy of John the Baptist in Matthew 3: 11, which Jesus later echoed in Acts 1: 5, was now fulfilled. The Day of Pentecost had come and, according to the view mentioned earlier, baptism with the Holy Spirit had been experienced. That, however, is not the end of it. The phenomenon described here is mentioned one other time in Scripture. A few years later Peter was summoned to Caesarea to the house of Cornelius, a Gentile. It was there that he, and those accompanying him, witnessed a similar outpouring of the Holy Spirit on those in Cornelius' house (Acts 10: 44-46). In the eleventh chapter of Acts, Peter, while he was recalling the incident for the Jews in Jerusalem, recounted how these Gentiles had received the Holy Spirit in a manner similar to what the apostles had experienced on the Day of Pentecost (Acts 11: 15-16).

Pentecost and Caesarea: One View – Two Perspectives

Within the proposition that baptism with the Holy Spirit is represented by the events of Pentecost and the manner in which the Gentiles received the Spirit at Caesarea, there are two discrete opinions. Some believe that this supernatural manifestation of the Spirit was common among Christians in the apostolic age and may be received today in the same manner that it was experienced in the first century. There are, of course, some distinct biblical flaws with this belief.

The first problem with this position is that receiving the Spirit in this manner was actually a most uncommon event in the first century. Scripture reveals that it occurred only twice. If this kind of manifestation of the Holy Spirit was commonplace in the first century, as some would have us believe, Peter would have recognized it as a widespread development among the Jewish Christians. In Caesarea, however, Peter is reminded of Jesus' prophecy and how they had received the Holy Spirit *'at the beginning'* (Acts 11: 15-16). The very fact that Peter sees this as an *anomaly* should erase the notion that episodes such as this were routine in the Christian community.

Furthermore, beyond these two incidents, no mention is made of the Spirit falling on anyone without the touch of an apostle. There are those who turn to 1 Corinthians 12: 13 and suggest that Paul is discussing this phenomenon, but this view of the passage stretches biblical interpretation beyond reasonable limits. According to Paul's words in that passage, *'we are all baptized by one Spirit.'* He was speaking of a baptism common to all Christians. However, when Peter was with the Gentiles, he acknowledged the fact that he had only witnessed that phenomenon once before. His astonishment convinces us that this was something most rare as opposed to the common baptismal experience discussed by Paul.

* * * * *

The alternate stand taken by many who accept that Pentecost and Caesarea demonstrate true baptism with the Spirit holds that these two episodes represent *complete and final* fulfillment of all prophecies regarding this kind of baptism in the church age. They believe that these prophecies were totally and completely fulfilled, never to recur, once the Gentiles had experienced baptism with the Spirit. Once again, however, there are some difficulties plaguing this position.

Paul, in his first letter to the Corinthians, indicated that baptism *by*, or *with*, the Spirit is something that was known to all Christians (1 Corinthians 12: 13). This experience is intended as a unifying element within the body of Christ. Therefore, we cannot limit baptism with (or by) the Spirit to these two occasions.

We also face a challenge from the prophecy offered by John the Baptist (Matthew 3: 11). Given the fact that Jesus' statement regarding power received on the Day of Pentecost was directed at the apostles (Acts 1: 8), we *could* argue that His prophecy regarding baptism with the Spirit at that time (Acts 1: 5) was given with the same focus – to the apostles. However, this is not true of John's prophecy. John the Baptist spoke his prophecy concerning baptism with the Spirit and with fire without focusing on any specific group. Additionally, John spoke these words prior to Jesus selecting those men who would later become apostles. In fact, he spoke these words prior to Jesus' own baptism. We must certainly accept, then, that when John said, *'He will baptize you with the Holy Spirit and with fire'* his words suggested a much larger sphere of inclusion than these two events. Therefore, while it would be foolish to deny that Pentecost and Caesarea represent a form of baptism with the Spirit, it seems narrow-minded to confine this baptism to these two incidents or to this kind of experience. Baptism with the Spirit must carry with it an even greater significance.

Gifts of the Spirit

Many men believe that the miraculous gifts (e.g., speaking in tongues, prophecy, etc.) that were present among first century Christians were a result of *baptism with the Spirit* as depicted in Jerusalem on the Day of Pentecost and later at the house of

Cornelius. This reveals a misunderstanding concerning the gifts of the Spirit that were distributed to these early Christians.

The means by which spiritual gifts were received in the first century was through the touch of an apostle's hands. Several passages of Scripture confirm that, with the exceptions of Pentecost and Caesarea, where Cornelius lived, an apostle's touch was necessary to bestow these extraordinary gifts (Acts 8: 14-17; 19: 6; Romans 1: 11-12; 2 Timothy 1: 6). While it was certainly the Spirit who distributed the gifts (1 Corinthians 12: 11), when the method of distribution is discussed it is always through the hands of the apostles. Pentecost and Caesarea were exceptional in that the Holy Spirit was received without an apostle's touch. Yet, even on those two occasions at least one apostle was present.

The fact that spiritual gifts were distributed through the apostles is one of the significant issues surrounding the identity of those who received the outpouring of the Spirit on the Day of Pentecost. The ability to distribute these gifts was evident among the apostles after they received the outpouring of the Holy Spirit (Acts 2: 1-4). This method of the distribution of spiritual gifts in the first century helps us better understand the relationship of the apostles and the work of the Spirit in the early church. The Holy Spirit worked specifically through the apostles. That is why Philip did not distribute spiritual gifts in Samaria. He could not. It was an ability exclusive to the apostles (Acts 8: 12-15) and indicative of their special role in the church.

The Moving of the Spirit – Acts 4: 29-31

Some may reasonably inquire about the fourth chapter of the book of Acts. Could this not be an example of baptism with the Holy Spirit? In this instance Peter and John were taken before the chief priests and elders, being accused of teaching about Jesus after they had healed the lame man at the temple. When they returned to their own and explained what had taken place, everyone began praising God and praying. As they continued, the place where they were gathered shook as in an earthquake and they were all filled with the Spirit (Acts 4: 29-31).

The information is somewhat sketchy in that no details are offered regarding those with whom Peter and John were meeting at the time. While it may have been only the apostles, it is also certainly possible, and perhaps likely, that more than the apostles were present. Information that is available to us, however, indicates that this is not equivalent to the outpouring of the Holy Spirit experienced in Acts 2: 1-4. First of all, the Holy Spirit did not *fall upon* these individuals as He had on the Day of Pentecost. Secondly, no miraculous gifts of the Spirit were evidenced at this time. Finally, at the house of Cornelius, Peter seems to only recollect the Day of Pentecost as a corresponding event.

It is possible that God did, at this time, send a refreshing of the Holy Spirit upon those present. Another, and perhaps a more reasonable, view is that the shaking of the house stirred the Holy Spirit who already dwelt in those who were there, causing them to speak the word of God boldly.

Water and Holy Spirit Baptism Together

The other prevailing view with respect to baptism with the Holy Spirit is that this takes place at the time of water baptism. The understanding from Scripture is that baptism with the Holy Spirit does not point to the Spirit *falling on* men and bestowing miraculous gifts, as was reported on the Day of Pentecost and later at the house of Cornelius. The belief is that these prophecies regarding baptism with the Holy Spirit (Matthew 3: 11; Acts 1: 6) are fulfilled as a penitent believer is baptized in water. It is at that time that he/she receives the promised gift (filling/saturation) of the Holy Spirit. Scripture reveals that this, too, first occurred on the Day of Pentecost (Acts 2: 38).

Those who believe baptism with the Holy Spirit occurs simultaneously with water baptism have determined that there is one baptism, as taught in Ephesians, but that the nature of that baptism is twofold. It is a baptism that has the capacity to unite the physical world of man with the spiritual world in which God dwells. Thus, when Paul explained that we are unified by baptism (1 Corinthians 12: 13), he recognized that the work of the Spirit that unites us in the body of Christ occurs during water baptism. Peter first presented the concept of the *'gift of the Holy Spirit'* on the Day of Pentecost. Not only did Peter teach that, at the time of baptism, each one would receive the gift of the Holy Spirit, but he also explained that this gift was promised to all obedient believers (Acts 2: 39).

Several Bible passages speak of a connection between the Holy Spirit and the act of water baptism. Paul confirmed this when he arrived at Ephesus and met with several disciples who had received the baptism of John.

> 1. And it happened, while Apollos was at Corinth, that Paul, having passed through the upper regions, came to Ephesus. And finding some disciples 2. he said to them, "Did you receive the Holy Spirit when you believed?" So they said to him, "We have not so much as heard whether there is a Holy Spirit." 3. And he said to them, "Into what then were you baptized?" So they said, "Into John's baptism." 4. Then Paul said, "John indeed baptized with a baptism of repentance, saying to the people that they should believe on Him who would come after him, that is, on Christ Jesus." 5. When they heard *this*, they were baptized in the name of the Lord Jesus. (Acts 19: 1-5)

Paul's discovery that these disciples had not *heard* of the Holy Spirit instantly led him to conclude that they had not been baptized in the name of Jesus. His question to them in verse three can leave no doubt in anyone's mind the point Paul was making. He recognized that, had they been baptized in the name of Jesus, they *would have known* the Holy Spirit. In like manner, Jesus explained to Nicodemus that being born again involves a birth of both water and Spirit (John 3: 3-5). Jesus' words suggest a direct link between the Holy Spirit and water as a man is born again, a connection confirmed by Paul in his letter to Titus (Titus 3: 4-7).

Paul once again binds together water and the Spirit as he addresses the Corinthians regarding sanctification and justification (1 Corinthians 6: 9-11). Pointing to the many evils by which men are so often consumed, he explained that the *Holy Spirit* separated them from such corruption as they were *washed* in baptism. No time sequence is offered in the statement. These works of the Spirit, done in the name of Jesus, are essentially accomplished simultaneously in baptism. The Corinthians were sanctified (consecrated) and justified (rendered innocent or free from sin) as they were washed (baptized). The washing to which Paul refers is unquestionably water baptism, to which the original Greek attests.

The word translated *washed* is απολουω (*apolouo*), which is derived from two other Greek words. The first of these words is απο (*apo*) meaning: *separation or departure.*[1] The second is λουω (*louo*), which means, *to bathe (the whole person).*[2] The New Strong's Exhaustive Concordance of the Bible, in its explanation of the word's meaning, draws an explicit distinction between this word and νιπτω (*nipto*), which suggests only a partial washing, such as the hands and/or feet. Thus it is a literal washing rather than a figurative use of the word. This passage, then, denotes a separation from the list of unrighteous acts by the Corinthians.

229

That separation from sins (justification and sanctification), as expressed in Titus 3: 5, is achieved in Jesus' name, by the Holy Spirit, through faith, in the washing of the entire person – in water.

Baptism of the Three Thousand

Many are convinced that Holy Spirit baptism was intended to replace water baptism. After all, John said he baptized with water but that Jesus would baptize with the Holy Spirit. Certainly *sounds* like replacement. However, the Holy Spirit did not discard water baptism when He came into the world, but incorporated Himself into water baptism. That is what happened on the Day of Pentecost. The Holy Spirit did not replace water baptism; He enhanced it.

If the baptism commanded by Peter was the same baptism with the Spirit that the apostles had received (Acts 2: 1-4), no water baptism would have been necessary *after* the Day of Pentecost. Why baptize each one with water when Jesus could baptize them with the Spirit as He had just done with the apostles? It was an opportune time to completely abandon the water baptism of John and Jesus that was administered prior to His death and replace it with baptism in the Spirit.

While many deny it, there is every reason to believe that the baptism received by the three thousand on the Day of Pentecost was baptism in water and no reason to believe that it was anything else. First of all, as previously stated, no mention is made of any other on that day receiving extraordinary gifts, such as speaking in tongues. Secondly, there is no record of the apostles ever *teaching* anyone to be baptized with the Holy Spirit. However, the Bible is filled with numerous accounts of the apostles both teaching and administering water baptism after the Day of Pentecost. Finally, the two times Scripture does record the Holy Spirit being *poured out* in this extraordinary manner it is not initiated by the apostles, but by God Himself.

The suggestion that Christian baptism in water in the name of Jesus might be abandoned on this particular day is especially unfounded since no one had yet been baptized in this manner. Christian baptism *first occurred* on the Day of Pentecost. It is a bit awkward to suggest that the apostles forsook this rite before it was ever administered. Many had received the baptism of John. That, however, was not baptism in the name of Jesus that was commanded by Jesus and taught by the apostles.

Peter and the other apostles on the Day of Pentecost were faithfully following the instructions they had received from Jesus in the Great Commission when He had charged them to '*go...make disciples...baptizing...teaching*' (Matthew 28: 19-20). Receiving the Holy Spirit was then promised as a result of repentance and baptism (Acts 2: 38). Christian baptism was not abrogated, but established, on the Day of Pentecost. Water baptism was not abolished; it was enriched as the Holy Spirit now insinuated Himself into this celebration of faith.

Baptism *in* the Spirit, *with* the Spirit, or *by* the Spirit?

Let us return to the challenges men face, which were mentioned earlier in this chapter, given these limited views of *baptism with the Spirit*. After all, what are we to do with a passage like the one from Paul where he states that we are baptized *by one Spirit into one body*? (1 Corinthians 12: 13). In such a case, is the Spirit the *administrator* of baptism or is He the one *into whom we are baptized*? In certain other passages (Matthew 3: 11; Acts 1: 5; 10: 45) essentially the same Greek phrase '$εν$ $ενι$ $πνευματι$' is translated '*with the Spirit*' or '*by the Spirit*'. Even within a specific passage various translations will offer a different rendering of the phrase. While other passages do not specify *one* Spirit, as does 1 Corinthians 12: 13, its inclusion by Paul at that time is undoubtedly meant to emphasize the central message of unity in that text. Yet one wonders, if we are baptized *by the Spirit*, how reconciliation can be found with baptism *in the Spirit* if we are to be true to the meaning of $βαπτιζο$ as immersion? All of this can be confusing.

Most scholars accept that the translation of this phrase in a particular setting relies heavily on the surrounding text. John the Baptist distinguishes baptism *in* (NIV) or *with* (NASB) water from baptism *in* (NIV) or *with* (NASB) the Holy Spirit in his introduction of the baptism that Jesus would provide. Generally, most translators accept that the words *by*, *in*, or *with*, could easily be used interchangeably in each of these settings. It seems the most consistent and most utilized translation is '*with the Spirit.*' This certainly offers flexibility concerning the role of the Spirit and allows that role to be whatever an individual ideology determines it to be. However, that seems to be the easy way out of a quandary without giving full explanation.

It is easy enough to understand how the *pouring out* of the Spirit on the Day of Pentecost and later in Caesarea could be viewed as baptism *'in the Spirit.'* Those involved were enveloped and overwhelmed by the Spirit in a mighty way. Surely they were immersed in every sense of the word. Yet if the Spirit becomes the administrator in baptism on Christ's behalf, according to the words of Paul (1 Corinthians 12: 13), how does this fit with the prophecy of John the Baptist (Matthew 3: 11)?

It is difficult for us, with our human limitations, to fully grasp the function of the Holy Spirit in water baptism. We find in Scripture that baptism is the time when the Holy Spirit indwells the new Christian (Acts 2: 38) and that the Holy Spirit plays a significant influential role in our lives from that moment. Given these facts, perhaps we should consider the possibility that *baptism with the Spirit* does not simply point to a specific spiritual event like Pentecost or water baptism, but characterizes a life that is *fully immersed in the Spirit*. Rather than depicting a one-time spiritual *experience*, it seems more reasonable that baptism with the Spirit aptly portrays our *continued* immersion in the Holy Spirit.

When John the Baptist mentioned that Jesus would baptize men *'with the Spirit'* (Matthew 3: 11), we automatically assume that he is contrasting the *events* of baptism in water and baptism in the Spirit. The comparison offered, however, may not have been intended to distinguish between specific incidents, but to the fact that one (water baptism) was an event while the other (Spirit baptism) was actually a way of life. This would explain why he considered baptism with (or in) the Spirit infinitely superior to the purification ceremony of water baptism.

As Jesus restated the prophecy of John the Baptist concerning water and Spirit baptism, rather than speaking of a specific incident, perhaps He was depicting the manner in which their lives would be immersed in the Spirit, an immersion that would *begin* in a few days (Acts 1: 5). As Peter considered the spiritual experience of the Gentiles, we look to the gift of tongues they received and automatically determine that his reference to baptism with the Holy Spirit is specific to that moment. Yet it is at least as harmonious to conclude that he was contemplating not only that particular episode, but the fact that a life immersed in the Spirit was also available to the Gentiles.

The picture of the early Christians offered up in the New Testament reveals people who seemed to *walk in the Spirit* (Galatians 5: 25). These were not people who simply received a momentary baptism with the Spirit, but people who were continually immersed in the Spirit and were being renewed on a daily basis (2 Corinthians 4: 16). This fits nicely with Paul's remark to the Corinthians concerning unity in the body as they were immersed with one Spirit into that body. That spiritual immersion continued as they walked and lived in the body of Christ. Limiting baptism with the Spirit to an event seems to diminish the significance both Christ and the apostles intended. The Christian, according to Scripture, is to be immersed in the Spirit each and every day. Surely this is the nature of baptism with the Spirit.

What we are seeking, then, is not necessarily the time of baptism with the Spirit, since we cannot legitimately limit it to a specific moment. Baptism with the Spirit, like faith, is a journey – a way of life. Immersion in the Spirit is the seal that continues with us in our daily walk (Ephesians 1: 13). The question to which we seek an answer, then, is this: *At what time does baptism with the Spirit begin?*

Instruction Vs Narrative Concerning Baptism

Teaching that baptism with the Holy Spirit occurs, or begins, independent from water baptism as depicted on the Day of Pentecost and in Caesarea, is founded upon certain incidents in the book of Acts rather than the baptismal instruction available throughout God's Word. One major flaw with this approach is that those passages upon which this doctrine is based cannot be considered didactic (instructional), but are narrative passages chronicling certain events. Instruction concerning baptism on the day of Pentecost is not found in the incident where the Holy Spirit was poured out upon the apostles (Acts 2: 1-4), but in Peter's sermon to the crowd (Acts 2: 38). It is imprudent to view an event in Scripture and determine that it represents doctrine unless corroborating support can be found in passages where the words are intended to teach, especially when the event smacks of divine intervention. We have no legitimate reason to derive a baptismal creed from those narratives where the Holy Spirit manifest Himself in such an extraordinary fashion since we are offered no instruction concerning this phenomenon.

A number of historical events are related to us throughout Scripture upon which no doctrine has been formed. We find in the book of Luke, as Jesus met Zaccheus, that the man vowed to offer half of all he owned to the poor. In response Jesus stated, *'Today salvation has come to this house...'* (Luke 19: 9). Yet who has developed a doctrine that salvation comes by giving away half of all that we own? A doctrine such as this would be inconsistent with the teaching of Scripture. The account details an event that occurred, providing information on the life of Christ and His followers. Certainly we must give generously as we are *taught* in Scripture (2 Corinthians 9: 6), but a doctrine of salvation in exchange for half of one's wealth would be erroneous.

Prior to Paul's conversion, as he traveled on the Road to Damascus, God removed his sight with a bright light from heaven. Yet no one to date has developed a doctrine claiming physical blindness as a prerequisite to salvation. The reason is that this was a moment of divine revelation intended to call Paul to be an apostle to the Gentiles. It is not presented as a matter of biblical doctrine concerning the manner in which men are saved.

The belief that baptism with the Holy Spirit occurs at a time other than water baptism regards the manner in which the Spirit arrived on the Day of Pentecost as instruction concerning baptism with the Holy Spirit. This event, however, should not be considered instructional since it cannot, then, be reconciled with the events at the house of Cornelius (Acts 10: 44) where no tongues of fire were present. The occasion of Pentecost is also dissimilar to other instances such as Samaria (Acts 8: 14-16) or Ephesus (Acts 19: 6) where the Spirit fell upon no one without the touch of the apostles' hands.

Throughout the New Testament, when the apostles offered *instruction* with respect to baptism, the subject was consistently immersion in water. Jesus, looking ahead to the establishment of the church, commanded His disciples to baptize in water (Matthew 28: 19-20). Peter taught that this was the manner in which men are saved (1 Peter 3: 21). Paul addressed the significance of water baptism in his letters to the various churches (Romans 6: 1-10; 1 Corinthians 1: 12-17; 12: 13; Galatians 3: 27; Ephesians 4: 5; Colossians 2: 12). These instructional words found throughout Scripture provide tremendous consistency regarding the role of baptism in the church.

What is the Biblical Answer Concerning Spirit Baptism?

When does baptism with the Holy Spirit begin? Biblical support falls in favor of baptism with the Spirit that begins at the time of water baptism. This is the kind of baptism with the Spirit that is portrayed by Peter, Paul, and Luke in their inspired writings (Acts 2: 38; 19: 1-5; Romans 6: 3-4; 1 Corinthians 6: 11; 12: 13; Colossians 2: 11-12; Titus 3: 5; Hebrews 10: 22; 1 Peter 3: 21). The Holy Spirit entered the world of man and incorporated Himself into water baptism on the Day of Pentecost. If God intended the receiving of the Holy Spirit to occur at a time other than water baptism, no reasonable explanation can be given for the Holy Spirit to be associated *with* water baptism. Additionally, the Bible offers no instruction suggesting that God, through the apostles, ever modified this relationship between the Holy Spirit and immersion in water.

That is not to say that we should not consider those occasions when the Spirit was poured out on men as baptism with the Holy Spirit. That would be a foolish denial based on Jesus' prophecy as He spoke with the apostles (Acts 1: 5) and Peter's reference to that prophecy at the house of Cornelius. If Peter deemed what occurred on the Day of Pentecost to be baptism with the Holy Spirit (Acts 11: 15-16), and if we are to be true to Scripture, then the incident in Caesarea, at the house of Cornelius, must be viewed in the same manner.

However, the outpouring of the Holy Spirit that was experienced on these two occasions should not be perceived as the manner by which all first century Christians received the Holy Spirit into their lives. On the contrary, if Peter considered the episode with Cornelius as some kind of rare incident, so, too, should we. Scripture offers considerable instruction that identifies water baptism as the time the Holy Spirit insinuated Himself into each one's life.

Paul indicates that *all* Christians are *baptized by one Spirit into one body* (1 Corinthians 12: 13). The *one baptism* that was common to all Christians was not the outpouring of the Spirit that was experienced by a few on two separate occasions, but water baptism in which the gift (indwelling) of the Spirit was promised (Acts 2: 38; Titus 3: 5-6). In each case, the outpouring of the Holy Spirit that was experienced by the few seems to have served its divinely intended purpose fully at the time it occurred. On the day of Pentecost the apostles were endowed with powers and the gift of tongues in order to teach and persuade men that Jesus was truly the Messiah. Peter and his associates were convinced by this outpouring of the Spirit upon the Gentiles at the house of Cornelius that the gospel message was no longer limited to those of Jewish descent. These uncommon manifestations of the Spirit were not intended to depict the manner in which baptism with the Spirit would be experienced. These incidents should be recognized for their incomparable status. They were exceptional events for extraordinary times and should be viewed with that in mind. According to Scripture, immersion in the Spirit that is intended for the church age begins with our immersion in water.

NOTES FOR CHAPTER 14

1. James Strong, LL.D., S.T.D., The New Strong's Exhaustive Concordance of the Bible, Greek Dictionary of the New Testament, p. 14, 1990, Thomas Nelson Publishers

2. James Strong, LL.D., S.T.D., The New Strong's Exhaustive Concordance of the Bible, Greek Dictionary of the New Testament, p. 45, 1990, Thomas Nelson Publishers

Chapter XV
In Whose Name Must I Be Baptized?

Occasionally someone will notice a peculiarity in the Bible and wonder about its significance. The charge by Jesus to baptize *'in the name of the Father and of the Son and of the Holy Spirit'* (Matthew 28: 19) is one that is all too familiar. It seems curious, then, that through the balance of the New Testament, including the Day of Pentecost shortly after Jesus extended this Great Commission, the apostles *appear* to baptize simply in the name of Jesus (Acts 2: 38; 10: 47-48; 19: 5).

The few examples mentioned above are representative of New Testament instruction regarding baptism. Nowhere does the New Testament give account that anyone is actually baptized in the name of the Father, Son, and Holy Spirit. This appears to be a potential incongruity between the words of Jesus and the actions of the apostles. The possible explanations are somewhat limited. It could reflect a misunderstanding by the apostles of the words uttered by Jesus; or perhaps the apostles fell into disobedience by failing to abide by Jesus' instructions.

If this apparent inconsistency represented disobedience on the part of the apostles to the command of Christ, no doubt it would have been accentuated aptly within the pages of Scripture. An errant apostle was not to be taken casually. Such was the case with Peter when, we are told, he used rather poor judgment in one particular instance (Galatians 2: 11-13). Paul's rebuke of Peter and others for wrongfully disassociating themselves from the uncircumcised Gentiles was carried out before our eyes in the Bible. Rather than concealing such an episode, God's approach is to take the opportunity to provide a lesson. Therefore, if the seeming discrepancy on the part of the apostles to baptize in the name of Jesus is not depicted as an error or waywardness, another explanation must be found. Thus we are left with only two possibilities.

The first possibility concerning this seeming disparity is that the apostles never baptized in the name of the Father, Son, and Holy Spirit, but in the name of Jesus alone. The authority of Jesus is truly genuine and irrefutable. He holds within His being *all the authority of heaven and earth* (Matthew 28: 18). To believe that He is a Savior who has the ability to take away sins is to believe that all authority is His. If He did not have the authority He claimed He must be considered an impostor, at which point everything He ever said could be called into question. He would be a sinner (a liar) and as such would lack the standing to take away sins. Thus, one option is that God considers baptism in the name of Jesus equivalent with baptism in the name of the Father, Son, and Holy Spirit.

Several passages speak of the oneness of the Father and Son (John 8: 19; 14: 6-9; Acts 4: 12). That is essentially the exclusive theme of the entire fourteenth chapter of the Gospel of John. Still other passages reveal the unity between Jesus and the Holy Spirit (Luke 4: 18; John 4: 24; 2 Corinthians 3: 17). Upon close examination, it is evident that the idea of the Father and the Son and the Holy Spirit cannot be easily separated into three individual entities.

> And Jesus came and spoke to them, saying, "All authority has been given to Me in heaven and on earth." (Matthew 28: 18)

> ...yet for us *there is* one God, the Father, of whom *are* all things, and we for Him; and one Lord Jesus Christ, through whom *are* all things, and through whom we *live*. (1 Corinthians 8: 6)

> For in Him (Christ) dwells all the fullness of the Godhead bodily. (Colossians 2: 9)

> 9. Therefore God also has highly exalted Him and given Him the name which is above every name, 10. that at the name of Jesus every knee should bow, of those in heaven, and of those on earth, and of those under the earth, 11. and *that* every tongue should confess that Jesus Christ *is* Lord, to the glory of God the Father. (Philippians 2: 9-11)

It is through honoring the Son that we truly honor and worship God the Father. The name of Jesus is to be placed above all other names. God the Father awaits us as we come to Him in the name of Jesus. Thus, there seems to be little difficulty in recognizing that the name of Jesus carries with it sufficient authority that we might be baptized in that name. Another look at that passage in Matthew that mentions the Father, Son, and Holy Spirit may offer additional perspective that could help explain this apparent disparity.

> 19. Go therefore and make disciples of all nations, baptizing them in the name of the Father and of the Son and of the Holy Spirit, 20. teaching them to observe all things I have commanded you; and lo, I

am with you always, *even* to the end of the age. Amen. (Matthew 28: 19-20)

An interesting point from this passage is the manner in which the Father, Son, and Holy Spirit are addressed. The disciples are instructed to baptize in the *name* of the Father and of the Son and of the Holy Spirit. They are not told to baptize in the *names* of the Father and of the Son and of the Holy Spirit. The word *name* is singular, not plural. Father, Son, and Holy Spirit are not designations held by three entities, but rather, three titles or positions attributed to the Godhead (Acts 17: 29; Romans 1: 20; Colossians 2: 9). The apostles were not to baptize into three names, but in the three as one. That one was Jesus. The apostles obviously understood what Jesus expected of them and moved forward, baptizing in the name of Jesus.

* * * * *

The second possible resolution to the question of *in whose name* one should be baptized is this: the apostles did, in fact, baptize *'in the name of the Father and of the Son and of the Holy Spirit.'* This may affect a raised eyebrow, but this prospect deserves serious consideration.

Mere days after Jesus issued the Great Commission the Holy Spirit ushered in the Day of Pentecost. On that day Peter instructed the crowd that they must be baptized in the name of Jesus. Shall we attribute this discrepancy to poor memory on the part of the apostles? Did they simply fail to grasp the command given to them by Christ, or was it possibly an act of defiance since Jesus had left them? How about *none of the above*?

The Jews in Jerusalem were not unversed in baptism. Even prior to the time of John the Baptist they had observed the practice of proselyte baptism for those Gentiles who desired to convert to Judaism. As John the Baptist appeared on the scene, baptizing with water, the Bible makes no mention of people asking him to explain the meaning of baptism. They perceived that it was the zenith of a life-changing decision.

In addressing the Jews on the Day of Pentecost and explaining that they should be baptized in the name of Jesus, it makes sense that Peter's intent was to distinguish Christian baptism from any other baptism they may have witnessed in the past (e.g., the baptism performed by John). This does not mean that they would not be baptized in the name of the Father and of the Son and of the Holy Spirit, but that he was presenting this baptism to them through (by the authority of) Jesus Christ about whom Peter had just finished speaking. This clarification is made even more apparent as Paul met with the men in Ephesus (Acts 19: 1b-3). When Paul realized these men had not heard of the Holy Spirit, he assumed they had not been baptized in the name of Jesus. He naturally responded by inquiring of them exactly what baptism they had received (Acts 19: 3). Here he is clearly using the name of Jesus to contrast the baptism of John and Christian baptism. Had they been baptized in the name of Jesus, they would have undoubtedly known of the Holy Spirit since the name of the Father and the Son and the Holy Spirit would have been invoked at the time of their immersion.[1] Later, during Paul's appeal for unity in his letter to the Corinthians, he again denotes the association between the Holy Spirit and baptism (1 Corinthians 6: 11; 12: 13).

The notion that the apostles baptized in the name of the Father, Son, and Holy Spirit is certainly sustained by other writers in the first and second centuries. Justin Martyr, a man from the second century recognized as one of the Ante-Nicene Fathers, indicated the baptism that was practiced at that time.

> For, in the name of God, the Father and Lord of the universe, and of our Saviour Jesus Christ, and of the Holy Spirit, they then receive the washing with water.[2]

Perhaps the quandary of *whose name* should be invoked in baptism derives from the fact that many view this in terms of a precise *formula* of words that must, in conformity to biblical proclamation, be uttered at the time one is immersed. This does not seem to be the intention of Scripture. While Jesus does speak of baptism *'in the name of the Father and of the Son and of the Holy Spirit,'* and the apostles teach baptism *in Jesus' name,* the two need not be seen as antagonistic, but emphatic, in nature. Of prime importance in the gospel message is *recognition* that our salvation comes through Jesus and it is at the time of baptism that His blood is applied to our sins (Colossians 2: 11; Hebrews 10: 19-22), washing them into nothingness. That is the marrow of these two statements.

When Jesus told the disciples to baptize *'in the name of the Father and of the Son and of the Holy Spirit'* He predicated the statement with a remark concerning His own authority. He was presenting them instructions that were to be carried out in His name, or by His authority. Thus baptism *in Jesus' name* was never intended to identify a specific verbal expression to be invoked during baptism; rather it was the manner in which the apostles regarded Jesus' authority to command baptism of those who would follow Him. We find the apostles performing various other acts in the New Testament *in Jesus' name*. Most often this came in a form of physical healing or casting out demons (Acts 3: 6; 4: 10, 30; 16: 18). They also preached the *name of Jesus* (Acts 11: 20). These were not about a formula of words, but pointed to the source of authority by which these things were accomplished. Everything the apostles did from Pentecost forward was founded upon that authority, including baptism. Since Jesus ordained baptism in His name or by His own authority, perhaps we should baptize invoking the *name* specifically commanded by Him (Matthew 28: 19).

What, then, is the answer? Should men be baptized *in the name of Jesus* or *in the name of the Father and of the Son and of the Holy Spirit*? Certainly the name of Jesus carries with it the power of justification that would save us from our sins. Yet, Jesus specifically commanded that we should baptize in the latter. There also appears to be plausible evidence, implicitly stated, that the apostles did baptize in the name of the Father and of the Son and of the Holy Spirit. Paul clearly associated the recognition of the presence of the Holy Spirit with the rite of Christian baptism. When the Ephesians explained that they had not even, *'...heard whether there is a Holy Spirit,'* (Acts 19: 2), Paul assumed they had not received Christian baptism. His statement offers a direct link between the recognition of the Holy Spirit and water baptism. Given this kind of testimony, as well as the witness of others from the early church, baptism in the name of the Father, Son, and Holy Spirit, is what also makes the most sense for us today.

NOTES FOR CHAPTER 15

1. The suggestion that Paul's comment, "Into what then were you baptized?" denotes baptism in the name of the Father, Son, and Holy Spirit, is noted in the *New Advent Catholic Encyclopedia, Baptism, VI, Matter and Form of the Sacrament*.

2. The First Apology of Justin Martyr, Chapter LXI.-Christian Baptism.

Chapter XVI
Paedobaptism: Scriptural?

While the subject of baptism often provokes dissension among believers on a variety of levels, perhaps no point is more contentious than that of paedobaptism (infant baptism). It is a ritual that is performed by many and, accordingly, merits serious consideration. The founding principles of infant baptism derive from two dissimilar perspectives. Some view baptism as the time when sins are blotted out, a principle solidly founded in Scripture. This naturally results in a query regarding why sinless beings such as children would need sins removed from their lives. The notion is based upon the principle of original sin, the belief that each one who enters this world carries inherently the guilt of sin. If then, children are born guilty of sin, and baptism is the manner in which sin is remitted, baptism of children is reasonable.

There are those, however, who embrace the doctrine of infant baptism yet do not believe that sins are erased at the time of baptism. Instead, this rite is regarded as the mechanism that admits the child into the body of believers. Each of these viewpoints (forgiveness or membership into the body) relies heavily on what is seen as a sense of parity between water baptism in the new covenant and Jewish circumcision in the first covenant.

Original Sin
The myriad of arguments offered in support of, or opposition to, infant baptism must be able to withstand biblical scrutiny. A creed that is not supported by Scripture and does not harmonize with the fullness of God's Word must be deemed unreliable and dismissed accordingly. The Catholic Encyclopedia offers considerable discourse on the topic of original sin. This is only natural since it is a fundamental teaching that is embraced in full by practicing Roman Catholics.

> Original sin may be taken to mean: (1) the sin that Adam committed; (2) a consequence of this first sin, the hereditary stain with which we are born on account of our origin or descent from Adam.
>
> From the earliest times the latter sense of the word was more common, as may be seen by St. Augustine's statement: "the deliberate sin of the first man is the cause of original sin" (De nupt. et concup., II, xxvi, 43).

> It is the hereditary stain that is dealt with here. As to the sin of Adam we have not to examine the circumstances in which it was committed nor make the exegesis of the third chapter of Genesis.[1]

It is challenging to establish unequivocally the *guilt* of original sin from Scripture, notwithstanding the numerous voices making the assertion; and the phrase *original sin* does not appear in the Bible. In order for us to conclude anything with respect to this subject, the question as to whether or not such a doctrine blends with the message that is provided in God's Word must be answered satisfactorily.

> 12 Therefore, just as through one man sin entered the world, and death through sin, and thus death spread to all men, because all sinned — 13 (For until the law sin was in the world, but sin is not imputed when there is no law. 14 Nevertheless death reigned from Adam to Moses, even over those who had not sinned according to the likeness of the transgression of Adam, who is a type of Him who was to come. 15. But the free gift is not like the offense. For if by the one man's offense many died, much more the grace of God and the gift by the grace of the one Man, Jesus Christ, abounded to many. 16. And the gift is not like that which came through the one who sinned. For the judgment which came from one offense resulted in condemnation, but the free gift which came from many offenses resulted in justification. 17. For if by one man's offense death reigned through the one, much more those who receive abundance of grace and the gift of righteousness will reign in life through the one, Jesus Christ). 18. Therefore, as through one man's offense judgment came to all men, resulting in condemnation, even so through one man's righteous act the free gift came to all men, resulting in justification of life. 19. For as by one man's disobedience many were made sinners, so also by one man's obedience many will be made righteous. (Romans 5: 12-19)

This is a cumbersome passage to be sure. Yet the thoughts are a bit easier to take in when we recognize the fact that the proposition of verse twelve is answered in verses eighteen and nineteen, while everything in between is essentially a parenthetic comment offering further insight into the problems caused by Adam's sin and the solution wrought by Christ's sacrifice.

Death entered into the world through Adam and consequently spread to all of mankind (Romans 5: 12-13). Yet certain actualities must be taken into consideration in order to determine Paul's intent. The first is that it is death, rather than sin, that ultimately spread from Adam to all men. Death crept into the world through Adam's sin and ultimately extended to men everywhere. Death is a consequence of sin. Yet, according to Paul's words the death of an individual, such as an infant, is not necessarily due to *guilt* that is ascribed to him/her. He notes that there are those who die not having sinned as Adam sinned (v. 14). How might we classify the *manner* of Adam's sin, you may ask? What is it that distinguishes Adam's sin – the sin that brought death upon mankind? In his letter to Timothy Paul points out that, unlike Eve's sin, where she was deceived by Satan, Adam's sin was *deliberate* (1 Timothy 2: 14). Paul identifies Adam's sin in the Romans passage cited previously as *disobedience* (v. 19), depicting the voluntary nature of the act. Still, it is certainly true that all men were condemned to death as a consequence of Adam's sin.

Note that, *'sin is not imputed when there is no law.'* Exactly what law, then, would apply to an infant? No awareness of right or wrong exists at that stage of life. An infant is even incapable of evil thoughts. Actually, Paul addresses that very issue immediately prior to his utterance that all have sinned in Romans 3: 23.

> 20. Therefore by the deeds of the law no flesh will be justified in His sight, for by the law is the knowledge of sin. 21. But now the righteousness of God apart from the law is revealed, being witnessed by the Law and the Prophets, 22. Even the righteousness of God through faith in Jesus Christ, to all and on all who believe. For there is no difference; 23. for all have sinned and fall short of the glory of God. (Romans 3: 20-23)

Without law there is no knowledge of sin (Romans 3: 20). For the infant there is no law, nor is there any knowledge of sin. Paul is specifically talking about the availability of God's righteousness *'through faith…to all and on all who believe.'* His remarks are not concentrated on the innocent newborn, but on those who have the capacity to make life decisions.

> For I, the Lord your God, am a jealous God, visiting the iniquity of the fathers upon the children to the third and fourth generations of those who hate Me... (Exodus 20: 5)

> The Lord is longsuffering and abundant in mercy, forgiving iniquity and transgression; but He by no means clears the guilty, visiting the iniquity of the fathers on the children to the third and fourth generation. (Numbers 14: 18)

While God may visit *'the iniquity of the fathers on the children...'* the sin is still that of the father, and not the children. In truth, what more effective reproof exists to penalize the guilty than by punishing his descendants for his sin? Such was the case with King David. The child he fathered with Bathsheba died, not because of anything the child had done, but as a direct result of David's sin (2 Samuel 12: 14). Ezekiel addressed directly the biblical principle that one is not held responsible, as a matter of judgment, for the sins of others.

> The soul who sins shall die. The son shall not bear the guilt of the father, nor the father bear the guilt of the son. The righteousness of the righteous shall be upon himself, and the wickedness of the wicked shall be upon himself. (Ezekiel 18: 20)

There is, of course, David's claim that he was conceived in sin (Psalm 51: 5). David is not suggesting that the manner of conception is evil. Nor do we have reason to believe that David was conceived out of wedlock as a matter of sin. Of all biblical passages, the language here could be construed to denote original sin if the backdrop for the wording is not considered. David's lament is perhaps twofold. First, he seems to be alluding to the fact that he can remember no time when sin was absent from his life. His grief stems from his sorrow over his separation from God because of sin. Yet the sins about which David is overwrought (v. 5) are sins he consciously committed against God (v. 4) rather than the sins of others (such as Adam). Secondly, and perhaps even more relevant, is David's recognition that men are prone to succumb to temptation. That is to say, men are predisposed to sin when temptation presents itself. That fact is true from the moment one is conceived, even though temptation and sin are still at a distance. For that reason Paul could boldly proclaim that *'all have sinned.'* (Romans 3: 23)

It is important to consider the context of David's words – that is the symbolic as well as the poetic character of the Psalms where hyperbole and metaphor are the rule rather than the exception. Such is the case here. Nothing connected with David's conception or birth would be considered evil or sinful even in the eyes of God. As David considered his own sinful nature, he served up a lament to God for his own sinful *choices* of which he was keenly aware. The passage apparently denotes David's compunction specifically over his fornication with Bathsheba and the murder of her husband Uriah – sins far removed from his own conception.

When Noah exited the ark, God promised to *'never again curse the ground for man's sake, although the imagination of man's heart is evil from his youth...'* (Genesis 8: 21). This passage speaks of man's evil heart *beginning with his adolescence* (מנעריו), or pre-adulthood, not in conception or infancy.

If, as many claim, all are conceived in a sinful state, then Jesus, born of woman, would necessarily have been conceived in like manner. Yet the passage from Ezekiel plainly denies the claim that the *guilt* of sin passes from father to son. Therefore, when a man or woman enters this world through childbirth, God sees that person as an innocent being.

It appears that these passages (Romans 3: 20; Ezekiel 18: 20) provide us with a qualification of Romans 3: 23. When Paul states that *all have sinned*, which he echoes in Romans 5: 12, it is reasonable to conclude, given the scriptural landscape, that all men who have the *opportunity* for sin have, at least once, fallen short. His remarks lie within the context of those who have the capacity for faith (Romans 3: 26). Ezekiel, however, indicates that God considers each man and woman to be perfect from the moment of conception until his/her first sin.

* * * * *

While the concept of original sin conflicts with instruction found in God's Word, it would be foolish to maintain that we are not affected by Adam's sin. Even though we do not bear the *guilt* of Adam's sin, it seems clear from Paul's words (Romans 5: 12-18) that there is an *effect* on all men that originates from that sin whereby *'many were made sinners'* (v. 19). Adam's disobedience has left a mark on the face of mankind, although the nature of that mark is not entirely clear. Of course, it is the ambiguity of the remarks from which we can deduce that, if the sin of Adam is charged to his descendents in some manner, God has not placed upon the shoulders of men the obligation to remove that particular blemish. There is no call within the pages of Scripture for man to do anything to eradicate *that* sin.

Paul recognizes the effect of Adam's sin on other men and then immediately distinguishes between the impact of that kind of stain and the sin Adam actually committed. Adam's sin was a sin of choice. He was disobedient. In whatever manner his sin has touched other men the effect on them is not the same as that realized by Adam. He alone is responsible for his sin while others are responsible for sins they have committed (Ezekiel 18: 20).

These things having been said, we need to ask ourselves a question concerning the role of baptism. We must address whether we should consider baptism appropriate for infants *even if* we bear in any way the burden of Adam's sin. While we learn from Paul that, as a result of Adam's disobedience, *'many were made sinners'* (Romans 5: 19), we discover in that same passage that all men have been conversely affected by Christ's obedience. Paul indicates that the obedience of Christ on the cross has an offsetting effect on those who may be affected by Adam's sin. We also learn that Jesus' obedience is not equal to, but far superior to, Adam's disobedience. Paul says it is *'much more'* (v. 15). Concerning the obedience and disobedience of Jesus and Adam respectively, Paul repeats himself several times in order to make his point clear (Romans 5: 12-19). Death came through Adam while life comes through Christ (v. 17). Condemnation came through Adam while justification comes through Jesus (v. 16). Our sinful nature came through Adam while righteousness comes through the Lord (v. 19).

We also discover from Paul's words that the counteraction of Jesus' obedience affects us *in like manner* as the disobedience of Adam. Consequently, if Adam's sin is *automatically* assigned to men in some fashion, it seems that Christ's sacrifice, providing the opposite, albeit more forceful, effect is also intended to *automatically* apply in blotting out that sin. This is the essence of Paul's comment, *'as by one man's offense...so through one man's righteous act'* (v. 18). Again we find, *'as by one man's disobedience...so also by one man's obedience'* (v. 19).What is true of Adam's offense is conversely true of Christ's righteous act. In the face of the consequence of Adam's offense, this would explain a great deal concerning God's view of the innocence of infants and children.

In that same vein, when sin becomes a matter of choice, as was true of Adam's sin, the man who succumbs to temptation is held accountable for the sin committed. In that case, it stands to reason that the appeal for forgiveness must also be by choice – an appeal made via repentance and baptism (Acts 2: 38, 1 Peter 3: 21).

As we consider New Testament instruction concerning baptism, we discover that it serves a specific purpose in that it is the moment of forgiveness of sins. Yet baptism is *always* conjoined with belief and repentance when it comes to forgiveness. Baptism, combined with repentance, is relational in that repentance gives forgiveness a sense of *meaning* for those who submit to the Lord in baptism. By this we understand that baptism is designed to forgive sins committed *'in the likeness of the transgression of Adam'* (Romans 5: 14). That is the precise focus of the baptism of the New Testament.

New Testament Omission of Infant Baptism

The New Testament does not provide instruction regarding the baptism of infants and this absence in Scripture is a key factor in any discussion of the subject. It does not find support either through *direct command* or *necessary inference*. The single conclusion that can be drawn from an honest examination of relevant passages regarding this rite is that infant baptism is ineffectual. Matthew recorded the words of Jesus when He spoke concerning children. Jesus not only clearly recognized, but also markedly focused upon, their innocence.

> 1. At that time the disciples came to Jesus, saying, "Who then is the greatest in the kingdom of heaven?" 2. Then Jesus called a little child to Him, set him in the midst of them, 3. and said, "Assuredly, I say to you, unless you are converted and become as little children, you will by no means enter the kingdom of heaven." (Matthew 18: 1-3)

> But Jesus said, "Let the little children come unto Me, and do not forbid them; for of such is the kingdom of heaven." (Matthew 19: 14)

Contrary to the notion that children should be held accountable for sins they had not committed, Jesus testifies that we, as adults, must become *like* them in their guilelessness in order to enter the kingdom of heaven. Children are the epitome of innocence. He did not call them to Himself to be baptized, although Jesus' disciples had by this time been performing baptisms (see John 3: 22; 4: 1-2). Rather than suggesting baptism, these children are portrayed as the example of what we are to become when we are converted.

The Candidate for Baptism

Numerous passages offer additional insight into whether or not infant baptism might be effective for salvation. While these do not speak specifically regarding infants, they provide direction about the characteristics of someone who would be considered an acceptable candidate for baptism.

> And he went into all the region around Jordan, preaching a baptism of repentance for the remission of sins. (Luke 3: 3)
>
> I indeed baptize you with water unto repentance. (Matthew 3: 11)
>
> Then Peter said to them, "Repent, and let every one of you be baptized in the name of Jesus Christ for the remission of sins..." (Acts 2: 38)

The baptism depicted in Scripture was *for* forgiveness. Accompanying baptism, each believer was to repent for the sins he/she had committed. Jesus' remarks[2] suggest that children would not be held accountable for sins until they were perhaps of an age when they would truly understand the concept of sin. Jesus viewed small children as innocent beings. It is impossible for a small child or infant to repent of sins of which he has no understanding. This is a primary reason the biblical authors failed to address infant baptism.

Exploring these passages, a scriptural pattern develops. That pattern is this: in every case those who were baptized made a clear decision in favor of baptism based upon the teaching they had received. Philip told the Ethiopian eunuch that he could be baptized *if he believed*. Those on the Day of Pentecost (Acts 2: 41) *'gladly received his word'* prior to baptism. Jesus commanded that belief on the part of the one being baptized was an essential predicate to baptism. (Mark 16: 16)

Explaining, then, how an infant could *gladly receive* the word or *believe* on Jesus, with no ability to perceive the teaching, presents a particularly difficult problem for those who wish to teach infant baptism. Combined with the fact that Jesus acknowledges a purity of heart with respect to children, it is difficult to establish biblical justification or support for this practice.

In quoting Jesus' words concerning baptism, it has been suggested that Mark may not be placing the precept of belief *prior* to baptism (Mark 16: 16) in a chronological sense, but perhaps offers the statement in a manner that simply places emphasis upon belief. Therefore, the infant who is baptized and later believes would satisfy this imperative. Throughout the whole of Scripture, however, belief is presented as the initial step a man must take toward salvation (Acts 8: 36-37; 16: 31-33; Romans 10: 10). The proposition that one might repent or confess prior to belief is, of course, unimaginable. Additionally, Scripture places the responsibility for repentance and confession squarely upon the believer as a matter of decision (Acts 2: 38; Romans 10: 9). A parent cannot repent or confess Jesus as Savior on behalf of an infant since the Bible portrays these as subject to the decision-making of the person involved. So it is with baptism. God's Word portrays baptism as a matter of personal conviction – a matter of choice (Acts 18: 8; Galatians 3: 27).

What Is a Household?

Vital to the defense of the doctrine of infant baptism is the use of the word *household* in certain narratives within the book of Acts (Acts 16: 14-15, 30-33; 18: 8). Those men who practice infant baptism have concluded that this *could* indicate that a decision *may* have been made by the head of the house to have each one baptized, and that this *may* have even included infants. The story of Lydia (Acts 16: 15) affirms that her entire household was baptized. An unsupported assumption must be made to conclude that small children who were not old enough to understand and make an informed decision participated in this baptism. No such representation can be found in the text. In the words of Alexander Campbell, *'Positive ordinances demand positive proof....'*[3] If Scripture provides no such evidence the claim is unfounded, especially since it seems utterly contrary to the instructions provided by the apostles.

In the account of the Philippian jailer (Acts 16: 30-33) *'...they spoke the word of the Lord to him and to all who were in his house.'* The fact that the word was spoken *'to all who were in his house'* seems a reliable indication that they all had the ability to hear and understand the word being spoken. They, therefore, would also have the ability to respond, on a personal level, to the message being taught. The incident does not lend itself to the *conclusion* that infants were baptized.

As Crispus listened to the gospel message from Paul, he *'believed on the Lord with all his household.'* The testimony is that those in the house had the capacity to discern and believe. We are not told that Crispus believed on behalf of others. On the contrary, those who were *baptized* were those who *believed*. The fact that Crispus was a ruler of the synagogue indicates that he was probably not a young man with small children. A position of such prominence was reserved for men who had proven themselves over time.

Quite often the mention of *household* is not even a reference to direct family, but to others (servants, etc.) who abide there, as was the case with Cornelius when he called his *'household servants'* ($των$ $οικετων$) (Acts 10: 7). This is the more reasonable conclusion with respect to the household of Crispus. This may also be the case with Lydia. Yet it is not the means by which infants can be ruled out since a household can also include infants. Rather, it is the statement regarding the belief of those who were baptized that is the overriding determinant.

While the absence or presence of infants in these households cannot be firmly established, we can state resolutely that they are not mentioned. This fact limits us to three specific possibilities. Either (1) no children who were too young to understand the gospel message were present at the time or (2) they were not given consideration in the text because they were not viable candidates for belief and baptism or (3) they were baptized without being mentioned. In order to draw any conclusion we must consider the greater landscape of Scripture.

Concerning those episodes where many were gathered, such as Pentecost, there is insistence by many that children (infants) must not only have been present, but baptized, suggesting that, in such a great crowd the absence of infants is unlikely. Yet, when we do encounter a crowd where the message is proclaimed and, arguably, infants *must have been* present, baptism was limited to men and women. For instance, as Philip preached in Samaria, he preached to crowds of people.

> 5. Then Philip went down to the city of Samaria and preached Christ to them. 6. And the multitudes with one accord heeded the things spoken by Philip, hearing and seeing the miracles which he did…12. But when they believed Philip as he preached the things concerning the kingdom of God and the name of Jesus Christ, both men and women were baptized. (Acts 8: 5-6, 12)

As Philip spoke to *multitudes*, and the likelihood of the presence of small children and infants is strong, it was still men and women who were baptized. Since no indication of the baptism of infants is given, and the recipients of baptism are specifically identified as men and women, proclaiming the baptism of infants from the silence of other episodes (e.g., the jailer, Lydia, or Crispus) seems a considerable leap. So, too, when Paul preached in Corinth, it was those who *heard* and *believed* who were baptized (Acts 18: 8). We would be wise to follow this apostolic pattern today concerning the relationship between belief and baptism.

Baptism and Circumcision

In the third chapter of this book we considered briefly the weaknesses of the creed that regards baptism in the new covenant as a replacement of circumcision in the first covenant. The presumed association between the two lies at the heart of the doctrine of infant baptism. In an effort to combat entrenched beliefs concerning this commonly accepted view, a more in-depth examination of the deficiencies surrounding this position is offered at this time.

On the eighth day after a male Israelite was born he would be circumcised according to the law (Genesis 17: 12). Many believe that since circumcision might be considered, in essence, initiation into the old covenant, the ceremony that initiates into the new covenant must have replaced it. That initiation ceremony is viewed as baptism. This assumption, then, is the basic premise for the institution of infant baptism. Just as Israelite male infants were acknowledged in the old covenant through circumcision, so may the child of today be *recognized* as a faithful member of the new covenant through baptism. Yet, Mont W. Smith draws a clear distinction between a covenant sign, such as circumcision, and the oath taken in a covenant as a matter of conviction.

> There is a difference between the oath or pledge of a covenant and the "sign" of a covenant. The Hebrew for oath was *alah*. It was also used for "the curse of covenant," because an oath was both a commitment and a self-curse. The sign of a covenant was *'ot*. The oath was walking between the halves of the slain animals, touching "the blood of the covenant." A sign was a visible representation or memorial to that ceremony. It may have been a pile of rocks (Gen. 31:44f), or a rainbow (Gen. 9:13), or others. The oath swearing of God and Abraham was passing between the halves (Gen. 15:17, 18). The sign of the covenant that night was circumcision (17:11). The sign of the Mosaic covenant was the Sabbath (Exod. 31-13). The sign of the Christian covenant was possessing the holy Spirit or living the kind of life Jesus did (Eph. 1: 13).[4]

Circumcision in the Old Testament was performed on any male born into the Israelite lineage. It was a sign of the covenant God established with Abraham. God declared concerning circumcision, *'...and it shall be a sign of the covenant between Me and you'* (Genesis 17: 11). This rite was intended as a constant memorial, or reminder, of the covenant. While circumcision was a sign of the Abrahamic covenant, membership was recognized as a birthright (Genesis 17: 1-8). In like manner, just as membership in the first covenant came through childbirth, in the New Testament we are told that entry into the kingdom of heaven comes through a second birth (John 3: 3; Galatians 4: 21-31; 1 Peter 1: 23; Titus 3: 5). What we must consider is whether baptism is a covenant sign in the likeness of circumcision, or the oath (*alah*) through which we are reborn, thus establishing us in the new covenant.

In the Old Testament, not every covenant was given a sign (e.g., the Davidic covenant) and not every sign was a covenant sign. While we read of many *signs* in God's Word, the truth is that a covenant sign was/is a rare commodity. Signs were often given in witness of God's handiwork (1 Kings 13: 2-3; 2 Kings 19: 29-31; Isaiah 66: 19; Ezekiel 4: 3). These, however, were not established as covenant signs. Jonah's adventure, as he spent three days in the belly of a fish, was a sign of Jesus' burial (Matthew 12: 39), yet it was not a covenant sign. In the New Testament, the baby Jesus *'...wrapped in swaddling cloths, lying in a manger'* (Luke 2: 12) was a sign for the shepherds, but it cannot be regarded as a covenant sign.

For an event or object to be considered a covenant sign it must exhibit certain characteristics. First of all, in a forthright manner its station as a sign must be made manifest. Arnold G. Fruchtenbaum, an expert in the Old Testament and Hebrew culture, remarks *"what is a sign of a covenant is what God calls a sign of a covenant and therefore, I would agree that 'a sign must be formally declared.'"* [5] Furthermore, as we examine the nature of these signs in Scripture, we discover one more common trait. A steadfast feature of a covenant sign, such as the Sabbath Day (Exodus 31: 13-17), is that it *persists* throughout the life of the covenant, either perpetually or repeatedly, as a reminder of promises that have been made. Since the purpose of a *covenant* sign is remembrance, its continuation is vital.

When a man and woman marry they exchange rings as a *sign or seal* of the covenant they have made. The continued presence of those rings serves as a daily reminder to them. When God made His covenant with Noah, He stated, *'I set My rainbow in the cloud....'* The rainbow was the sign of that covenant. Each time a rainbow appears it serves as a token not only to men, but also to God, concerning His promise to never again flood the entire earth (Genesis 9: 11-17). Finally, when God established a sign with Abraham it was the sign of circumcision, which a man would carry with him permanently in full recognition that his inheritance, including the promise of the coming Messiah, was through Abraham's seed. No *covenant* sign in the Bible fails to meet the qualifications of declaration and continuance.

It is perhaps a great deal more reasonable in linking baptism to the first covenant that it should be most closely associated with a child's birth into that covenant, a point made in Chapter II. This is true for a couple of very important reasons. The first is the fact that, within the teaching of Jesus and the apostles, the implication that baptism is a *sign* cannot be found. It is certainly emblematic of the death, burial, and resurrection of Jesus (Romans 6: 1-4; Colossians 2: 11-12), but this rite of baptism completely lacks the characteristics of a covenant sign. The presence of symbolism does not automatically confer the status of *covenant sign* to an object or event. A covenant sign is installed as a continuing memento of the constitution of that covenant.

Secondly, baptism in the new covenant, like childbirth before it, is recognized in Scripture, not as a sign, but as the passageway through which man becomes a participant in the covenant. Just as men are physically born only once, so they are born once spiritually. Thus, baptism is no more a sign in the new covenant than a child's birth was a sign in the first covenant.

Honest consideration of the connection between baptism in the new covenant and childbirth into the old covenant is both imperative and enlightening. Their relationship becomes even more visible when we reconsider God's covenant with Noah. Peter declared the waters of baptism an *antitype* to the waters of the flood (1 Peter 3: 21). Yet the rainbow, not the water, was the *sign* of the covenant between God and Noah just as circumcision was the sign between God and Abraham. The water, on the other hand, represented an immersion, resulting in regeneration and renewal of the world God had created. If God intended for us to consider baptism as a covenant sign, as many people maintain, it seems

Peter would have likened baptism, not to the *waters* of the flood, but to the rainbow, which was/is the sign of that covenant.

One question consistently remains unanswered by those who hold to the circumcision/baptism connection, and it is a question that begins with the baptism performed by John the Baptist. John's was a baptism for the forgiveness of sins that was performed on none other than the Israelites. Yet a baptism in replacement of circumcision would have abolished the rite of circumcision. However, no elimination of circumcision can be found during the period of time that John baptized. Those who were baptized also practiced circumcision faithfully. Upon the institution of Christian baptism, no thought was given to the rite of circumcision. The Israelites, including those who were converted Gentiles, practiced circumcision without consideration that it may have been replaced. Not until several years later, with respect to Gentiles in the church, did the topic of circumcision even arise within the new covenant.

In Antioch, a dispute arose regarding circumcision, a narrative that can be found in the fifteenth chapter of Acts. Some Jews believed and taught that circumcision was essential for both Jews and Gentiles within the new covenant. As the issue came before the apostles and elders in Jerusalem it was determined that circumcision was not pertinent in the covenant of grace.

Of note in this episode is the fact that the subject of baptism never surfaces. In a setting where the entire focus is the requirement of circumcision in the new covenant, if baptism should be considered its replacement it is inconceivable that these pages of Scripture would be silent on the matter. If this reflected apostolic understanding, that association would necessarily have emerged at this time since it was incumbent upon the apostles to teach the full truth of God. Their staggering silence concerning any connection between the two at the time of the Jerusalem Council wholly repudiates the claim.

When the church leaders were approached concerning circumcision in the new covenant, instead of teaching baptism as the new circumcision, they *'came together to consider this matter'* (Acts 15: 6). Thus they weighed the necessity of circumcision even in the presence of baptism. The bigger issue, of course, encompassed the commandments of the Mosaic Law and their relevance to the covenant of grace. Yet, during their deliberations we find not even the slightest insinuation of a relationship between baptism and circumcision. Baptism was simply not a factor in the decision to dismiss circumcision for Gentiles. Furthermore, Christian Jews continued to practice circumcision faithfully after the Jerusalem Council even as they submitted to Christ in baptism. Thus the early church consisted of both circumcised and uncircumcised Christians. It is evident, then, that an association between baptism and the circumcision of Israelite infants was never contemplated in the first century church.

What *is* clear from Scripture is that the role of baptism in the covenant of grace differs significantly from the role of circumcision in the old covenant. We have already seen that the precedent for baptism lies, not in circumcision, but in the various washings of the old covenant as well as God's use of water for the creation (birth and rebirth) of life.

Circumcision and the Death of Christ

Perhaps the best association between the circumcision of the old covenant and its correspondent in the new covenant can be found in the death of Christ. This is not to suggest that Jesus' death should be considered some kind of sign of the covenant, but circumcision is certainly represented within this setting. Paul states, *'In Him you were also circumcised with the circumcision made without hands, by putting off the body of the sins of the flesh, by the circumcision of Christ'* (Colossians 2:11). Note that Paul does not state that this is the circumcision of baptism, but the circumcision of Christ, as our sins are removed by means of His death. Once again we turn to Mont W. Smith for clarification on this point:

> A passage in Colossians used the words circumcision, sinful nature, the circumcision of Christ, and baptism as burial together in a discussion. Paul did not equate circumcision with baptism. He did not use them in parallel. The "circumcision not done with hands," that is, "the circumcision of Christ," was His death. He was cut off. His entire body on the cross was "circumcised." The Christian joined Christ at baptism when he participated in that death and resurrection.[6]

In this case, like childbirth and circumcision in the first covenant, Paul's remark concerning circumcision and the ceremony of baptism are in such close proximity that many fail to recognize the distinction between them in this passage. The *'circumcision made without hands'* is the removal of our sins that is promised at the time of baptism (Acts 2: 38). The decision to be baptized is ours to make. The circumcision (cutting off or removal) of our sins is the work of God that occurs as we submit in the waters of baptism, making us holy in His eyes.

Infant Baptism and the Day of Pentecost

Often those who attempt to make the case for infant baptism turn to the Day of Pentecost, and Peter's remarks there, in defense of their view. The following statement is considered very significant with respect to the role of the children of Christian parents within the new covenant:

> For the promise is unto you, and to your children, and to all who are afar off, as many as the Lord our God will call. (Acts 2:39)

The first relevant point we must recognize from this verse is that those to whom Peter was speaking were not yet Christians. Since the point regarding paedobaptism is understood to be for children of parents who are already established within God's covenant, this passage must not apply since Peter's words here cannot be seen as speaking of the children of Christian parents. In the ensuing verses we learn that, of the crowd gathered, only *'those who gladly received his words were baptized; and that day about three thousand souls were added to them'* (Acts 2: 41). Those to whom Peter spoke these words did not all accept Christ. He also mentioned *'all who are afar off,'* men and women who had yet to hear the gospel and even those who were yet to be born. These are timeless words spoken by Peter, and they must apply equally to *'you'* (including those who did not accept Christ) and to *'your children'* and to *'all who are afar off.'*

The word *'children'* in this instance is not limited to the immediate children of those present in the crowd. Peter has in view generations, not infants and adolescents. The expanse of the remark is made clear as we realize that the promise is also to *'all who are afar off.'* For all time the call is from God to all those who are able to respond to the message Peter had just delivered, and are able to do so in the manner in which Peter calls upon them to respond; that is, *repent and be baptized.*

The Unnecessary Inference of Infant Baptism

God views marriage as a covenant and, therefore, does not take it lightly. Paul recognized that some believers, having accepted

Jesus as Savior, could find themselves married to someone who was an unbeliever (1 Corinthians 7: 12-19). This was undoubtedly a common situation in the early church as people learned the message of the gospel and some believed while others did not. It is not that uncommon in our own day and age. It was not God's desire, however, that the marriage would decay in such a circumstance. While the choice between God and spouse must clearly result in a choice for God, Paul suggested that if that choice was not necessary, the marriage might endure.

Offering what Paul describes as his own words, we learn that those who believe have a sanctifying effect upon the unbelieving spouse. This should not be construed as salvation for the unbeliever. Sanctification does not automatically presume justification. It appears, however, that simply having such an intimate relationship with one of God's children, and loving that person, results in a sense of consecration and blessing for the unbelieving spouse. Of interest in this passage is Paul's view of the children. They are holy (v. 14). While this is perhaps a reference to the holiness of the child with respect to the relationship of the parents, since it is a loving relationship within the framework of marriage, in a passage that features the child of a believer, no suggestion of baptism can be found.

Infant baptism is an excellent example of doctrine that has been conceived upon a foundation of scriptural silence. While the old covenant assigns infant circumcision its rightful place within the scope of that covenant, no such teaching regarding baptism can be found within the pages of the covenant of grace, which is the New Testament. Passages that are employed in defense of this practice seem to be considered valid by many despite the fact that infant baptism is mentioned in none of them. In order to reach a conclusion in favor of infant baptism based upon these writings, certain assumptions must be ascribed to the text - assumptions that cannot be supported by the fullness of God's Word.

Infant baptism, then, is concluded, not from the teaching of the Word, but from unspoken inferences that are drawn from certain passages. The objection to this doctrine lies in the fact that no passage exists where one must *necessarily* conclude through *inference* that infant baptism even occurred, much less that it was ordained or commanded as part of the gospel message. Yet there are numerous passages of Scripture that clearly indicate the unreasonableness of this principle (Mark 16: 16; Acts 2: 38; 8: 37;

16: 31). The Catholic Encyclopedia does not cite much Scripture on the subject (only Romans 5: 12 and 1 Corinthians 12: 12). Most support is drawn from writers beginning in the late second century and beyond when the doctrine of infant baptism was just beginning to develop. The same is true of all pro-paedobaptism literature. Even John Calvin, a zealous advocate of infant baptism, did not offer his defense of the rite based upon scriptural example. His approach to the subject was founded on a personal view that, *'...whatever belongs to circumcision, except the difference of the visible ceremony, belongs also to baptism.'* [7]

Paedobaptism and Immersion

As we contemplate the baptism of infants, we often find men insisting that this was a practice handed down by the apostles. Yet it is plain that the baptism of Scripture was by immersion in water. This is a reality recognized even by those who postulate infant baptism. John Calvin recognized the baptism of the New Testament as immersion in water, stating, *"The word baptize signifies to immerse, and the rite of immersion was practiced by the ancient church."* [8] So, too, John Wesley and Martin Luther both acknowledged immersion as the baptism of Scripture. In keeping with their awareness that immersion was the baptism of the first century, these men granted that it was *highly* unlikely that paedobaptism was a practice of the apostles. In fact, Luther even went as far as to concede that proof of infant baptism by the apostles was clearly lacking in Scripture as he remarked:

> "It can not be proved by the sacred Scriptures that infant baptism was instituted by Christ, or began by the first Christians after the apostles." [9]

If we are to maintain that infant baptism was a practice of the early church, we must be able to reconcile this with the immersion that was practiced at that time. Did Jesus and the apostles immerse infants as a matter of baptism? Scripture offers no evidence that this ever occurred, much less that it was commanded. The practice of immersion in the early church, combined with the attributes of a baptismal candidate that are depicted in God's Word (e.g., belief, repentance, etc.), simply prohibit the establishment of the doctrine of infant baptism from apostolic instruction.

Forgiveness through Baptism Alone

Those who profess infant baptism have mistakenly ascribed to this rite a characteristic that Scripture does not. Man is not able to obtain forgiveness of sins through baptism alone any more than through faith alone. When forgiveness of sins is attributed to baptism, it is consistently portrayed in conjunction with the other precepts God has established, such as belief and repentance. In fact, repentance is depicted in Scripture as at least as relevant to forgiveness as baptism (Acts 3: 19; 13: 24; 17: 30). Peter taught forgiveness, not for those who were *baptized*, but for those who *repented and were baptized* (Acts 2: 38). Jesus did not declare that those who were *baptized*, but that those who *believed and were baptized*, would be saved (Mark 16: 16). Placing the whole of forgiveness upon submission to baptism simply does not harmonize with the role of baptism that is displayed in God's Word.

No compelling debate in favor of infant baptism is encountered in the New Testament. The general theme of baptism in Scripture, which involves belief, repentance, and the human decision making process, provides impressive evidence that New Testament baptism was never intended to be performed on infants. A relevant question, however, is whether or not infant baptism does any harm.[10] Even if infant baptism provides no justification, since the newborn has not sinned, what damage can it do? Perhaps it is better to proactively baptize the infant rather than take the risk that he/she might die and not go to heaven. It is a legitimate point that should be given suitable consideration.

Infants are not immersed – the one mode of baptism taught and practiced in the Bible. Yet the child who is sprinkled as an infant may be raised with the understanding that he/she has been baptized and, therefore, has no need for the one true baptism of repentance and forgiveness. The Bible teaches repentance and baptism (immersion) as the mechanism in which we receive forgiveness of sins and the indwelling of the Holy Spirit. While this presumably occurs at a time of confirmation later in the child's life, this is not the manner of events portrayed in Scripture, nor is the teaching of confirmation displayed there. In God's Word, repentance is accompanied by baptism. Could infant baptism be harmful? There is no doubt about the possible implications.

In short, infant baptism cannot be supported in an honest search of the Scriptures. Why some practice this rite when no appreciable encouragement can be found in God's Word is puzzling. It is disconcerting that such a practice could cost the souls of many who might have been saved.

NOTES FOR CHAPTER 16

1. New Advent. Catholic Bible. Original Sin.

2. Campbell, in a <u>REVIEW OF BISHOP KENRICK'S TREATISE</u>, regarding infant baptism, states the following in answer to Kenrick's argument. First is stated the argument in favor of infant baptism, and then Campbell's response:

> *Bible Argument, No. 1.*--"Who," says the bishop, "would venture to deny that they can be saved of whom Christ has said, 'Suffer the little children to come to me, and forbid them not, for of such is the kingdom of God!'"
>
> To this argument I have four objections:-- [315].
>
> 1. It changes the subject of discussion. It is *baptism*, and not salvation, for which the bishop pleads; and now he talks of salvation, and asks, "Who can deny that infants can be *saved.*"
>
> 2. These children were brought to the Messiah, neither for baptism nor for salvation, but for his blessing.
>
> 3. They were brought to Jesus *before* Christian baptism was ordained; and, therefore, their case can have no logical nor scriptural connection with baptism.
>
> 4. Jesus does not say that the kingdom of God is composed of *little children;* but of such as are, in some respects, *like them.* The English Hexapla, in all its versions, even including the Rheims, has "of such," and not *of them.* The late Polyglot, containing eight languages, which I have just examined, also favours this version. The French version expresses the full sense of them all. It reads in Matt. xix. 13; Mark x. 14; Luke xv2i.15, *Qui lour ressemblent.* The kingdom of God is of those who *resemble* them. There is not, then, a single version of the New Testament, in either Bagster's Hexapla, or in Bagster's recent splendid Polyglot Bible, containing the Greek, Hebrew, Latin, English, French, German, Italian, and Spanish approved versions, that justifies the bishop's gloss. Alexander, Campbell, <u>Christian Baptism, with Its Antecedents and Consequents</u> B O O K S I X T H. CHAPTER I. (1851).

3. Campbell's continued <u>REVIEW OF BISHOP KENRICK'S TREATISE</u> addresses the issue regarding the conversion of households. First the claim and then the rebuttal:

> "We are challenged to show that the Apostles baptized infants. Had we a detailed enumeration of their ministerial acts, the challenge would be reasonable; but the book styled their Acts contains only some of the chief facts which marked the origin and proved the divine authority of the Christian church. Yet even there it is said that Lydia 'was baptized and her household,' and the jailer 'was baptized and presently all his family;' and St. Paul testifies that he 'baptized also the household of Stephanas.' It cannot indeed be proved that infants were in these families; but the presumption is that there were, and the general expressions naturally lead us to consider the baptism of all the children as following the conversion of the parent." [319].

> Our resolute champion for the infant rite, in his self-respect and candour, is, it appears, in the end of his enumeration of households baptized, constrained to give up his own argument deduced from them, and to acknowledge that an infant cannot be found in any one of them. So these, too, are abandoned, and his dernier resort is to tradition--ecclesiastic tradition. He, of course, desires to find in the first century or second century some case that would favour the idea. Beginning with Justin Martyr, who flourished about the middle of it, and then proceeding to Irenæus, who flourished at the end of it, he cannot find a clear allusion to it, much less a positive proof of it; for infant baptism is not so much as named in any fragment of ancient tradition during the first and second centuries. No living man can find any allusion to it, or account of it, till in the third century, and even then there is little certain and less indicative that it had obtained in the Christian church so called.
>
> Positive ordinances demand positive proof as certain as divine ordinances require the proof of divine authority. But neither he nor any other man can, from the oracles of God, or from ecclesiastical history, produce any direct, positive proof, human or divine, for infant baptism during the first two hundred years of the Christian age. Alexander, Campbell,Christian Baptism, with Its Antecedents and Consequents BOOKSIXTH CHAPTER I. (1851).

4. Smith, Mont W, "What the Bible Says About Covenant", page 309-310, College Press, 1981.

5. This quote was received in a personal e-mail from Mr. Frutchenbaum to the author of this book.

6. Smith, Mont W, "What the Bible Says About Covenant", page 310, College Press, 1981.

7. Calvin, John, Institutes of Christian Religion, Book 4, Chapter 16.

8. Brants, T.W., The Gospel Plan of Salvation p 223, Nashville: Gospel Advocate, reprint, 1977.

9. Brants, T.W., The Gospel Plan of Salvation p 315, Nashville: Gospel Advocate, reprint, 1977.

10. Campbell takes a somewhat more assertive approach in opposing infant baptism, referring to it as The Evil of Infant Baptism. His point, first and foremost, is that God seeks what Campbell calls will-worship:

> HAVING been able to find *no good* in infant baptism, nor in infant sprinkling, (for I must always consider them as distinct things,) I now proceed to inquire, Is there any *evil* in it? In answering this question, I desire to be guided by three things only--Scripture, reason, and fact: neither by passion nor by prejudice; nor, I trust, will the fear of the frown of any mortal ever deter me from declaring the truth on this, or any other topic on which I am fairly called to express my sentiments. I answer the question now proposed, with the utmost coolness and deliberation; and feel no hesitation in declaring that infant sprinkling is a *manifold evil*. This I shall instance in a few respects:--
>
> 1st. It is "*will-worship.*" By the term *will-worship*, I understand worship founded upon the *will* of man, and not on the *will* of God. "In vain do they

worship me," saith Christ, "teaching for doctrines the commandments of men." The preceding pages show that the rite of infant sprinkling is as much a tradition of men as the *scrutiny*, the *exsufflation* by which devils are expelled, the *insufflation* by which the Spirit of God is communicated, the *consecration* of the wafer, the *chrismal unction*, the *lighted taper*, and the *milk* and *honey*, which are but seven of the twenty-two appendages to infant sprinkling, made by the church of Rome. Now, as all will-worship is a disparagement of the worship appointed of God, it is, consequently, a reflection upon his wisdom, and obnoxious to his displeasure. It is as contrary to his revealed will as the presenting of "strange fire" upon his altar was in the days of Nadab and Abihu. And, indeed, every religious practice which is not founded upon an explicit revelation of the will of Heaven, is will-worship. The [405] language of it is this, "Thou shouldst have appointed this, and we are supplying a defect in thy wisdom or goodness." Such is the spirit of every innovation in divine worship. Alexander, Campbell, Christian Baptism, with Its Antecedents and Consequents BOOK SIXTH CHAPTER V21. (1851).

Chapter XVII
Baptism and Biblical Harmony

The lesson that man is saved by grace through faith in Jesus permeates the pages of Scripture. Because this message is so profound, many have difficulty reconciling the physical properties of baptism with a plan of salvation that appears spiritual in its nature. The resulting struggle brings many to a crisis of discernment concerning baptism and how it does or does not affect our relationship with God. This has led a number of believers to conclude that, if man is saved by grace through faith, baptism must be allowed no role within the framework of redemption.

Of course, the greatest obstacle facing anyone who denies the efficacy of baptism lies in the numerous instances within Scripture where the rite of baptism is recognized as a condition of salvation (Mark 16: 16; Acts 2: 38; 22: 16; Romans 6: 1-4; 1 Peter 3: 21). Bringing these passages into harmony with a view of salvation that precludes baptism provides a tremendous challenge. In essence, these various passages must be addressed almost with a sense of antagonism and the assumption that they cannot possibly mean what they literally proclaim. The presumption is that passages linking baptism to salvation, if accepted at face value, conflict with the gospel message of salvation by grace through faith that is presented in the Bible. Rather than seeking a natural harmony within Scripture concerning baptism and the message of salvation, men have turned to redefining any passage that presents baptism in that light; the ideological equivalent of attempting to place a square peg in a round hole. The truth of the matter is that passages linking baptism to redemption fully harmonize with the message of grace through faith when they are allowed the uncomplicated meaning provided in a common reading of the text.

Baptism in Harmony with Grace

The grace of God toward men that is depicted in the Bible is the only grace recognized by many people. This is, of course, understandable. It is safe to assert that the idea of grace originated from God. Yet, the essence of grace given is not always associated directly with salvation or eternal life. Created in His image, men have the capacity to show grace toward one another. However, men are unable to bestow eternal life or cleanse a man from his sins. Still, grace can be present among men without the consequence of redemption or any relationship to things spiritual. The true nature of the grace of man, which is a reflection of the grace of God, is related directly to one's unselfish giving and/or sacrifice for the good of another.

That grace pertains to giving is an undeniable truth that few would ever care to challenge. However, the image of grace transcends the concept of simply giving a gift or sacrificing for the good of another. Many men offer gifts (birthday, anniversary, etc.) or willingly sacrifice for others daily without offering grace to the recipient. That is because simply giving a gift or offering a sacrifice does not automatically qualify as an act of grace. For example, the Old Testament Israelites, in sacrificing to God, were certainly not offering God grace. Often gifts are given where grace is absent.

It is important to recognize that the true nature of a gift – any gift – is that it is unearned. Whether grace is present or absent does not change this unalterable truth. If it is a gift it is, by definition, unmerited. Once something is earned by any means it immediately relinquishes its personification as a gift and becomes a wage. A *gift* must be offered freely and not as a matter of obligation.

What, then, constitutes an act of grace and what is it that separates mere gifting from what may be considered a gift of grace? Grace is realized when a gift (often in the form of good will or kindness) is not only freely given, but when it is offered to someone who is *least deserving* of that gift. The less deserving someone is, the greater the gift of grace becomes (Luke 7: 41-43). In fact, the effect of grace is maximized when the recipient actually *merits* exactly the opposite of what he/she receives. It is showing compassion and mercy when retribution is warranted. Because of this, grace must be considered as mysterious as it is uncommon. Offering something precious to someone who is least deserving of the gift makes no sense to the human mind. Yet this is what God has done. Grace finds no greater manifestation than the grace of God that is revealed in Scripture. What could be a more charitable act of grace than offering life to those who have earned death? (Romans 6: 23)

The concept of grace suggests that, in the giving of a gift, there is some risk to the giver. This truth lies in the fact that, where grace is concerned, the gift given often involves the benefactor's participation on a personal level. If we give to someone a gift that holds little meaning for us, while the recipient may appreciate the gesture, what occurs with that gift once it is given will likely be of little concern to the giver. However, it is when we give something that is precious to us, and that is perhaps a part of us, that we seek assurance that the gift given will be cared for just as we would care for it. The more personal and precious the gift is, the greater will be the concern over its care once it has been given. When the gift is given in grace, the concern over the care of the gift tends to escalate. Giving to someone something very special when that person has shown little regard in the past for things precious is certainly cause for anxiety.

Men have a startling opportunity to have a relationship with God for which we are most undeserving. That opportunity, which is grace, is founded upon the very personal sacrifice of God's only Son made on our behalf. It simply cannot get more personal than that. With this gift there is risk involved even for God since the sacrifice could be for naught. It is possible that no one would be willing to receive this gift of grace. Therefore, when someone does accept what God has offered – that which is so personal – the heavens rejoice over the one reconciled to God (Luke 15: 7) because the angels realize exactly what God has given up.

The relationship on earth that most closely resembles the bond between Christ and His church is that of a marriage. The portraiture of the marriage relationship, while not exact in its nature, provides a reasonable analogy of the familial spiritual relationship that God has always intended to have with His people. At various times in Scripture the covenant between Christ and the church is likened to marriage (John 3: 29; Ephesians 5: 25), which could be considered the most precious of relationships among men.

A wedding ring is symbolic of many elements of the relationship between a man and woman in the covenant of marriage. The ring represents not simply love, but a life-long commitment to the one from whom the ring is received. That commitment encompasses much more than a mere promise to wear the ring as a reflection of that love. Acceptance of the ring seals the promise to treat with respect and honor the life of the giver. The ring symbolizes the life of the giver who is, in essence, offering his/her life to its recipient as a free gift. How much more precious can any gift be than the gift of one's life?

Accepting a wedding ring, then, places upon the shoulders of the prospective husband/wife the responsibility to care for the life given in a manner that recognizes the extraordinary nature of the gift. In marriage, it is both the privilege and responsibility of the husband to treat his wife in a manner that offers her greater happiness than she would have known without him. Conversely, it is the wife's opportunity, as well as her responsibility, to bring a joy into her husband's life that would have been unattainable in her absence.

As a man and woman exchange vows and rings in the wedding ceremony, it is the privilege of those in attendance to witness a most extraordinary event. It is an event that, according to Scripture, may be considered somewhat spiritual, especially since it takes place in a manner invisible to the naked eye. As vows are exchanged and commitments are made, Scripture tells us that *'they shall become one flesh.'* (Genesis 2: 24) The man and woman, then, are united in marriage with a bond that truly transcends man's physical nature. No doubt this was God's design from the beginning.

Each couple tends to design the marriage ceremony to their own specifications. Still, there are certain elements that most deem significant, and these are included in nearly every wedding ceremony. There are, of course, the vows and the ring exchange. Many will include a unity candle that symbolizes the fact that these are no longer two individuals, but a family of two. The kiss, then, is the seal that completes the transformation of the two into one.

Beyond these rather traditional characteristics of a wedding, the bride and groom will undoubtedly add to the ceremony those elements of a personal nature that are intended to attach special meaning to the day. Perhaps they will introduce a video of the history of their relationship or a song that carries with it a very special meaning. Regardless of the intricacies of the day, there can be no doubt that the design of the wedding is intended to represent things significant to the bride and groom.

The fact that rings and life-long commitments are given within the setting of the wedding ceremony in no way diminishes either the gift or the commitment. On the contrary, the ceremony is the very manner in which these are given a place of special honor. Men view the wedding as a thing of joy and an opportunity to recognize that something remarkable occurs at that time. The wedding ceremony is the time when everyone understands that the union between the bride and groom is made complete. In recognition of that fact, the bride then takes the name of the groom as her own, taking on his likeness. His name is not hers prior to the ceremony. However, the transformation that occurs during the service gives her the right to identify with him, and he with her.

The wedding ceremony effectively raises the stakes for those who have decided to engage in the commitment of marriage. Submitting to one another in wedlock compels the participants to seriously consider the nature of that commitment as well as the consequences of breaking the vows that are spoken at that time.

God has chosen a ceremony as the time when He will give the gift of life through His only begotten Son to those who are willing to receive it. That fact does not in any way diminish the nature of the gift any more than the wedding ceremony diminishes the gift of the bride to the groom or vice versa. On the contrary, it is one's willing participation in this ceremony that accords the gift the highest of honors.

It is important to realize that, within the framework of the rite of baptism, the gifts given and received are not completely one-sided. It is not simply a matter of God bestowing upon us the gift of eternal life while He receives nothing in return. What God seeks is reconciliation with mankind. That reconciliation is not possible as long as sin separates man from God. It is at the time of baptism that those sins are removed (Acts 2: 38; Colossians 2: 11) as a barrier between God and His creation. This reconciliation, as well as the offering of one's own life to God as a living sacrifice (Matthew 10: 39; Romans 12: 1), are what He receives in return.

Just as the wedding couple designs a ceremony that symbolizes those things considered most significant and most personal, so God has designed the ceremony of baptism. No doubt His aim in baptism is to reflect the imagery of the death, burial, and resurrection of Christ. This intent is understandable given the substance of the gift. For Him it is personal, representing the unequaled nature of the sacrifice He has made. Paul attests to the personal nature of this ceremony from God's perspective as he explains to the Romans:

> 3. Or do you not know that as many of us as were baptized into Christ Jesus were baptized into His death? 4. Therefore we were buried with Him through baptism into death, that just as Christ was raised from the dead by the glory of the Father, even so we should walk in newness of life. 5. For if we have been united together in the likeness of His death, certainly we also shall be *in the likeness of His* resurrection, 6. Knowing this, that our old man was crucified with *Him*, that the body

of sin might be done away with, that we should no longer be slaves of sin. (Romans 6: 3-6)

The ceremony of baptism has assuredly been designed in a manner that makes participation very personal, both for the believer and for the Father. It reflects those elements that God deems most significant as we are buried in water where, according to Paul, the desired unity with Christ actually occurs. As that unity takes place and we rise from the water, just as the bride takes on the likeness of the groom by accepting his name as her own, so the new Christian takes the identity of Christ, walking *'in newness of life.'* His name is not ours prior to baptism. However, the transformation that occurs during the ceremony gives us the right to identify with Him according to His promise (Acts 2: 38).

It is certainly unjust to view baptism as something that men have added to Christ's sacrifice, thereby disparaging the meaning and efficacy of the blood. On the contrary, Baker's Dictionary of Theology states:

> ...the action itself is divinely ordained as a means of grace, i.e., a means to present Christ and therefore to fulfil the attesting work of the Spirit. It does not do this by the mere performance of the prescribed rite; it does it in and through its meaning.[1]

If then, this ceremony of baptism is, by God's own design, *divinely ordained* as the time when we are united with Christ, we must learn to accept that truth. Baptism must be recognized as the time when we are both united with Christ and reconciled to the Father. Receiving God's gift of grace in a ceremony designed by Him specifically for that purpose cannot depreciate the value of the gift that is received. On the contrary, the ceremony is the very manner in which Jesus' sacrifice is most genuinely honored. Baptism is mentioned more than one hundred times in the New Testament. This fact undoubtedly reflects the significance of the baptismal waters from God's perspective. It is understandable, then, why Jesus would proclaim to His disciples:

> He who believes and is baptized will be saved...(Mark 16: 16)

Baptism in Harmony with Faith
While we are saved *by* grace, which is the means of salvation, we are also saved *through* faith, the pathway to salvation

(Ephesians 2: 8). However, the biblical teaching of salvation through faith seems to present an additional dilemma for a great many men. While Paul's statement concerning salvation *'by grace through faith'* is straightforward, other passages of Scripture present teaching concerning a variety of conditions for salvation. Believing that face value acceptance of these passages would destroy the very fabric of *grace through faith* that Paul presents, the unfortunate reaction of some men is to reconstruct forthright biblical teaching concerning faith so that it might fit their own doctrinal views.

The prominent cry within evangelical circles is not that salvation comes by grace through faith, as Paul states so clearly; rather the appeal is to salvation by grace through faith *only*. The doctrine of salvation through faith only ultimately views saving faith as intellectual and emotional acceptance of, and trust in, the deity of Christ as well as His crucifixion for our sins and His resurrection to conquer death. This, however, is not the apostolic portrayal of faith in Scripture. Instead, it is simply a description of the moment of one's initial recognition and acceptance of the fact that Jesus is the Son of God. It is best that we allow Scripture to define for us the true nature of faith through which eternal life is ultimately granted.

In his proclamation that men are saved by grace through faith (Ephesians 2: 8), Paul does not define for us the character of saving faith. He certainly tells us what it is not (works), but falls short of explaining in the Ephesians passage the exact make-up of saving faith. He does not state that it is purely mental assent to Jesus as Lord, but he also fails to intimate that it may be more than this. Therefore, based solely upon Paul's words to the Ephesians, we could determine that the faith that offers eternal life is equivalent to belief only. However, we cannot necessarily discern what faith *is* from a passage that simply tells us what it *is not*. If we are to be honest students of the Word, should we not take the time to discover whether or not, within the pages of Scripture, saving faith is defined? Paul has provided additional insight in other epistles concerning what constitutes redemptive faith.

Paul differentiates between works and faith when it comes to salvation (Ephesians 2: 8). Yet, we discover that God's Word associates faith with human activity more often than with salvation, although it is true that these two elements (faith and works) are essentially inseparable (James 2: 20). In fact, despite modern perceptions, at no point does the New Testament define the time of initial faith as the time of initial salvation. That is because faith is not simply about an initial moment of belief in Jesus. Instead, faith identifies our participation in life as our deeds reflect our commitment to God (Romans 1: 17). It is those things that we *do*, through faith, that ultimately bring about salvation. The image of faith that we find in Scripture is really a picture of faithfulness.

In the book of Romans, a book consisting of sixteen chapters, the word faith ($\pi\iota\sigma\tau\iota\varsigma$) appears thirty-eight times. We can rightfully conclude, then, that faith is the core issue Paul addresses in his words to the Romans. In a tenor comparable to his letter to the Ephesians, Paul establishes in Romans a theme of grace through faith, reiterating that grace does not come by works (Romans 3: 20-31). Those who view the first few chapters of this letter as Paul's full declaration of the gospel attempt to draw a line of demarcation between chapters five and six, a proposition that defeats Paul's objective. The first verses of the sixth chapter are decidedly intimate with the last verses of chapter five, offering an uninterrupted flow of Paul's instructions concerning the difference between justification by the law or by grace. It is a theme that envelops the entire epistle.

In this letter we learn that Paul was sent to teach all nations to be obedient to the gospel message (Romans 1: 5; 15: 18-20). Much of Paul's teaching in chapters six through sixteen of the book of Romans is spent demonstrating the faith that he has addressed in the first few chapters. Despite his emphasis on the contrast between faith and works as a means to salvation, we discover that Paul most deliberately teaches the *necessity* of obedience as a matter of salvation (Romans 2: 8; 6: 16-18). Some form of the word *obey* (obedience, etc.) appears in Romans no less than thirteen times. Therefore, we cannot honestly maintain that *obedience* to the gospel is in any way commensurate with the *works* of Ephesians 2: 8. Given the ideological principle supporting the book of Romans that distinguishes between obedient faith and works of merit, we must openly reject the proposition that Paul's remark concerning faith *not of works* somehow equates to faith *not of obedience*.

As Paul considers the nature of saving faith, he never discusses the initial moment of faith – that is to say, he does not identify faith as something that occurs at a specific time. Instead, he views faith in terms of activity. Paul begins his portrayal of the nature of saving faith with our obedience in the waters of baptism (Romans 6: 1-23). This is most appropriate since the spiritual activity that occurs at the time of baptism is, according to Paul, reliant upon our faith (Colossians 2: 11-12). In the eighth chapter of the book of Romans Paul identifies faith in terms of our walk with God. Because the Holy Spirit dwells in us through faith, we *'do not walk according to the flesh, but according to the Spirit'* (Romans 8: 1).

As we reach the tenth chapter of Romans, Paul explains how we come to faith. We learn that faith comes by hearing the gospel message (Romans 10: 17). Faith is once again defined in terms of our response to that message, as a matter of salvation, as we believe the gospel and confess Jesus as Lord (Romans 10: 9-10). The general theme of the eleventh chapter of Romans regards obedient faith as the means by which we are grafted as branches to the tree of eternal life, while the twelfth chapter recognizes that not all men have an equal portion of faith. In the fourteenth chapter the apostle completes this thought, urging the Romans to always consider the influence of their actions upon those who may be weaker in the faith. Paul closes his letter to the Romans, exhorting his readers to remain obedient to the commands of God and faithful to the gospel message through which their relationship with God was established (Romans 16: 25-26).

Instruction concerning faith that is obedient to the gospel message is hardly limited to the book of Romans. It is a central theme from Acts through Revelation. Luke wrote of priests who, in their acceptance of Jesus, were *'obedient to the faith'* (Acts 6: 7). Paul told the Thessalonians that God would punish eternally *'those who do not obey the gospel'* (2 Thessalonians 1: 8). Peter challenged the salvation status of *'those who do not obey the gospel'* (1 Peter 4: 17).

Paul instructed the Philippian jailer to, *'Believe on the Lord Jesus Christ, and you will be saved...'* (Acts 16: 31). This statement is as beautiful as it is true. Believing on Jesus is absolutely central in our path to salvation. The belief ($\pi\iota\sigma\tau\epsilon\upsilon\sigma\upsilon\nu$) of which Paul spoke in teaching the Philippian jailer (Acts 16: 31) may be considered closely associated with the faith ($\pi\iota\sigma\tau\epsilon\omega\varsigma$) of Ephesians 2: 8. In the Greek, while the word *'believe'* ($\pi\iota\sigma\tau\epsilon\upsilon\omega$) is a derivative of *faith* ($\pi\iota\sigma\tau\iota\varsigma$), the slight distinction that exists between them must be recognized. Belief, as Paul taught the jailer, suggests the placing of one's trust in Jesus. The faith through which salvation is received is belief carried to its logical conclusion of *faithfulness*. It is obedient belief. This distinction is well demonstrated in the story of the rulers who actually believed on Jesus but failed to follow through with their conviction.

> Nevertheless even among the rulers many believed ($επιστευσαν$) in Him, but because of the Pharisees they did not confess Him, lest they should be put out of the synagogue. (John 12: 42)

Here the apostle John employs a form of the same word that Paul told the jailer was the *belief* by which he could be saved. According to John these men did believe. Yet, despite their conviction, these rulers did not carry that belief through to the conclusion of faithfulness since *'they did not confess Him.'* Their priorities were such that maintaining a position in the synagogue took precedence. We can biblically conclude that without a willingness to confess Jesus as Savior, men cannot be saved (Romans 10: 9). We can also presume that there is a distinction between trusting that Jesus is the Son of God (belief) and the level of faithfulness necessary to receive salvation.

Based upon this episode we can ascertain that, had the Philippian jailer believed on Jesus, as did the rulers at the synagogue, but never carried that belief forward to the point of the faithfulness of Ephesians 2: 8, he would not have received salvation. Paul certainly recognized that fact and would have fully explained to the jailer that faithfulness was essential in answer to his question, *'Sirs, what must I do to be saved?'* (Acts 16: 32) Had Paul taught the man to merely believe *($πιστευω$)* in Jesus, he would have remained in the same condemned state of the believing rulers in the synagogue.

In the New Testament, we find that the benefits received by obedient faith are also recognized as benefits of the combination of belief, repentance, confession, and baptism – these four ultimately constituting obedience to the gospel message (1 Peter 4: 17).[2] So exact are these characteristics and benefits that the sum of these four might be considered interchangeable with the idea of *saving faith* as it develops within apostolic instruction. We receive forgiveness of our sins through baptism (Acts 2: 38; Romans 6: 6; 1 Corinthians 6: 11), repentance (Acts 3: 19), and faith (Galatians 2: 16). Sanctification is attained through the work of the Spirit and by our obedience (1 Peter 1: 2), by our belief in the truth (2

Thessalonians 2: 13), and by baptism (1 Corinthians 6: 11). Rebirth/renewal comes by baptism (John 3: 5; Romans 6: 5; Titus 3: 5) through faith in the work of the Holy Spirit (John 3: 5; Colossians 2: 11; Titus 3: 5). Just as we are united with Christ in faith (Ephesians 3: 17), we are also united with Him in baptism (Romans 6: 5). Receiving the Holy Spirit is a matter of faith (Galatians 3: 2), baptism (Acts 2: 38), and obedience (Acts 5: 32). Salvation is attained by faith (Ephesians 2: 8), obedience (Hebrews 5: 9), baptism (1 Peter 3: 21), repentance of our sins (2 Corinthians 7: 10), and confession of Jesus as Lord (Romans 10: 9). Adoption by the Father comes both through baptism and by faith (Galatians 3: 26-27).

The story of Noah parallels God's plan of salvation for the church on a number of levels, some of which are discussed in this book. One such similarity can be found in the grace/faith duo by which Noah was saved. God looked upon a world where, *'the wickedness of man was great ...every intent of the thoughts of his heart was only evil continually.'* (Genesis 6: 5) However, God looked down upon Noah and offered grace to Him (Genesis 6: 8). The fact that Scripture describes Noah as a just man should not be construed to imply that he was deserving of grace since Noah was not sinless (Romans 3: 23). Yet he did stand out from all others and for this God offered him the opportunity to escape His wrath.

Unlike everyone else in his day, Noah actually had faith in God (Hebrews 11: 7). Yet it is the nature of that faith that is most notable. Noah spent decades building an ark to prepare for a flood. There is no indication that Noah ever complained about building the ark, insisting that God could save him and his family without it if He wished. He simply obeyed the clear command of God.

What is important is that Noah's faith was a faith that built the ark. Had Noah's faith fallen short of obedience to God's command concerning the ark he, along with his family, would have perished despite the magnitude of Noah's faith or God's grace. Neither grace nor faith would have saved Noah absent his obedience. He was not saved by mere intellectual/emotional faith, but by faithfulness. God's grace offered Noah an opportunity to be saved *if he built an ark*. Noah was saved by grace, but not by grace *alone*. Nor was he saved by faith *alone*. Instead, he was saved through faithfulness. The grace of God made contact with the faith of Noah as he obediently constructed the ark.

The teaching that obedience to any command of God is conditional for salvation is challenged fervently. Some men who oppose such a proposition submit that mandatory obedience to *any* of God's commands *as a matter of salvation* necessarily translates into requisite adherence to *all* of His commands, and that anything short of this would leave a man condemned. They reason that, since it is impossible for men to be obedient in all things, no command may be considered essential.

What shall we say, then, concerning belief and repentance, both of which God requires from those who seek salvation? Since they are specific commands we obey in seeking redemption can we, in like manner, conclude that if these commands are essential, all commands must be obeyed? The truth is not all Godly commands are required in the initial course of redemption.

Peter commands his readers to *be holy* (1 Peter 1: 16). However, without the grace of God at the time of our salvation we are incapable of holiness. We can only be partakers of God's holiness (Hebrews 12: 10). Yet at no time did the apostles teach holiness as a prerequisite to salvation. Holiness is bestowed upon us as we clothe ourselves with Christ (Galatians 3: 27) and receive the Holy Spirit (Acts 2: 38). Those to whom Peter wrote with the command to *be holy* were already Christians. His plea was for them to honor Jesus by living holy lives.

Jesus commanded that we *'...love one another; as I have loved you.'* (John 13: 34) Yet who on earth has the capacity for such love? Nor is this depth of love incorporated into the plan of salvation that is revealed in Scripture. Holiness and Christ-like love are ideals toward which we are commanded to strive. They are not treated in the Bible as precepts for one's salvation.

Those commands taught in Scripture as essential for our initial salvation (belief, repentance, confession, and baptism) are commands to which mankind has the capacity to be *fully obedient*. They are commands that fall considerably short of building an ark. We have the *capacity* to believe that Jesus is the Messiah. We are *capable* of repenting of our sins and confessing Jesus as Savior. We also have the *ability* to be baptized for the remission of sins. That is what God has asked of us *in order to be saved*. He has not placed on our shoulders a hopeless task by asking for obedience to things unachievable. It is most likely the utter simplicity of the commands that will ultimately bring judgment upon those who refuse to obey the gospel.

Peter, in his first epistle, declares baptism to be a matter of salvation (1 Peter 3: 21). Even more than this, he identifies baptism as that which saves. Yet Paul tells us that we are *'saved by grace through faith...not of works'* (Ephesians 2: 8-9). What approach can we then use to balance the teachings of two men whose work is inspired by God? There are a couple of options open to us. One approach would be to determine that in one of these two cases the writer did not mean exactly what he said. We could conclude that Peter did not intend to identify baptism as a matter of salvation *or* that Paul did not mean that we are saved by faith. However, we would then face the challenge of determining the intent of the apostle who wrote in error. That would be a formidable task since the words and teaching of each are direct and are supported in other apostolic writings.

Our second option is to treat the meaning of these two teachings from Peter and Paul as harmonious and complementary. In other words, let us discover how *both* statements, as they are written, might be true rather than intruding upon the integrity of one so that it agrees, however awkwardly, with the other. This would inevitably lead us to a search through Scripture to better understand how the two elements, faith and baptism, are linked within God's plan.

For the Christian, faith and baptism are complementary. Together they represent faithfulness. In the pages of Scripture, baptism is always presented as a response of faith to the gospel message. (Acts 16: 15; Romans 6: 3-4; Galatians 3: 26-27; Colossians 2: 12). If baptism is an act of faith, Scripture harmonizes fully as Peter proclaimed that we must *'be baptized...for the remission of sins'* (Acts 2: 38). As it was with Noah in building the ark, this is the time when the grace of God makes contact with the obedient faith of man (Colossians 2: 12). Since we have already considered the parallel characteristics and benefits of faith and baptism, it seems pointless to reiterate. It is sufficient to say that when men view baptism as a work, as though it was in conflict with Paul's words that teach salvation by grace through faith, passages such as these *cannot* be satisfactorily reconciled. It is *only* when we view baptism as an act of faithfulness in God's divine plan that we find harmony in passages concerning faith and baptism.

NOTES FOR CHAPTER 17

1. Harrison, Everett F., Editor, Baker's Dictionary of Theology, p. 84-85, Baker Book House, 1960.

2. In his work, **Baptism in the New Testament**, G. R. Beasley-Murray has solidly examined the scriptural link between the benefits of faith and baptism, as have other authors. However, in God's plan of salvation the obedience of repentance and confession cannot be divorced from faith or baptism. That is not to say this was his intent since it surely was not, but these are no less relevant when it comes to saving faith. If we are to associate faith with baptism we must also recognize its association with repentance and confession in obedience to the gospel message.

Chapter XVIII
Baptism and Doctrinal Purity

Doctrinal Significance

Doctrine, as it is presented in Scripture, is frequently assigned subordinate status in modern times as men contemplate what is or is not acceptable, scripturally speaking. In fact, it seems that quite often little attention is given to the idea of biblical doctrine. Multitudes have come to conclude that what we believe doctrinally is relatively unimportant, reasoning that essentially any belief in God/Jesus is sufficient. Exactly what is doctrine? Doctrine is teaching. Jesus' doctrine is the set of teachings He gave us in His own words and through the writings of the apostles. If a doctrine, or teaching, is not supported by God's Word, it should not be considered the doctrine of Christ.

Not all doctrine involves direct commands from God. We find that much doctrine in the pages of Scripture appears in the form of sage advice or direction on how to live a holy life. Furthermore, we are plainly instructed in the Bible that not every decision we face carries with it eternal consequences. Regarding certain choices, it is clear that having varied opinions will not necessarily interfere directly with our fellowship with God (Romans 14: 6-14). Paul and Barnabas were very close in their relationship. Nonetheless, the two were not always of one mind. Facing a decision regarding who would travel with them on a particular journey, they parted ways and traveled separately due to a disagreement over one young man (Acts 15: 36-40).

Just as the choice of companionship on a particular journey need not alter our relationship with God, many other choices do not necessarily have eternal consequences. Doctrinal commands are not the *determining* factor in choosing a spouse or vocation, the number of children one desires, or in what town a person will live. Still, Scripture certainly offers guidelines (*doctrine in the form of sage advice*) to assist God's children in facing decisions such as these, and it is always wise to seek guidance through prayer. Electing to engage in an honorable vocation is germane to Christian living, but countless moral and ethical careers are available for our choosing. When choosing a life partner we may wish to contemplate the wisdom of being yoked together with someone who shares our beliefs (2 Corinthians 6: 14). Yet our freedom to make these kinds of choices is evident throughout God's Word. Likewise, in Paul's letter to the Christians at Thessalonica, he advised them regarding a Christian way of life rather than offering doctrinal commands.

> 15. See that no one renders evil for evil to anyone, but always pursue good both for yourselves and for all. 16. Rejoice always, 17. pray without ceasing. (1 Thessalonians 5: 15-17)

Since many decisions we face are not addressed through doctrinal commands, why would the author of the book of Hebrews caution his readers to beware of strange doctrines (Hebrews 13: 9)? Why would the apostles place such a strong emphasis on *adherence* to true doctrine (2 Timothy 4: 3-4)?

New Testament passages like those listed above indicate that abiding in the doctrine of Christ, as it is spelled out in Scripture, is paramount. Exhortations such as these provide fair warning that certain teachings are completely unacceptable to God. Jesus has specific expectations of His followers. While a measure of doctrine comes in the form of wise instruction regarding living a holy life, Jesus and the apostles regarded as critical certain elements of biblical doctrine.

Since certain biblical teachings *must* be followed, men must learn to differentiate between those decisions involving freedom of choice and those that simply demand obedience. Honest and thorough biblical study is crucial in the search for discernment. In Scripture we learn the doctrine of Christ, those teachings that are the substructure of His kingdom here on earth. These are the teachings that men who truly seek Christ must not ignore. For instance, salvation is attainable through Jesus alone. Worshipping other gods is forbidden (John 14: 6; Acts 4: 12). This is a doctrine that is not optional. It is a requirement.

Distinguishing between those elements of biblical doctrine that are meant to simply guide us and those that are commands of eternal consequence can prove rather challenging. False teachers often present a very convincing case that a belief is scriptural when, upon close examination, it may not be. Thus, in the same book where Paul warns Timothy of false doctrines, he encourages Him to:

> Be diligent to present yourself approved to God, a worker who does not need to be ashamed, rightly dividing the word of truth. (2 Timothy 2: 15)

Like Timothy, all men are to be diligent in the study of the Bible in order to attain a true understanding of God's Word. Honest, devoted study is the vaccine that can prevent the *itching ears* (2 Timothy 4: 3) so willingly responsive to false teachers. God's Word holds within its pages all doctrinal authority. The only means to fully grasp biblical doctrine and defend against those beliefs that lead astray is to faithfully and honestly study as the Holy Spirit guides us to an even greater understanding.

The word doctrine(s) appears roughly fifty times in the New Testament. Jesus even termed His own teaching as doctrine.

> 16. Jesus answered them and said, "My doctrine is not Mine, but His who sent Me. 17. If anyone wills to do His will, he shall know concerning the doctrine, whether it is from God or whether I speak on My own authority." (John 7: 16-17)

He also noted that there existed doctrine (teaching) His disciples must be sure to avoid. He told them:

> 11. ...but to beware of the leaven of the Pharisees and Sadducees. 12. Then they understood that He did not tell them to beware of the leaven of bread, but of the doctrine of the Pharisees and Sadducees. (Matthew 16: 11b-12)

That the Pharisees were descendants of Abraham and worshipped the same God as the disciples was not in doubt. Yet, as Cain's offering was unbefitting true worship in days of old, so the doctrine of these men was not acceptable to God. They did not live in His way or keep the commands as God intended.

The apostles were keenly aware of false doctrines and continuously warned others to beware of those who might teach anything contrary to what was taught by both Jesus and the apostles:

> ...that we should no longer be children, tossed to and fro and carried about by every wind of doctrine, by the trickery of men, in the cunning craftiness of the deceitful plotting... (Ephesians 4: 14)

> As I urged you when I went into Macedonia -- remain in Ephesus that you may charge some that they teach no other doctrine. (1 Timothy 1: 3)
>
> Do not be carried about with various and strange doctrines. (Hebrews 13: 9)

Biblically sound teachings are crucial to the fitness of the body of Christ. While it is true that men are given freedom in Christ, spiritual freedom cannot invade doctrinal purity. Once a teaching conflicts with the Bible, false doctrine results.

If there are doctrines that are false it can be reasoned, and we are told in Scripture, that there is a doctrine that is true. That is the doctrine of Christ. The apostles charged the people to continue in the doctrine of Christ and offered greatly encouraging words to those who held fast:

> If you instruct the brethren in these things, you will be a good minister of Jesus Christ, nourished in the words of faith and of the good doctrine which you have carefully followed. (1 Timothy 4: 6)

There can be no question about the importance that was placed by both Jesus and the apostles upon following the teachings, or doctrine, they provided. In fact, Timothy was commended by Paul for applying the *'good doctrine'* that he had *'carefully followed.'* Should we not follow the doctrine of Christ just as *carefully* as Timothy?

The Doctrine of Baptism

Among men there is a popular view suggesting that, since God is such a gracious God, He would never *really* send anyone to the eternal flames of hell. If what one believes is not important as long as it is bathed in sincerity, this teaching could be considered as legitimate as anything we might learn from Scripture. And yet, we know that it is unacceptable since it stands in direct contrast to biblical principles.

Repentance and belief in Jesus are essential in man's quest for eternal life (Acts 3: 19; 4: 12), a fact very few would ever dispute. Among those who profess Christ, essentially no one would consider belief in any deity other than Jesus as a means to salvation. Baptism is the single precept ordinarily deemed by men to be inconsequential despite the words of the apostles.

There is a distinction that can be drawn between gospel and doctrine. The gospel is the message that reveals Jesus and leads men to accept Him as Savior. The honest presentation of the gospel message is an indispensable component of scriptural doctrine. The apostles clearly taught that men must abide in undistorted biblical doctrine (2 Timothy 4: 3; 2 John 9) and Peter demonstrated that a critical element of scriptural doctrine is faithful obedience to the gospel (1 Peter 4: 17). Baptism is, within the pages of the Scripture, presented as a significant ingredient in our obedience to the gospel message.

Scripture is replete with testimony concerning the efficacy of baptism. Beginning with the ministry of John the Baptist and on through the epistles, this rite is identified as the point of forgiveness of sins (Acts 2: 38; 22: 16; Colossians 2: 11-13). It is also called the moment of regeneration or rebirth (John 3: 5; Romans 6: 4; Titus 3: 5). It is in baptism that we are freed from our slavery to sin (Romans 6: 17-18). Jesus commanded baptism as a matter of both becoming a disciple (Matthew 28: 19) and attaining salvation (Mark 16: 16), a truth that is confirmed by the apostle Peter (1 Peter 3: 21). Paul noted that baptism is the moment we clothe ourselves with Christ (Galatians 3: 27). Both Paul and Luke recognized baptism as the point of entry into the body (Acts 2: 42; 1 Corinthians 12: 13). It is the time of cleansing (Ephesians 5: 26), justification and sanctification (1 Corinthians 6: 11).

Immersion in water represents the death, burial, and resurrection of Christ. Through our participation we are united with Christ in His sacrifice (Romans 6: 4-5). Just as the flood eradicated evil, offering a fresh start for mankind, baptism is a time of renewal. Peter recognized baptism as the means to salvation *through the resurrection of Christ* (1 Peter 3: 21) as Jesus' sacrifice is applied to our lives. This is the doctrine of baptism.

Men are commanded by both Jesus and the apostles to be baptized. Additionally, we are provided abundant biblical evidence that the baptism established in the Bible was baptism by immersion in water for the forgiveness of sins. Thus, it stands to reason that any other doctrine concerning baptism would conflict with the doctrine of Christ that is established in God's Word.

The sentiment has often been put forth that the teaching of any strict doctrine, such as baptism, effectively places limits upon God in His relationship with man. If, however, these teachings constitute restrictions on God, they are limitations He has placed upon Himself. Each time God has established a covenant with men, He has limited Himself to the provisions of that covenant. God's covenant with Abraham restricted the *seed* through which Jesus would come to earth (Genesis 18: 18). The covenant with Noah assured that God would never again destroy all life with a flood (Genesis 9: 11-13). Such covenants placed boundaries and requirements not only on the deeds of men, but on God's actions as well. These limitations, however, were not set by the hands and minds of men, but by God. So it is with baptism. If God has chosen to establish certain conditions for us in our relationship with Him, even if those tenets seem to limit what He will or will not do, history reveals a God with the resolve to abide by His own decision.

Is it conceivable that someone in the church age might be saved without the benefit of immersion for forgiveness of his sins? We cannot determine the answer to that question with full conviction since we have no clear vision beyond the moment of death. What we can substantiate, however, is that within the New Testament, baptism is identified as a matter of salvation. While it will continually be a matter of contention, Jesus' words to Nicodemus indicate that those who choose to forego immersion in water will not enter heaven (John 3: 5).

The manner by which men receive justification and salvation, according to God's Word, involves man's submission in baptism for forgiveness of sins as a matter of spiritual birth (Mark 16: 16; John 3: 5; Acts 2: 38; Romans 6: 3-6; Colossians 2: 11-2). God has sanctioned no other teaching. Therefore, if someone in this age sees heaven without baptism, this could occur only by God's own prerogative, for reasons that He deems appropriate, as an exception to biblical doctrine. No man has the authority to teach exemption from the command since God has not given men license to dismiss baptism. Unfortunately, many simply refuse to accept immersion as a part of God's plan of salvation. This has led to a philosophy that God *will* redeem that person who is not immersed despite scriptural instruction. Based upon this rationale, many have developed, and boldly teach, a gospel message that deliberately disregards the biblical role for baptism.

Doctrinal Purity Vs Sincerity of Heart

The argument is often raised that the eternal life of one who earnestly seeks God could not possibly hinge upon obedience to a specific command, such as baptism, especially if that person simply misunderstands what is expected of him. Surely sincerity of heart is the thing God desires rather than ritualistic compliance.

A book that attempted to address this issue arrived on the shelves of bookstores a few years ago. John Mark Hicks and Greg Taylor published their book <u>Down in the River to Pray</u>, a work that actually respects the significance placed upon baptism within the pages of Scripture. There is no question that this book offers valuable insights into the baptism of apostolic doctrine. It is a must read for any and all who care to have a better understanding of the value that the biblical authors have placed upon water baptism.

While the book contributes much to the discussion of baptism, especially in contrasting baptism and works, the authors have taken a precarious stance when considering the need for baptism. In essence, they have established a scenario that recognizes the salvation status of those whom they have labeled *'transformed unimmersed believers.'*[1] This proposition, based upon an Old Testament incident involving Hezekiah's observance of the Passover, suggests that God might overlook disobedience in response to a man's honest desire to please Him.

Hezekiah, a Godly man who also happened to be king of Israel, wished to reinstate the Passover Feast that the Israelites had ignored for so long (2 Chronicles 30: 1-36). Unfortunately, the Israelites were unable to celebrate the feast at the time God had established for the Passover (v. 3). While God had allowed for an alternate season for the festival (Numbers 9: 11), it is difficult to say whether or not that exception might apply here. Yet, the timing of the celebration was not the only issue that the Israelites faced in honoring God with their commemoration, since some of those who came to participate were ceremonially unclean. This, too, was prohibited by law.

Recognizing the fact that they were not acting in accord with God's instructions concerning the Passover, Hezekiah sought God's blessing upon the celebration even though they were not observing it in the exact manner, or at the specific time, God had commanded (v. 18). God, who has a passion for His people and a desire to commune with them, heard this prayer and accepted their worship despite the fact that they had not kept the *letter* of the law (v. 19). Hicks and Taylor have argued a correlation between this episode and obedience, or disobedience, with respect to baptism. They have likened the sincere un-immersed believer to these

Israelites who, while they did not obey the commands of God precisely, worshiped Him honestly and sought His blessing. Even among those who embrace the biblical model of baptism as the moment of forgiveness and salvation, this proposition has certainly made an impact.

As enticing as this proposal may be, it seems to be a sizeable leap to compare the prayer offered by Hezekiah, and answered by God, with the situation we face concerning baptism in modern times. In order to derive commonality between this event and man's present treatment of baptism, it would have been necessary for Hezekiah, and those who celebrated with him, to question whether God had actually established a specific time, or any rules concerning ceremonial cleanliness, with respect to the Passover. Then, progressing in a manner of their own choosing, by either neglecting the Passover completely or by disregarding God's established rules, they would need to assume that God would honor their decision, all the while insisting that they had not disobeyed any of His commands.

This may seem to be an insensitive commentary on the modern view of baptism, but it is not offered with malice or hardness of heart. Rather, it is given out of an honest concern for the souls of men. Modern man has not earnestly sought exemption from baptism, or its meaning, on the grounds that he has been prohibited from participating. Instead, he has presumed exemption. The general consensus is that God has not established baptism for the purposes designated in Scripture (Acts 2: 38; 1 Peter 3: 21). Thus, men have developed a view of the baptism that challenges what is taught in God's Word, insisting that God must honor their belief.

We find no presumption among the Jews in Jerusalem that God would respect their decision concerning celebration of the Passover Feast. What we do find is a humble heart in Hezekiah, a man of God, who beseeched Him to accept their worship at this time *despite the inappropriateness of their actions*. Present-day dismissal of God's call to baptism as a requisite for salvation is hardly akin to Hezekiah's prayer for God to make an exception. However, it does seem to offer hope for the man who seeks exemption from baptism due to circumstances that might prevent him from obedience.

Despite the compatibility issues that exist between this Old Testament account and modern views on baptism, Hicks and Taylor have suggested that there are those who appear to have been transformed into Christ's image despite the fact that they have never received immersion in water for remission of sins. This transformation, they argue, gives us reason to hope these men and women are, indeed, children of God.

The assertion that certain un-immersed men and women appear to have been transformed from their previous life into a life that emulates Christ is, admittedly, unarguable. There are certainly those among us who proclaim Jesus as Lord who have never been baptized; yet their way of life does seem to reflect that of Christ. They appear to be devoted to God and are giving toward other people, even to the point of sacrifice. Exactly how can we reconcile this very peculiar reality?

The first truth we must recognize when considering this question is the fact that baptism is not defined in Scripture as the moment of one's transformation into a Christ-like being. Instead, it is presented as the moment of rebirth, forgiveness of sins, and receiving of the Holy Spirit as an integral part of our lives. Transformation into the image of Christ is a separate matter that cannot be confined to, or defined by, the moment of baptism, or even limited to those who have been immersed. Just as there are those who remain un-immersed who do undergo transformation, there are also those who are immersed who do not.

God does not zap us into a Christ-like existence at the moment of immersion in water. Baptism is simply the time appointed by God when we are offered the opportunity to start over as His children, having been adopted by Him (Galatians 4: 5) and united with Christ (Romans 6: 4). It is our opportunity to pursue, with a clean conscience from sin (1 Peter 3: 21), the transformation that God desires to see in us. Our transformation increases as we seek God through His Word. It is there that we discover the character of Christ that we are meant to imitate. Through reading the Bible and earnestly seeking God we are, over time, transformed. Although the Romans were already immersed believers (Romans 6: 1-4), Paul still beseeched them to be (or continue to be) transformed by the renewing of their minds rather than conforming to the ways of the world (Romans 12: 2).

It is certainly possible, and perhaps even inevitable, that we as men would become more and more Christ-like as we spend time in God's Word. Those who commit any significant amount of time to studying the Bible cannot help but be impacted by these inspired writings. That is a truth that eclipses obedience in baptism.

Scripture is undeniably powerful (Hebrews 4: 12) and has that effect on men notwithstanding their baptismal status. God's Word has the capability, in itself, to affect one's transformation toward the character of Christ. Therefore, a man can be noticeably transformed without being baptized. Indeed, by the time someone chooses to receive Christ in baptism, his/her transformation may be well underway as a result of the discipleship (Matthew 28: 19) that has led to this very decision.

The greatest difficulty we face in establishing the redemption of *'transformed unimmersed believers'* is that God's Word recognizes no time other than baptism when a man's sins are forgiven and he becomes a new creature in Christ. The apostles offer no instruction about a time other than baptism when a man would receive the Holy Spirit or experience adoption as a child of God. In his letters, Paul consistently recognizes the members of the body as men and women who had submitted to Christ in Christian baptism. While a man may experience a marked transformation of character as a result of constant immersion in the Word, salvation for the un-immersed believer simply has no scriptural warrant despite any visible transformation that may have occurred.

What shall we say about the person who, having been raised to believe that baptism has no salvation value, embraces that teaching with honest intentions? After all, it is a most difficult step for any man to reconsider theological views to which he has become accustomed – views he has learned since childhood. It is like someone who, for many years, views a painting through a tinted lens. The shade of the lens affects his perspective. Observing the same image absent that lens, he may very well insist that it is a forgery.

The answer to this question is not an easy one. It is the hope of everyone who believes in Jesus as the Son of God that all men would be saved. However, Scripture does not offer greatly encouraging words for those who are disobedient, despite the circumstances. As Jesus completed the Sermon on the Mount, He addressed the matter of certain disciples who failed to obey God's commands (Matthew 7: 21-27). Jesus did not say that their condemnation was due to insincerity, but disobedience. John proclaimed that those who accept doctrine from men that does not harmonize with Jesus' teaching actually share in their *'evil deeds'* (2 John 9). We cannot judge the salvation or condemnation of anyone. Even so, it is true that Scripture offers no promise of salvation to the un-immersed; a reality that was stated eloquently by F. D. Srygley more than one hundred years ago.

> As I understand the N.T., the 'pious unimmersed' ought to be immersed. And in case they are not immersed, I know of no promise in the N.T. that they will be saved. But as to whether God will make allowance for honest mistakes, and save those who think they are obeying him when in reality they are doing something he has not commanded in lieu of what he has commanded, is a question for God to settle, and I decline to take any part in it.[2]

The greatest challenge, however, concerns those who present themselves as teachers of God's doctrine, but fail to teach it appropriately. For these men, God seems to allow no excuses (Galatians 1: 6-9). Once a man lifts himself to the position of teacher in the eyes of men, he places upon himself a greater responsibility than that of other men, at least in the eyes of God. For this reason it is best for that man to be confident that his doctrine harmonizes completely with the fullness of Scripture.

Of course, no man will see heaven without an honest desire to please and honor God (2 Timothy 2: 22; 1 John 3: 19-20). Yet the Bible also places considerable emphasis upon doctrinal purity (Romans 6: 17; Ephesians 4: 14; 1 Timothy 1: 3; Titus 1: 9). Neither a sincere heart nor devoted obedience to the commands of God may be dismissed as we seek a relationship with Him and salvation through the blood of Christ. That being the case, perhaps we should regard purity of doctrine, including the doctrine of baptism, with the respect it is given in God's Word.

NOTES FOR CHAPTER 18

1. Hicks, John Mark, and Taylor, Greg, Down in the River to Pray, p. 180, Leafwood Publishers, 2004.

2. F. D. Srygley, 'From the Papers,' Gospel Advocate 32, March 26, 1890, p. 193.

Chapter XIX
The Apostles: Baptized in Jesus' Name?

Other than Paul, the baptism of the apostles *in Jesus' name* is not addressed within the pages of Scripture. It is, however, the baptism *taught* by the apostles. What conclusion may be reached from this curious scriptural silence? One of two determinations is possible. The first is that these men did receive the baptism they taught. The second option views their foundational role in the establishment of the church (Ephesians 2: 20) as an indication that they may not have been required by God to submit to baptism in Jesus' name.

The baptism of the apostles *in Jesus' name* is a challenging subject simply because it is a topic not discussed specifically in Scripture. This lack of illumination suggests that witnessing the apostles' baptism is not a critical matter in our relationship with God. Nonetheless, we will address it is in a manner that considers all available counsel.

Baptized by John

We can easily determine that the apostles received the baptism of John. As John's disciples questioned him concerning the baptism performed by Jesus' disciples, it was not a question regarding the *authority* of these men, but seems to intimate jealousy on the part of John's disciples (John 3: 25). Additionally, it would be foolish to suspect that these men were among those who, in opposition to the will of God, refused to participate in John's baptism (Luke 7: 30).

An unqualified indicator that the apostles experienced the baptism of John the Baptist can be found in the first chapter of the book of Acts. When Peter called together the many disciples in Jerusalem in an effort to replace Judas, one requirement for that individual was that he must have been with them beginning with John's baptism (Acts 1: 21-22). Many look to this statement by Peter and assume that he is referring to the event of Jesus' baptism by John. However, the gospel writers do not place these men with Jesus at the time of His baptism.

When Jesus went to John to be baptized by him it was His first public appearance as the Messiah (Matthew 3: 13-17). After He had been baptized, Jesus went to the dessert where He fasted and was tempted by Satan (Matthew 4: 1-11). It was after His time in the dessert that Jesus traveled to Galilee where He selected those men who would later become apostles. Therefore, when Peter spoke of selecting a replacement for Judas, declaring that the man should have been with them *'beginning from the baptism of John'* (Acts 1: 22), it is unrealistic to conclude that he was speaking of Jesus' baptism by John. These men were not present with Jesus at that time. Consequently, the only possible conclusion is that Peter had in mind either the period of time during which John baptized or the apostolic candidate's immersion in water as performed by John. Since these men were certainly not among those who refused to receive baptism (Luke 7: 30), the latter conclusion is unquestionably the correct one.

Baptized in the Name of Jesus

When considering the apostles' baptism, the first point we must examine is whether the apostles *needed* to experience baptism in Jesus' name. In addressing this question we look to Paul's encounter with the Ephesians who had received the baptism of John (Acts 19: 1-7). Realizing that these men had not met the Holy Spirit in baptism, Paul baptized them *in Jesus' name*. The logical conclusion from this episode is that the baptism of John was insufficient within the covenant of grace, and that those who submitted to John's baptism had not received the Holy Spirit.

A point of interest concerning Paul's re-baptism of these men in Ephesus is what occurs in the verses just prior to this incident. At an earlier time, while Aquila and Priscilla were in Ephesus, a Jewish man by the name of Apollos made his way there fervently teaching what he knew concerning the Lord. However, where baptism was concerned we find that *'he knew only the baptism of John'* (Acts 18: 25). Yet, as Aquila and Priscilla instructed him more fully in the things of God, there are no details concerning his baptism in Jesus' name. This seems to be a possible incongruity between the actions and understanding of Paul and that of Aquila and Priscilla.

Some have suggested that the men of Ephesus with whom Paul met may have received John's baptism sometime after the Day of Pentecost. Of course, John was executed prior to Pentecost, but the baptism of John could have been administered by one of his disciples after his death and after Pentecost – disciples like Apollos. If this was the case, it might mean that those who received the baptism of John before Pentecost may not need to be baptized in Jesus' name. If Apollos had received his baptism prior to Pentecost, this rationale would explain why we have no record of his re-baptism in Ephesus.

One difficulty with this reasoning is found in Paul's motive for re-baptizing the men at Ephesus. When they were originally baptized they had not received the Holy Spirit (Acts 19: 3-4). The promise of the Spirit is found only in baptism performed *in Jesus' name*. Additionally, Paul did not ask these men *when* they had been baptized. He was only curious as to the nature of their baptism. Also, when Peter commanded baptism of his listeners on the Day of Pentecost, while there were surely those in the crowd who had received John's baptism (e.g., the one hundred twenty disciples), he commanded baptism for every willing believer within the sound of his voice (Acts 2: 38). Those who had been baptized by John were apparently baptized in Jesus' name at this time. Peter made no distinction, in his petition to the crowd, between those who had receive John's baptism, and those who had not.

Since Apollos had received the baptism of John, his condition paralleled those on the Day of Pentecost. We can also liken his situation to that of the men at Ephesus in that, through the baptism of John, he would not have received the Spirit. Additionally, although we are not told that Apollos was baptized in Jesus' name while at Ephesus, neither are we told that he failed to receive Christian baptism at that time. The absence of the mention of baptism in the narrative does not preclude it from occurring.

From Luke's observation that Apollos knew *only* John's baptism, we can surmise that there exists a baptism of greater significance – baptism in Jesus' name. Luke underscores Apollos' perspective on baptism as his primary shortcoming. He indicates that this was the chief issue they would need to address with Apollos. When Aquila and Priscilla *'took him aside and explained to him the way of God more accurately'* (Acts 18: 26), it is not difficult to picture Apollos receiving Christian baptism at that time, especially since he would later baptize others in the name of Jesus (1 Corinthians 1: 12). Since his situation mirrored both the disciples in Jerusalem and Ephesus, this is the most sensible conclusion.

Furthermore, we can surmise from the Luke's terminology and the context of the passage that Apollos *knew (επισταμαι)* the baptism of John in the same fashion that the Colossians *knew* the grace of God, in that he had experienced it (Colossians 1: 6). The word *epistamai* (ɛπισταμαι) represents not just his knowledge of, but also his familiarity with, John's baptism. That is to say, he *understood and had experienced* only John's baptism. This was the baptism upon which his conversion and teaching were based. Thus, Luke's observation that he *knew* John's baptism indicates that both Apollos' perception of baptism and his baptismal experience were deemed by Aquila and Priscilla to be incomplete in the new covenant.

Reading the account of Apollos, we note that he was *'fervent in spirit'* (Acts 18: 25). Certain men have suggested that this reflects him having received the Spirit at some time prior to Ephesus. However, this phrase concerning the *spirit* is not a reference to the Holy Spirit, but to Apollos' *spirit of enthusiasm*. This is why translators do not treat the word *spirit*, in this instance, as a proper name or title. However, when Paul taught the Ephesians, and as Peter addressed the crowd on the Day of Pentecost, the word points directly to the Holy Spirit in relation to Christian baptism.

What does all of this mean with respect to the baptism of the apostles? Since the narrative in these passages points to the inadequacy of John's baptism in the new covenant, and in the absence of any Scripture specifically exempting the apostles, we have every reason to believe that this same pattern would equally apply to them. While this is the most reasonable determination, based solely on what we know concerning John's baptism, there is actually additional evidence in the New Testament that speaks to the baptism of the twelve.

It is true that the apostles, on the Day of Pentecost, did not need to be baptized in Jesus' name in order to receive the Holy Spirit. They received the Spirit while *'they were all with one accord in one place'* (Acts 2: 1). However, at the house of Cornelius, when Peter saw that these Gentiles had received the Holy Spirit in a manner similar to what he and the others had experienced on the Day of Pentecost, his immediate response was to command them to be baptized in water (Acts 10: 45-47). Peter did not view the outpouring of the Spirit as license to dismiss the waters of baptism. Additionally, we are taught in Scripture that forgiveness of sins is provided at the time of baptism (Acts 2: 38). Since the apostles were not sinless they were undoubtedly obedient in seeking forgiveness in the manner commanded by God, which is baptism (Acts 2: 38). While they had surely received forgiveness at the time of John's baptism, this was a new day and a new covenant.

It is doubtful that the apostles would have taught baptism to others as a command of God while resisting that command for themselves. We also find that, in the early stages of the church, a valiant effort was made to discredit the work of the apostles. The very fact that no one ever questioned, within the pages of Scripture, why the apostles had not received the baptism they taught gives us reason to believe that they were baptized. Had such a question been raised, no doubt Paul would have addressed it in one of his epistles. Arguably, then, Scripture presumes, by its very silence on such an important subject as the baptism of the twelve, that the apostles were indeed baptized according to God's will.

Some may inquire, *'If scriptural silence concerning the apostles' baptism leads us to believe they were, indeed, baptized, why would this not hold true for infants as well?'* The primary answer is that the baptism of the apostles does not conflict with apostolic instruction concerning the relationship between belief and baptism. This relationship is fundamental in New Testament instruction about baptism. Furthermore, we find no concrete example of infant baptism in Scripture.

However, we know that the apostle Paul was baptized in Jesus' name (Acts 22: 16). While he was bestowed with the same powers and fulfilled the same role as the other apostles who had received the outpouring on the Day of Pentecost, God saw fit that he should be baptized in water. Given the fact that we are provided a biblical example of a baptized apostle, there is no reason to question the baptism of the rest. In fact, the testimony of a baptized apostle should settle any argument to the contrary. Apostles were baptized. It seems, then, that the Bible is not completely silent on the subject.

Apparently the topic of the baptism of the apostles did arise during the life of Tertullian, a church leader who lived in the late second century. His response to those who accused the apostles of not receiving the baptism of Christ was very direct.

> When, however, the prescript is laid down that "without baptism, salvation is attainable by none" (chiefly on the ground of that declaration of the Lord, who says, "Unless one be born of water, he hath not life"), there arise immediately scrupulous, nay rather audacious, doubts on the part of some, "how, in accordance with that

prescript, salvation is attainable by the apostles, whom-Paul excepted-we do not find baptized in the Lord? Nay, since Paul is the only one of them who has put on *the garment of* Christ's baptism, either the peril of all the others who lack the water of Christ is prejudged, that the prescript may be maintained, or else the prescript is rescinded if salvation has been ordained even for the unbaptized." I have heard-the Lord is my witness-doubts of that kind: that none may imagine me so abandoned as to ex-cogitate, unprovoked, in the licence of my pen, ideas which would inspire others with scruple.

And now, as far as I shall be able, I will reply to them who affirm "that the apostles were unbaptized." For if they had undergone the human baptism of John, and were longing for that of the Lord, *then* since the Lord Himself had defined baptism to be *one*; (saying to Peter, who was desirous of being thoroughly bathed, "He who hath once bathed hath no necessity *to wash* a second time; "which, of course, He would not have said at all to one *not* baptized;) even here we have a conspicuous proof against those who, in order to destroy the sacrament of water, deprive the apostles even of John's baptism. Can it seem credible that "the way of the Lord," that is, the baptism of John, had not then been "prepared" in those persons who were being destined to *open* the way of the Lord throughout the whole world? The Lord Himself, though no "repentance" was due from *Him*, was baptized: was baptism not necessary for *sinners*? As for the fact, then, that "others were not baptized"-they, however, were not companions of Christ, but enemies of the faith, doctors of the law and Pharisees. From which fact is gathered an additional suggestion, that, since the *opposers* of the Lord *refused* to be baptized, they who *followed* the Lord *were* baptized, and were not like-minded with their own rivals: especially when, if there were any one to whom they clave, the Lord had exalted John above him (by the testimony) saying," Among them who are born of women *there is* none greater than John the Baptist."

Others make the suggestion (forced enough), clearly "that the apostles then served the turn of baptism when in their little ship, were sprinkled and covered with the waves: that Peter himself also was immersed enough when he walked on the sea." It is, however, as I think, one thing to be sprinkled or intercepted by the violence of the sea; another thing to be baptized in obedience to the discipline of religion. But that little ship did present a figure of the Church, in that she is disquieted "in the sea," that is, in the world, "by the waves," that is, by persecutions and temptations; the Lord, through patience, sleeping as it were, until, roused in their last extremities by the prayers of the saints, He checks the world, and restores tranquillity to His own.

Now, whether they were baptized in any manner whatever, or whether they continued unbathed to the end-so that even that saying of the Lord touching the "one bath" does, under the person of Peter, merely regard *us*-still, to determine concerning the salvation of the apostles is audacious enough, because on *them* the prerogative even of first choice, and thereafter of undivided intimacy, might be able to confer the compendious grace of baptism, seeing they (I think) followed Him who was wont to promise salvation to every believer. "Thy faith," He would say, "hath saved thee; "and, "Thy sins shall be remitted thee," on thy believing, of course, albeit thou be not *yet* baptized. If that was wanting to the apostles, I know not in the faith of what things it was, that, roused by one word of the Lord, *one* left the toll-booth behind for ever; *another* deserted father and ship, and the craft by which he gained his living; *a third*, who disdained his father's obsequies, fulfilled, before he heard it, that highest precept of the Lord, "He who prefers father or mother to me, is not worthy of me." Tertullian, On Baptism, Chapter X2. - Of the Necessity of Baptism to Salvation.[1]

Tertullian's view was that if, for some reason, the apostles who received the initial outpouring of the Spirit on the Day of Pentecost did not receive water baptism, what we must recognize is the unequaled characteristics of their relationship with Jesus. These were the very men through whom the Holy Spirit would make known His presence. Theirs was an unparalleled role at a unique time in history – a role that would/could never be equaled. Nonetheless, concluding that these men did not receive water baptism is a stretch given their leading role in the early church.

Baptism of the Apostles – A Most Reasonable Conclusion

Finally, it is reasonable to believe that the apostles were baptized *in Jesus' name* simply because this is the most sensible conclusion. The apostles walked before the people as examples of what God expected from His disciples (2 Thessalonians 3: 9). Since the apostles taught baptism there is no reason to question whether or not they experienced it. That is certainly the case with repentance. Who would even think of questioning whether or not the apostles actually repented of their sins? Repentance, like baptism, is a fundamental teaching of the apostles throughout the New Testament. However, the occasion of the apostles' repentance for their sins is not detailed in Scripture. Nevertheless, we can, and do, assume that the apostles repented. In fact, they almost certainly repented on a daily basis.

While we are not told exactly *when* the apostles received baptism, it is plausible that it occurred on Pentecost since others who were baptized that day were *'added to them'* (Acts 2: 41). Prior to others becoming part of Christ's body, the foundation of the apostles must first have been laid (Ephesians 2: 20).

Questioning whether or not the apostles were baptized essentially profits nothing. The only imaginable reason for doubt is the opportunity to somehow discredit the redemptive value of baptism. The baptism of the apostles, however, is not a matter that relates to our salvation or the efficacy of baptism. Knowing exactly when the apostles received water baptism in Jesus' name has no bearing on our salvation. Our charge is to respond to the instructions provided regarding baptism and the normal pattern of salvation as it is presented in Scripture.

NOTES FOR CHAPTER 19

1. Anti-Nicene Fathers, Volume III, Chapter XII - Of the Necessity of Baptism to Salvation.

Tertullian suggests that it is unimportant to our salvation whether or not the apostles received baptism in water in the name of Jesus. This is because they received the Spirit as a matter of this divine manifestation of the Spirit similar to the manner by which the Spirit was received by Cornelius and the other Gentiles. If, indeed, the apostles were not baptized (other than John's baptism) divine intervention/revelation is the only reason.

Chapter XX
At the Feet of the Apostles

The Apostolic Fathers

Imagine how educational and inspirational it would have been to sit at the feet of the apostles and listen as they taught those in the first century. The apostles were not merely men who carried out an assignment for God. These men were specially selected to carry on the work that would help establish the very kingdom of God here on earth. Each one had spent considerable time with Jesus and understood things that go far beyond the grasp of other human beings.

Some men did have the unparalleled opportunity to study under the direct leadership and guidance of the apostles. These men, known as the apostolic fathers, were given the task of carrying forward the teachings of Jesus as the apostles, one by one, lost their lives. Living and working alongside the apostles offered these men the opportunity to not only read the words they had written, but have intimate conversations regarding the meaning of the written word. Perusing their various works affords us the opportunity to take a look at the views of these men who had direct or indirect instruction from the apostles. This should provide a better perspective as to the apostles' intended meaning in their writings on baptism.

It is always risky to cite writings outside of Scripture in an effort to buttress apostolic edification. Often the works of other men reveal personal prejudices and doctrinal disparity. It is true that those who followed after the apostles occasionally drifted from scriptural instruction. Therefore, the following excerpts are not intended to portray these men as authoritative on doctrinal issues. The Bible is, and must remain, our sole source of doctrine. Nonetheless, a review of the works of these men provides insight into the consistent and unified view of the efficacy of baptism in the early church, despite any doctrinal divergence that may have occurred in other areas.

Early on <u>The Epistle of Barnabas</u> was credited to Barnabas, Paul's companion. More recently, however, some scholars have claimed that the work was possibly penned by either Barnabas of Alexandria or another apostolic student of the same name. Nevertheless, many of the early church fathers, staunchly attributing the work to Barnabas of Cyprus, considered the letter equivalent with Scripture, believing it might easily have been added to the canon. In it we discover these words concerning the rite of baptism:

> Now let us see if the Lord has been at any pains to give us a foreshadowing of the waters of Baptism and of the cross. Regarding the former, we have the evidence of Scripture that Israel would refuse to accept the washing which confers the remission of sins and would set up a substitution of their own instead [Jer 22:13; Isa 16:1-2; 33:16-18; Psalm 1:3-6]. Observe there how he describes both the water and the cross in the same figure. His meaning is, "Blessed are those who go down into the water with their hopes set on the cross." Here he is saying that after we have stepped down into the water, burdened with sin and defilement, we come up out of it bearing fruit, with reverence in our hearts and the hope of Jesus in our souls. This He saith, because we go down into the water laden with sins and filth, and rise up from it bearing fruit in the heart, resting our fear and hope on Jesus in the spirit.[1]

* * * * *

One of the earliest and certainly better known students of the apostles was a man named Ignatius. It is unknown exactly when he was born and when he died, although it is evident that he died somewhere around AD 110 between the ages of 75 and 85. Known as Ignatius of Antioch, he was a student of the apostle John and probably did some studying under Paul. During his final journey to Rome, which ended in his martyrdom, he wrote several letters to churches and individuals. In <u>The Epistle of Ignatius to the Ephesians</u> we read the following passage:

> For our God, Jesus Christ, was, according to the appointment of God, conceived in the womb by Mary, of the seed of David, but by the Holy Ghost. He was born and baptized, that by His passion He might purify the water.[2]

In <u>The Epistle of Ignatius to the Trallians</u> we find:

> Wherefore also, ye appear to me to live not after the manner of men, but according to Jesus Christ, who died for us, in order that, by believing in His death, ye may by baptism be made partakers of His resurrection.[3]

On that same journey he wrote to his dear friend, Polycarp, these encouraging words:

> Let your baptism endure as your arms; your faith as your helmet; your love as your spear; your patience as a complete panoply. Let your works be the charge assigned to you, that ye may receive a worthy recompense. Be long-suffering, therefore, with one another, in meekness, as God is towards you. May I have joy of you for ever![4]

Once again, as with the writing of the apostles, one would be challenged to make the leap between these two letters which were, in essence, written simultaneously, that the baptism referred to in the letter to Polycarp was a different baptism than that addressed to the Ephesians. And what was the baptism to which he referred in his letter to the Ephesians? It was baptism in water. In fact, in his letter to the Trallians, he states plainly that this baptism is the very means by which we are, *'...made partakers of His resurrection.'* This is quite reminiscent of Paul's remarks to the Romans and Colossians regarding baptism.

* * * * *

Polycarp, known as Polycarp of Smyrna, who was just mentioned in association with Ignatius, was another student of the apostle John. Born in AD 69, he was raised in the church and it is believed he was baptized around the age of 10 or 11. Although Polycarp was considerably younger than Ignatius, their difference in age could not prevent the two men from becoming very close friends.

Little is available in the way of written documents from Polycarp. Much of his teaching, however, is revealed in the writings of his best known student – a man named Irenaeus. The only confirmed writing directly from Polycarp is a letter he penned to the church at Philippi. He does not directly address the issue of baptism, presumably because he was writing to those who had already been baptized. In his letter, however, it is interesting to note this particular excerpt:

> The letters of Ignatius which were sent to us by him, and others as many as we had by us, we send unto you, according as ye gave charge; the which are subjoined to this letter; from which ye will be able to gain great advantage. For they comprise faith and endurance and every kind of edification, which pertaineth unto our Lord. Moreover

> concerning Ignatius himself and those that were with him, if ye have any sure tidings, certify us.[5]

Polycarp sent the letter written to him by Ignatius so that they *'will be able to gain great advantage.'* He wrote that these letters contained *'every kind of edification.'* He appears to find no fault with anything in the letter from Ignatius, including his reference to baptism.

The Ante-Nicene Fathers

The Ante-Nicene Fathers were a group of early Christian leaders who led the church in the post-apostolic period until the First Council of Nicea in AD 325. These men did not have the advantage of sitting at the feet of the apostles, but some of the earlier Ante-Nicene Fathers were students of men who were students of the apostles.

Irenaeus, born around AD 130, studied under the guiding hand of Polycarp. When confronted with those who, in his time, tried to deny the salvation value of water baptism, he wrote the following:

> And we come to refute them, we shall know in its fitting-place, that this class of men have been instigated by Satan to a denial of that baptism which is regeneration to God, and thus to a renunciation of the whole faith...For the baptism instituted by the visible Jesus was for the remission of sins.[6]

He also wrote:

> As we are lepers in sin, we are made clean from our old transgressions by means of the sacred water and the invocation of the Lord. We are thus spiritually regenerated as newborn infants, even as the Lord declared: "Except a man be born again through water and the Spirit, he shall not enter the kingdom of heaven."[7]

It may be beneficial and worthwhile, at this point, to reiterate that the writings of Irenaeus were based on the teachings of Polycarp. Polycarp had studied under the Apostle John. The Apostle John is the author of the gospel of John where we find the account of Nicodemus, which we find referenced in the last quote. It is reasonable to conclude, then, that Polycarp, who did study under the Apostle John, understood Jesus' phrase *'born of water'* to be a direct reference to water baptism. Irenaeus also emphatically states that, *'...a denial of that baptism...'* is equivalent to, '*...a renunciation of the whole faith...*' He also wrote:

> Moreover, those things which were created from the waters were blessed by God, so that this might also be a sign that men would at a future time receive repentance and remission of sins through water and the bath of regeneration -- all who proceed to the truth and are born again and receive a blessing from God.[8]

* * * * *

Justin Martyr was born very near the time of the death of the apostle John. He was not raised in a Christian home but, in his early manhood, converted to Christianity. While it is true he could not have studied directly under the apostles, he was most certainly influenced by those who had heard the apostles. His First Apology was addressed to Emperor Marcus Aurelius.

> I will also relate the manner in which we dedicated ourselves to God when we had been made new through Christ; lest, if we omit this, we seem to be unfair in the explanation we are making. As many as are persuaded and believe that what we teach and say is true, and undertake to be able to live accordingly, are instructed to pray and to entreat God with fasting, for the remission of their sins that are past, we praying and fasting with them. Then they are brought by us where there is water, and are regenerated in the same manner in which we were ourselves regenerated. For, in the name of God, the Father and Lord of the universe, and of our Saviour Jesus Christ, and of the Holy Spirit, they then receive the washing with water. For Christ also said, "Except ye be born again, ye shall not enter into the kingdom of heaven." Now, that it is impossible for those who have once been born to enter into their mothers' wombs, is manifest to all. And how those who have sinned and repent shall escape their sins, is declared by Esaias the prophet, as I wrote above; he thus speaks: "Wash you, make you clean; put away the evil of your doings from your souls; learn to do well; judge the fatherless, and plead for the widow: and come and let us reason together, saith the Lord. And though your sins be as scarlet, I will make them white like wool; and though they be as crimson, I will make them white as snow. But if ye refuse and rebel, the sword shall devour you: for the mouth of the Lord hath spoken it."[9] (Chapter LXI.- Christian Baptism.)

> 'For at that time they obtain for themselves the washing in water in the name of God the Master of all and Father, and of our Savior Jesus Christ, and of the Holy Spirit. For Christ also said, "Unless you are regenerated, you cannot enter the kingdom of heaven."'[10]

Once again we find another reference to Jesus' conversation with Nicodemus and the true meaning of the phrase *'born of water.'* In his <u>Dialogue with Trypho</u>, we read the following:

> "By reason, therefore, of this laver of repentance and knowledge of God, which has been ordained on account of the transgression of God's people, as Isaiah cries, we have believed, and testify that that very baptism which he announced is alone able to purify those who have repented; and this is the water of life. But the cisterns which you have dug for yourselves are broken and profitless to you. For what is the use of that baptism which cleanses the flesh and body alone? Baptize the soul from wrath and from covetousness, from envy, and from hatred; and, lo! the body is pure."[11]

Justin was a true believer in the spiritual effect of immersion in water. He claimed that if water only cleanses the flesh and body and is not accompanied by a truly repentant heart, it is of no use spiritually. His remark parallels Peter's statement regarding baptism that saves, but *'not the removal of the filth of the flesh, but the answer of a good conscience toward God'* (1 Peter 3: 21). Certainly it was a fundamental belief by Justin Martyr that water baptism was a requirement based on the teachings of the apostles.

* * * * *

Tertullian was a Christian leader in the second half of the second century and into the third century. He wrote letters on special topics, including baptism. Consider the following writing regarding Paul, the Apostle:

> But they roll back *an objection* from *that* apostle himself, in that he said, "For Christ sent me not to baptize", as if by this argument baptism were done away! For *if so*, why did he baptize Gaius, and Crispus, and the house of Stephanas? However, even if Christ had not sent Him to baptize, yet He had given *other* apostles the precept to baptize. But these words were written to the Corinthians in regard of the circumstances of that particular time; seeing that schisms and dissensions were agitated among them, while one attributes *everything* to Paul, another to Apollos. For which reason the "peace-making" apostle, for fear he should seem to claim all *gifts* for himself, says that he had been sent "not to baptize, but to preach." For preaching is the prior thing, baptizing the posterior. Therefore the preaching came *first*: but I think baptizing withal was *lawful* to Him to whom preaching was.[12]

For those who argue against immersion as the *one baptism* addressed by Paul, consider the following excerpts from the works of Tertullian. They are very revealing with respect to Paul's statement.

> Thus, too, in *our* case, the unction runs carnally, (*i.e.* on the body,) but profits spiritually; in the same way as the *act* of baptism itself too is carnal, in that we are plunged in water, *but* the *effect* spiritual, in that we are freed from sins.[13]

> There is to us one, and but one, baptism; as well according to the Lord's gospel as according to the apostle's letters, inasmuch as *he says*, "One God, and one baptism, and one church in the heavens." We enter, then, the font *once: once* are sins washed away, because they ought never to be repeated. But the Jewish Israel bathes daily, because he is daily being defiled: and, for fear that *defilement* should be practiced among *us* also, therefore was the definition touching the one bathing made. Happy water, which *once* washes away; which does not mock sinners (with vain hopes); which does not, by being infected with the repetition of impurities, again defile them whom it has washed![14]

* * * * *

Clement of Alexandria, an early Greek theologian, was a contemporary of Tertullian. While his date of birth is unknown it is believed he died circa AD 215. He, too, wrote regarding the purification that could be found in baptism alone and saw in Jesus' words to Nicodemus a call to rebirth involving baptism.

> 'It is the washing through which we are cleansed of our sins...We who have repented of our sins, renounced our faults, and are purified by baptism.'[15]

> But you will perhaps say, "What does the baptism of water contribute toward the worship of God?" In the first place, because that which has pleased God is fulfilled. In the second place, because when you are regenerated and born again of water and of God, the frailty of your former birth, which you have through men, is cut off, and so ...you shall be able to attain salvation; but otherwise it is impossible. For thus has the true Prophet [Jesus] testified to us with an oath: "Verily, I say to you, that unless a man is born again of water....he shall not enter into the kingdom of heaven."[16]

* * * * *

The intent here is not to portray these writings as anything other than what they are: writings of the early leaders in the decades of the church following the death of the apostles. However, they do provide important confirmation that the apostles continued teaching immersion as the baptism of the Scripture as long as they lived. Additionally, they affirm the efficacy of baptism that is taught in the epistles. While these early Christian leaders did not agree in *all* things, and occasionally even strayed dramatically from some apostolic principles, especially near the end of the second century, there does seem to be unanimity on one topic in particular. That agreement involves immersion in water as the biblical means to receive forgiveness of sins and enter the kingdom of God.

These writings also seem to offer implicit confirmation that the idea of infant baptism would be fruitless, as was discussed earlier. Justin Martyr wrote, *'that very baptism which he announced is alone able to purify those who have repented...'* He also noted that baptism was for, *'As many as are persuaded and believe that what we teach and say is true....'* Again he wrote that those who would be baptized *'are instructed to pray and to entreat God with fasting.'* Infants are incapable of repentance. Infants are incapable of belief. Infants are incapable of fasting and prayer.

As a side note, it is of interest that many of these men quoted here were eventually martyred for their beliefs. Marcus Aurelius beheaded Justin Martyr in AD 165 for his refusal to worship pagan gods. Ignatius was condemned and devoured by wild beasts in Rome somewhere around AD 110. In AD 155 Polycarp was burned at the stake in Smyrna at age 86. Irenaeus, in AD 202, was martyred under the rule of Emperor Lucius Septimus Severus.

The quotes offered in this chapter are but a small token of the literature available from the early church fathers concerning the efficacy of baptism. More would have been presented if it were possible that it would have any additional impact. The apostles taught and practiced water baptism (immersion) until the end of their physical lives. We have good witnesses who have been able to confirm this. For those who assert that water baptism was discarded during the ministry of Paul, it seems that these Christian teachers/historians disagree.

NOTES FOR CHAPTER 20

1. Barnabas, THE EPISTLE OF BARNABAS (c. A.D. 70), (11:1-10) – While some ascribe this letter to Barnabas of Alexandria, an early church father, most scholars agree that it is the work of Paul's companion.

2. Ignatius, The Epistle of Ignatius to the Ephesians, Chapter XV2I, THE GLORY OF THE CROSS.

3. Ignatius, The Epistle of Ignatius to the Trallians, Chapter 2, BE SUBJECT TO THE BISHOP, ETC.

4. Ignatius, THE DUTIES OF THE CHRISTIAN FLOCK, Chapter VI.

5. Polycarp, The Epistle of Polycarp 13: 2.

6. Irenaeus, CHAP. XXI.--THE VIEWS OF REDEMPTION ENTERTAINED BY THESE HERETICS.

7. Irenaeus, Cited by J. Pelikan, The Emergence of the Catholic Tradition (100-600), p. 164.

8. Irenaeus, ST. THEOPHILUS OF ANTIOCH (c. A.D. 181), (To Autolycus 2:16).

9. Justin Martyr, Chapter LXI.-Christian Baptism.

10. Justin Martyr, Apology I, 61.

11. Justin, Martyr, Dialogue with Trypho, Chapter XIV -- RIGHTEOUSNESS IS NOT PLACED IN JEWISH RITES, BUT IN THE CONVERSION OF THE HEART GIVEN IN BAPTISM BY CHRIST.

12. Tertullian, On Baptism, Chapter XIV-Of Paul's Assertion, that He Had Not Been Sent to Baptize.

13. Tertullian, Chapter V2.-Of the Unction.

14. Tertullian, Chapter XV.-Unity of Baptism. Remarks on Heretical And Jewish Baptism.

15. Clement, Clement Of Alexandria Instructor I. vi. 32:1.

16. Clement, *RECOGNITIONS OF CLEMENT* (c. A.D. 221), **(Recognitions 6:9).**

Conclusion

Many will read this book out of curiosity, seeing it as an opportunity to explore a different point of view. Most will already have refined their own doctrine with respect to the role of baptism within God's plan of salvation, and this book will not sway them. Given the prevailing view of baptism in the modern world, a vast number will undoubtedly consider this book provocative while others will vigorously decry the teaching presented here.

It is true that the point of view expressed in this book is uncompromising when it comes to the teaching of baptism. That persistence is founded upon the words of Scripture. Paul, in his letter to the Galatians, defined baptism as the time we cover ourselves with Jesus (Galatians 3: 27). He taught the Romans that we begin our new life as we rise from the baptismal waters (Romans 6: 4). Peter taught that baptism is necessary for forgiveness of sins (Acts 2: 38) and identified it as a matter of salvation (1 Peter 3: 21). Jesus told the apostles, prior to His ascension, that it is the one who believes and is baptized who will be saved (Mark 16: 16). He explained to Nicodemus, *'unless one is born of water and the Spirit, he cannot enter the kingdom of God'* (John 3: 5). We find that Jesus' words, too, are unyielding. Therefore, if we believe that one who is not *born of water* cannot be saved, how can anything less be proclaimed?

Challenging nearly five centuries of beliefs about baptism may appear on the surface to be a hopeless undertaking since apparently so few wish to hear it. Perhaps, however, there are those who will be influenced and make the decision to be baptized for the forgiveness of sins, as the Bible teaches. At the very least, it is my hope that men will take it upon themselves to seriously reconsider, with an open and honest heart, biblical instruction related to baptism. It is for this reason and for my own conscience that this book has been written.

What is remarkable is the fact that so very few ever question the teaching of men that denies the role of baptism as it is presented in Scripture. Most men simply accept the contention that clear biblical instruction concerning baptism does not mean what it says. Rarely does anyone ask how it could possibly be that Spirit-inspired teaching about baptism is faulty.

The establishment of baptism as an essential precept of God is readily determined from a candid study of God's Word. Baptism is recognized as a vital ingredient of the saving faith of which the apostles wrote. It is upon our shoulders, then, to set aside the doctrine of men concerning baptism, as difficult as that may be, and found our beliefs on God's Word alone. It is the responsibility of each man to examine Scripture to discern God's will. If the apostles taught that we could be saved by baptism with the Holy Spirit alone, this book would not exist. Nor would it have been written if the apostles' teaching proclaimed that we *only* needed to believe or to repent or to confess to be saved. But, alas, that is not the lesson of Scripture.

Does God have the authority to redeem someone who has never received immersion in water? God's authority is not, and never has been, in question. He has the authority to do what He wills. Consequently, God has the power to save anyone He chooses in any manner He chooses. With that in mind, we must also acknowledge that He has the authority to establish baptism as essential for those who would receive forgiveness of sins and eternal life. In truth, that is exactly what He has done.

While God has the authority to select how men will be saved, He has not granted us that same latitude. So the real issue when it comes to baptism is not God's authority, but the authority of mankind. We have not been given license to choose how we might be saved or to neglect God's commands. At no time have we been given authority to dismiss immersion as the method of baptism or to introduce the Sinner's Prayer as a means to salvation. In the end, we have no reason to believe that we will be measured by any scale, or any plan of salvation, established by men. When judgment comes, the only scale that really matters is God's and the only commands that matter are those proclaimed in Scripture.

These things having been said, it is important to note that it is not the aim of this book to identify, from a personal perspective, those who will or will not be saved. No man has that prerogative. However, it is fully meant to portray what God has to say, through Scripture, about who will receive eternal life. The intent is not to judge, but to teach. We as men can do no more, but we can certainly do no less. That is the mission with which we have been charged. Scripture depicts baptism as vital for the man or woman who earnestly seeks salvation. God's Word is so straightforward on this issue that it is actually difficult to understand how modern views of the role of baptism have become so popular. The numerous passages that identify baptism as a matter of justification (Acts 2: 38; 1 Corinthians 6: 11), rebirth/renewal (John 3: 5; Romans 6: 1-4; Titus 3: 5), and ultimately salvation (Mark 16: 16; 1 Peter 3: 21) are so uncomplicated that it seems like it would take considerable resolve to come to any other conclusion. If we are to remain faithful to the message of the gospel, it is critical that we recognize the role for baptism that God has revealed in His Word.

For those who are reading this book, I ask that you consider the value placed upon immersion as it has been presented to us in Scripture. Is it Jesus' teaching? Certainly it is. Is a doctrine that resists baptism or diminishes its value a doctrine that is contrary to the teaching of Christ? I believe it is. What do you believe?

Bibliography

Ante-Nicene Fathers, On Baptism [Online], http://www.ccel.org/fathers2/ANF-03/anf03-49.htm .

Araujo, Luzia and Valerie Grundy, Larouse Portuguese English Pocket Dictionary, Larousse/VUEF, 2003.

Atkerson, Steven, 2003, Baptism's Practice [Online] http://www.ntrf.org/regen.html, (Accessed 01 June 2004) .

Barclay, William, 1976, The Daily Study Bible Series, The Acts of the Apostles, The Westminster Press, Philadelphia, PA.

Beasley-Murray, G. R., 1994, Baptism in the New Testament, William B. Eerdsman Publishing Company, Grand Rapids, MI.

Brants, T. W., 1977, The Gospel Plan of Salvation, Gospel Advocate, reprint, Nashville, TN.

Brown, Robert K. & Comfort, Philip W., 1990, The New GREEK ENGLISH Interlinear New Testament, Tyndale House Publishers, Wheaton, IL.

Campbell, Alexander, 1839, The Christian System, Forrester & Campbell, Pittsburgh, PA.

Campbell, Alexander, 1851, Christian Baptism With Its Antecedents And Consequents, Alexander Campbell.

Chalmers, Marianne and Martine Pierquin, 2000, Pocket Oxford Hachette French Dictionary Second Edition, p. 337, Oxford University Press.

Conant, Thomas Jefferson, 2002, The Meaning and Use of Baptizein, The Wakeman Trust, London.

Copeland, Mark A., 2002, Baptism in the Preaching of the Apostles [Online] http://www.bible.ca/eo/ba/ba_01.htm, (Accessed 24 Feb 2005).

Copeland, Mark A., 2002, "Baptism in the Teaching of Paul" [Online] http://www.bible.ca/eo/ba/ba_02.htm, Mark A. Copeland, (Accessed 24 Feb 2005).

Copeland, Mark A., 2002, Baptism in the Teaching of Peter [Online] http://www.bible.ca/eo/ba/ba_03.htm, (Accessed 24 Feb 2005).

Cottrell, Jack, 1989, Baptism A Biblical Study, College Press Publishing Company, Joplin, MO.

Cox, Jack, 2000, What the Bible Says About Baptism, Star Bible Publications, Inc., Ft Worth, TX.

Dixon, Danny, 1901, Essential Christian Baptism, Star Bible Publications, Ft. Worth, TX.

Elliot, Jim, "Rightly Interpreting the Bible", [Online] http://www.ovrlnd.com/Apologetics/interpreting.html, (Accessed February 19, 2006).

Fletcher, David W., ed., 1992, Baptism and the Remission of Sins, College Press, Joplin, MO.

Goodrick, Edward W. & Kohlenberger, John R. 2I, 1990, The NIV Exhaustive Concordance, Zondervan Publishing House, Grand Rapids, MI.

Hall, Steve and Vickie, Principles for Understanding the Bible, [Online] http://www.aboundingjoy.com/hermeneutics.htm, (Accessed February 19, 2006).

Harrison, Everett F., ed., 1960, Baker's Dictionary of Theology, Baker Book House, Grand Rapids, MI.

Henry, Matthew, 2001, Matthew Henry's Commentary on the Whole Bible, Hendrickson Publishers, Inc., United States.

Hicks, John Mark and Greg Taylor, 2004, Down in the River to Pray, Leafwood Publishers, Siloam Springs, AR.

Johnson, B. W., 1891, The People's New Testament, [Online] http://www.ccel.org/j/johnson_bw/pnt/PNT00A.HTM, 11 Feb. 2005.

Kieszonkowy, Stownik, 2004, Larouse Polish English Pocket Dictionary, p. 116, Larousse/SEJER.

Luther, Martin, 1978, Luther's Large Catechism, Saint Louis, MO: Concordia.

Miller, David, 2005, "Is Mark 16: 9-20 Inspired?" Apologetics Press. Org, [Online] http://www.apologeticspress.com/articles/2780, (Accessed December 6, 2007).

Padfield, David, "Baptism for the Remission of Sins", [Online] http://www.padfield.com/1995/sins.html, (Accessed August 15, 2007).

Practical Christianity Foundation, 2004, The General Epistles: A Practical Faith, Green Key Books, Holiday, FL.

Reese, Gareth, 2002, New Testament History Acts, Scripture Exposition Books, Moberly, MO.

Reese, Gareth, 1992, The New Testament Epistles – Hebrews, Scripture Exposition Books, Moberly, MO.

Simpson, D. P., 1987, Cassell's Latin English Dictionary, p. 111, Hungry Minds, Inc., © Macmillan Publishing, New York, NY.

Smith, Mont W., 1981, What the Bible Says About Covenant, College Press, Joplin, MO.

Southall, Timothy A. & Kimberly B., 1998, 1999, "A Biblical Look at Salvation", [Online] http://www.bright.net/~1wayonly/biblical.html, 18 Feb 2005.

Srygley, F. D., Gospel Advocate 32, March 26, 1890.

Staten, Steven Francis, "The Sinner's Prayer", [Online] http://www.bible.ca/g-sinners-prayer.htm, (Accessed June 20, 2006).

Staten, Steven Francis, "Where Did We Get The Sinner's Prayer? Is it Biblical?", [Online] http://s8int.com/sinnersprayer.html, (Accessed June 20, 2006).

Strong, James, 1990, The New Strong's Exhaustive Concordance of the Bible, Thomas Nelson Publishers, Nashville, TN.

Thayer, Joseph Henry, D.D., Thayer's Greek-English Lexicon of the New Testament, Baker Book House, 1977.

Thompson, Della, The Oxford Russian Dictionary, p. 43, The Berkley Publishing Group, Oxford University Press, 1997.

Tertullian, On Baptism, Chapter X2I. - Another Objection: Abraham Pleased God Without Being Baptized. Answer Thereto. Old Things Must Give Place to New, and Baptism is Now a Law.

Webster's Everyday Spanish - English Dictionary, p. 129, Federal Street Press, 2002.

Welty, William, Acts 2:38 — "Baptism for Forgiveness?", [Online] http://isv.org/musings/musing15.htm, (Accessed June 24, 2006).

Zwingli, Huldreigh, "Of Baptism," in Zwingli and Bullinger, "Library of Christian Classics," Vol. 24, ed. And tr. G. W. Bromiley (Philadelphia Westminster Press), 1953.